THE ANNUAL DIRECTORY OF AMERICAN
AND CANADIAN BED & BREAKFASTS

Mid-Atlantic Region

Includes
ONTARIO

2000 EDITION • VOLUME II

THE ANNUAL DIRECTORY OF AMERICAN AND CANADIAN BED & BREAKFASTS

Mid-Atlantic Region

Includes

ONTARIO

2000 EDITION   •   VOLUME II

Tracey Menges, *Compiler*

BARBOUR
PUBLISHING, INC.
Uhrichsville, Ohio

Copyright © 1989, 1990, 1991, 1992, 1993, 1994, 1995, 1996, 1997, 1998, 1999 by Barbour Publishing, Inc.

ISBN 1-57748-772

Published by Barbour Publishing, Inc., P.O. Box 719, Uhrichsville, Ohio 44683
http://www.barbourbooks.com

Cover design and book design by Harriette Bateman
Page composition by Roger A. DeLiso, Rutledge Hill Press®

Printed in the United States of America.

1 2 3 4 5 6—02 01 00 99

Contents

Introduction

The 2000 edition of *The Annual Directory of Mid-Atlantic Bed & Breakfasts* is one of the most comprehensive directories available today. Whether planning your honeymoon, a family vacation or reunion, or a business trip (many bed and breakfasts provide conference facilities), you will find what you are looking for at a bed and breakfast. hey are all here just waiting to be discovered.

Once you know your destination, look for it, or one close by, to see what accommodations are available. Each state has a general map with city locations to help you plan your trip efficiently. There are listings for all 50 states, Canada, Puerto Rico, and the Virgin Islands. Don't be surprised to find a listing in the remote spot you thought only you knew about. Even if your favorite hideaway isn't listed, you're sure to discover a new one.

How to Use This Guide

The sample listing below is typical of the entries in this directory. Each bed and breakfast is listed alphabetically by city and establishment name. The description provides an overview of the bed and breakfast and may include nearby activities and attractions. *Please note that the descriptions have been provided by the hosts. The publisher has not visited these bed and breakfasts and is not responsible for inaccuracies.*

Following the description are notes that have been designed for easy reference. Looking at the sample, a quick glance tells you that this bed and breakfast has four guest rooms, two with private baths (PB) and two that share a bath (SB). The rates are for two people sharing one room. Tax may or may not be included. The specifics of "Credit Cards" and "Notes" are listed at the bottom of each page.

GREAT TOWN_____

Favorite Bed and Breakfast

123 Main Street, 12345
(800) 555-1234

This quaint bed and breakfast is surrounded by five acres of award-winning landscaping and gardens. There are four guest rooms, each individually decorated with antiques. It is close to antique shops, restaurants, and outdoor activities. Breakfast includes homemade specialties and is served in the formal dining room at guests' leisure. Minimum stay of two nights.

Hosts: Sue and Jim Smith
Rooms: 4 (2 PB; 2 SB) $65-80
Full Breakfast
Credit Cards: A, B
Notes: 2, 5, 8, 10, 11, 12, 13

For example, the letter A means that MasterCard is accepted. The number 10 means that tennis is available on the premises or within 10 to 15 miles.

In many cases, a bed and breakfast is listed with a reservation service that represents several houses in one area. This service is responsible for bookings and can answer other questions you may have. They also inspect each listing and can help you choose the best place for your needs.

Before You Arrive

Now that you have chosen the bed and breakfast that interests you, there are some things you need to find out. You should always make reservations in advance, and while you are doing so you should ask about the local taxes. City taxes can be an unwelcome surprise. Make sure there are accommodations for your children. If you have dietary needs or prefer nonsmoking rooms, find out if these requirements can be met. Ask about check-in times and cancellation policies. Get specific directions. Most bed and breakfasts are readily accessible, but many are a little out of the way.

When You Arrive

In many instances you are visiting someone's home. Be respectful of their property, their schedules, and their requests. Don't smoke if they ask you not to, and don't show up with pets without prior arrangement. Be tidy in shared bathrooms, and be prompt. Most places have small staffs or may be run single-handedly and cannot easily adjust to surprises.

With a little effort and a sense of adventure you will learn firsthand the advantages of bed and breakfast travel. You will rediscover hospitality in a time when kindness seems to have been pushed aside. With the help of this directory, you will find accommodations that are just as exciting as your traveling plans.

We would like to hear from you about any experiences you have had or any inns you wish to recommend. Please write us at the following address:

Barbour Publishing, Inc.
P.O. Box 719
Uhrichsville, Ohio 44683

THE ANNUAL DIRECTORY OF AMERICAN
AND CANADIAN BED & BREAKFASTS

Mid-Atlantic Region

Includes
ONTARIO

2000 EDITION • VOLUME II

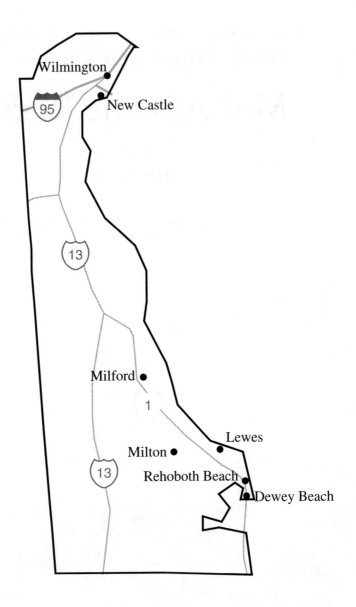

Delaware

Delaware

Barry's Gull Cottage Bed & Breakfast

116 Chesapeake Street, 19971
(302) 227-7000 (phone/FAX)
(302) 645-1575 (off-season)
e-mail: innkeeper@gullcottage.com
www.gullcottage.com

Wild Swan Inn

Contemporary Nantucket cottage one and one-half blocks to ocean. Gourmet breakfast, hot tub, afternoon tea, free parking, bicycles, cable TV in each room. Ten percent discount off low off-season rate—May, June, September, October—if booked by March 15. Ten percent discount off stays of five days or longer anytime. Close to fine dining, antiquing, shopping, and nature walk in state park. Picked as one of best stays at beach by *Washingtonian* magazine. Two rooms share a bath, with half-bath in room.

Hosts: Bob and Vivian Barry
Rooms: 4 (2 PB; 2 SB) $100-150
Full Breakfast
Credit Cards: None
Notes: 2, 7, 9, 10, 11, 12

LEWES

Wild Swan Inn

525 Kings Highway, 19958-1421
(302) 645-8550; e-mail: wildswan@udel.edu

This classic Queen Anne Victorian is a wonderful, romantic, special-occasion getaway. Memorable breakfasts—Innkeeper Mike's recipes featured in Gail Greco's *Tea Time at the Inn* and Laura Zahn's *Innkeepers' Best*

Muffins—and attention to detail are Wild Swan hallmarks. The inn has private baths, queen-size beds, air conditioning, bicycles, and spacious verandas. The quiet patio/swimming pool is a delight. Lewes has expansive beaches, nature trails, museums, great antiquing. Wild Swan was selected for the National Trust for Historic Preservation 1998 Historic America calendar.

Hosts: Michael and Hope Tyler
Rooms: 3 (PB) $85-150
Full Breakfast
Credit Cards: None
Notes: 2, 5, 7, 9, 10, 11, 12

MILFORD

Amanda's Bed & Breakfast Reservation Service

3538 Lakeway Drive, Ellicott City, MD 21042-1226
(443) 535-0008; (800) 899-7533
FAX (443) 535-0009; e-mail: AmandasRS@aol.com
www.Amandas-BBRS.com

193. A unique Victorian, built in 1873 with whimsical architectural detail, stained-glass windows, towers, turrets, porches, balconies, and gables mounted in fantastic confusion. Minutes from the ocean and beach. Modern

NOTES: Credit cards accepted: A MasterCard; B Visa; C American Express; D Discover; E Diner's Club; F Other; 2 Personal checks accepted; 3 Lunch available; 4 Dinner available; 5 Open all year; 6 Pets welcome; 7 No smoking; 8 Children welcome; 9 Social drinking allowed; 10 Tennis nearby; 11 Swimming nearby; 12 Golf nearby; 13 Skiing nearby; 14 May be booked through a travel agent; 15 Handicapped accessible.

conveniences in rooms. Dinner and additional accommodations in sister property nearby. $95-125.

MILTON

Amanda's Bed & Breakfast Reservation Service

3538 Lakeway Drive, Ellicott City, MD 21042-1226
(443) 535-0008; (800) 899-7533
FAX (443) 535-0009; e-mail: AmandasRS@aol.com
www.Amandas-BBRS.com

313. Welcoming guests with a distinctly English accent, the hosts will make them feel at home and serve afternoon tea. The house is an eclectic mix of pre-Victorian, Victorian, and modern architecture. The Delaware coast offers an amazing array of wading birds so bird watchers and cyclists are welcome. In the historic district, this bed and breakfast is just a block from the scenic Broadkill River and a short drive to either the Delaware Bay or the Atlantic Ocean. Two rooms at the back of the house each have a private bath, a queen-size bed, air conditioning, and ceiling fan. $70-95.

NEW CASTLE

Armitage Inn

2 The Strand, 19720
(302) 328-6618; FAX (302) 324-1163
e-mail: armitageinn@earthlink.net

Built in 1732, the Armitage Inn is on the banks of the Delaware River. Elegantly furnished air-conditioned guest rooms, all with private baths, and most with whirlpool tubs, overlook the picturesque vistas of the grand Delaware River, the acres of parkland surrounding the inn, and a peaceful walled garden. The gourmet-buffet breakfast is served in the grand dining room. New Castle, established in 1651, is in the heart of the Brandywine Valley with its numerous museums and attractions. Children over 12 welcome.

Hosts: Stephen and Rina Marks
Rooms: 5 (PB) $105-150
Full Breakfast
Credit Cards: A, B, C, D
Notes: 2, 5, 7, 10, 12, 14

The Terry House

130 Delaware Street, 19720
(302) 322-2505

Walk on the brick sidewalks and cobblestone streets William Penn saw when he first landed in America. This is an 1860 Federal-style home built by a banker in the heart of New Castle's historic district. Spacious rooms overlooking the town square or Battery Park. Private baths, cable TV, porches for relaxing. Step back to a town as it was in the 1800s. Children over 12 welcome.

Hosts: Evelyn Weston; Margaret and Gregory Bell
Rooms: 4 (PB) $90-98
Continental Breakfast
Credit Cards: A, B, C
Notes: 2, 5, 7, 9, 10

William Penn Guest House

206 Delaware Street, 19720
(302) 328-7736

Choose one of four guest rooms in this beautifully restored 1682 guest house in the center of historic New Castle, 20 minutes from museum and public gardens. Private bath and king-size beds available. Children over 12 welcome.

Hosts: Richard and Irma Burwell
Rooms: 4 (PB or SB) $60-90
Continental Breakfast
Credit Cards: A, B
Notes: 2, 7, 9, 10

REHOBOTH BEACH

Lord & Hamilton Seaside Inn

20 Brooklyn Avenue, 19971
(877) 227-6960
e-mail: lordandhamilton@erols.com
www.lordhamilton.com

NOTES: Credit cards accepted: A MasterCard; B Visa; C American Express; D Discover; E Diner's Club; F Other; 2 Personal checks accepted; 3 Lunch available; 4 Dinner available; 5 Open all year; 6 Pets welcome;

One-half block from the ocean and steps away from shopping, fine dining, and the beach, the Lord and Hamilton Seaside Inn is a vintage Victorian home built in 1871. The house has been restored and retains its 19th-century charm and atmosphere. The restoration includes a combination of Victorian decor and English country comfort, and is furnished with family heirlooms and antiques. Each room has its own distinct personality. Bedrooms are tasteful and cheerful and include designer linens. Several provide ocean views. All rooms have private baths and air conditioning. Parking included. Breakfast fare includes a selection of fresh fruit in season, juice, coffee, tea, and freshly baked pastries. Rates are seasonal. Smoking permitted on porch only. Children 15 and older are welcome.

Hosts: Robert Thompson and Stephen Grady
Rooms: 6 (PB) $95-155
Continental Breakfast
Credit Cards: A, B
Notes: 2, 9, 10, 11, 12

The Boulevard

The Rose Bud

100 Laurel Street, 19971
(800) 226-2314
e-mail: therosebud@worldnet.att.net
www.beach-fun.com/rosebud.html

Air conditioning. Afternoon lemonade and iced tea. One block to ocean and boardwalk. Proximity to shopping, dining, and churches. Walking distance to Main Street. Parking for guests. Back yard. Grill use—steamer use for cookouts. Shower outside off the beach. Sun porch.

Host: Rose Mary Sheeto, innkeeper
Rooms: 6 (1 PB; 5 SB) $115-130
Full Breakfast
Credit Cards: A, B, C
Notes: 2, 5, 7

WILMINGTON

The Boulevard Bed & Breakfast

1909 Baynard Boulevard, 19802
(302) 656-9700; FAX (302) 656-9701
e-mail: blvdbb@wserv.com

This beautifully restored city mansion was originally built in 1913. Impressive foyer and magnificent staircase lead to a landing complete with window seat and leaded-glass windows flanked by 15-foot columns. Breakfast is served on the screened porch or in formal dining room. Central air conditioning. Close to the business district and area attractions.

Hosts: Charles and Judy Powell
Rooms: 6 (4 PB; 2 SB) $70-85
Full Breakfast
Credit Cards: A, B, C
Notes: 2, 5, 7, 8, 9, 10, 12

Darley Manor Inn

3701 Philadelphia Pike, 19703
(302) 792-2127; (800) 824-4703
FAX (302) 798-6143
e-mail: darley@claymontde.org

Darley Manor offers elegant accommodations in a suburban historic register manor house, circa 1790. There are a full breakfast, canopied queen-size beds, private baths, TV, telephones,

7 No smoking; 8 Children welcome; 9 Social drinking allowed; 10 Tennis nearby; 11 Swimming nearby; 12 Golf nearby; 13 Skiing nearby; 14 May be booked through a travel agent; 15 Handicapped accessible.

and air conditioning. Winterthur, Longwood Gardens, and the Brandywine River Museum are nearby. I-95 and I-495 provide easy access to Philadelphia and Wilmington. Southern-style hospitality abounds and special attention is given to the business traveler's needs. Three-star rating from Mobil. Truly "close to everything, yet a century away."

Hosts: Ray and Judith Hester
Rooms: 6 (PB) $95-139
Full Breakfast
Credit Cards: A, B, C, D, E, F
Notes: 2, 5, 7, 9, 12, 14

Darley Manor Inn

District of Columbia

Amanda's Bed & Breakfast Reservation Service

3538 Lakeway Drive, Ellicott City, MD 21042-1226
(443) 535-0008; (800) 899-7533
FAX (443) 535-0009; e-mail: AmandasRS@aol.com
www.Amandas-BBRS.com

133 & 134. Two small inns in the Adams Morgan area of District of Columbia are near the zoo. Each room with private bath. One Art Deco, the other Jeffersonian. Rooms and suites available. Space for a small meeting. TV and dial direct telephones. About eight blocks to Dupont Circle Metro. Continental breakfast. $79-150.

160. On a prominent corner in the historic district of Dupont Circle stands an impressive mansion in the Victorian style. The elaborate mantels, fluted woodwork, and crown moldings add to the ambiance and spacious rooms. Use the Metro for easy access to the Mall. Restaurants are within walking distance. $125-250.

Bed & Breakfast Accommodations, Ltd.

P.O. Box 12011, 20005
(202) 328-3510; FAX (202) 332-3885
e-mail: BNBACCOM@AOL.COM
www.BNBACCOM.COM

104. Azalea Manor II Bed and Breakfast. This beautiful Mediterranean-style stucco home was built in 1930. The main floor features antique furnishings, hardwood floors and palladium windows. The second floor features two guest rooms. One room has two twin beds and it shares the bath with a room that has a four-poster double bed. Resident cat. Plenty of free parking. Six blocks to a bus line connecting to the Friendship Heights Metro station, and close to shopping, National Institutes of Health, and the National Naval Medical Center. $65-75.

107. Right in the heart of Georgetown, this is a relatively new townhouse. The guest room features a queen-size bed and private bath. Guests also have access to a den with a color TV and a small kitchenette. One-half block to major bus line. Street parking with permit. No smoking. $75-90.

111. Victoria and Maxwell Bed and Breakfast. On General's Row, a row of townhouses constructed in the late 1880s. This house is just three blocks from Dupont Circle, second only to Georgetown as a neighborhood for the trendy, offering good restaurants, boutiques, and theaters. Three guest rooms with shared baths. Two rooms have double beds and one room has twin beds. On the second floor, a queen-size room with private hall bath. All rooms with TV and telephone. Two resident cats. Parking available. $75-85.

124. The Smithmont Bed and Breakfast. The hosts have designed the award-winning 1994 renovations for this 1908 stucco home. The second-floor guest room features a queen-size bed, TV, telephone, and private hall bath. The home also features a fully equipped, second-story studio. It features a queen-size bed, kitchen, full bath, telephone, and TV. The family dog is in residence. Four blocks to the Friendship Heights Metro. Monthly rates available. $100.

7 No smoking; 8 Children welcome; 9 Social drinking allowed; 10 Tennis nearby; 11 Swimming nearby; 12 Golf nearby; 13 Skiing nearby; 14 May be booked through a travel agent; 15 Handicapped accessible.

District of Columbia

125. This Victorian townhouse was built in 1890 and is filled with an eclectic mix of period pieces, oriental and contemporary art. Four gracefully appointed bedrooms share two baths on the second floor. Two large bedrooms, each with private bath, on the third floor. In the heart of the city, this home is one mile north of the White House and six blocks from Dupont Circle Metro stop on the Red Line. No smoking. $70-110.

126. The Grant House Bed and Breakfast. This house is a Georgian-style brick Colonial with a slate roof. A wide, tree-lined avenue in a residential neighborhood, Tenley Circle is between Georgetown and Chevy Chase, Maryland. Guests have easy access to downtown business areas and major bus routes and are within two blocks of many restaurants, shops, movie theaters, tennis courts, and an indoor pool. Two large guest rooms each have a private bath with a tiled shower. Guest pets and smoking are not permitted. $75-90.

128. A lovely restored Victorian built in 1894. The house is furnished with period antiques. Parlor and dining room feature gas lights from the mid-1800s and guests are invited to use the walled back yard garden with fountain. The guest room has a full-size four-poster bed with a private bath that includes an antique clawfoot tub. $100.

132. Designed in the style of a classic 18th-century manor, this award-winning inn is in historic Old Town Alexandria. The decor includes fine Federal Period reproductions, including four-poster beds and decorative fireplaces. Forty-five rooms include some suites. Weekend packages include breakfast and parking. $160-295.

133. Rebecca Garrett House. This beautifully restored Victorian home was built in 1859. The house is full of lovely antiques, including antique beds in the guest rooms, and features

a lovely garden area with koi pond and fountain, which has been the site of several weddings. One guest room has an antique armoire, ceiling fan, stained-glass window, dressing room, and private bath with a large walk-in double shower. The other guest room has antique furnishings, including handmade rugs from North Carolina. The room is decorated in Laura Ashley wallpaper, linens, and fabrics, and has its own private attached bath. Resident cat. $100-120.

138. A professionally decorated efficiency apartment in Dupont Circle. In one of the turn-of-the-century townhouses, with a bay front and gas lamps, it offers a fully equipped kitchen, a double size Murphy bed, sofa, desk, TV, and telephone. Perfect for weekly or monthly stays. Two blocks from Dupont Circle Metro. No smoking. $85.

139. This spacious five-bedroom house was designed by famed Washington architect Harry Wardman, who developed this elegant, tree-lined district adjacent to Rock Creek Park. One guest room has twin beds, a sitting room, and a private bath. The second guest room has a twin bed and shared bath. The third floor has one room with double bed and private bath. Pets in residence. $75-85.

145. The "Settle" Bed and Breakfast. This beautifully restored Victorian dates back to around the 1850s. The bayfront living room features twin fireplaces, original artwork, crystal chandeliers, and comfortable furnishings. The second-floor guest room features a brass bed, private hall bath, and access to a sunlit sitting room with a sofa bed for an extra person. Across from the Library of Congress and four blocks to the Capitol South Metro station. $100.

155. A 19th-century inn in historic Virginia just 45 minutes from downtown has been lovingly restored as a beautiful, cozy bed and

NOTES: Credit cards accepted: A MasterCard; B Visa; C American Express; D Discover; E Diner's Club; F Other; 2 Personal checks accepted; 3 Lunch available; 4 Dinner available; 5 Open all year; 6 Pets welcome; 7 No smoking; 8 Children welcome; 9 Social drinking allowed; 10 Tennis nearby; 11 Swimming nearby; 12 Golf nearby; 13 Skiing nearby; 14 May be booked through a travel agent; 15 Handicapped accessible.

breakfast. There are 14 unique rooms furnished with antiques and reproductions, and each is named for a noteworthy Virginian. The dining room was inspired by Belvoir, the home of William Fairfax. Lovely gardens designed to reflect the era when the inn was constructed have been added to both the front and back of the building. Full breakfast and high tea are both served. $130-299.

158. Waterfront Row Bed and Breakfast. A four-story brick townhouse at Tiber Island is right in the heart of the city on Washington's waterfront. Guests have an easy stroll to the Smithsonian Institution, the Jefferson Memorial, and the Tidal Basin. Accommodations include a queen-size bed, private hall bath, and music/video room. $110.

160. This beautiful Colonial estate was built prior to the Civil War. On a horse farm in the Virginia countryside. Seven unique rooms, each appointed with period antiques and reproductions, each with private bath. Some rooms feature fireplaces and luxurious whirlpool tubs. Homemade breakfast included. Special holiday packages available. $125-295.

165. Virginia Fieldstone Inn. Built in 1938, this stone and brick house sits on large professionally landscaped grounds with a natural brook. Under two miles from the heart of historic Old Town Alexandria. The antique-filled house features a room with double bed and private hall bath. There is an additional room that can accommodate another person in the same party. $85-100.

167. Home on the Hill Bed and Breakfast. A restored red brick townhouse with glass solarium-garden area. The home is antique filled and features a wood-burning fireplace. Two rooms share a bath with whirlpool tub. One room has a double bed, the other a twin bed. In addition, a self-hosted English basement-level studio apartment with double bed and private bath. Resident pets. $65-85.

170. The Painted Lady of Capitol Hill. The house is a beautifully restored Victorian retaining most of the original architectural details. It faces Pennsylvania Avenue and is furnished with American antiques throughout. Guests are invited to use the Florida Room where breakfast is served, as well as the Florentine Room and garden. There are two large guest rooms sharing a bath, one with a period antique double bed and one with a queen-size bed. $65-80.

199. This small, elegant hotel is in the heart of Georgetown on the C&O canal. It has 143 guest rooms, including two-level carriage suites and four pool-side bungalow rooms. Rooftop swimming pool, sun deck, and world-class restaurant. Packages include parking and breakfast. $99-250.

200. Each of the 54 guest rooms and suites is unique. Many contain historical features. Each guest room is individually decorated with original art work and authentic period furnishings, complemented by custom-designed and hand-crafted pieces. Guest room features include maid service twice a day, including turn-down service; convenient in-room bar and refreshments; baths with marble vanities and personal toiletries; many rooms with bay windows and some with porches; individually controlled heating and air conditioning; telephones, computer access data ports; color TV and in-room movies; and AM/FM radios. Valet parking is available. $89-139.

The Bed & Breakfast League, Ltd./Sweet Dreams & Toast, Inc.

P.O. Box 9490, 20016-9490
(202) 363-7767; FAX (202) 363-8396
e-mail: bedandbreakfast-washingtondc@erols.com

296. The Madison House, built in 1849, is one block from the Capitol South Metro stop. It is decorated with antiques, oriental rugs, and Waterford chandeliers. One guest suite has two bedrooms, sitting room, and bath. The master suite has a bedroom with private bath with

---

NOTES: Credit cards accepted: A MasterCard; B Visa; C American Express; D Discover; E Diner's Club; F Other; 2 Personal checks accepted; 3 Lunch available; 4 Dinner available; 5 Open all year; 6 Pets welcome;

Jacuzzi. Three other bedrooms have private baths. The apartment has a bedroom, living room with extra bed and pull-out bed, kitchen, and bath. Parking available. Credit cards and personal checks accepted. Open year-round. No smoking. Children welcome. Social drinking permitted. Full breakfast. $88-150.

297. On a quiet street near Dupont Circle and downtown, the Swann Bed and Breakfast is a Victorian house with 15-foot ceilings, original crown moldings, brass light fixtures, tiled fireplaces, and an interesting history—one previous owner operated an after-hours jazz club and hotel in the house during the 1930s, 1940s, and 1950s. The guest room has a queen-size bed, sitting area, color TV, and newly renovated private hall bath. Off-street parking. Four-block walk to the Dupont Circle Metro stop. Credit cards and personal checks accepted. Open year-round. No smoking. Social drinking allowed. Continental breakfast. $78-95.

396. This Victorian is decorated with period furnishings, wallpaper, linens, and antique light fixtures. Four guest rooms have one queen-size bed or one queen-size and one twin, and they share two baths. A fifth guest room has one queen-size bed, a queen-size sofa bed, private bath. The sixth guest room has a queen-size and a twin bed, private bath. Guests may use the parlor, library, or deck. Ten-minute walk to Dupont Circle Metro. Credit cards and personal checks accepted. Open year-round. No smoking. Social drinking allowed. Continental breakfast. $75-125.

397. A garden apartment in the prestigious Woodley Park area offers a living room/ bedroom with queen-size bed and queen-size pull-out bed, private bath, kitchen with eating area, private deck, off-street parking, TV, and telephone. The kitchen is stocked for a Continental breakfast. Walk to the Washington National Cathedral in 10 minutes; the zoo, the Woodley Park Metro, Washington Sheraton and Omni

Shoreham Hotels in 20 minutes. Credit cards and personal checks accepted. Open year-round. No smoking. Social drinking allowed. $90-100.

497. A beautifully designed and decorated efficiency apartment in Cleveland Park is six blocks from the Washington National Cathedral and a 15-minute walk to two Metro stops. The living/bedroom has an antique three-fourths double bed, sitting and dining areas, and full kitchen, which is stocked for a Continental breakfast. Also included are a private bath, telephone line, and color cable TV. Parking is easy and unrestricted. Credit cards and personal checks accepted. Open year-round. No smoking. Social drinking allowed. $85-100.

796. Georgetown is the oldest section of the city, home to some of the city's best restaurants and renowned for its world-class shopping. This quiet, secluded suite offers the use of a sitting room with TV, a wet bar, bedroom with queen-size bed, private bath. All the shops and restaurants are within easy walking distance, as are Georgetown University and Dumbarton Oaks. Credit cards and personal checks accepted. Open year-round. No smoking. Social drinking allowed. Continental breakfast. $78-95.

896. This unhosted apartment is part of a turn-of-the-century home on one of the prettiest blocks on Capitol Hill. It is three blocks from the Eastern Market Metro and eight blocks east of the Capitol. The apartment has a bedroom with queen-size bed, private bath, living room with queen-size pull-out bed, and kitchen. The kitchen is stocked for a Continental breakfast, and there is off-street parking. Credit cards and personal checks accepted. Open year-round. No smoking. Children welcome. Social drinking. $88-105.

996. Just 10 minutes from Georgetown and 5 minutes from American University is this

7 No smoking; 8 Children welcome; 9 Social drinking allowed; 10 Tennis nearby; 11 Swimming nearby; 12 Golf nearby; 13 Skiing nearby; 14 May be booked through a travel agent; 15 Handicapped accessible.

The Bed & Breakfast League, Ltd.

handsome house built on a hillside in one of the best parts of Washington. One guest room has a queen-size bed and private bath; the second has twin-size beds and private bath. Parking is on-street. The hosts, an artist and a defense policy analyst, serve a much-admired breakfast and often drive their guests to the Metro stops nearby. Credit cards and personal checks accepted. Open year-round. No smoking. Social drinking allowed. Continental breakfast. $78-88.

1096. This Victorian townhouse is on Capitol Hill, a 10- or 15-minute walk to the Capitol, Supreme Court, and Union Station Metro. The interior retains its antique charm enhanced by the original brick walls and new skylights. It is furnished with family antiques and mementos from the host's travels while in the Peace Corps. The guest accommodations are a bedroom with double bed, adjoining bedroom with twin-size beds, and private bath. Credit cards and personal checks accepted. Open year-round. No smoking. Social drinking allowed. Continental breakfast. $83-105.

1296. This completely furnished, full daylight, English basement apartment on Capitol Hill draws guests back again and again because the hosts have thought of everything their guests might need. The suite includes a private entrance, living/dining room, complete kitchen, bedroom with queen-size bed, private bath, color cable TV, and private telephone line. There is off-street parking. The Eastern Market Metro stop is a 10-minute walk away, and the Capitol is 11 blocks away. Credit cards and personal checks accepted. Open year-round. No smoking allowed. Social drinking allowed. Continental breakfast. $95-105.

1596. This turn-of-the-century townhouse is one minute from the Dupont Circle Metro and many restaurants, but the street is secluded and

quiet. The spacious rooms have high ceilings and wonderful furnishings, many from the Far East. The guest bedroom has queen-size bed, stereo, TV, telephone, and private bath. The first-floor apartment can accommodate four people and has a living/dining room, bedroom, kitchen, and private bath. Credit cards and personal checks accepted. Open year-round. No smoking. Social drinking allowed. Continental breakfast. $88-125.

1996. This Cape Cod-style home is in Cleveland Park, the most beautiful and sought-after historic district in the city. Filled with family antiques, this light, airy home offers quiet and tranquility close to downtown. The Metro stop, shops, and restaurants are a 10- or 15-minute walk from the house. The master bedroom has a queen-size bed and private bath. Two other rooms have one twin bed each and share a hall bath. Credit cards and personal checks accepted. Open year-round. No smoking. Social drinking allowed. Continental breakfast. $78-88.

2096. This Victorian home in Cleveland Park was built as a summer home and later converted to year-round use. It has wraparound porches, high ceilings, beautiful wood paneling, and antique furniture. One guest bedroom has an antique double sleigh bed and private bath; the second guest room has an antique three-fourths double bed and shared bath. There is off-street parking, and the Cleveland Park Metro stop is a six-minute walk away. Credit cards and personal checks accepted. Open year-round. No smoking. Children welcome. Social drinking allowed. Continental breakfast. $78-88.

2196. Sitting on the porch or in the library of this large, rambling Victorian home in Cleveland Park, it's hard to believe it is an 8-minute walk from the Cleveland Park Metro stop and a number of restaurants and a 6-minute Metro ride to downtown. The house is furnished with handsome English and American antiques. The

NOTES: Credit cards accepted: A MasterCard; B Visa; C American Express; D Discover; E Diner's Club; F Other; 2 Personal checks accepted; 3 Lunch available; 4 Dinner available; 5 Open all year; 6 Pets welcome;

guest bedroom has an extra-large double bed and private bath. Off-street parking is available. Credit cards and personal checks accepted. Open year-round. No smoking. Social drinking allowed. Continental breakfast. $78-88.

2396. The Lucky Bed and Breakfast is near the new Embassy District and American University and a four block walk to the Van Ness Metro stop. The house and guest rooms are furnished with fine 18th- and 19th-century furniture and oriental rugs. There are three guest bedrooms with twin, double, or queen-size beds, private or shared baths, color TVs, and telephones. Off-street parking is available, and there are numerous restaurants within walking distance. Credit cards and personal checks accepted. Open year-round. No smoking. Social drinking allowed. Continental breakfast. $75-90.

Capitol Hill Guest House

101 Fifth Street Northeast, 20002
(202) 547-1050; (800) 261-2768

The Capitol Hill Guest House is a 19th-century Queen Anne-style row house only three blocks behind the U.S. Supreme Court on historic Capitol Hill. There are 10 moderately priced rooms with the flavor of a bygone era when all visitors to the nation's capital stayed in the many guest houses that dotted Capitol Hill.

Hosts: Bryan and Rikk
Rooms: 9 (3 PB; 6 SB) $45-125
Continental Breakfast
Credit Cards: A, B, C, D
Notes: 5, 7, 9, 11, 14

The Dupont at the Circle

1604 19th Street, Northwest, 20009
(202) 332-5251; FAX (202) 332-3244
www.dupontatthecircle.com

The Dupont at the Circle is a charming Victorian bed and breakfast inn in Washington, D.C.'s premier location. Our neighborhood is safe and convenient, just steps from the effi-

cient Metrorail and Dupont Circle—making all the area's restaurants, museums, and the downtown business district easily accessible. Beautifully appointed rooms with private baths, telephones, and ironed bed linens will pamper guests in Washington, D.C.'s only AAA rated bed and breakfast. All room rates include a Continental plus breakfast.

Hosts: Anexora and Alan Skvirsky
Rooms: 7 (PB) $130-190
Suites: 1 (PB) $250
Continental Breakfast
Credit Cards: A, B, C
Notes: 2, 5, 7, 9, 14

The Embassy Inn

1627 16th Street Northwest, 20009
(202) 234-7800; (800) 423-9111
FAX (202) 234-3309

A nice home away from home, the Embassy Inn offers great rates in a charming, intimate hotel. Complimentary evening sherry, cable TV with free HBO, and a library of books and free magazines are all available to guests. Metro, sights, and restaurants are within walking distance.

Rooms: 38 (PB) $69-129
Continental Breakfast
Credit Cards: A, B, C, E
Notes: 5, 8, 9, 10, 11, 14

Hereford House Bed & Breakfast

604 South Carolina Avenue, Southeast, 20003
(202) 543-0102 (Direct line to hostess. No
  Reservation Service fee)

A 1915 brick townhouse on wide tree-lined
avenue on historic Capitol Hill, one block from
Metro. U.S. Capitol, Congressional Library,
Smithsonian Institution,
and ethnic restaurants
within walking dis-
tance. British host-
ess and resident
dog offer a warm
and friendly wel-
come to this cozy,
convenient, afford-
able bed and break-
fast with single rates
$50-64. One addi-
tional room with private
bathroom is available at a second home six
minutes' walk from Hereford House. A full
breakfast is available at the hosted house for
those staying at the second home. Pets welcome with prior arrangement. Children 12 and
older welcome.

Host: Ann Edwards
Rooms: 4 (SB) $66-74; 1 (PB) $80
Full Breakfast
Credit Cards: None
Notes: 2, 5, 7, 9, 10, 11, 14

Kalorama Guest House at Kalorama Park

1854 Mintwood Place Northwest, 20009
(202) 667-6369; FAX (202) 319-1262

A charming Victorian inn in a quiet downtown
residential neighborhood is only a short stroll
to the underground Metro and a potpourri of
ethnic restaurants and shops. Enjoy the hospitality of the innkeepers, a complimentary Continental breakfast, and evening apéritif. Just 10
minutes from the Mall, White House, and most
attractions. Economical rates bring guests back

again and again. Smoking permitted in very
limited areas.

Hosts: Michael, Stephen, Karin, and Adris
Rooms: 30 (12 PB; 18 SB) $45-130
Continental Breakfast
Credit Cards: A, B, C, D, E
Notes: 5, 8, 9, 14

Kalorama Guest House at Woodley Park

2700 Cathedral Avenue Northwest, 20008
(202) 328-0860; FAX (202) 328-8730

This turn-of-the-century Victorian townhouse
offers guests a downtown residential home
away from home. Decorated in period
antiques, the guest house is a short walk to the
underground Metro, restaurants, and shops.
Only 20 minutes from the Smithsonian and the
White House, yet offering guests the relaxation and hospitality of a country inn. Enjoy a
complimentary Continental breakfast and
evening apéritif.

Hosts: Michael, Mary Ann, and Carol
Rooms: 19 (12 PB; 7 SB) $45-105
Continental Breakfast
Credit Cards: A, B, C, D, E
Notes: 5, 7, 8, 9, 10, 14

Maison Orleans Bed n' Breakfast

414-5th Street Southeast, 20003-2051
(202) 544-3694; e-mail: maisonorln@aol.com
www.bbonline.com/dc/maisonorleans/
www.innsnorthamerica.com

This charming Edwardian-style bed and
breakfast on historic Capitol Hill is just five
blocks from the Capitol. Three bedrooms, all
with private baths, are available along with
telephone, TV, and off-street parking. The
furnishings are family pieces from the '30s
and '40s, which give guests the feeling of
Grandmother's house. Guests are invited to
use the French Quarter-style patio directly off
the living room. Eastern Market Metro one
block away.

NOTES: Credit cards accepted: A MasterCard; B Visa; C American Express; D Discover; E Diner's Club;
F Other; 2 Personal checks accepted; 3 Lunch available; 4 Dinner available; 5 Open all year; 6 Pets welcome;

Maison Orleans

Host: Bill Rouchell
Rooms: 3 (PB) $90-95
Continental Breakfast
Credit Cards: None
Notes: 2, 5, 7, 9, 10, 11

Morrison–Clark Inn & Restaurant

1013-1015 L Street, NW, Massachusetts and 11th
    Street, 20001
(202) 898-1200; (800) 332-7898

The restored Morrison–Clark Inn preserves the elegance of Victorian design and creates the feel of an elegant turn-of-the-century Washington home. The guest rooms and suites are individually decorated with authentic period furnishings. Breakfast, lunch, and dinner are served in the restaurant. *Condé Nast's Traveler* rates the restaurant as one of the best in Washington; "one of the top 10 restaurants in Washington" rating by *Gourmet* magazine. The inn is just six blocks from the White House near downtown shopping, Chinatown, and the convention center. Complimentary Continental breakfast served daily. Weekend rates are available. Nonsmoking rooms available. Fitness center on property.

Host: Josette Shelton
Rooms: 54 (PB) $115-195
Continental Breakfast
Credit Cards: A, B, C, D, E, F
Notes: 2, 3, 4, 5, 8, 9, 10, 11, 12, 14

The Reeds

P.O. Box 12011, 20005
(202) 328-3510

A 100-year-old Victorian mansion has been carefully and extensively restored and has original wood paneling, stained glass, chandeliers, and porch. Each room has a color TV and telephone; laundry facilities are available. Adjoins Logan Circle Historic District, with excellent transportation and easy parking. This beautiful home was selected as a part of the "Christmas at the Smithsonian" festivities and was featured in the *Washington Post* in December when it was decorated for Christmas. Ten blocks from the White House. The hosts speak English and French. Personal checks accepted two weeks prior to arrival. Also available is a fully equipped one-bedroom apartment.

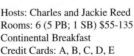

Hosts: Charles and Jackie Reed
Rooms: 6 (5 PB; 1 SB) $55-135
Continental Breakfast
Credit Cards: A, B, C, D, E
Notes: 2, 5, 7, 8, 9, 14

7 No smoking; 8 Children welcome; 9 Social drinking allowed; 10 Tennis nearby; 11 Swimming nearby; 12 Golf nearby; 13 Skiing nearby; 14 May be booked through a travel agent; 15 Handicapped accessible.

The Windsor Inn

1842 16th Street, Northwest, 20009
(202) 667-0300; (800) 423-9111
FAX (202) 667-4503

Charming and convenient bed and breakfast hotel right in the heart of Washington, D.C. Wonderful value and extras, such as cable and free HBO; complimentary evening sherry; books and free magazines for guests. Close to Metro, sights, and a variety of restaurants. Several suites and a small conference room available. Enjoy the atmosphere of an inn with the conveniences of a hotel.

Rooms: 46 (PB) $69-159
Continental Breakfast
Credit Cards: A, B, C, E
Notes: 5, 8, 9, 14

Maryland

ANNAPOLIS

Amanda's Bed & Breakfast Reservation Service

3538 Lakeway Drive, Ellicott City, 21042-1226
(443) 535-0008; (800) 899-7533
FAX (443) 535-0009; e-mail: AmandasRS@aol.com
www.Amandas-BBRS.com

163. This 10-room bed and breakfast is on the main street in downtown Annapolis, just steps away from the docks, shops, and historic buildings. All rooms have private baths. As the inn is above a famous deli, breakfast may be chosen from a special menu. Full breakfast. $75-95.

172. Just one block from the city docks, Market Square, or a five-minute walk to the Naval Academy. In the heart of historic district. Guests can also walk to the many historic buildings, shops, and many fine restaurants. Take a cruise around the harbor in one of several tour boats. There are two suites, each with a private bath. Both rooms abound with old-time creature comforts and childhood memorabilia. Full breakfast. $125.

213. A five-room guest house in the historic district of Annapolis with off-street parking. Each room has a private bath. The library with a fireplace for use by the guests contains a collection of original naval and yachting art. Relax after a day of sightseeing and enjoying the docks on the front porch swing. Enjoy a large English breakfast served in the dining room. $140-160.

218. Two older homes and a newer addition are in the heart of the historic district of Annapolis.

There is a total of 21 guest rooms. Parlors, dining and meeting rooms are all lovingly furnished with beautiful antiques. $78-125.

230. A lovely contemporary home set in the woods near Manresa, about five minutes from downtown Annapolis. A deck looks out into the woods offering a quiet place to relax after the day's activities. Wonderful views from every window. An outdoor hot tub also offers a relaxing end to guests' day. $125.

306. A quaint four-room bed and breakfast residence, decorated with a European country flavor. Walk to everything in Anna-polis: restaurants, historic sites, naval academy, and shops. Four rooms, all with private baths. Full breakfast. $95-120.

307. A brick mansion dating from the 18th century with period furnishings. Off-street parking. Walk the brick streets to the many interesting historical attractions, the naval academy, shops, restaurants, or the tour boats around the harbor. Four spacious rooms, several with fireplaces and Jacuzzi tubs, each with a private bath. There is a lovely garden area to enjoy after a tour around town. $125-160.

319. A lovely location on a cliff with a panoramic view of the water. Beautiful views along with a pool and deep-water dock. Breakfast is served on the glass-enclosed porch overlooking the water. The swimming pool is an inviting way to end or start the day. About 10 minutes from downtown in a quiet neighborhood. There is a sitting room on the second floor, which also has a water view. Whole house rental or three rooms with a two-night minimum. $100-135.

7 No smoking; 8 Children welcome; 9 Social drinking allowed; 10 Tennis nearby; 11 Swimming nearby; 12 Golf nearby; 13 Skiing nearby; 14 May be booked through a travel agent; 15 Handicapped accessible.

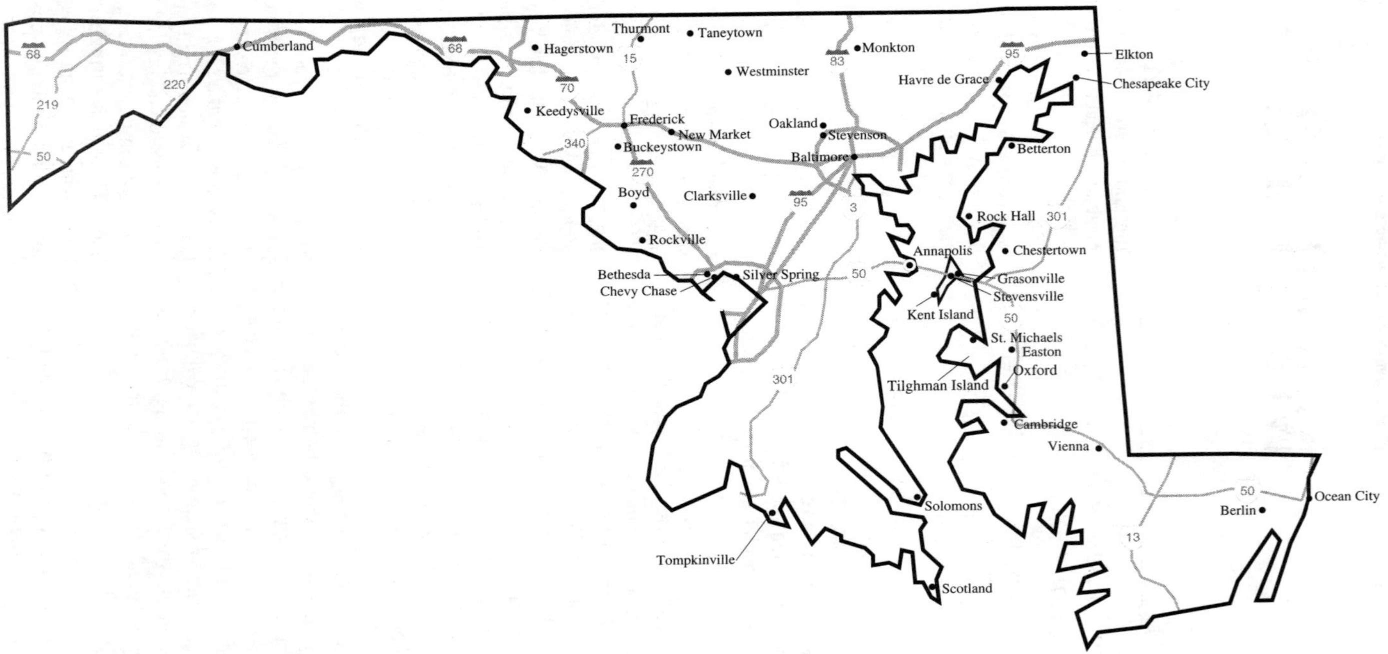

Maryland

Ocean City
Berlin
50
13
Elkton
Chesapeake City
Betterton
301
Chestertown
Rock Hall
Grasonville
Stevensville
Havre de Grace
95
St. Michaels
Easton
50
Oxford
Vienna
Cambridge
Annapolis
Kent Island
Tilghman Island
Monkton
Solomons
Scotland
Stevenson
Westminster
83
Oakland
Baltimore
3
Taneytown
50
Silver Spring
301
Frederick
New Market
Clarksville
Thurmont
Buckeystown
Rockville
Bethesda
Hagerstown
15
Chevy Chase
270
Boyd
Keedysville
70
340
Tompkinsville
Cumberland
66
220
219
68
50

334. Just north of the city in a quiet wooded area. A ranch-style home built by the owners. Inside some furniture made by the men of the family. A private entrance wing with queen-size bed and sitting area overlooking dogwood garden. Walking trail just behind the house. Full breakfast. $85.

355. Only 15 minutes from downtown Annapolis on the water. Enjoy the water and a pool at this small, comfortable cottage set off from the main house. Private entrance. Double bed. Also two rooms in main house available, one with whirlpool tub. Full breakfast. $85-105.

366. A private space with a large room, sitting area, kitchenette, double bed, and bath. Just steps from the water and minutes from downtown Annapolis. Very quiet and peaceful. Self-catered breakfast provided. $85.

The Barn on Howard's Cove

500 Wilson Road, 21401
(410) 266-6840

A renovated 1850 horse barn on a secluded cove of the Severn River, two miles from the center of this historic state capital, sailing center of the United States and home of the U.S. Naval Academy. Convenient to Baltimore and Washington, D.C. Beautiful gardens, rural setting. Country decor with antiques, Noah's Ark collection, handmade quilts. The room with

The Barn on Howard's Cove

deck and loft now has an added bedroom to make a suite. Both the suite and other bedroom overlook the river. Breakfast is served in flower-filled solarium overlooking river.

Hosts: Dr. and Mrs. Graham Gutsche
Rooms: 2 (PB) $100+5.00 tax
Full Breakfast
Credit Cards: F
Notes: 2, 5, 7, 8, 9, 10, 14

Chez Amis Bed & Breakfast

85 East Street, 21401
(410) 263-6631

Renovated 70-year-old corner store offers four guest rooms combining yesteryear ambiance with today's conveniences—air conditioning, TVs, and beverage centers. The 19th-century American antiques, original oak store counter, tin ceilings, and Georgia pine floors blend with European and country decor. In historic district, one block from city dock, state capitol, and the U.S. Naval Academy. Enjoy romance and warm hospitality in America's sailing capital at "the House of Friends." Closed for the month of January.

Hosts: Don and Mickie Deline
Rooms: 4 (PB) $105-130
Full Breakfast
Credit Cards: A, B
Notes: 2, 7, 14

College House Suites

One College Avenue, 21401-1603
(410) 263-6124

This historic district townhouse, nestled between the U.S. Naval Academy and St. John's College, features two suites: the Annapolitan Suite has a fireplace and private entrance through the ivy-covered courtyard; the Colonial Suite has superb oriental rugs, antiques, and views of naval academy grounds.

NOTES: Credit cards accepted: A MasterCard; B Visa; C American Express; D Discover; E Diner's Club; F Other; 2 Personal checks accepted; 3 Lunch available; 4 Dinner available; 5 Open all year; 6 Pets welcome; 7 No smoking; 8 Children welcome; 9 Social drinking allowed; 10 Tennis nearby; 11 Swimming nearby; 12 Golf nearby; 13 Skiing nearby; 14 May be booked through a travel agent; 15 Handicapped accessible.

College House Suites

Fresh flowers, bathrobes, toiletries, fruit baskets, and chocolates enhance the romantic atmosphere. A "breakfast-out" option is available at a $20-rate reduction. AAA-approved. Three-star award. Two-night minimum stay. Adult nonsmokers only.

Hosts: Don and Jo Anne Wolfrey
Suites: 2 (PB) $193
Continental Breakfast
Credit Cards: A, B
Notes: 5, 7, 9, 10, 11, 12, 14

Distinguished Accommodations in the Potomac Region— (Amanda's Bed & Breakfast Reservation Service)

3538 Lakeway Drive, Ellicott City, 21042-1226
(443) 535-0008; (800) 899-7533
FAX (443) 535-0009; e-mail: AmandasRS@aol.com
www.Amandas-BBRS.com

237. Enjoy the sailing capital of the United States. Less than a block from the historic State House and across the street from St. John's College and a short walk to the Naval Academy. Restaurants, unique shops, and other historic sites are within walking distance. The house was completely renovated in 1998 with furnishings reflecting the naval history of the house. Three very gracious and well-appointed rooms, each with a private bath. One room has a Jacuzzi tub and another has a hot tub on the porch roof. $150-175.

398. Romantic guest rooms decorated in the original Federal period style. Cozy fireplaces, queen-size beds, private baths, several with whirlpool tub or an antique claw-foot tub with shower. In the heart of the historic district just a half-block from restaurants, shopping, the docks, and three blocks from the U.S. Naval Academy. A large brick patio and garden are available for relaxing, sometimes breakfast, or a reception event. Full breakfast. $150-200.

The Dolls' House Bed & Breakfast

161 Green Street, 21401
(410) 626-2028

Enjoy this circa 1900 Victorian home fully decorated with antiques and filled with memo-

The Dolls' House

ries of childhood past. Bedrooms have cozy cottage ambiance. Two queen-size bedroom suites plus large family-size suite. Central air, TVs, private baths. Front porch swing, English flower garden. Full breakfast. In historic district. Close to all city amenities. Children over six welcome.

Hosts: Barbara and John Dugan
Rooms: 3 (PB) $115-150
Full Breakfast
Credit Cards: None
Notes: 2, 5, 7, 9, 12

Gibson's Lodgings of Annapolis

110 Prince George Street, 21401
(410) 268-5555

Gibson's Lodgings Bed and Breakfast Inn in the heart of historic Annapolis is a distinctive and internationally known inn with 21 rooms, courtyard parking, and a unique conference facility, all one-half block from the city dock.

Host: Beverly Snyder
Rooms: 21 (7 PB; 14 SB) $68-125
Continental Breakfast
Credit Cards: A, B, C
Notes: 5, 7, 8, 9, 12, 14, 15

Gibson's Lodgings of Annapolis

Maryrob Bed & Breakfast

243 Prince George Street, 21401-1631
(410) 268-5438; FAX (410) 268-9623

Maryrob Bed and Breakfast, elegant Victorian Italianate villa (circa1864), is in the heart of

Maryrob

historic district. Close to U.S. Naval Academy, city docks, state capital, St. Johns College, Wm. Paca House, and all other historic sites. All attractions are within a few minutes of pleasant, leisurely walking. The house is beautifully furnished and decorated with antiques and reproduction pieces and objets d'art. Lovely private garden with fountain. Breakfast is to-order in spacious dining room with bay window. Central air conditioning. Free off-street parking.

Hosts: Mary-Stuart Taylor and Robert E. Carlson
Rooms: 2 (PB) $95-120
Full Breakfast
Credit Cards: A, B
Notes: 2, 5, 7, 10, 11, 12

William Page Inn

8 Martin Street, 21401
(410) 626-1506; (800) 364-4160
FAX (410) 263-4841; e-mail: wmpageinn@aol.com
www.williampageinn.com

Built in 1908, this gracefully restored turn-of-the-century, four-square, cedar-shaker Shingle home was handsomely renovated into a bed and breakfast in 1987. The inn is in the historic district of Annapolis, convenient to all major attractions. Within easy walk of Maryland

7 No smoking; 8 Children welcome; 9 Social drinking allowed; 10 Tennis nearby; 11 Swimming nearby; 12 Golf nearby; 13 Skiing nearby; 14 May be booked through a travel agent; 15 Handicapped accessible.

State House, historic homes, landmarks, St. Johns College, and the Naval Academy. Special occasion packages available. Gift certificates, and meeting facilities for small corporate groups may also be arranged.

Host: Robert Zuchelli
Rooms: 5 (3 PB; 2 SB) $95-195
Full Breakfast
Credit Cards: A, B
Notes: 2, 5, 7, 9, 10, 11, 12, 14

BALTIMORE

Abacrombie Badger Bed & Breakfast

58 West Biddle Street, 21201
(410) 244-7227; FAX (410) 244-8415
e-mail: ABadger722@aol.com
www.badger-inn.com

Elegant lodgings in the heart of Baltimore's cultural center. Twelve beautifully decorated rooms in the 162-year-old mansion of Major Thomas Biddle, all with private baths and private telephones. Restaurant on premises. Free parking, Continental breakfast, cable TV. Next door to Meyerhoff Symphony Hall. Walk to the opera, Antique Row, University of Baltimore, Light Rail, and Penn Station (Amtrak). Near the Inner Harbor, art galleries, University of Maryland, and Maryland Institute, College of Art.

Hosts: Paul Bragaw and Collin Clarke
Rooms: 12 (PB) $105-145
Continental Breakfast
Credit Cards: A, B, C, D, E
Notes: 2, 3, 4, 5, 7, 9

Amanda's Bed & Breakfast Reservation Service

3538 Lakeway Drive, Ellicott City, 21042-1226
(443) 535-0008; (800) 899-7533
FAX (443) 535-0009; e-mail: AmandasRS@aol.com
www.Amandas-BBRS.com

102. A four-story row house in historic Mount Vernon neighborhood has two rooms with shared bath on third floor and two rooms with shared bath on fourth floor. Ride the new Light Rail to Oriole Park at Camden Yards and Inner Harbor. Only minutes away from the Inner Harbor, shopping, and restaurants. Continental breakfast. $65-80.

119. Elegant Victorian mansion is decorated with imported antiques and is in the historic Mount Vernon area near Antique Row. All 24 guest rooms/suites have kitchenettes, private baths, and meeting facilities. Ride the Light Rail to Camden Yards and Inner Harbor or walk to the harbor just 10 blocks away. Fine dining is nearby. Continental breakfast. $99-129.

128. Enjoy this historic row house in downtown Baltimore. The neighborhood is called Otterbein and is within walking distance to the Inner Harbor, convention center, and Oriole Park at Camden Yards, Ravens Stadium, shops, water taxi to Fells Point and many attractions around the Harbor including restaurants. In nice weather have a cool drink in the side garden, where breakfast may be served, weather permitting. Two rooms each with a private bath. $90.

131. Downtown historic neighborhood townhouse is furnished with antiques and is on a quiet street facing a park. Public transportation, cultural center, and churches are all nearby. The guest room is a large king-size suite all with a private kitchenette. $85.

179. A very nice private home in Federal Hill. Guests step outside the front door and turn the corner and have a view of the harbor which is just a short walk to the many attractions, restaurants, and shops. The water taxi is nearby which guests can ride to other points around the harbor. There are restaurants and shops in Federal Hill also. There is a king-size bed and private bath. Breakfast is self-catered. $100.

199. A small apartment on the ground floor of the owners' building in Federal Hill, the historic neighborhood, just south of the Inner Harbor. Guests can walk to the many attractions and restaurants in the Inner Harbor or Oriole Park at Camden Yards and the new football stadium. There is a bedroom with a double bed, bath, sitting room with sleeper-sofa, and small kitchen. For guests' convenience there is a telephone and TV. Breakfast is self-catered. $95.

216. Federal Hill, Baltimore's Inner Harbor neighborhood. Federal Hill is a historic neighborhood, walking distance to Inner Harbor, Oriole Park at Camden Yards, or the water taxi to Fells Point and other Inner Harbor attractions. A Baltimore townhouse with three floors and garden in rear. Double bedroom, sitting room with TV, private bath, and a suite with sitting room with a gas-fired fireplace. $125.

226. Built in 1897, the official guest house of the city of Baltimore is comprised of three townhouses in historic Mount Vernon. Guests are treated to personalized service, private baths, ornate and unusual decor. Great location with guest parking. Continental breakfast. $95-140.

265. This Federal-style townhouse was built in 1982 between two existing buildings to match. Features include three stories, patio, garden in back, fireplace in den, and living room. Two rooms with double beds and shared bath. Walk to Inner Harbor and Camden Yards. Continental breakfast is served in the dining room. $75-85.

347. A small two-level row house unhosted. The first floor has a living room with fireplace, kitchen, washer and dryer, and access to a small patio. On the second floor is a bedroom with a fireplace and a bath. Walk to the Inner Harbor and all of the many attractions and events, including the water taxi to Fells Point. The convention center and associated hotels are also within walking distance. $125.

The Biltmore Suites

205 West Madison Street, 21201
(410) 728-6550; (800) 868-5064
FAX (410) 728-5829

Built before the turn-of-the-century, the Biltmore Suites offers 26 antique-appointed guest rooms, all with private modern baths. Other modern amenities include in-room coffee makers, remote-controlled color cable TV, and mini-refrigerators. Guests are treated to a deluxe Continental breakfast each morning.

Host: Rajen Patel
Rooms: 26 (PB) $99-139
Continental Breakfast
Credit Cards: A, B, C, D, E
Notes: 5, 6, 7, 8, 14

Celie's Waterfront

Celie's Waterfront Bed & Breakfast

Historic Fell's Point, 1714 Thames Street, 21231
(410) 522-2323; (800) 432-0184
FAX (410) 522-2324; e-mail: celies@aol.com
www.bbonline.com/md/celies/

On Baltimore Harbor. Ideal for business or pleasure. Seven air-conditioned guest rooms, one wheelchair accessible, others also accessible to a private garden and harbor-view roof deck. Some with whirlpools, fireplaces, private balconies, and harbor views in a relaxed

7 No smoking; 8 Children welcome; 9 Social drinking allowed; 10 Tennis nearby; 11 Swimming nearby; 12 Golf nearby; 13 Skiing nearby; 14 May be booked through a travel agent; 15 Handicapped accessible.

atmosphere. Private telephones with answering machines, modem capability, fax, satellite TV, VCRs, irons and ironing boards, and hair dryers. Marina nearby. Minutes to Harbor Place, central business district, and Oriole Park by water taxi. Children over 10 are welcome.

Host: Celie Ives
Rooms: 7 (PB) $115-200
Continental Breakfast
Credit Cards: A, B, C, D
Notes: 2, 5, 7, 9, 14, 15

Distinguished Accommodations in the Potomac Region— (Amanda's Bed & Breakfast Reservation Service)

3538 Lakeway Drive, Ellicott City, 21042-1226
(443) 535-0008; (800) 899-7533
FAX (443) 535-0009; e-mail: AmandasRS@aol.com
www.Amandas-BBRS.com

190. Rooms with a view of the water or facing the charming English country garden, each with a private bath and nicely appointed furniture, all within an easy walk of Fells Point or the water taxi to the Inner Harbor. At the tip of Fells Point, this century old brick building is a national historic landmark. Walk the cobblestone streets past the row houses that once were home to sea captains and merchants that founded the community in the mid-1700s. Renovated to maintain its historical integrity, the lobby and rooms are furnished with period furnishings. Treasure the waterfront ambiance and enjoy your stay. $139-189.

346. A unique private house, circa 1860, which has been carefully restored and preserved. Downtown Baltimore in the Inner Harbor, close enough to walk to the many attractions, restaurants, and shops in Federal Hill, the convention center, Oriole Park at Camden yards, PSI Stadium home of the Baltimore Ravens. A roof deck overlooks the garden, with a fireplace in the living room, smoke-free, and furnished in the style of the period. A fully equipped kitchen stocked for a self-catered breakfast. Enjoy the cable TV, telephone, and fireplace. $125-165.

Mr. Mole

Mr. Mole Bed & Breakfast

1601 Bolton Street, 21217
(410) 728-1179; FAX (410) 728-3379

"Maryland's only four-star award-winning bed and breakfast" (1995-1999 Mobil Travel Guide). Decorated like a designers' showcase home. Amid quiet, tree-lined streets on historic Bolton Hill, two miles north of Inner Harbor. This 1870 row house has 14-foot ceilings, some two-bedroom suites. Private telephone and bath, garage parking (with automatic garage door opener). Near symphony, opera, museums, art galleries, Antique Row, universities, Penn Station, Light Rail, Metro, and Oriole Park.

Hosts: Collin Clarke and Paul Bragaw
Rooms: 5 (PB) $105-135
Continental Breakfast
Credit Cards: A, B, C, D, E
Notes: 2, 5, 7, 9, 14

NOTES: Credit cards accepted: A MasterCard; B Visa; C American Express; D Discover; E Diner's Club; F Other; 2 Personal checks accepted; 3 Lunch available; 4 Dinner available; 5 Open all year; 6 Pets welcome;

BALTIMORE (ESSEX)

Distinguished Accommodations in the Potomac Region— (Amanda's Bed & Breakfast Reservation Service)

3538 Lakeway Drive, Ellicott City, 21042-1226
(443) 535-0008; (800) 899-7533
FAX (443) 535-0009; e-mail: AmandasRS@aol.com
www.Amandas-BBRS.com

201. Historic waterfront manor house built in the early 1900s by the owner of a local successful brewery. A spacious home with two large rooms for bed and breakfast. One with a king-size bed, private bath with whirlpool tub and fireplace. The other, also a spacious room with a queen-size bed, fireplace, and a steam sauna shower in the private bath. A full breakfast is served. The house is decorated with antiques and collectibles. There is a swimming pool to cool down after a day in town around Baltimore. $125-140.

BERLIN

Atlantic Hotel Inn & Restaurant

2 North Main Street, 21811
(410) 641-3589; (800) 814-7672

Restored Victorian hotel with 16 period-furnished rooms. A national register building in

Atlantic Hotel Inn

the historic district. Elegant dining and piano lounge on the premises. Eight miles west of Ocean City and Assateague Island National Seashore. Walk to nearby antique shops, gallery, and museum.

Rooms: 16 (PB) $65-165
Full Breakfast
Credit Cards: A, B, C
Notes: 3, 4, 5, 7, 8, 9, 10, 11, 12

Distinguished Accommodations in the Potomac Region— (Amanda's Bed & Breakfast Reservation Service)

3538 Lakeway Drive, Ellicott City, 21042-1226
(443) 535-0008; (800) 899-7533
FAX (443) 535-0009; e-mail: AmandasRS@aol.com
www.Amandas-BBRS.com

164. Spacious grounds, quiet peaceful setting near great restaurants and the ocean. Beautifully restored early 19th-century Victorian with wraparound porch. All rooms are decorated with quality antiques. Honeymoon suite with Jacuzzi. Two-night minimum on weekends. Full breakfast. $150-175.

Merry Sherwood Plantation

8909 Worchester Highway, 21811
(410) 641-2112; (800) 660-0358
www.merrysherwood.com

Merry Sherwood Plantation, circa 1859, was listed in the National Register of Historic Places in 1991. A wonderful blend of Greek Revival. Classic Italianate, and Gothic architecture, this elegant 27-room mansion has nine Victorian-style fireplaces, private baths, ballroom, 19 acres of 19th century lush private gardens, and authentic period antiques. Convenient to Ocean City and many historic and resort attractions. Full gourmet breakfast is included. Smoking permitted in designated areas only.

7 No smoking; 8 Children welcome; 9 Social drinking allowed; 10 Tennis nearby; 11 Swimming nearby; 12 Golf nearby; 13 Skiing nearby; 14 May be booked through a travel agent; 15 Handicapped accessible.

Merry Sherwood Plantation

Host: Kirk Burbage
Rooms: 8 (6 PB; 2 SB)
Full Breakfast
Credit Cards: A, B
Notes: 2, 5, 8, 10, 11, 12

BETTERTON

Lantern Inn

115 Ericsson Avenue, P.O. Box 29, 21610
(410) 348-5809; (800) 499-7265

This restored 1904 inn is in a quiet town on
Maryland's Eastern Shore. One and one-half
blocks to a nice sand beach on the Chesapeake
Bay. Near historic Chestertown, sporting clays,
horseback riding, hiking trails, and three
wildlife refuges. Miles of excellent biking roads,
with detailed maps provided. Antiquing and
good seafood restaurants abound. Children over
12 welcome. Chair stair lifts to rooms only.

Lantern Inn

Hosts: Ray and Sandi Sparks
Rooms: 13 (4 PB; 9 SB) $75-90
Full Breakfast
Credit Cards: A, B, C
Notes: 2, 5, 7, 9, 10, 11

BOYD

Amanda's Bed & Breakfast Reservation Service

3538 Lakeway Drive, Ellicott City, 21042-1226
(443) 535-0008; (800) 899-7533
FAX (443) 535-0009; e-mail: AmandasRS@aol.com
www.Amandas-BBRS.com

116. An 18th-century historic log cabin, lovingly restored, crooked walls, and exposed
original beams and seams. Listed in the
national historic registry. A private place on 32
acres of herb gardens, woodland paths, ponds,
sheep, and country meadows. Host has a small
adjacent yarn shop where she dyes her own
wool. Bring own bicycles for cycling around
the beautiful countryside. There is a fireplace
in the sitting area of the cabin along with a
queen-size bed and bath. For additional people
the floor has a room with a double bed for a
family or two couples. Full breakfast. $150.

BUCKEYSTOWN

Amanda's Bed & Breakfast Reservation Service

3538 Lakeway Drive, Ellicott City, 21042-1226
(443) 535-0008; (800) 899-7533
FAX (443) 535-0009; e-mail: AmandasRS@aol.com
www.Amandas-BBRS.com

154. A family-owned and operated bed and
breakfast inn on four acres with sweeping
views of the historic village of Buckeystown
and the Catoctin Mountains. Afternoon tea is
served. Relax by the marble fireplace in the
spacious library. The guest rooms are uniquely
decorated with queen-size beds, private baths
with modern comforts such as cable TV, telephone, and air conditioning. Several rooms

have fireplaces and one features a whirlpool tub. A variety of attractions surround the area in addition to the beautiful countryside. Full breakfast. $95 and up.

The Catoctin Inn

3619 Buckeystown Pike, P.O. Box 243, 21717
(301) 694-0555; (301) 874-5555; (800) 730-5550
FAX (301) 874-2026; www.catoctininn.com

The Catoctin Inn is a historic country inn. Established 1780-1800s. The rooms in the inn offer antique decor, queen-size beds, and private baths. Or stay in one of the cottages or the king deluxe rooms, each with king-size beds, fireplaces, and two-person whirlpool baths. All of the rooms offer telephones, TVs, and VCRs, and include a full breakfast. There is also meeting space available up to 200 persons. Dinner available on Fridays and Saturdays only. A full restaurant will open by fall of 1999. One room is available for smoking. One room is handicapped accessible.

Rooms: 20 (19 PB; 1 SB) $95-175
Full Breakfast
Credit Cards: A, B, C, D, E
Notes: 2, 5, 6, 8, 9, 10, 11, 12, 13, 14

The Inn at Buckeystown

3521 Buckeystown Pike, P.O. Box 546, 21717
(301) 874-5755; (800) 272-1190

The Inn at Buckeystown is a Victorian village inn opened in 1981 to provide, bed, board, and

The Inn at Buckeystown

luxury to the traveler. Located on two acres just one hour from Baltimore and Washington, the inn is central to a variety of historic sites, natural environs, and antique market places. Emphasis is placed on learning, meeting, and exceeding our guests needs and expectations. Modified American Plan available on weekends, two-night minimums apply to certain holidays.

Hosts: George Richardson and Debbie Maltrotti
Rooms: 7 (5 PB; 2 SB) $110-165
Full or Continental Breakfast
Credit Cards: A, B, C, D
Notes: 2, 5, 7, 9, 12, 13, 14

CHESAPEAKE CITY

The Blue Max Inn

300 Bohemia Avenue, 21915
(410) 885-2781; FAX (410) 885-2809

Beautiful Georgian Federal-style inn built in 1854. The inn, fondly called, "the house with generous porches," rests among restored shops and restaurants. Sumptuous gourmet breakfasts served in fireside dining room or solarium overlooking picturesque fishpond. Seven elegant guest rooms, each with private bath and air conditioning. One block to C&D canal. Historic district.

Rooms: 7 (PB) $85-130
Credit Cards: A, B, C, D
Notes: 2, 5, 7, 9, 15

CHESTERTOWN

Amanda's Bed & Breakfast Reservation Service

3538 Lakeway Drive, Ellicott City, 21042-1226
(443) 535-0008; (800) 899-7533
FAX (443) 535-0009; e-mail: AmandasRS@aol.com
www.Amandas-BBRS.com

126. In the heart of Chestertown, this bed and breakfast was built in 1876. An easy walk to Washington College, shops, and restaurants.

7 No smoking; 8 Children welcome; 9 Social drinking allowed; 10 Tennis nearby; 11 Swimming nearby; 12 Golf nearby; 13 Skiing nearby; 14 May be booked through a travel agent; 15 Handicapped accessible.

Near Rock Hall and other interesting towns on the Eastern Shore. Three rooms with private bath. $105-110.

136. The inn sits on the Chester River, four miles below town. The original part of the house was built in the 1830s and was completely renovated prior to its opening as an inn in 1985. Five acres of waterfront make up the grounds, and a marina offers deep-water slips. Five rooms and one suite, all with private baths, are available. Continental breakfast served. $95-115.

204. This Victorian inn was built in 1877 and is in the heart of town. Restored to its original charm. The dining room and double parlor feature plaster moldings. Walk to historic Washington College and shops. Seven rooms with private baths. Continental breakfast. $95-110.

Widow's Walk Inn

402 High Street, 21620
(410) 778-6455; www.chestertown.com/widow/

In Chestertown's historic district, the inn is within a short walking distance of many homes and buildings of historic significance, as well as quaint gift and antique shops and restaurants. At the inn, guests will find comfortable

Widow's Walk Inn

lodging with the atmosphere and warmth of an 1877 circa Victorian home.

Hosts: Bob and Sue Lathroum
Rooms: 5 (3 PB; 2 SB) $90-115
Continental Breakfast
Credit Cards: A, B
Notes: 2, 5, 7, 9, 11, 12

CHEVY CHASE

Chevy Chase Bed & Breakfast

6815 Connecticut Avenue, 20815
(301) 656-5867 (phone/FAX)

Enjoy gracious hospitality and the convenience of being close to the sights of Washington, D.C., and conferences in Bethesda, in a charming beamed-ceiling turn-of-the-century house and garden in historic Chevy Chase. Furnished with rare tapestries, oriental rugs, and native crafts from around the world. Special breakfasts of European hot breads, jams, cheeses, fresh fruits, and a special blend of Louisiana coffee.

Host: S. C. Gotbaum
Rooms: 1 (PB) $60-65
Continental Breakfast
Credit Cards: None
Notes: 2, 5, 7, 8, 10, 11, 12, 14

CLARKSVILLE

Amanda's Bed & Breakfast Reservation Service

3538 Lakeway Drive, Ellicott City, 21042-1226
(443) 535-0008; (800) 899-7533
FAX (443) 535-0009; e-mail: AmandasRS@aol.com
www.Amandas-BBRS.com

350. A renovated antique shop in an old barn. Pleasantly created space with sitting and eating area with kitchenette. Gas-fired fireplace in sitting area. Separate bedroom and bath. Plank floors and beamed ceilings. Furnished with country antiques. Scenic trails and picnic by pond. $145.

NOTES: Credit cards accepted: A MasterCard; B Visa; C American Express; D Discover; E Diner's Club; F Other; 2 Personal checks accepted; 3 Lunch available; 4 Dinner available; 5 Open all year; 6 Pets welcome;

CUMBERLAND

Inn at Walnut Bottom

120 Greene Street, 21502
(301) 777-0003; (800) 286-9718
FAX (301) 777-8288; e-mail: iwb@iwbinfo.com
www.iwbinfo.com

Historic Cumberland's finest lodging. Twelve lovely guest rooms and family suites. Two cozy sitting rooms for reading and relaxing. Afternoon refreshments and a full breakfast included with lodging. Excellent restaurant on premises. A small shop offers beautiful and unique items by local artisans. Stroll to the Western Maryland Scenic Railroad, the historic district, and antique shops. Families welcome. Scenic train packages. Extraordinary hiking, biking, and sightseeing close by. Free bike use. Short drive to Frank Lloyd Wright's Fallingwater. AAA three-diamond-rated and Mobil three-star-rated.

Hosts: Grant M. Irvin and Kirsten O. Hansen
Rooms: 12 (8 PB; 4 SB) $79-125
Suites $120-190
Full Breakfast
Credit Cards: A, B, C, D
Notes: 2, 4, 5, 7, 8, 9, 10, 11, 12, 13

Inn at Walnut Bottom

EASTON

Amanda's Bed & Breakfast Reservation Service

3538 Lakeway Drive, Ellicott City, 21042-1226
(443) 535-0008; (800) 899-7533
FAX (443) 535-0009; e-mail: AmandasRS@aol.com
www.Amandas-BBRS.com

137. This lovely Victorian bed and breakfast, in the historic district of Easton, offers current amenities with former charm. Nineteenth-century oak, walnut, and mahogany antiques decorate the guest rooms enhanced by private baths with a whirlpool tub and/or a fireplace. Off-street parking and secured storage for bicycles. Walk to historic sites, restaurants, and boutiques. Easton is just a short drive to St. Michaels and other interesting places on the Eastern Shore. Full breakfast. $85-120.

202. Great wraparound porch with swing enhancing an old Victorian-style home in Easton, the colonial capital on Maryland's Eastern Shore. This eight-room bed and breakfast inn is within walking distance of the Academy of Arts, historical points of interest, restaurants, and antique shops. There is secure storage for bicycles. Six rooms have private baths, two share a bath. Continental breakfast. $75-110.

380. Cottage on the water near Easton has a beautiful view from private deck. Separate from main house, with equipped kitchen, bath, sitting area with pull-out sofa, and bedroom. TV. Air conditioned. Continental breakfast. $125.

The Bishop's House Bed & Breakfast

214 Goldsborough Street, P.O. Box 2217,
   21601-2217
(410) 820-7290 (phone/FAX); (800) 223-7290
e-mail: bishopshouse@skipjack.bluecrab.org

Experience the elegance of a lovingly restored, historic district, in-town Victorian, circa 1880. Romantically furnished in period style, with working fireplaces, whirlpool tubs, air conditioning, off-street parking, secured overnight storage for bicycles, bicycle rentals for guests, wraparound porch for relaxation, and hot sumptuous breakfasts. Within 10 miles of historic Oxford and St. Michaels, the Bishop's House provides an excellent location for visiting all points of interest in Talbot County.

7 No smoking; 8 Children welcome; 9 Social drinking allowed; 10 Tennis nearby; 11 Swimming nearby; 12 Golf nearby; 13 Skiing nearby; 14 May be booked through a travel agent; 15 Handicapped accessible.

Within three blocks of restaurants, specialty shops, and boutiques.

Hosts: Diane M. Laird-Ippolito and John B. Ippolito
Rooms: 5 (PB) $85-120
Full Breakfast
Credit Cards: None
Notes: 2, 7, 9, 10, 11, 12, 14

ELKTON

The Garden Cottage

234 Blair Shore Road, 21921
(410) 398-5566

In a setting with an early plantation house, including a 400-year-old sycamore, the Garden Cottage nestles at the edge of a meadow

The Garden Cottage

flanked by herb gardens and an old restored barn with gift shop. It has a sitting room with working fireplace, air conditioning, bedroom, and bath. Freshly ground coffee and herbal teas are offered with the full country breakfast. Longwood Gardens and Winterthur Museum are 50 minutes away. Near historic Chesapeake City. Twenty-five-dollar charge for a third person in the room.

Hosts: Bill and Ann Stubbs
Cottage: 1 (PB) $93
Full Breakfast
Credit Cards: A, B
Notes: 2, 5, 6, 7, 8, 9, 10, 12. 14

FREDERICK

Amanda's Bed & Breakfast Reservation Service

3538 Lakeway Drive, Ellicott City, 21042-1226
(443) 535-0008; (800) 899-7533
FAX (443) 535-0009; e-mail: AmandasRS@aol.com
www.Amandas-BBRS.com

106. This inn's 26-acre grounds include a picturesque garden and henhouse. Each room offers a delightful 19th-century ambiance, and all rooms have private baths and air conditioning. A stone fireplace, stained-glass windows, and skylights highlight the keeping room where guests can relax. Four rooms, all of which have private baths, are available. Continental breakfast. $110.

Middle Plantation Inn

9549 Liberty Road, 21701
(301) 898-7128; e-mail: BandB@MPInn.com
www.MPInn.com

A charming bed and breakfast built of stone and log. Drive through horse country to the village of Mount Pleasant. Several miles east of Frederick, on 26 acres. Each room has furnishings of antiques with private bath, air conditioning, and TV. Nearby are antique shops, museums, and many historic attractions. Children over 15 welcome.

NOTES: Credit cards accepted: A MasterCard; B Visa; C American Express; D Discover; E Diner's Club; F Other; 2 Personal checks accepted; 3 Lunch available; 4 Dinner available; 5 Open all year; 6 Pets welcome;

Middle Plantation Inn

Hosts: Shirley and Dwight Mullican
Rooms: 4 (PB) $95-110
Continental Breakfast
Credit Cards: A, B, C
Notes: 2, 5, 7, 9, 10, 11, 12, 14

GRASONVILLE

Distinguished Accommodations in the Potomac Region— (Amanda's Bed & Breakfast Reservation Service)

3538 Lakeway Drive, Ellicott City, 21042-1226
(443) 535-0008; (800) 899-7533
FAX (443) 535-0009; e-mail: AmandasRS@aol.com
www.Amandas-BBRS.com

394. Looking out on the water, this country French manor house sits on 17 secluded acres surrounded by water. A very gracious and spacious house with numerous fireplaces, lovely solarium, swimming pool, and fantastic sunsets. A gourmet full breakfast is served. Three spacious rooms. One has a working fireplace. $110-160.

HAGERSTOWN

Amanda's Bed & Breakfast Reservation Service

3538 Lakeway Drive, Ellicott City, 21042-1226
(443) 535-0008; (800) 899-7533
FAX (443) 535-0009; e-mail: AmandasRS@aol.com
www.Amandas-BBRS.com

156. An 1890 Queen Anne Victorian on a tree-lined street of grand old homes. Furnished in antiques that provide a tranquil setting. Three rooms, each with private bath. Full breakfast. $95-125.

Beaver Creek House Bed & Breakfast

20432 Beaver Creek Road, 21740
(301) 797-4764; (888) 942-9966

A turn-of-the-century country home filled with family antiques and memorabilia. Five centrally air-conditioned guest rooms. A full country breakfast is served on the screened porch or in the elegantly decorated dining room. A sitting room has reading material of local interest. Guests can enjoy a country garden with fish pond and fountain. Visiting historic sites, hiking, biking, skiing, golf, and antiquing are popular recreational pursuits.

Hosts: Don and Shirley Day
Rooms: 5 (PB) $75-95
Full Breakfast
Credit Cards: A, B, C
Notes: 2, 5, 7, 9, 10, 11, 12, 13, 14

Beaver Creek House

Blue Ridge Bed & Breakfast

2458 Castleman Road, Berryville, VA 22611
(540) 955-1246; (800) 296-1246
FAX (540) 955-4240
e-mail: blurdgbb@shentel.net
www.blueridgebb.com

A. Large 1890 Victorian filled with beautiful antiques. A culinary delight. Close to downtown

7 No smoking; 8 Children welcome; 9 Social drinking allowed; 10 Tennis nearby; 11 Swimming nearby; 12 Golf nearby; 13 Skiing nearby; 14 May be booked through a travel agent; 15 Handicapped accessible.

shopping. Corporate rates and packages available. $75-115.

B. Turn-of-the-century farmhouse filled with antiques and collectibles in the middle of 125 acres, 40 of which are woods. Hosts speak Spanish, German, and Italian. Close to I-70 and I-81, Antietam battlefield, C&O Canal, Crystal Grottoes Caverns, Potomac River, outlet stores, and antique shops. Children are always welcome. $50-95.

Sunday's

Lewrene Farm

Lewrene Farm Bed & Breakfast

9738 Downsville Pike, 21740
(301) 582-1735

Spacious Colonial country farm home near I-70 and I-81. Large living room, fireplace, piano, and antique family heirlooms. Deluxe bedrooms with canopied poster beds and other antique beds. Bedside snacks, shared and private baths, one of which has a whirlpool. Full breakfast. Home away from home for tourists, business people, families. Children welcome. Peacocks, old-fashioned swing, and a gazebo. Quilts for sale. Antietam battlefield, Harpers Ferry, C&O Canal, and antique malls nearby. Seventy miles to Washington and Baltimore.

Hosts: Lewis and Irene Lehman
Rooms: 5 (3 PB; 3 SB) $50-115
Full Breakfast
Credit Cards: None
Notes: 2, 5, 7, 8, 10, 11, 13

Sunday's Bed & Breakfast

39 Broadway, 21740
(800) 221-4828

In historic Hagerstown, this romantic 1890 Queen Anne Victorian is distinctively furnished with antiques. One suite has a large two-person whirlpool to soothe your spirit. Guests may want to explore the national historic parks of Antietam, Harpers Ferry, and the C&O Canal. Antique shops, museums, golfing, fishing, skiing, and shopping outlets are all nearby. Full breakfast, afternoon tea and desserts, evening wine and cheese, late-night cordial and chocolate, fruit basket, and more await guests.

Host: Bob Ferrino
Rooms: 4 (PB) $65-135
Full Breakfast
Credit Cards: A, B, E
Notes: 2, 5, 7, 9, 10, 11, 12, 13, 14

HAVRE DE GRACE

Amanda's Bed & Breakfast Reservation Service

3538 Lakeway Drive, Ellicott City, 21042-1226
(443) 535-0008; (800) 899-7533
FAX (443) 535-0009; e-mail: AmandasRS@aol.com
www.Amandas-BBRS.com

302. Explore historic Havre de Grace, the upper Chesapeake Bay region, while spending nights in a turn-of-the-century Victorian house, little changed from its original construction. Visit the Concord Point Lighthouse, a decoy museum, canal museum, and a state park; enjoy local seafood and the bay. Four rooms, one with private bath, are available in the main house. A newly renovated cottage with queen-size bed, TV/VCR, kitchenette, antiques, Jacuzzi, and fireplace is also available for $125. $65-85.

Vandiver Inn

Vandiver Inn

301 South Union Avenue, 21078
(800) 245-1655; www.vandiverinn.com

Turn-of-the-century charm and Victorian hospitality await the visitor to the unprecedented Vandiver Inn, historic Havre de Grace's finest guest inn. Enjoy tastefully appointed rooms, fireplaces, and a gourmet breakfast. Journey back to the heyday of gracious Maryland living, Chesapeake Bay style, when visiting the Vandiver Inn. The inn is surrounded by historic sites, museums, and four full-service marinas. Catering site available.

Host: Suzanne Mottek
Rooms: 9 (PB) $85-125
Full Breakfast
Credit Cards: A, B, C, D, F
Notes: 2, 5, 7, 8, 9, 10, 12, 14, 15

KEEDYSVILLE

Antietam Overlook Farm

P.O. Box 30, 21756
(800) 878-4241; FAX (301) 432-5230

Ninety-five acres of mountaintop tranquility overlooking the Antietam National Battlefield,

with a four-state view. Accommodations feature queen-size beds, fireplaces, screened porches, big quiet bubble bath tubs, and, best of all—privacy. Huge country breakfast and complimentary beverages. Reservations in advance. Call for availability and directions.

Hosts: Barbara and John Dreisch
Rooms: 6 (PB) $115-165
Full Breakfast
Credit Cards: A, B, C, D
Notes: 2, 5, 7, 9, 10, 11, 12, 13, 14

KENT ISLAND

Amanda's Bed & Breakfast Reservation Service

3538 Lakeway Drive, Ellicott City, 21042-1226
(443) 535-0008; (800) 899-7533
FAX (443) 535-0009; e-mail: AmandasRS@aol.com
www.Amandas-BBRS.com

376. This newly constructed Victorian on the water on the most northern point of Kent Island has a stunning, breathtaking view of the bay. A hot tub built into the side of a cliff overlooks the water. Guests may enjoy a pool, decks, and many excellent seafood restaurants nearby on the island. Two rooms. Continental breakfast. $110.

MONKTON

Amanda's Bed & Breakfast Reservation Service

3538 Lakeway Drive, Ellicott City, 21042-1226
(443) 535-0008; (800) 899-7533
FAX (443) 535-0009; e-mail: AmandasRS@aol.com
www.Amandas-BBRS.com

209. Warm hospitality and exceptional accommodations are offered on this working farm. Pond with fishing privileges (catch and throw back), bicycling and hiking trails, and tubing on Gunpowder River. Near North Central Railroad, Ladew Gardens, and Amish country. One room is offered to guests, and it features a

7 No smoking; 8 Children welcome; 9 Social drinking allowed; 10 Tennis nearby; 11 Swimming nearby; 12 Golf nearby; 13 Skiing nearby; 14 May be booked through a travel agent; 15 Handicapped accessible.

private bath and fireplace. Continental or full breakfast. $85.

NEW MARKET

The Strawberry Inn

17 West Main Street, P.O. Box 237, 21774
(301) 865-3318

The first bed and breakfast in the state of Maryland, the Strawberry Inn has been in the business of hospitality for 26 years. It is furnished with antiques passed down from generations, truly a compliment to New Market, the antiques capital of Maryland. Guests have a variety of choices, type of beds, personal sitting room, private porches overlooking the beautiful landscaped gardens and gazebo. Full breakfast is served in the dining room or on the grapevine-covered porch. It's a hub for sightseeing to Washington, D.C., Baltimore, Civil War sites. An excellent restaurant just across the street.

Hosts: Jane and Bud Rossig
Rooms: 5 (PB) $95-125
Full Breakfast
Credit Cards: None
Notes: 2, 5, 7, 9, 10, 12, 13, 15

OAKLAND

Amanda's Bed & Breakfast Reservation Service

3538 Lakeway Drive, Ellicott City, 21042-1226
(443) 535-0008; (800) 899-7533
FAX (443) 535-0009; e-mail: AmandasRS@aol.com
www.Amandas-BBRS.com

108. A 65-acre working farm with horses, crops, pond, ducks, etc. Near Deep Creek Lake with seasonal activities like skiing, swimming, boating, hiking, biking, snow boarding, ice skating. Walk to the woods, sit by the lake, relax by the log fire in the great room. Five guest rooms, each with a private bath. $85-100.

157. Recreation land! Water, ice, and snow for year-round fun. Colonial Revival with a large lawn and mature trees in a historic district. Five rooms available, three with private baths. Fireside breakfast in dining room. Relax after sporting day in cozy TV room. $65-95.

The Oak and Apple Bed & Breakfast

208 North Second Street, 21550
(301) 334-9265
e-mail: oakapplebb@mail2.gcnet.net

Built circa 1915, this restored Colonial Revival sits on a beautiful large lawn with mature trees and includes a large columned front porch, enclosed sun porch, parlor with fireplace, and cozy gathering room with TV. Awake to a fresh Continental breakfast served fireside in the dining room or on the sun porch. The quaint town of Oakland offers a wonderful small-town atmosphere; and Deep Creek Lake, Wisp Ski Resort, and state parks with hiking, fishing, swimming, bicycling, boating, and skiing are nearby.

Host: Jana Brown
Rooms: 5 (3 PB; 2 SB) $75-100
Continental Breakfast
Credit Cards: A, B
Notes: 2, 5, 7, 9, 10, 11, 12, 13

OCEAN CITY

Amanda's Bed & Breakfast Reservation Service

3538 Lakeway Drive, Ellicott City, 21042-1226
(443) 535-0008; (800) 899-7533
FAX (443) 535-0009; e-mail: AmandasRS@aol.com
www.Amandas-BBRS.com

170. In old Ocean City near the boardwalk and beach. An 11-room bed and breakfast, originally a rooming house for young women. Current owners are local natives. Caring and new decorating are a plus. Some private baths. Enjoy good weather off-season. Near Fifth and Boardwalk in the older section of Ocean City.

NOTES: Credit cards accepted: A MasterCard; B Visa; C American Express; D Discover; E Diner's Club; F Other; 2 Personal checks accepted; 3 Lunch available; 4 Dinner available; 5 Open all year; 6 Pets welcome;

Parking available. In-season and off-season rates available. $95-145.

252. On the ocean with all rooms magnificently decorated for luxury and comfort. Enjoy the breathtaking views from the very private oceanfront location or just relax in the gracious living room. Watch the waves pound the shore from the wraparound porch. Enjoy the sea breezes and sunset. The boardwalk is just outside the front door. An adult smoke-free accommodation. $150-215.

OXFORD

Distinguished Accommodations in the Potomac Region— (Amanda's Bed & Breakfast Reservation Service)

3538 Lakeway Drive, Ellicott City, 21042-1226
(443) 535-0008; (800) 899-7533
FAX (443) 535-0009; e-mail: AmandasRS@aol.com
www.Amandas-BBRS.com

396. A gracious combination of restored 18th-century splendor with touches of luxury designed for unsurpassed comfort and privacy. Set among magnolias and arching willows on the banks of Island Creek. All rooms provide splendid water views. There are several rooms in the main house as well as a private cottage which features a Jacuzzi, full kitchen, and fireplace in the living room. Prices start at $250.

ROCK HALL

Amanda's Bed & Breakfast Reservation Service

3538 Lakeway Drive, Ellicott City, 21042-1226
(443) 535-0008; (800) 899-7533
FAX (443) 535-0009; e-mail: AmandasRS@aol.com
www.Amandas-BBRS.com

299. Nestled between the Eastern Neck Wildlife Refuge and the small town of Rock Hall, a water village on the upper Eastern Shore. Visit the unspoiled shoreline of the Chesapeake Bay and the watermen at the docks. The manor house is 100 years old. Six rooms with a cottage in rear. $85-155.

Distinguished Accommodations in the Potomac Region— (Amanda's Bed & Breakfast Reservation Service)

3538 Lakeway Drive, Ellicott City, 21042-1226
(443) 535-0008; (800) 899-7533
FAX (443) 535-0009; e-mail: AmandasRS@aol.com
www.Amandas-BBRS.com

360. A very private place in the quaint village of Rock Hall, small watermen's village with lots of outdoor activity. Local antique and gift shops with places to taste the area cuisine. Swimming pool on premises. Simple elegance along with luxury and comfort on 30 acres of waterfront property. A nice restaurant on premises.

The Inn at Osprey

20786 Rock Hall Avenue, 21661
(410) 639-2194; FAX (410) 639-7716

Enjoy a relaxing getaway on the Eastern Shore of Maryland at this reproduction Colonial inn on the shores of scenic Swan Creek. Seven spacious, well-appointed guest rooms are available, some with water views and all with private baths and TVs. Full service restaurant and bar serving dinner only. Picnic grounds, swimming pool, bicycles, and marina. Close to antiquing, fishing, hunting, boating, and bird sanctuary. An easy two-hour drive from Philadelphia, Baltimore, and Washington, D.C. Seasonal rates.

Host: Christine Will
Rooms: 7 (PB) $105-160
Continental Breakfast
Credit Cards: A, B, D
Notes: 2, 4, 5, 7, 8, 9, 10, 11, 12

7 No smoking; 8 Children welcome; 9 Social drinking allowed; 10 Tennis nearby; 11 Swimming nearby; 12 Golf nearby; 13 Skiing nearby; 14 May be booked through a travel agent; 15 Handicapped accessible.

ROCKVILLE (DERWOOD)

Amanda's Bed & Breakfast Reservation Service

3538 Lakeway Drive, Ellicott City, 21042-1226
(443) 535-0008; (800) 899-7533
FAX (443) 535-0009; e-mail: AmandasRS@aol.com
www.Amandas-BBRS.com

177. Suburban Washington, near Rockville/ Bethesda, just two minutes from Shady Grove Metro Station into Washington. Colonial-style with a wing that includes a suite, bedroom/ bath with whirlpool and sun porch. Public golf nearby. Also two other rooms available. $80-85.

ST. MICHAELS

Amanda's Bed & Breakfast Reservation Service

3538 Lakeway Drive, Ellicott City, 21042-1226
(443) 535-0008; (800) 899-7533
FAX (443) 535-0009; e-mail: AmandasRS@aol.com
www.Amandas-BBRS.com

245. This historic house, dating back to 1805, with period furnishings, working fireplaces, and four-poster canopied beds, is in a historic watermen's village on the Eastern Shore of the Chesapeake Bay. Within walking distance of shops, restaurants, and the museum, this inn offers seven rooms and one cottage with private and shared baths. Two-night minimum on weekends March through December. Continental breakfast. $80-120.

Chesapeake Wood Duck Inn

Gibsontown Road, P.O. Box 202 Tilghman Island, 21671
(410) 886-2070; (800) 956-2070

Award-winning "Southern hospitality on the Chesapeake Bay" is a way of life for owners/innkeepers Dave and Stephanie. This romantically restored 1890 Victorian overlooks Dogwood Harbor, home of the last fleet of antique skipjack sailing vessels in North America. According to the *New York Times*, the Wood Duck Inn is "luxurious…immaculate…well appointed." Period furnishings, oriental rugs, original art, luxurious linens, and fresh flowers. Water views abound. On Maryland's Eastern Shore and the Chesapeake Bay, in a quaint fishing village offering spectacular scenery, serenity, and a forgotten way of life. Within walking distance of restaurants and shops. Bikes available. AAA three-diamond and Mobil three-star rating.

Hosts: Stephanie and Dave Feith
Rooms: 7 (PB) $139-219
Suite: 1
Full Breakfast
Credit Cards: A, B
Notes: 2, 5, 7, 9, 10, 11, 12, 14

The Inn at Christmas Farm

8873 Tilghman Island Road, Wittman, 21676
(800) 987-8436; FAX (410) 745-5618

This waterfront farm near St. Michaels offers a unique combination of solitude at the water's edge, broad lawns, meticulously restored two-room suites (including Christmas Cottage and Riverview with Jacuzzi), while fine restaurants, antiques, and historic towns are but minutes away. Enjoy gourmet breakfasts while watching peacocks, waterfowl, and the tiny horse, James, meander nearby. Walk along the creek or simply spend a lazy afternoon pondside with magnificent views of marsh, field, and farm. Member of Professional Association of Innkeepers of America. Children welcome.

Hosts: David and Beatrice Lee
Rooms: 5 (PB) $155-175
Full Breakfast
Credit Cards: A, B
Notes: 2, 3, 4, 5, 9, 10, 11, 12, 14

The Inn at Christmas Farm

Kemp House Inn

412 Talbot Street, P.O. Box 638, 21663-0638
(410) 745-2243

Built in 1807 by Colonel Joseph Kemp, this superbly crafted home is one of a small collection of large Federal-period brick structures in St. Michaels. Elegant Federal details are evident throughout the house. Each of the rooms is tastefully furnished with period decor. Cozy antique four-poster rope beds with patchwork quilts, down pillows, wing-back sitting chairs, and Queen Anne tables grace each room. Old-fashioned nightshirts, low-light sconces, candles, and working fireplaces create an ambiance of the early 19th century.

Hosts: Diane and Steve Cooper
Rooms: 8 (6 PB; 2 SB) $80-120
Continental Breakfast
Credit Cards: A, B, D
Notes: 2, 5, 7, 9, 10, 12, 14

Kemp House Inn

Parsonage Inn

210 North Talbot Street, Route 33, 21663
(410) 745-5519; (800) 394-5519

Late Victorian bed and breakfast, circa 1883, lavishly restored in 1985 with eight guest rooms, private baths, king- or queen-size brass beds with Laura Ashley linens. Parlor and dining room in European tradition. Gourmet restaurant next door. Two blocks to Chesapeake Maritime Museum, shops, and harbor. Ten percent off midweek for AARP or retired

Parsonage Inn

officers. ABBA, AAA, and Mobil three-star award-winner.

Hosts: Walt and Jane Johnson
Rooms: 8 (PB) $90-160
Full Breakfast
Credit Cards: A, B
Notes: 2, 5, 7, 8, 9, 10, 11, 12

Wades Point Inn on the Bay

P.O. Box 7, 21663
(888) 923-3466

On the Eastern Shore of Chesapeake Bay, this historic country inn is ideal for those seeking country serenity and bay splendor. The main house, circa 1819, was built by a noted shopwright. From 1890 to the present the inn has provided a peaceful setting for relaxation and recreation, such as fishing, crabbing, and a

Wades Point Inn on the Bay

7 No smoking; 8 Children welcome; 9 Social drinking allowed; 10 Tennis nearby; 11 Swimming nearby; 12 Golf nearby; 13 Skiing nearby; 14 May be booked through a travel agent; 15 Handicapped accessible.

one-mile nature and jogging trail on 120 acres. Chesapeake Bay Maritime Museum, cruises, sailing charters, fine shops, and restaurants are nearby.

Hosts: Betsy and John Feller
Rooms: 24 (17 PB; 7 SB) $110-230
Continental Breakfast
Credit Cards: A, B
Notes: 2, 7, 8, 9, 10, 11, 12, 15

SCOTLAND

St. Michael's Manor
Bed & Breakfast

50200 St. Michael's Manor Way, 20687
(301) 872-4025

The land belongs to St. Michael's Manor (1805) and was originally patented to Leonard Calvert in 1637. The house, on Long Neck Creek, is furnished with antiques. Boating, canoeing, a swimming pool, bikes, and wine-tasting are available. Near Point Lookout State Park, Civil War monuments, and historic St. Mary's City. Open February through December. Smoking permitted in designated areas only. Inquire about accommodations for children.

Hosts: Joseph and Nancy Dick
Rooms: 4 (SB) $50-75
Full Breakfast
Credit Cards: None
Notes: 2, 9, 10, 11, 12

SILVER SPRING

Amanda's Bed & Breakfast
Reservation Service

3538 Lakeway Drive, Ellicott City, 21042-1226
(443) 535-0008; (800) 899-7533
FAX (443) 535-0009; e-mail: AmandasRS@aol.com
www.Amandas-BBRS.com

325. Easy commute to Washington, D.C. Wooded park setting in an older residential neighborhood. Tudor-style home with Euro-

pean antiques. Walk to local restaurants. One suite with queen-size bed and private bath. One twin bedroom. Shared bath. Continental breakfast. $70-90.

SOLOMONS

Back Creek Inn Bed & Breakfast

Alexander Lane and Calvert Street, P.O. Box 520, 20688-0520
(410) 326-2022; FAX (410) 326-2946
www.bbonline.com/md/backcreek/

Established gardens and water surround this 1800s waterman's home. The view includes a lily pond and Back Creek with deep water slips at the inn's private prier. Walk or bike to island stops, gallery, maritime museum, restaurants, and antique shops. Garden tea on Wednesdays by RSVP and picnic baskets can be catered. This inn serves as a perfect respite or corporate retreat.

Hosts: Carol Pennock and Lin Cochran
Rooms: 7 (PB) $95-145
Full Breakfast
Credit Cards: A, B
Notes: 2, 5, 7, 9, 10, 11, 12

STEVENSON

Distinguished Accommodations
in the Potomac Region—
(Amanda's Bed & Breakfast
Reservation Service)

3538 Lakeway Drive, Ellicott City, 21042-1226
(443) 535-0008; (800) 899-7533
FAX (443) 535-0009; e-mail: AmandasRS@aol.com
www.Amandas-BBRS.com

115. A large Tudor mansion on 45 acres. Five spacious rooms used for bed and breakfast. Each room has a special feature. Whirlpool tub, steam sauna shower, fireplace, double Jacuzzi, suite with sun porch. A gourmet

---

NOTES: Credit cards accepted: A MasterCard; B Visa; C American Express; D Discover; E Diner's Club; F Other; 2 Personal checks accepted; 3 Lunch available; 4 Dinner available; 5 Open all year; 6 Pets welcome;

breakfast is served in several different places according to the weather. $165-275.

STEVENSVILLE

Amanda's Bed & Breakfast Reservation Service

3538 Lakeway Drive, Ellicott City, 21042-1226
(443) 535-0008; (800) 899-7533
FAX (443) 535-0009; e-mail: AmandasRS@aol.com
www.Amandas-BBRS.com

180. This historic manor is on Kent Island on the Eastern Shore side of the Bay Bridge. This grand mansion, circa 1820, is in the Maryland historic register. The inn is surrounded by 226 acres of land and is one and one-half miles from the waterfront. The Victorian decor will make any stay here memorable. Restaurant has a four-star rating. Continental breakfast. $130-225.

TANEYTOWN

Distinguished Accommodations in the Potomac Region— (Amanda's Bed & Breakfast Reservation Service)

3538 Lakeway Drive, Ellicott City, 21042-1226
(443) 535-0008; (800) 899-7533
FAX (443) 535-0009; e-mail: AmandasRS@aol.com
www.Amandas-BBRS.com

161. This restored 1844 mansion sits on 24 acres with clay tennis courts, croquet, gardens, a view of the Catoctin Mountains, and gourmet dinners provided with reservations. Winner of "Baltimore's Most Romantic Getaway," this inn offers 14 rooms, all with private baths, some with fireplaces, and Jacuzzis. Excellent dining facilities. Two-night minimum on weekends. Full breakfast. $150-350.

THURMONT

Amanda's Bed & Breakfast Reservation Service

3538 Lakeway Drive, Ellicott City, 21042-1226
(443) 535-0008; (800) 899-7533
FAX (443) 535-0009; e-mail: AmandasRS@aol.com
www.Amandas-BBRS.com

240. A registered landmark with the Frederick County Historical Society. Near Catoctin Mountains, a state park, a zoo, skiing, and a golf course. Also near Gettysburg, Antietam, orchards, wineries, antiques, and shops. A spacious room with a view of the garden. Queen-size beds and private baths. A variety of restaurants within walking distance or a short drive. Continental breakfast. $85-95.

TILGHMAN ISLAND

Amanda's Bed & Breakfast Reservation Service

3538 Lakeway Drive, Ellicott City, 21042-1226
(443) 535-0008; (800) 899-7533
FAX (443) 535-0009; e-mail: AmandasRS@aol.com
www.Amandas-BBRS.com

378. An intimate resort with tennis courts, pools, and croquet court, fishing, biking, docking, and both formal and casual dining. Take a tour of the bay on a lock skipjack to get a feel for the many water communities that make up the Eastern Shore of Maryland. Enjoy the blue herons, Canada geese, and tundra swans that inhabit the Island. Beautiful country with many rooms having water views. All rooms have private baths. There are special weekend packages or regular rates. $100-225.

7 No smoking; 8 Children welcome; 9 Social drinking allowed; 10 Tennis nearby; 11 Swimming nearby; 12 Golf nearby; 13 Skiing nearby; 14 May be booked through a travel agent; 15 Handicapped accessible.

TOMPKINVILLE

Distinguished Accommodations in the Potomac Region— (Amanda's Bed & Breakfast Reservation Service)

3538 Lakeway Drive, Ellicott City, 21042-1226
(443) 535-0008; (800) 899-7533
FAX (443) 535-0009; e-mail: AmandasRS@aol.com
www.Amandas-BBRS.com

168. More than 100 acres with two miles of waterfront along Cuckold Creek, a navigable tributary of the Potomac River. Adjacent to the manor home are the pool house and the guest cottage. The breathtaking sunsets over the water and the boxwood-filled gardens beckon a distant past of unmatched serenity. There are a swimming pool, pier, bird watching, hiking, horseback riding, carriage rides, golf at Swan Point Golf Club, and many seafood restaurants. The guest house is a private place with a double bed and view of the water. The fireplaces, mini-kitchen, TV, and telephone enhance the tranquil setting for relaxing and rejuvenating. The pool house also faces the pool and the water. Sleep four to six people with three fireplaces, two baths, dining area, wet bar, and sitting area. Available for weekends or weekly. $150.

VIENNA

The Tavern House

Box 98, 21869
(410) 376-3347

A Colonial tavern on the Nanticoke River featuring the simple elegance of colonial living and special breakfasts that are a social occa-

The Tavern House

sion. A glimpse into Michener's Chesapeake for those who love colonial homes, the peace of a small town, or watching osprey in flight. Children over 12 are welcome.

Hosts: Harvey and Elise Altergott
Rooms: 4 (SB) $65-75
Full Breakfast
Credit Cards: A, B
Notes: 2, 5, 9, 10, 12, 14

WESTMINSTER

Amanda's Bed & Breakfast Reservation Service

3538 Lakeway Drive, Ellicott City, 21042-1226
(443) 535-0008; (800) 899-7533
FAX (443) 535-0009; e-mail: AmandasRS@aol.com
www.Amandas-BBRS.com

219. This Victorian inn is a former schoolhouse 45 minutes from northwest Baltimore. All guest rooms have queen-size beds and Jacuzzis. An athletic club, which includes swimming, jogging, racquetball, and weight machines, available to guests. Historic Union Hills Homestead and museums are all nearby. Hearty breakfast buffet. $145-195.

New Jersey

Candlewick Inn

AVON-BY-THE-SEA

Candlewick Inn

28 Woodland Avenue, 07717
(732) 774-2998; FAX (732) 774-4348
www.bbianj.com/candlewick

An 1890s ocean retreat, steps to the beach. Light, airy, cozy. A mix of antiques, wicker, and traditional motif. Full breakfast. Afternoon refreshment. Midweek and quiet season specials. An hour from New York City and Philadelphia. Guests say it's warm and comfortable. Make Candlewick Inn "your home away from home."

Host: Kathleen Ostermann
Rooms: 9 (5 PB; 4 SB) $85-175
Full Breakfast
Credit Cards: A, B, C
Notes: 2, 5, 7, 8, 9, 11, 12

Cashelmara Inn

22 Lakeside Avenue, 07717
(732) 776-8727; (800) 821-2976
e-mail: cashelmara@monmoutn.com
www.belmar.com/cashelmara

Oceanside/lakefront Victorian inn allows guests to enjoy views of the Atlantic from bed. Rooms decorated in beautiful Victorian antiques and a rocker-filled veranda overlooking the ocean make stays here memorable. Two suites with a fireplace and Jacuzzi are also available. Visit Mulligan's grand Victorian theater. Only 55 minutes from New York City and one hour from Philadelphia. Singles $10 less. Minimum stay summer weekends: three nights; summer holidays: four nights.

Host: Mary E. Wiernasz
Owner: Martin J. Mulligan
Rooms: 12 (PB) $83-193
Suites: 2 (PB) $193-276
Full Breakfast
Credit Cards: A, B, D
Notes: 2, 5, 7, 8, 9, 10, 11, 12

BARNEGAT

The Dynasty

Pebble Beach, 248 Edison Road, 08005
(609) 698-1566

A quiet bayside air-conditioned home on a peninsula with dock space. Breakfast is served around an award-winning pool amid beautiful foliage. Enjoy a picturesque view of the sunset and wildlife reserve, the warmth of a designer's fireplace, and the ultimate in antiques collected from around the world. All bedrooms have

Glenwood

Newton

80 Stanhope

Hope

Chatham

78

Plainfield

Flemington 287

Franklin
Park

Highlands

Princeton

Lambertville

PKY

TPK

Ocean Grove
Avon-By-The-Sea

Cream Ridge 195

Belmar
Spring Lake

Beverly

Bay Head

Island Heights

Barnegat

Pemberton

Haddonfield

TPK

EXP

Woodstown 40

Ocean City

Woodbine

PKY

North Wildwood

Wildwood Crest

Cape May

New Jersey

The Dynasty

twin or king-size beds. Just minutes to the world's largest playground, Atlantic City. Closed October 16 through May 5.

Host: Stanley Finkelstein
Rooms: 3 (1 PB; 2 SB) $95-135
Full Breakfast
Credit Cards: None
Notes: 2, 7, 8, 9, 10, 11, 12, 13, 14, 15

BAY HEAD

Conover's Bay Head Inn

646 Main Avenue, 08742
(732) 892-4664; (800) 956-9099
www.conovers.com

The 12 romantic, antique-filled bedrooms have views of the ocean, bay, marina, or gardens. The aroma of inn-baked biscuits, muffins, or coffeecake awakens guests each morning. Enjoy a large collection of original art or swim at the private ocean beaches. Collect seashells and sea glass. Walk to Twilight Lake and feed the ducks or relax in the garden. Try the new Jacuzzi spa in the south garden.

Hosts: Carl and Beverly Conover
Rooms: 12 (PB) $140-225
Full Breakfast
Credit Cards: A, B, C
Notes: 2, 5, 7, 9, 10, 11, 12

BEACH HAVEN

Amanda's Bed & Breakfast Reservation Service

3538 Lakeway Drive, Ellicott City, MD 21042-1226
(443) 535-0008; (800) 899-7533
FAX (443) 535-0009; e-mail: AmandasRS@aol.com
www.Amandas-BBRS.com

568. Step through the stained-glass front doors into another era. Built in 1876 with its Victorian charm and filled antiques. Nine guest rooms, five of which have ocean views. Breakfast is served as well as afternoon tea. Enjoy the sunsets and the ocean breeze from the wraparound veranda. Available for garden weddings.

Victoria Guest House

126 Amber Street, 08008
(609) 492-4154

This gracious guest house offers the warmth of a friendly late 19th-century family atmosphere and the refreshment of a "home away from home" in the heart of beautiful Long Beach Island. Between the ocean and the bay, the Victorias offer the comfort of spacious guest rooms, attractively decorated, some with four-poster beds and all with cheerful exposure and comfortably decorated. The guest house is across the street from the Bicentennial Park and convenient to Summer Stock theater, concerts, and day cruises to Atlantic City.

Hosts: Marilyn and Leonard Miller
Rooms: 23 (21 PB; 2 SB) $140-160
Credit Cards: None
Notes: 2, 7, 10, 11, 12

BELMAR

Amanda's Bed & Breakfast Reservation Service

3538 Lakeway Drive, Ellicott City, MD 21042-1226
(443) 535-0008; (800) 899-7533

NOTES: Credit cards accepted: A MasterCard; B Visa; C American Express; D Discover; E Diner's Club; F Other; 2 Personal checks accepted; 3 Lunch available; 4 Dinner available; 5 Open all year; 6 Pets welcome; 7 No smoking; 8 Children welcome; 9 Social drinking allowed; 10 Tennis nearby; 11 Swimming nearby; 12 Golf nearby; 13 Skiing nearby; 14 May be booked through a travel agent; 15 Handicapped accessible.

FAX (443) 535-0009; e-mail: AmandasRS@aol.com
www.Amandas-BBRS.com

A private home with three rooms for bed and breakfast. This home is newly built and decorated. Guest living room is large with a front porch to enjoy the summer breezes. One block to the beach. A full breakfast is served. One mile from town, marinas, or restaurants. $85-100.

The Inn at the Shore

The Inn at the Shore

301 Fourth Avenue, 07719
(732) 681-3762; FAX (732) 280-1914
e-mail: tomvolker@aol.com
www.bbianj.com/innattheshore

Enjoy the inn's casual Victorian child-friendly ambiance on the expansive wraparound porch, where a rocking chair takes one back to the seashore of days gone by. Relax in the spacious common areas, including a café-style brick patio ready for barbecues or refreshing beverages after a day at the beach. The large living room with its lovely stone fireplace and state-of-the-art entertainment center, the grand dining room, and the library are perfect for reading, writing, or just unwinding. The beach is only a short walk away, as is Silver Lake, home of the first flock of swans bred in America. Bedrooms are air conditioned. Beach badges included.

Hosts: Rosemary and Tom Volker
Rooms: 12 (3 PB: 9 SB) $95-125
Full Breakfast
Credit Cards: A, B, C
Notes: 2, 5, 7, 8, 9, 10, 11, 12, 14

BEVERLY

Whitebriar Bed & Breakfast

1029 South Cooper Street, Edgewater Park, 08010
(609) 871-3859

Historic Whitebriar is now two German salt-box-style homes. It has been added on to many times in its 280 years. An English conservatory shipped from Beverly, England, a cedar and plate glass room, overlooks the pool and spa on the east side of the house. Complemented by the neighboring Dunks Ferry Inn, this complex of Revolutionary historic homes is just 20 minutes from center city Philadelphia, three hours from Washington, and one hour and a half from the Big Apple, just eight minutes off I-295 and the New Jersey Turnpike. Orderly pets welcome. Ponies, pigs, puppies, and many different animals.

Hosts: Carole and Bill Moore; Liz and Ed Horner;
Carrie and Scott Ramage
Rooms: 9 (3 PB; 6 SB) $50-85
Full Breakfast
Credit Cards: F
Notes: 2, 3, 4, 5, 6, 7, 8, 9, 10, 11, 12

Whitebriar

CAPE MAY

The Abbey

34 Gurney Street at Columbia Avenue, 08204
(609) 884-4506

The Abbey consists of two restored Victorian buildings in the heart of Cape May's historic

NOTES: Credit cards accepted: A MasterCard; B Visa; C American Express; D Discover; E Diner's Club; F Other; 2 Personal checks accepted; 3 Lunch available; 4 Dinner available; 5 Open all year; 6 Pets welcome;

The Abbey

district. The main house is an elegant Gothic Revival villa with a 65-foot tower. Line drawings of the main house are on file in the Library of Congress. The cottage is a delightful example of Second Empire Mansard Revival style. All rooms have private baths, double or queen-size beds, and are furnished with period Victorian antiques; they have small refrigerators. Most have air conditioning in season. On- or off-site parking. Beach chairs and tags included. Afternoon tea. Two-, three-, or four-night minimum stays on weekends, depending on the season. Closed January through March. Personal checks for deposit only. Children 12 and over welcome.

Hosts: Jay and Marianne Schatz
Rooms: 14 (PB) $100-275
Full Breakfast
Credit Cards: A, B, D
Notes: 7, 9, 10, 11, 12

Amanda's Bed & Breakfast Reservation Service

3538 Lakeway Drive, Ellicott City, MD 21042-1226
(443) 535-0008; (800) 899-7533
FAX (443) 535-0009; e-mail: AmandasRS@aol.com
www.Amandas-BBRS.com

503. Built in 1840 and enlarged in 1900, this Victorian mansion retains the ambiance and grandeur of the era. Enjoy elegance and comfort, period reproduction wallpapers, and the original furnishings of the Wilbraham family. Heated swimming pool available to guests. Four blocks from the beach, and beach passes are available. Ten accommodations, all with private baths. Full breakfast. $100-200.

504. In the prime historic district of this wonderful seaside town, this gem of an inn has spacious rooms, exceptional period furniture and woodwork. Some of Cape May's finest stained glass remains for guests enjoyment. Wintertime is the coziest by the parlor fire or in summer sun and shade on the porches. Just one block from the beach. $85-250.

506. Just a half-block from the ocean with beach passes for guests. Comfortable and cozy with several porches to enjoy the ocean breeze and relax. Near the mall and restaurants. Victorian decor, ceiling fans, air conditioning, and some parking. Full breakfast. $85-200.

507. One of many lovely Victorian inns in Cape May, just two blocks from the beach or the mall. Romantic and relaxing. A full breakfast is served. Beach tags, towels, chairs, and parking. $85-175.

508. A very nice 24-room Victorian summer cottage. Eight of these rooms are used for bed and breakfast. Some off-street parking available. Two blocks from the beach or the mall. Beach tags available. Full breakfast. Two- and three-night minimum during busy season. $85-175.

539. A beautiful Colonial Revival home with large open living room with fireplace and French doors to outside covered patio. On-site parking. Two blocks from the beach in a quiet area. All rooms have private baths and a full breakfast is served. Afternoon snacks available. Beach passes provided. $75-125.

7 No smoking; 8 Children welcome; 9 Social drinking allowed; 10 Tennis nearby; 11 Swimming nearby; 12 Golf nearby; 13 Skiing nearby; 14 May be booked through a travel agent; 15 Handicapped accessible.

621. Comfortable elegance in a classic Second Empire inn with a grand entrance hall and spiral staircase. Built in 1882, one of Cape May's original guest houses. A full breakfast is served with afternoon snacks. Outdoor showers, beach tags, towels, and parking. $150-165.

Angel of the Sea

Angel of the Sea
Bed & Breakfast

5-7 Trenton Avenue, 08204
(800) 848-3369; FAX (609) 884-3331
e-mail: innkeeper@angelofthesea.com
www.angelofthesea.com

The Angel of the Sea was built in 1850 and renovated in 1989. There are 27 guest rooms, all with private baths and many with views of the Atlantic Ocean. A full breakfast, afternoon sweets, and wine and cheese are served daily. The Angel was awarded the second place Best B&B in North America in 1996. Enjoy the charm of this Victorian "painted lady." Children over eight welcome. Smoking permitted outside on the veranda only.

Hosts: Gregory and Lorie Whissell
Room: 27 (PB) $95-285
Full Breakfast
Credit Cards: A, B, C
Notes: 2, 5, 7, 10, 11, 12

Bedford Inn

805 Stockton Avenue, 08204
(609) 884-4158; FAX (609) 884-6320
e-mail: info@bedfordinn.com

Fully restored Victorian bed and breakfast—romantic and elegant. All rooms and honeymoon suites are furnished with authentic antiques and have private bath, TV, and air conditioning in season; most with queen-size bed. Rates include gourmet breakfast and afternoon tea and treats, beach passes, beach chairs, and free on-site parking. Great location—very close to beach and center of town. Parlor fireplace and two-story porch. Children over seven welcome.

Hosts: Cindy and James Schmucker
Rooms: 11 (PB) $85-195
Full Breakfast
Credit Cards: A, B, C, D
Notes: 2, 7, 9, 10, 11, 12, 14

The Brass Bed Inn

719 Columbia Avenue, 08204
(609) 884-2302

Circa 1872—a collection of antique brass beds, lace curtains, gasoliers, oriental carpets. We offer gourmet breakfasts, elegantly served. One and one-half blocks to ocean—two blocks to the walking open-air mall. Carriage rides, trolley, sight-seeing. Both casual and fine dining are within walking distance. Come and enjoy the rockers. The inn is in the historical district.

Hosts: Marilyn and Tony Codario
Rooms: 9 (7 PB; 2 SB) $100-170
Full Breakfast
Credit Cards: A, B
Notes: 2, 7, 9, 10, 11, 12, 14

Captain Mey's Inn

202 Ocean Street, 08204
(609) 884-7793; (800) 981-3702
www.captainmeys.com

Charming 1890 Victorian inn, in historic district, named after the Dutch explorer Capt.

NOTES: Credit cards accepted: A MasterCard; B Visa; C American Express; D Discover; E Diner's Club; F Other; 2 Personal checks accepted; 3 Lunch available; 4 Dinner available; 5 Open all year; 6 Pets welcome;

Captain Mey's Inn

Cornelius Mey. The Dutch heritage is evident from the Persian rugs to the Delft blue china to European antiques. All queen-size beds, private baths, and air conditioning. Guest rooms with a two-person whirlpool tub, brass-footed Victorian whirlpool tub, and two beds available. A full country breakfast is served along with afternoon tea. On-site parking; walk to beach, shops, and restaurants.

Hosts: George and Kathleen Blinn
Rooms: 7 (PB) $85-225
Full Breakfast
Credit Cards: A, B, C
Notes: 2, 5, 7, 9, 10, 11, 12

The Carroll Villa Bed & Breakfast Hotel

19 Jackson Street, 08204
(609) 884-9619; FAX (609) 884-0264
e-mail: mbatter@cyberenet.net

Restored Victorian bed and breakfast/hotel, circa 1882, on one of the oldest streets, in the center of the historic district. One-half block from beach and ocean, and one-half block down from outdoor walking mall. Fifty minutes from Atlantic City. All rooms are on second and third floors. The Mad Batter Restaurant is on the first floor where guests can choose either to dine in the dining room, on the garden terrace, or on the popular front porch. All rooms include full breakfast each morning. Closed January.

Hosts: Mark Kulkowitz and Pamela Huber
Rooms: 22 (PB) $80-170
Full Breakfast
Credit Cards: A, B, C, D
Notes: 3, 4, 7, 8, 9, 10, 11, 12, 14

Chalfonte Hotel

301 Howard Street, 08204
(609) 884-8409; FAX (609) 884-4588
e-mail: chalfontnj@aol.com; www.chalfonte.com

Built in 1876, the Chalfonte remains a time capsule of Victorian charm and southern hospitality. A summer hotel with gingerbread trim and wraparound porches. Open Memorial Day to Columbus Day. Breakfast buffet and family-style dinner included. Separate supervised dining room for children six and under. Three blocks from the beach, the Chalfonte is the perfect spot for family vacations. No smoking permitted in bedrooms.

Chalfonte Hotel

7 No smoking; 8 Children welcome; 9 Social drinking allowed; 10 Tennis nearby; 11 Swimming nearby; 12 Golf nearby; 13 Skiing nearby; 14 May be booked through a travel agent; 15 Handicapped accessible.

Hosts: Anne LeDuc and Judy Bartella
Rooms: 70 (10 PB; 60 SB) $100-200
Full Breakfast
Credit Cards: A, B, C
Notes: 2, 4, 8, 9, 10, 11, 12, 14

Cliveden Bed & Breakfast Inn and Cottage

709 Columbia Avenue, 08204
(609) 884-4516

Comfortable and attractively restored Victorian accommodations with private baths and air conditioning. In the historic district, within easy walking distance to the beach, shops, tours, and fine restaurants. Take pleasure in the relaxing atmosphere of the large wraparound veranda while enjoying a hearty full homemade buffet breakfast and afternoon tea and treats. Cozy Victorian cottage available year-round.

Hosts: Sue and Al De Rosa
Rooms: 10 (PB) $100-165
Full Breakfast
Credit Cards: None
Notes: 2, 5, 8, 9, 10, 11, 12, 14

Colvmns by the Sea

1513 Beach Drive, 08204
(609) 884-2224; e-mail: colvmns@bellatlahtic.net
www.colvmns.com

In a private enclave at the eastern tip of historic Cape May Island and secluded at Sewell's

Colvmns by the Sea

Point is an exclusive four-star oceanfront Renaissance Revival mansion, Colvmns By The Sea. We offer an oasis of tranquillity in an authentic turn-of-the-century Victorian atmosphere with breathtaking ocean views. Private baths, air conditioning, TV.

Host: Bernadette Kaschner
Rooms: 12 (PB) $150-265
Full Breakfast
Credit Cards: A, B
Notes: 2, 3, 4, 5, 7, 8, 9, 10, 11, 12, 14

The Duke of Windsor Inn

The Duke of Windsor Inn

817 Washington Street, 08204
(609) 884-1355; (800) 826-8973
FAX (609) 884-1887

Sense the romance of a classic Queen Anne Victorian bed and breakfast inn. The Duke of Windsor Inn, built in 1896 with a 45-foot tower, has a large, central foyer with a three-story, carved oak staircase and Tiffany stained-glass windows. The parlor with a corner fireplace, two formal dining rooms, and 10 guest rooms decorated with lovely antique furnishings extend a feeling of warmth and elegance. Gourmet breakfasts, afternoon tea and treats, on-site parking, and air conditioned rooms await guests. Open year-round.

NOTES: Credit cards accepted: A MasterCard; B Visa; C American Express; D Discover; E Diner's Club; F Other; 2 Personal checks accepted; 3 Lunch available; 4 Dinner available; 5 Open all year; 6 Pets welcome;

Host: Patricia Joyce (new owner)
Rooms: 10 (PB) $85-200
Full Breakfast
Credit Cards: A, B
Notes: 2, 5, 7, 10, 11, 12

Gingerbread House

Gingerbread House

28 Gurney Street, 08204
(609) 884-0211; www.gingerbreadinn.com

The Gingerbread House is a meticulously and elegantly restored 1869 Victorian seaside cottage in the historic district, one-half block from the beach. Period antiques, original Cape May watercolor paintings, classical music, Fred's photographs, and exquisite woodwork combine with friendly service and attention to detail. Breakfast, afternoon tea and goodies, beach passes, fireplace, and guest veranda overlooking the quaint garden. Inquire about midweek and off-season specials.

Hosts: Fred and Joan Echevarria
Rooms: 6 (3 PB: 3 SB) $98-240
Full Breakfast
Credit Cards: A, B
Notes:, 2, 5, 7, 8, 9, 10, 11, 12, 14

The Humphrey Hughes House

29 Ocean Street, 08204
(609) 884-4428; (800) 582-3634

Nestled in the heart of Cape May's historic section is one of its most authentically restored inns—perhaps the most spacious and gracious of them all. Until 1980 it was the Hughes family's home. While the house is filled with magnificent antiques, it still feels more like a home than a museum. All rooms have private baths, air conditioning, and cable TV.

Hosts: Lorraine and Terry Schmidt
Rooms: 11 (PB) $105-235
Full Breakfast
Credit Cards: A, B
Notes: 2, 5, 7, 10, 11, 12, 15

The Inn at Journey's End

710 Columbia Avenue, 08204
(609) 884-9899; FAX (609) 898-8939

Experience the charm of this seaside Victorian cottage built in 1878. Located in Cape May's primary historic district, beaches, shops, and restaurants are just a stroll away. A peaceful retreat where guests can escape the pressures of everyday life. "We'll pamper you with delicious breakfasts, delightful afternoon teas, three beautiful porches, and authentic claw-foot tubs." In-room amenities include hair dryers, glycerin soaps, shampoo, conditioner, body wash, moisturizer, and bath salts.

The Inn at Journey's End

7 No smoking; 8 Children welcome; 9 Social drinking allowed; 10 Tennis nearby; 11 Swimming nearby; 12 Golf nearby; 13 Skiing nearby; 14 May be booked through a travel agent; 15 Handicapped accessible.

Hosts: Joe and Fran Geores
Rooms: 5 (3 PB; 2 SB) $75-175
Full Breakfast
Credit Cards: A, B
Notes: 2, 5, 7, 9, 10, 11, 12

The Inn on Ocean

25 Ocean Street, 08204
(609) 884-7070; (800) 304-4477
FAX (609) 884-1384; www.theinnonocean.com

An intimate, elegant Victorian inn. Fanciful
Second Empire style with an exuberant personality. King- and queen-size beds. Private baths.
Centrally air conditioned. Color cable TV. Full
breakfast. Wicker-filled ocean-view porches.
Billiard room. Free on-site parking. Steps to
the beach. Seasonal rates. Open all seasons.

Hosts: Jack and Katha Davis
Rooms: 5 (PB) $129-299
Full Breakfast
Credit Cards: A, B, C, D, E
Notes: 7, 9, 10, 11, 12

The Inn on Ocean

The John F. Craig House

609 Columbia Avenue, 08204
(609) 884-0100; FAX (609) 898-1307

The 1866 John F. Craig House, a carpenter
Gothic beauty, in the historic district, close to
the ocean, shops, and great dining. Dressed in
lacy gingerbread, it has a wraparound veranda
with swing and two glass-enclosed porches,
plus views of the front perennial garden and

The John F. Craig House

the tranquil sight of sleeping cats, Heckle and
Jeckle. The innkeepers invite guests to relax
and enjoy their period-decorated, antique-filled
dining room, parlor, library, and guest rooms.
Trademarks of the inn include great food, hospitality, and positively outrageous service.
Closed January and February. Children over 12
welcome. Air conditioned in the summer.

Hosts: Frank and Connie Felicetti
Rooms: 8 (PB) $85-180
Full Breakfast
Credit Cards: A, B, D
Notes: 2, 7, 9, 10, 11, 12, 14

The Linda Lee Bed & Breakfast

725 Columbia Avenue, 08204
(609) 884-1240; FAX (609) 884-6762
e-mail:lindale@bellatlantic.net

In Cape May's historic district, this charming
1872 carpenter Gothic house is one of three
Cape May Victorians featured in *America's*

The Linda Lee

NOTES: Credit cards accepted: A MasterCard; B Visa; C American Express; D Discover; E Diner's Club;
F Other; 2 Personal checks accepted; 3 Lunch available; 4 Dinner available; 5 Open all year; 6 Pets welcome;

Painted Ladies. The Linda Lee is a few short blocks from the beach and shopping areas. Furnished with many period antiques, the inn features a full, served breakfast and afternoon tea. The five elegantly appointed rooms are air conditioned. Beach tags, towels, chairs, and free on-site parking are available.

Hosts: Lynda and Corbin Cogswell
Rooms: 5 (PB) $80-160
Full Breakfast
Credit Cards: A, B
Notes: 2, 5, 7, 9, 10, 11, 12, 14

The Mainstay Inn

Mainstay Inn

635 Columbia Avenue, 08204
(609) 884-8690; www.mainstayinn.com

Selected one of the "Top 100 Inns and Resorts in the USA" in the 1995 *Zagat Survey.* Spacious rooms and suites with fine antiques, some with fireplaces and private porches. All private baths, some with whirlpool tubs. Luscious breakfasts and afternoon teas.

Hosts: Tom and Sue Carroll
Rooms: 16 (PB) $95-295
Full and Continental Breakfast
Credit Cards: None
Notes: 2, 5, 7, 9, 10, 11, 12, 15

The Manse Bed & Breakfast

510 Hughes Street, 08204
(609) 884-0116

The Manse is an elegant turn-of-the- century home in the heart of Cape May's historic district. It boasts spacious rooms, natural floors, Persian rugs, lace curtains, antiques, and two generations offering unsurpassed hospitality. Breakfast is a special occasion with homemade delights served in a formal dining room or on the veranda. High tea is served every afternoon and guests are invited to enjoy the comfortable living room with fireplace and the grand wraparound porch. One block from the Victorian Mall and less than two blocks from the best beaches on the Jersey coast.

Hosts: Karsten and Anita Dierk
Rooms: 6 (4 PB; 2 SB) $115-175
Full Breakfast
Credit Cards: None
Notes: 2, 5, 7, 10, 11, 12, 14

The Mason Cottage

625 Columbia Avenue, 08204
(609) 884-3358; (800) 716-2766 (reservations)

The Mason Cottage was built in 1871 as the summer residence for a Philadelphia entrepreneur and his family. In the historic district, the inn is Second Empire with a concave mansard roof. Within the inn, guests discover elegance, meticulous restoration, and warm hospitality. Guest room accommodations include four air-conditioned suites, some with whirlpool baths and fireplaces. Nearby attractions: house tours, antique shops, and Victorian shopping mall. The inn is one block from the beach. Children over 12 welcome.

Hosts: Joan and Dave Mason
Rooms: 9 (PB) $95-285
Full Breakfast

The Mason Cottage

7 No smoking; 8 Children welcome; 9 Social drinking allowed; 10 Tennis nearby; 11 Swimming nearby; 12 Golf nearby; 13 Skiing nearby; 14 May be booked through a travel agent; 15 Handicapped accessible.

Credit Cards: A, B, C
Notes: 2, 7, 9, 10, 11, 12, 14

The Mooring

801 Stockton Avenue, 08204
(609) 884-5425; FAX (609) 884-1357

Built in 1882, one of Cape May's original guest houses. Comfortable elegance in a classic Second Empire inn, with grand entrance hall and wide spiral staircase leading to spacious guest rooms; each with private bath, ceiling fan, and period furnishings; most with air conditioning. Enjoy breakfast and afternoon tea in the dining room or on the front veranda. One block from the beach. Open April 1 through New Year's Day. Children over six welcome.

Host: Leslie Valenza
Rooms: 12 (PB) $75-150
Full Breakfast
Credit Cards: A, B
Notes: 2, 7, 9, 10, 11, 12, 14

The Mooring

The Queen Victoria

102 Ocean Street, 08204
(609) 884-8702

The Wells family welcomes guests as friends and treats them royally with unpretentious service and attention to detail. Three restored buildings furnished with antiques are in the center of the historic district. Nationally recog-

The Queen Victoria

nized for its special Christmas. One suite is handicapped accessible.

Hosts: Dane and Joan Wells
Rooms: 14 (PB) $100-300
Suites: 7 (PB)
Full Breakfast
Credit Cards: A, B
Notes: 2, 5, 7, 8, 9, 10, 11, 12

Sea Holly Bed & Breakfast

815 Stockton Avenue, 08204
(609) 884-6294; FAX (609) 884-5157

"Victorian but comfortable...like coming to your aunt's," says *New Jersey Monthly*. The Sea Holly is known for making one of the best breakfasts in town and killer chocolate chip cookies with afternoon tea. Guests will find all rooms have air conditioning. Some rooms have ocean views; all have TVs. For guests' comfort the Sea Holly supplies large bath towels, soap, shampoo, beach tags with deposit, beach towels, porch rockers, and outside showers for after beach. Nonmetered street parking; one-half block to ocean; four blocks to town center. Personal checks accepted for deposit only. Smoking permitted on porch only.

Host: Christy Lacey-Igoe
Rooms: 8 (PB) $50-200
Full Breakfast
Credit Cards: A, B, C
Notes: 9, 10, 11, 12, 14

NOTES: Credit cards accepted: A MasterCard; B Visa; C American Express; D Discover; E Diner's Club; F Other; 2 Personal checks accepted; 3 Lunch available; 4 Dinner available; 5 Open all year; 6 Pets welcome;

White Dove Cottage

White Dove Cottage

619 Hughes Street, 08204
(609) 884-0613; (800) 321-3683

This elegant little bed and breakfast, circa 1866, is in the center of the historic district on a quiet, tree-lined, gaslit street. Four rooms plus two suites offer cheerful accommodations for guests. Bicycle rental, golf course, ocean, and beach are all nearby. Tea and snacks are served every afternoon, and a full breakfast starts the day. AAA-, PAII-, and NJBBA-approved. Children over 12 welcome.

Hosts: Frank and Sue Smith
Rooms: 6 (PB) $85-215
Full Breakfast
Credit Cards: None
Notes: 2, 5, 7, 9, 10, 11, 12, 14

Wilbraham Mansion

133 Myrtle Avenue, 08204
(609) 884-2046; fax (609) 884-2099

Antique-furnished Victorian mansion with period wallpaper and five magnificent gilded mirrors. A warm, hospitable staff presides over a delicious breakfast and refreshing afternoon tea. Bicycles, beach tags, 10 air-conditioned bedrooms, and best of all, an indoor heated swimming pool. A glassed-front porch abounds with plants and flowers year-round. Smoking permitted in designated areas only.

Host: Patty Carnes
Rooms: 10 (PB) $110-210
Full Breakfast
Credit Cards: A, B
Notes: 2, 5, 10, 11, 12

Windward House

24 Jackson Street, 08204
(609) 884-3368

All three stories of this gracious Edwardian-style seaside inn contain antique-filled rooms. Beveled and stained glass cast rainbows of flickering light from the windows and French doors, while gleaming chestnut and oak paneling sets off the museum- quality furnishings and collectibles. Spacious guest rooms have king- or queen-size beds, private baths, refrigerators, air conditioning, and TV. Enjoy spectacular summer porches and wintertime coziness fireside. Prime historic district. A half-block to beach, shopping, mall, and restaurants. Rates include afternoon tea. Smoking in designated areas only. Children over eight welcome.

Hosts: Sandy and Owen Miller
Rooms: 8 (PB) $90-182
Full Breakfast
Credit Cards: B
Notes: 2, 5, 9, 10, 11, 12, 14

Windward House

The Wooden Rabbit

609 Hughes Street, 08204
(609) 884-7293

Built in 1838 and on one of the prettiest streets in Cape May, the Wooden Rabbit is nestled in the heart of the historic district. Two blocks to sandy beaches and one block to shopping and

7 No smoking; 8 Children welcome; 9 Social drinking allowed; 10 Tennis nearby; 11 Swimming nearby; 12 Golf nearby; 13 Skiing nearby; 14 May be booked through a travel agent; 15 Handicapped accessible.

The Wooden Rabbit

within easy walking distance to many fine restaurants. The decor is American country furnished with antiques and reproductions to the period of the house. A full breakfast is served each morning. All rooms are air conditioned in summer, private baths, and TVs. Afternoon refreshments from 4:00 until 5:00 P.M. each day. Beach tags, chairs, bicycles, and on-site parking available.

Hosts: Nancy and Dave McGonigle
Rooms: 4 (PB) $85-180
Full Breakfast
Credit Cards: A, B
Notes: 2, 5, 7, 10, 11, 12, 14

Woodleigh House

808 Washington Street, 08204
(609) 884-7123; (800) 399-7123

Victorian, but informal, with off-street parking, beach bikes, comfortable parlor, courtyard, and gardens. Full breakfast and afternoon refreshments. Walk to everything: marvelous restaurants, sights galore, nearby nature preserve, dinner theater, and craft and antique shows. Queen-size beds, private baths. Air conditioned. Inquire about accommodations for children.

Hosts: Joe and Jo Anne Tornambe
Rooms: 4 (PB) $95-185
Suite: 1
Full Breakfast
Credit Cards: A, B
Notes: 2, 7, 9, 10, 11, 12

CHATHAM

Parrot Mill Inn at Chatham

47 Main Street, 07928
(973) 635-7722; FAX (973) 701-0620

Built in 1790 as a mill house. Today the inn hosts weddings, rehearsal dinners, small parties, receptions, and business meetings. English country decor. Private baths, TVs, and telephones. Continental breakfast includes homemade breads or muffins, freshly squeezed juice, and hot coffee or tea. Outstanding restaurants, shopping, antiquing, and points of historical interest nearby. New York is 40 minutes away, and the Newark airport is within 12 minutes.

Host: Betsy Kennedy
Rooms: 11 (10 PB; 1SB) $105-115
Continental Breakfast
Credit Cards: A, B, C, D
Notes: 2, 5, 7, 8, 14

CREAM RIDGE

Earth Friendly Bed & Breakfast

17 Olde Noah Hunt Road, 08514
(609) 259-9744

Small family-oriented bed and breakfast on an eight-acre organic farm just two miles from Six Flags Great Adventure. Children of all sizes free to wander through the woods, fish in the pond, gather eggs from the chickens, pick fruit in season from the unsprayed trees, bushes, and vines. Convenient to dozens of restaurants, excellent shopping, the ocean, New York City, and Philadelphia, yet out in the country with lots of clean fresh air.

Host: Jim Schmitt
Rooms: 3 (1 PB; 2 SB) $65-95
Full Breakfast
Credit Cards: None
Notes: 2, 5, 8, 9, 12, 14, 15

NOTES: Credit cards accepted: A MasterCard; B Visa; C American Express; D Discover; E Diner's Club; F Other; 2 Personal checks accepted; 3 Lunch available; 4 Dinner available; 5 Open all year; 6 Pets welcome;

FLEMINGTON

Jerica Hill

Jerica Hill—
A Bed & Breakfast Inn

96 Broad Street, 08822
(908) 782-8234

Be warmly welcomed at this gracious country inn in the historic town of Flemington. Spacious, sunny guest rooms, each with private bath, telephone, TV, and air conditioning; living room with a fireplace, and a wicker-filled screened porch invite guests to relax. A guests' pantry offering beverages and snacks is available 24 hours a day. Champagne hot-air balloon flights are arranged, as well as country picnics and winery tours. A delightful full hot breakfast is served. Corporate and midweek rates available. Featured in *Country Inns Bed and Breakfast* and *Mid-Atlantic Country*.

Host: V. Eugene Refalvy
Rooms: 5 (PB) $85-125
Full Breakfast
Credit Cards: A, B, C
Notes: 2, 5, 7, 9, 10, 11, 12, 13, 14

FRANKLIN PARK

Amanda's Bed & Breakfast
Reservation Service

3538 Lakeway Drive, Ellicott City, MD 21042-1226
(443) 535-0008; (800) 899-7533
FAX (443) 535-0009; e-mail: AmandasRS@aol.com
www.Amandas-BBRS.com

501. About five miles south of the Brunswicks or Princeton and the numerous businesses that are in that area. A new townhouse with a master unit providing a professional atmosphere for guests' stay. A large room with amenities such as a telephone, TV/VCR, and a wide choice of tapes, CD player, and radio. Access use of the kitchen and a living room with a fireplace. $100.

GLENWOOD

Apple Valley Inn
Bed & Breakfast

Corner Routes 517 and 565, P.O. Box 302, 07418
(973) 764-3735; FAX (973) 764-1050

A Colonial mansion built in 1831 provides sunroom, porches, formal parlor, or extensive gardens and in-ground pool. Stroll through the apple orchard or fish the trout stream. This picturesque inn is four miles from Mountain Creek and Hidden Valley and exclusive ski slopes. The inn is on the fall foliage tour. The Appalachian Trail is one mile away. The New Jersey Botanical Gardens, Waterloo Village, and Skylands are a short drive away. West Point and the Hudson Valley make for a wonderful day. Guests start the day with a full country breakfast. Picnic lunches are available. Children over 13 are welcome. Rollaway available for an additional charge of $25.

Hosts: Mitzi and John Durham
Rooms: 7 (2 PB; 5 SB) $80-120
Full Breakfast
Credit Cards: A, B, D
Notes: 2, 5, 9, 10, 12, 13

Apple Valley Inn

7 No smoking; 8 Children welcome; 9 Social drinking allowed; 10 Tennis nearby; 11 Swimming nearby; 12 Golf nearby; 13 Skiing nearby; 14 May be booked through a travel agent; 15 Handicapped accessible.

HADDONFIELD

Haddonfield Inn

44 West End Avenue, 08033
(609) 428-2195; (800) 269-0014
FAX (609) 354-1273

This recently remodeled Victorian features elegant rooms and suites, many with whirlpools and fireplaces, and has in-room cable TVs and telephones, elevator, free parking, and concierge services. A gourmet breakfast is served in the fire-lit dining room or on the wraparound porch. Guests enjoy complimentary snacks and beverages. The picturesque village of Haddonfield is noted for its cultural attractions and more than 200 fine shops and restaurants. Walk to the train for fast transportation to Rutgers, the NJ Aquarium, Delaware Waterfront, and downtown Philadelphia. Catered affairs and conferences for up to 35. Children under 12 and dogs permitted subject to restrictions.

Hosts: Nancy and Fred Chorpita
Rooms: 8 (PB) $99-169
Suite: 1 (PB)
Full Breakfast
Credit Cards: A, B, C, D
Notes: 5, 7, 9, 10, 11, 12, 13, 14, 15

Haddonfield Inn

HIGHLANDS

Amanda's Bed & Breakfast Reservation Service

3538 Lakeway Drive, Ellicott City, MD 21042-1226
(443) 535-0008; (800) 899-7533
FAX (443) 535-0009; e-mail: AmandasRS@aol.com
www.Amandas-BBRS.com

513. Near the Twin Lighthouse historic site on the northeast shore of New Jersey. Elegant home, sheltered by trees, clings to the cliff and overlooks the ocean near Sandy Hook State Park. Beautiful views. A full gourmet breakfast is served on the deck or dining room. Rent a boat, go antiquing, and dine on excellent seafood. All rooms have private baths. $90-150.

573. A small family-run bed and breakfast offers guests home-like food and comfort. Being on the first ridge of the Highland Hills, provides a vista of the town below the bluffs, Sandy Hook, Raritan Bay, the ocean, and New York City. Listed with the Monmouth County Survey of historically significant places. Two rooms (eventually three) with a full breakfast. $115.

HOPE

The Inn at Millrace Pond

313 Johnsonburg Road, P.O. Box 359, 07844
(908) 459-4884; (800) 746-6467

The Inn was a grist mill from 1770 until 1952. Some of the old mill equipment is still in place. Hope originated as a Moravian village and several 18th-century stone buildings survived. Excellent antiquing nearby. Hiking in Delaware River Gap Park is 13 miles west. Public restaurant open nightly for fine dining. Hope is one mile south of I-80 (exit 12) and 63 miles from George Washington Bridge into New York City.

Hosts: Cordie and Charles Puttkamer
Rooms: 17 (PB) $110-160
Continental Breakfast
Credit Cards: A, B, C, D
Notes: 2, 4, 5, 6, 7, 8, 9, 10, 12

NOTES: Credit cards accepted: A MasterCard; B Visa; C American Express; D Discover; E Diner's Club; F Other; 2 Personal checks accepted; 3 Lunch available; 4 Dinner available; 5 Open all year; 6 Pets welcome;

ISLAND HEIGHTS

The Studio of John F. Peto

102 Cedar Avenue, 08732-0306
(732) 270-6058

Victorian home of famous still-life artist John
F. Peto. Front porch with rockers. large country
kitchen with full breakfast. Sailboat rentals at
foot of Hill. Great for joggers and bikers.
Island Beach State Park and ocean nearby—
also great adventure theme park.

Host: Joy Peto Smiley
Rooms: 4 (4 SB) $65-85
Full Breakfast
Credit Cards: C
Notes: 2, 5, 6, 8, 9, 10, 11, 12

KEMPTON

Amanda's Bed & Breakfast Reservation Service

3538 Lakeway Drive, Ellicott City, MD 21042-1226
(443) 535-0008; (800) 899-7533
FAX (443) 535-0009; e-mail: AmandasRS@aol.com
www.Amandas-BBRS.com

A country stone house where it is quiet and
restful. Swim in the pool, take a long walk,
and enjoy the nearby Hawk Sanctuary. A dining room for guests' pleasure as well as a
gourmet breakfast served in the common room
by the fireplace. Two rooms with fireplaces
and Jacuzzis. Several other rooms with private
baths. $100-140.

LAMBERTVILLE

Amanda's Bed & Breakfast Reservation Service

3538 Lakeway Drive, Ellicott City, MD 21042-1226
(443) 535-0008; (800) 899-7533
FAX (443) 535-0009; e-mail: AmandasRS@aol.com
www.Amandas-BBRS.com

582. Beautiful stone country estate, once a
designer's showcase. Just up the hill from
Lambertville/New Hope. The decorations are
lovely and are on well-kept grounds. A full
breakfast is served. A nice place for weddings.
Near shops, restaurants, theaters, and antique
shops. $125-160.

York Street House

York Street House

42 York Street, 08530
(609) 397-3007; (888) 398-3199
FAX (609) 397-9677; e-mail: yorksthse@aol.com

Exceptional in-town accommodations. Gracious 13-room manor house built in 1909. Featured in *House & Gardens* and *Country Living*.
The inn features a winding three-story staircase
leading to five relaxing guest rooms. Public
areas feature circa 1900 Waterford chandelier,
leaded glass and Mercer tile fireplaces, and
baby grand piano. Wicker rocking chairs on the
veranda. Candlelight gourmet breakfast served
in the oak trimmed dining room. Walk to
antiques shops, restaurants, and entertainment.
Homemade cookies, complimentary beverages.

Hosts: Nancy Ferguson and Beth Wetterskog
Rooms: 5 (PB) $105-185
Full Breakfast
Credit Cards: A, B, C, D
Notes: 2, 7, 9, 11, 14

7 No smoking; 8 Children welcome; 9 Social drinking allowed; 10 Tennis nearby; 11 Swimming nearby;
12 Golf nearby; 13 Skiing nearby; 14 May be booked through a travel agent; 15 Handicapped accessible.

MILFORD

Amanda's Bed & Breakfast Reservation Service

3538 Lakeway Drive, Ellicott City, MD 21042-1226
(443) 535-0008; (800) 899-7533
FAX (443) 535-0009; e-mail: AmandasRS@aol.com
www.Amandas-BBRS.com

545. A mountaintop estate overlooking Delaware River, with a vista of three states. Featured in *Country Living* magazine, has three-star AAA rating. Gourmet fireside breakfast or outside on the stone terrace. Close to good restaurants and shops. Beautifully decorated. Hiking trails. $95-120.

NEWTON

The Wooden Duck

140 Goodale Road, 07860
(973) 300-0395 (phone/FAX)
www.bbianj.com/woodenduck

A country Colonial mini-estate on 17 acres, furnished with antiques and reproductions. Seven spacious guest rooms, all with private baths, queen-size beds, TV/VCRs, telephones, air conditioning, sitting areas, and two with fireplaces and two-person soaking tubs. Guests will enjoy in-ground pool, game room, and living room with see-through fireplaces, complimentary self-service area in the kitchen. Very close to fine antiquing, golf, Waterloo Village, and contiguous to 1,200-acre state park offering excellent hiking and biking. Just over an

The Wooden Duck

hour's drive from New York City. The only bed and breakfast rated three stars by Mobil Travel Guide in the northern half of New Jersey. Children over eight welcome.

Hosts: Bob and Barbara Hadden
Rooms: 7 (PB) $100-175
Full Breakfast
Credit Cards: A, B, C, D
Notes: 2, 5, 7, 9, 11, 12, 13, 14

NORTH WILDWOOD

Candlelight Inn

Candlelight Inn

2310 Central Avenue, 08260
(609) 522-6200; e-mail: inn4pd@aol.com
www.candlelight-inn.com

"There is a quaint haven for those in a vintage romantic mood," wrote the *Philadelphia Inquirer* (July 1988). The Candlelight Inn is a beautifully restored bed and breakfast built at the turn of the century by Leaming Rice. This Queen Anne Victorian structure served as the family home for many years until it was purchased by its present innkeepers in 1985. Within minutes of Cape May and Atlantic City. Special touches and personalized service abound. Newly renovated carriage house with fireplaces and Jacuzzi tubs. AAA three-diamond-rated.

Hosts: Paul DiFilippo and Diane Buscham
Rooms: 10 (PB) $85-265
Suites: 3
Full Breakfast
Credit Cards: A, B, C, D
Notes: 2, 5, 7, 9, 10, 11, 12, 14

NOTES: Credit cards accepted: A MasterCard; B Visa; C American Express; D Discover; E Diner's Club; F Other; 2 Personal checks accepted; 3 Lunch available; 4 Dinner available; 5 Open all year; 6 Pets welcome;

OCEAN CITY

Barnagate Bed & Breakfast

637 Wesley Avenue, 08226
(609) 391-9366; FAX (609) 399-5048

The Barnagate offers the perfect spot to relax in one of five air-conditioned guest rooms decorated in country Victorian. After a full day of nearby antiquing or visiting Atlantic City (within 10 miles), guests are encouraged to kick off their shoes and relax on the front porch or in the cozy sitting room. Beach and boardwalk are within walking distance of the bed and breakfast, which offers its specialty of hospitality and extra-special breakfasts. Children 10 and older welcome.

Hosts: Lois and Frank Barna
Rooms: 5 (1 PB; 2 S1B) $85-170
Continental Breakfast
Credit Cards: A, B, C
Notes: 2, 5, 10, 11, 12, 14

Castle by the Sea

boardwalk. A stay here includes a gourmet three-course breakfast, afternoon tea and sumptuous sweets, turn-down service with bedside chocolates, evening soda, juice and snacks, complimentary beach passes, parking, and movie library. The exquisite bedrooms, one with a Jacuzzi and two with fireplaces, features private bath, air conditioning, hair dryers, TV, and VCR.

Hosts: Rene and Jack Krutsick
Rooms: 9 (PB) $109-239
Full Breakfast
Credit Cards: A, B, C, D
Notes: 5, 7, 9, 10, 11, 12, 14

Barnagate

Castle by the Sea

701 Ocean Avenue, 08226
(609) 398-3555; (800) 622-4894
www.castlebythesea.com

Experience the romance and elegance of the award-winning English-country bed and breakfast. Rated three diamonds by AAA, this magnificent inn is just a block from the beach and

The Ebbie

820 Sixth Street, 08226
(609) 399-4744; www.ebbie.com

The Ebbie, just 11 miles south of Atlantic City and one-half block to the beach and boardwalk, was established by the Warrington family in 1945. All of the rooms and apartments have been completely remodeled and come with air conditioning, color TV, refrigerator, and daily maid service. Guests can enjoy the large wrap-around porch with a view of the public recreation area including tennis, shuffle board, and family playgrounds. Member of Ocean City Chamber of Commerce. Also available are efficiencies and apartments. Coffee and doughnuts provided. Complimentary beach tags.

7 No smoking; 8 Children welcome; 9 Social drinking allowed; 10 Tennis nearby; 11 Swimming nearby; 12 Golf nearby; 13 Skiing nearby; 14 May be booked through a travel agent; 15 Handicapped accessible.

Hosts: Dave and Liz Warrington
Rooms: 7 (5 PB: 2 SB) $55-105
Credit Cards: A, B
Notes: 7, 8, 10, 11, 12

Scarborough Inn

720 Ocean Avenue, 08226
(609) 399-1558; (800) 258-1558
FAX (609) 399-4472
e-mail: cgbruno@earthlink.net

Serendipity

The Scarborough Inn, invitingly adorned in Wedgwood, rose, and soft cream, lends its special character to the neighborhood where it stands, just one and one-half short blocks from the beach and boardwalk of this island town. The Scarborough is reminiscent of a European-style inn—small enough to be intimate, yet large enough for privacy. Bedchambers are individually decorated and feature modern amenities like cable TV, private bath, and air conditioning plus signature toiletries and romantic decor. Scrumptious gourmet breakfasts and afternoon refreshments delight the palate. Featured in *Country Inns* magazine.

Hosts: Gus and Carol Bruno
Rooms: 23 (PB) $90-180
Full Breakfast
Credit Cards: A, B, C, D
Notes: 7, 8, 10, 11, 12, 14

Serendipity Bed & Breakfast

712 Ninth Street, 08226
(609) 399-1554; (800) 842-8544
FAX (609) 399-1527
e-mail: serendipitynj@prodigy.net
www.serendipitynj.com

Serendipity is a beautifully renovated, fully air-conditioned 1912 seashore inn decorated in wicker and pastels (all rooms have cable TV) where privacy, hospitality, and delicious, hearty breakfasts (fuests choice of entrée) and dinners (by reservation) are tastefully blended for a memorable getaway. Vegetarian, heart-healthy, and macrobiotic diets accommodated. Clara and Bill welcome guests year-round to snuggle in cozy flannel sheets and warm their

toes by the fireplace as fall turns to winter, or rise to a summertime breakfast on the vine-shaded veranda. One-half block to the island's beaches and boardwalk, within walking distance to shiatsu massage, restaurants, unique shops, and year-round events at the Music Pier, this light and airy inn is just eight miles south of the shows and casinos of Atlantic City. Off-street parking, beach passes, and complimentary refreshments. AAA- and Mobil-approved.

Hosts: Clara and Bill Plowfield
Rooms: 6 (4 PB: 2 SB) $80-139
Full Breakfast
Credit Cards: A, B, C, D
Notes: 2, 4, 5, 9, 10, 11, 12, 14

OCEAN GROVE

Cordova

26 Webb Avenue, 07756
(732) 774-3084 (in season); (212) 751-9577 (winter)
FAX (212) 207-4720

This delightful century-old Victorian inn in historic Ocean Grove has a friendly atmosphere exuding Old World charm. Guests feel like members of an extended family. The inn was listed in *Jersey* magazine as one of the seven best places to stay on the Jersey coast. Also listed in Heidi and Gilman's *O' New Jersey*. There are 15 guest rooms, three family suites, and two cottages. Less than a 90-minute bus or train ride to Manhattan, Philadelphia,

Cordova

the Atlantic Ocean. Centrally located within walking distance of all activities, shops, and restaurants. The innkeepers live here year-round and share their home from Memorial Day weekend to Labor Day. Recommended in *O'New Jersey* and *The Lonely Planet.*

Hosts: Sally and Alyn Heim
Rooms: 18 (10 PB; 8 SB) $60-110
Continental Breakfast
Credit Cards: None
Notes: 2, 7, 10, 11, 12

and Atlantic City. The weekly rate gives guests seven nights for the price of five. Midweek specials. Visit during murder mystery or tai chi or other special weekends. Continental plus breakfast. Open April through November.

Host: Doris Chernik
Rooms: 15 (5 PB; 10 SB) $45-80
Suites and Cottages: 5 (PB) $85-165
Continental Breakfast
Credit Cards: None
Notes: 2, 7, 8, 9, 10, 11, 14

House by the Sea

14 Ocean Avenue, 07756
(732) 775-2847; FAX (732) 502-0403
e-mail: housebysea@monmouth.com
www.travelguides.com/bb/house_by_the_sea

The style and hospitality of yesterday, with the comfort and personal service of today. House by the Sea is an oceanfront bed and breakfast with 18 rooms and three large porches facing

Manchester Inn

Manchester Inn Bed & Breakfast & Secret Garden Restaurant

25 Ocean Pathway, 07756
(732) 775-0616; e-mail: TheNJInn@aol.com
www.themanchesterinn.com

Magic embraces the charming elegance of the Manchester Inn and its fabulous 100-seat full-service restaurant. Circa 1880s, the Manchester boasts Victorian decor and 40 uniquely decorated rooms; just one block from the ocean. The spacious lobby features a Steinway piano and camel-back sofas. In this setting of Old World charm and gourmet dining, guests will be relaxed and elegantly pampered. The Secret Garden Restaurant can be reserved for private events. Exit 100B off the Garden State Parkway.

Hosts: Clark and Margaret Cate
Rooms: 40 (30 PB; 10 SB) $70-135
Continental Breakfast
Credit Cards: A, B, C, D
Notes: 2, 3, 4, 5, 7, 8, 10, 11

House by the Sea

7 No smoking; 8 Children welcome; 9 Social drinking allowed; 10 Tennis nearby; 11 Swimming nearby; 12 Golf nearby; 13 Skiing nearby; 14 May be booked through a travel agent; 15 Handicapped accessible.

PEMBERTON

Isaac Hilliard House

31 Hanover Street, 08068-1128
(609) 894-0756; (800) 371-0756
FAX (609) 894-7899; e-mail: ppaul@erols.com

On the fringe of New Jersey's scenic Pine Barrens, this 250-year-old, federal-era house features a suite with TV/VCR, canopied bed, fireplace, plus three other guest rooms. Each accommodation has a private bath and air conditioning. The hosts provide freshly prepared breakfasts, off-street parking, and private, in-ground swimming pool. Antiquing and canoeing are within walking distance. Golfing, hiking, and biking are nearby. Discount coupons available for many nearby restaurants. Open year-round.

Hosts: Phyllis Paul Davis and Gene R. O'Brien
Rooms: 4 (PB) $75-160
Full Breakfast
Credit Cards: A, B, C, D
Notes: 2, 3, 4, 5, 7, 9, 11, 12, 14

PLAINFIELD

The Pillars

922 Central Avenue, 07060-2311
(908) 753-0922; (888) PILLARS (phone/FAX)
(908) 753-7448 (guest phone)
e-mail: pillars2@juno.com
www.pillars2.com

Guests may make themselves at home in this restored 1880s mansion, on a secluded acre of trees. Luxurious private bath suites have queen-size bed, lounge chair, wood-burning fireplace, game table, telephone, TV. Full breakfast with Swedish baking. Evening wine and turn-down. Stained-glass windows, circular staircase. Play the organ in the music room, or read in the library. Close to New York City, Newark airport, Jersey Shore. Children under two and over 12 welcome. Cairn terrier on premises.

Hosts: Tom and Chuck Hale
Rooms: 4 (PB) $75-115
Full Breakfast

The Pillars

Credit Cards: A, B, C
Notes: 2, 5, 6, 7, 9, 10, 11, 12, 13, 14

PRINCETON

Amanda's Bed & Breakfast Reservation Service

3538 Lakeway Drive, Ellicott City, MD 21042-1226
(443) 535-0008; (800) 899-7533
FAX (443) 535-0009; e-mail: AmandasRS@aol.com
www.Amandas-BBRS.com

590. A charming and gracious 1740 in the historic register. A small working farm and home about four miles from Princeton University. One guest room with a fireplace. Full country breakfast served by the fireside or on the patio. In-ground pool, comfortable porch, organic fruits, and vegetable gardens.

RIDGEWOOD

Amanda's Bed & Breakfast Reservation Service

3538 Lakeway Drive, Ellicott City, MD 21042-1226
(443) 535-0008; (800) 899-7533
FAX (443) 535-0009; e-mail: AmandasRS@aol.com
www.Amandas-BBRS.com

546. Lovely home in an upscale community, with easy access to New York City. Public transportation available. Near the Meadowlands. Heart of the home is a rear screened porch area where breakfast and afternoon snacks are served, amid secluded woods. Hosts are very knowledgeable about the area. $75.

SPRING LAKE

Amanda's Bed & Breakfast Reservation Service

3538 Lakeway Drive, Ellicott City, MD 21042-1226
(443) 535-0008; (800) 899-7533
FAX (443) 535-0009; e-mail: AmandasRS@aol.com
www.Amandas-BBRS.com

522. A country lodge at the Jersey Shore. Log beams, knotty pine walls, and a massive stone fireplace. Overlooks Lake Como, near the beach, swimming, fishing, golf, and tennis. A full breakfast is served. Station pickup upon request. $90-150.

Ashling Cottage

106 Sussex Avenue, 07762
(732) 449-3553; (888) ASHLING

Under sentinel sycamores since 1877 in a storybook setting, Ashling Cottage, a Victorian seaside inn, has long served as a portal to an earlier time. A block from the ocean and just one-half block from a freshwater lake. Closed November through April.

Hosts: Goodi and Jack Stewart
Rooms: 10 (8 PB; 2 SB) $90-184

Ashling Cottage

Full Breakfast
Credit Cards: None
Notes: 2, 7, 9, 10, 11, 12, 14

The Carriage House Bed & Breakfast

208 Jersey Avenue, 07762
(732) 449-1332; (800) 349-1332
www.TheCarriageHouseInn.com

Built in 1893, the Carriage House has been renovated to reflect a cozy romantic inn. It is on a quiet, tree-lined street in this seaside village. Just two blocks from the boardwalk and the beautiful lake with its lovely wooden bridges. The rooms are accented with antiques, four-poster king-size beds, two Jacuzzis, one fireplace, air conditioning, ceiling fans, TV/VCRs, beach passes and chairs, and bikes upon availability. Rates quoted are for weekends in-season. Full breakfast served weekends; Continental breakfast served weekdays. Personal checks accepted for deposit only.

Hosts: Joyce and Dave Collins
Rooms: 8 (PB) $135-225
Full and Continental Breakfast
Credit Cards: A, B, C
Notes: 5, 7, 9, 10, 11, 12

La Maison— A Bed & Breakfast & Gallery

404 Jersey Avenue, 07762
(732) 449-0969; FAX (732) 449-4860
e-mail: LaMaisonSL@aol.com

"If you can't be in Paris, escape for a few days to our romantic and magical bed and breakfast!" Relax to soothing classics while sipping an apéritif. Serenity and a safe refuge await guests. Belgian waffles, crème brûlée, French toast, omelets, cappuccino, mimosas. Luxurious French beds with fluffy white duvets. Skylit Jacuzzi for two. Cozy year-round cottage. Free beach, pool, and premier fitness facility. Near ocean, shopping, and lake.

Host: Julie Corrigan
Rooms: 8 (PB) $130-325

7 No smoking; 8 Children welcome; 9 Social drinking allowed; 10 Tennis nearby; 11 Swimming nearby; 12 Golf nearby; 13 Skiing nearby; 14 May be booked through a travel agent; 15 Handicapped accessible.

Full Breakfast
Credit Cards: A, B, C, D
Notes: 5, 7, 9, 10, 11, 12, 15

The Normandy Inn

The Normandy Inn

21 Tuttle Avenue, 07762
(732) 449-7172; FAX (732) 449-1070
e-mail: normandy@bellatlantic.net
www.normandyinn.com

Guests' welcome begins in the spacious double parlors with their authentic Victorian splendor then continues in 19 totally different guest rooms and suites, all with antique Victorian furnishings. Guests' wake-up call combines the sound of the ocean and the aromas of the inn's legendary country breakfast—served at a private table in the gracious dining room. Built in 1888 this Italianate villa with Queen Anne modifications is the only Spring Lake bed and breakfast in the National Register of Historic Places.

Proprietors: Michael and Susan Ingino
Innkeepers: Mike and Jeri Robertson
Rooms: 19 (PB) $110-340
Full Breakfast
Credit Cards: A, B, C, D, E
Notes: 2, 5, 7, 8, 9, 10, 11, 12, 14

Ocean House

102 Sussex Avenue, 07762
(732) 449-9090; (888) 449-9094
FAX (732) 449-9092

Spring Lake, a magical seashore village, and the Ocean House, a perfect blend of past and pre-

sent. Guests may walk to the boards, stroll about the lakes, or browse through town, or enjoy the ocean breezes on the wraparound porch. Built in 1878 the building features a grand staircase from the 1873 Philadelphia exposition. Extensive renovation and interior design in 1999 include private baths, air conditioning, ceiling fans, telephone, cable TV. On-site parking, ocean views, and breezes are included.

Hosts: Nancy and Dennis Kaloostian
Rooms: 30 (PB) $100-325
Continental Breakfast
Credit Cards: A, B
Notes: 2, 5, 7, 10, 11, 12

Victoria House

214 Monmouth Avenue, 07762
(732) 974-1882; (888) 249-6252
FAX (732) 974-2132
e-mail: www.com/victoriahousebb@worldnet.att.net
www.bbianj.com/victoriahouse

The Victoria House provides the perfect retreat from today's hustle and bustle. This Eastlake-style residence exhibits typical Victorian appeal with its gingerbread accents, stained-glass windows, and Gothic shingles. Come and relax on the spacious wraparound porch and enjoy the cool ocean breezes. Some guest rooms with fireplaces and whirlpools. Stroll a few steps to the lake or beach or browse

Victoria House

through the quaint shops in the village. Spring Lake is easily accessible by car, bus, or train from both New York and Philadelphia. Featured on 1995 Historical Society house tour.

Hosts: Louise and Robert Goodall
Rooms: 9 (7 PB; 2 SB) $115-225
Full Breakfast
Credit Cards: A, B, C, D
Notes: 2, 5, 9, 10, 11, 12

STANHOPE

Whistling Swan Inn

110 Main Street, 07874
(973) 347-6369; FAX (973) 347-3391
e-mail: wswan@worldnet.att.net
www.bbianj.com/whistlingswan

A turn-of-the-century Queen Anne Victorian home renovated by the owners. The house features tiger-oak woodwork, fireplaces downstairs, and a huge sitting porch. Near Waterloo Village, International Trade Zone, skiing, wineries, antiques, museums, shops, and restaurants. Near to historic Morristown and just six miles north of Chester. This is a four-season region of New Jersey. Children over 12 welcome.

Hosts: Paula and Joe Williams Mulay
Rooms: 10 (PB) $95-150
Full Breakfast
Credit Cards: A, B, C, D
Notes: 2, 5, 7, 9, 10, 11, 12, 13, 14

Whistling Swan Inn

WILDWOOD CREST

Amanda's Bed & Breakfast Reservation Service

3538 Lakeway Drive, Ellicott City, MD 21042-1226
(443) 535-0008; (800) 899-7533
FAX (443) 535-0009; e-mail: AmandasRS@aol.com
www.Amandas-BBRS.com

533. Built in 1907 as a summer house, this lovely property with Victorian charm and modern conveniences is just three blocks from the beach or five blocks to the Boardwalk. Large comfortable veranda offers a place to relax and regroup. A full breakfast is served. Five rooms. $85-140.

WOODBINE

Amanda's Bed & Breakfast Reservation Service

3538 Lakeway Drive, Ellicott City, MD 21042-1226
(443) 535-0008; (800) 899-7533
FAX (443) 535-0009; e-mail: AmandasRS@aol.com
www.Amandas-BBRS.com

527. On a lake surrounded by woods. Romantic gazebo and canoes for guest use. Near beaches, historic areas, state parks, and antiquing. Romantic and relaxing. Bedroom fireplaces, handmade quilts, gourmet breakfast, and afternoon refreshments. $120-125.

WOODSTOWN

Victorian Rose Farm Bed & Breakfast

947 Route 40, 08098
(609) 769-4600; e-mail: m.stevens@waterw.com

This 1887 Gothic inn, on six beautiful acres, the Oakbarn Antiques and Uniques and, newly opened, Isabel's Cafe are a focal point of this historic area. Hosts, Isabel Leach and Mark

---

7 No smoking; 8 Children welcome; 9 Social drinking allowed; 10 Tennis nearby; 11 Swimming nearby; 12 Golf nearby; 13 Skiing nearby; 14 May be booked through a travel agent; 15 Handicapped accessible.

Stevens (a successful recording artist) keep this a happy and upbeat inn. Area attractions include: rodeo, polo, antiques, flea markets, Philadelphia (30 minutes away), Longwood Gardens, Jersey Shore (one hour away). Turnout for horses by reservation. Only eight miles from Exit 1 of the New Jersey Turnpike, I-95 and 295.

Hosts: Isabel Leach and Mark Stevens
Rooms: 4 (2 PB; 2 SB)
Full and Continental Breakfast
Credit Cards: A, B
Notes: 3, 5, 7, 9, 10, 12

New York

American Country Collection

1353 Union Street, Schenectady, 12308
(518) 370-4948; (800) 810-4948
FAX (518) 393-1634 (call first)
e-mail: Carolbnbres@msn.com
www.bandbreservations.com

097. This elegant turn-of-the-century Victorian home is on the bus route and just a few minutes' drive from all of the major area colleges, state buildings, and attractions. Six guest rooms are available; two rooms have private baths, and four rooms have shared baths. All rooms have telephones and air conditioning. Children over 12 are welcome. Continental breakfast served. Guests are welcome to use the TV in the living room. Off-street parking is provided. $64-79.

111. Once a residence for Albany's earliest extended families, this Victorian bed and breakfast also served as a tavern and grocery store. In the shadow of the Empire State Plaza. Twelve guest rooms with private baths, air conditioning, cable TV, and telephone. Award-winning restaurant on premises. Children are welcome. Smoking permitted. Cat resides in owner's apartment. $110-145.

248. In Slingerlands, a convenient suburb of Albany, travelers are close to downtown but removed from the busy city. This replica of a French Colonial farmhouse with plantation-style columns and full front porch offers two guests rooms that share a full hall bath. Both rooms are on the second floor as are guest common areas for TV viewing or playing billiards. Smoking permitted outside only. Children welcome by prior arrangement. Resident dog. Full breakfast. $75.

Pine Haven

Pine Haven Bed & Breakfast

531 Western Avenue, 12203
(518) 482-1574

A century-old Victorian home in the nicest residential area of Albany. Has five rooms, decorated in antiques, with feather mattresses on old iron/brass beds. Bus service to all areas of the city within 100 yards. Off-street parking. Four restaurants, a movie theater, and other shops within two blocks of bed and breakfast. Open front porch with wicker furniture for people watching in warm months. It's like going to Grandma's house. Continental plus breakfast served. Children over 12 welcome.

Host: Janice Tricarico
Rooms: 5 (2 PB; 3 SB) $64-79
Continental Breakfast
Credit Cards: A, B, C, D
Notes: 2, 5, 7, 9, 12, 14

---

7 No smoking; 8 Children welcome; 9 Social drinking allowed; 10 Tennis nearby; 11 Swimming nearby; 12 Golf nearby; 13 Skiing nearby; 14 May be booked through a travel agent; 15 Handicapped accessible.

New York

ALFRED

Saxon Inn

One Park Street, 14802
(607) 871-2650
e-mail: saxoninn@bigvax.alfred.edu

Distinctive lodging at historic Alfred University. Twenty elegantly appointed guest rooms and six fireside queen-size bedrooms. Richly furnished in deluxe cherry wood with a Colonial style. European breakfast is served fireside in the hospitality room. Smoke-free rooms available. All rooms have private baths.

Innkeeper: Kristen Jacobs
Rooms: 26 (PB) $85-110
Continental Breakfast
Credit Cards: A, B, C, D, E
Notes: 2, 5, 7, 8, 10, 11, 12, 13, 14, 15

AMENIA

Troutbeck

Leedsville Road, 12501
(914) 373-9681; FAX (914) 373-7080
e-mail: innkeeper@troutbeck.com
www.troutbeck.com

This English country house is on 600 gentle acres and was once a gathering place for literati and liberals. Nowadays, Troutbeck caters to corporate business groups during the week and inngoers and wedding and restaurant guests on the weekends. Just two hours from midtown Manhattan, Troutbeck has been nationally acclaimed for both its cuisine and ambiance. Guests also enjoy year-round swimming, tennis, beautiful gardens, and handsome furnishings. No smoking in the dining rooms; however, it is allowed in the public rooms. Children under 1 and over 12 are welcome. Rates are for two nights and include six meals and an open bar.

Owner and Innkeeper: Jim Flaherty; Garret Corcoran (general manager)
Rooms: 42 (37 PB; 5 SB) $650-1,050
Credit Cards: A, B, C, E
Notes: 2, 3, 4, 5, 9, 10, 11, 12, 13, 14, 15

AUBURN

Elaine's Bed & Breakfast Selections

4987 Kingston Road, Elbridge, 13060
(315) 689-2082 (call between 10:30 A.M.–7:00 P.M.)

1. This lovingly kept 1920 Colonial home has two guest rooms which share a modern bath with the owners. Guests may relax on the large front porch or on the equally comfortable rear deck by the swimming pool. Six miles to Skaneateles, 35 minutes from Syracuse, and convenient to all Finger Lake activities. Full breakfast. Open year-round. Moderate rates.

2. Spacious stucco Victorian in the historic section. Guests can choose what they would like for breakfast. Children welcome. Two guest rooms have private bath and one has a shared bath. Ample parking. Cats in residence. Open year-round. No smoking. Near Owasco lake, Merry-Go-Round Playhouse, Seward House, Cayuga County Museum, Schweinfurth Art Center, Cayuga Community College, and only seven miles to Skaneateles Village. Moderate rates.

AURORA

Elaine's Bed & Breakfast Selections

4987 Kingston Road, Elbridge, 13060
(315) 689-2082 (after 10 A.M.)

A historic brick inn, circa 1833, offers 15 rooms, including suites. A special handicap access room on the first floor offers a king-size bed, sitting area, private shower bath, and color TV with remote. All rooms have private baths and TVs. A complimentary breakfast is served from 8 to 10 a.m. The inn is smoke-free except the bar area. No pets. Rollaway cots and cribs available at extra charge. Seasonal rates. $75-135.

NOTES: Credit cards accepted: A MasterCard; B Visa; C American Express; D Discover; E Diner's Club; F Other; 2 Personal checks accepted; 3 Lunch available; 4 Dinner available; 5 Open all year; 6 Pets welcome; 7 No smoking; 8 Children welcome; 9 Social drinking allowed; 10 Tennis nearby; 11 Swimming nearby; 12 Golf nearby; 13 Skiing nearby; 14 May be booked through a travel agent; 15 Handicapped accessible.

AVERILL PARK

The Gregory House Country Inn & Restaurant

P.O. Box 401, 12018
(518) 674-3774; FAX (518) 674-8916
www.members.aol.com/gregoryhse

Near Albany and Troy and everything the capital city of New York State has to offer and more. Historic sites, cultural events, numerous mountain ranges, hiking, skiing, boating, swimming, golfing, summer theater, Saratoga racing, Performing Arts Center, and Tanglewood in the Berkshires. Great for the business traveler, too. Near RPI, Sage, Emma Willard. Inn and restaurant three stars in Mobil Travel Guide. Who could ask for anything more! Guests will be impressed.

Innkeepers: Bob and Bette Jewell
Rooms: 12 (PB) $85-110
Continental Breakfast
Credit Cards: A, B, C, D, E
Notes: 2, 4, 5, 9, 11, 12, 13, 14

The Gregory House

AVOCA

Patchwork Peace Bed & Breakfast

4279 Waterbury Hill, 14809
(607) 566-2443
e-mail: patchworkpeace@infoblvd.net

Enjoy the sights, sounds, and smells of a real farm. Visit dairy cows and calves. Observe the

Patchwork Peace

patchwork of fields in different hues of greens and golds. Take a delightful walk. This 1920 farmhouse with natural floors and woodwork and light, airy bedrooms affords a gentle night's sleep nestled in sun-dried linens. Heirloom quilts throughout. Individual thermostat and air conditioning. In-room telephone. Fishing and hunting very near. Country breakfast with hosts. Spend a night or a week. Special weekly rates.

Hosts: Bill and Betty Mitchell
Rooms: 3 (1 PB; 2 SB) $50-70
Full Breakfast
Credit Cards: None
Notes: 2, 7, 8, 9, 11, 12

BAINBRIDGE

Berry Hill Gardens Bed & Breakfast

242 Ward Loomis Road, 13733
(607) 967-8745; (800) 497-8745
FAX (607) 967-2227
e-mail: berryhill@excelonline.com
www.bbhost.com/berryhillgardens

A friendly, informal atmosphere. Sunrises, sunsets, stargazing, fresh air, views. Restored 1820s farmhouse on a hilltop surrounded by vegetable, flower, and herb gardens. On its 180 acres guests can hike, swim, bird watch, pick berries, skate, cross-country ski, or just sit on the wraparound porch and watch the nature parade. The rooms are furnished with comfortable antiques, and a scrumptious country

NOTES: Credit cards accepted: A MasterCard; B Visa; C American Express; D Discover; E Diner's Club; F Other; 2 Personal checks accepted; 3 Lunch available; 4 Dinner available; 5 Open all year; 6 Pets welcome;

Berry Hill Gardens

breakfast is served. A 10-minute drive takes visitors to restaurants, golf, tennis, auctions, and antique centers.

Hosts: Jean Fowler and Cecilio Rios
Rooms: 5 (1 PB; 4SB) $65-85
Full Breakfast
Credit Cards: A, B, C
Notes: 2, 5, 7, 8, 9, 10, 11, 12, 13, 14

BALDWINSVILLE

Elaine's Bed & Breakfast Selections

4987 Kingston Road, Elbridge, 13060
(315) 689-2082 (call between 10:30 A.M.–7:00 P.M.)

Spacious, historic Colonial in the village. The home was built around 1845 and, in keeping with its character, is decorated with many antiques and collectibles. Four guest rooms available, some with private bath and one with working fireplace. The house is on two acres high on a hill, a short walk to stores and the picturesque Seneca River. This bed and breakfast is also suitable for small wedding parties, teas, etc. Open year-round. Resident cat. $65-85.

Pandora's Getaway

83 Oswego Street, 13027
(315) 635-9571; (888) 638-8668
e-mail: pgetaway@worldnet.att.net

This beautiful restored Greek Revival home with sloping lawns is listed in the National Register of Historic Places and is only 20 min-

utes from Syracuse. Guests will find that they have easy access to the Thruway (I-90), NYS fairgrounds, Syracuse University, and Oswego College. Relax on the front porch or in front of a fire in the living room. Various decors and amenities throughout the house.

Host: Sandy Wheeler
Rooms: 4 (3 PB) $60-80
Full Breakfast
Credit Cards: A, B, C, D, E
Notes: 2, 5, 7, 8, 9, 10, 11, 12, 13, 14

BARNEVELD

Bed & Breakfast Leatherstocking Association, Inc.

5 Rundell House, Dolgeville, 13329
(315) 429-3416 (phone/FAX—call first)
(800) 941-BEDS (2337)
www.bedbreakfastnys.com

001. Grand-scale, 20-room farmhouse from the Victorian era, a former private boys academy, now graciously remodeled, restored with large entrance hall, formal living room, dining room, informal family rooms, several fireplaces. Just a short ride from Utica, close to Hamilton College, Utica College, ski centers of western Adirondacks. Private family suite, king-size/twin bed suite, double and singles, private and shared baths, full gourmet breakfasts, fresh flowers. Credit cards, no pets, children welcome, no smoking. $50-140.

BERLIN

American Country Collection

1353 Union Street, Schenectady, 12308
(518) 370-4948; (800) 810-4948
FAX (518) 393-1634 (call first)
e-mail: Carolbnbres@msn.com
www.bandbreservations.com

244. Charming farmhouse nestled in the Taconic Mountains on 150 acres of rolling hills, ponds, and wonderful views. Only 15 miles to Williamstown. Built in 1790, hand-hewn beams, brick fireplace transport guests back to earlier times. Modern amenities including a screened porch pamper guests. Hike to the pond to swim or cross-country ski the fields. Three guest rooms; one on the first floor has private bath, two others on the second share a hall bath. Full breakfast. No resident pets. $75-90.

BOLTON LANDING

American Country Collection

1353 Union Street, Schenectady, 12308
(518) 370-4948; (800) 810-4948
FAX (518) 393-1634 (call first)
e-mail: Carolbnbres@msn.com
www.bandbreservations.com

056. This 11-room farmhouse was built in 1926 as the caretaker's cottage for a large estate on Millionaires' Row along the west side of Lake George. Two second-floor rooms have their own private baths. On the grounds is a small private cottage available during the summer months. Furnished with queen-size bed, private bath, and kitchenette. Swimming, fishing and ice fishing, skating, parasailing, and boating are all available. Just 20-25 miles to Fort Ticonderoga and Great Escape Fun Park. Children over four are welcome. Pets in residence. Weekly rate for cottage $450. $65-80.

BOONEVILLE/ALDER CREEK

Bed & Breakfast Leatherstocking Association, Inc.

5 Rundell House, Dolgeville, 13329
(315) 429-3416 (phone/FAX—call first)
(800) 941-BEDS (2337)
www.bedbreakfastnys.com

043. Private guest house on a sprawling country estate, exclusively for guests. The house features a handsome living room with big

screen TV and VCR, open fireplace, a fully equipped kitchen, laundry, and dining area; sit on 2000 acres of hiking, biking, horseback trails. Two ponds and one and one-half miles of Black River for fishing—your catch will be cooked for you. Fly-fishing instructions available. Tennis court, volleyball, horseshoes. Pre-arranged air charter and antique dealers, performing art centers. Master suite has private bath with Jacuzzi. A twin suite or a double-size bedroom share a bath. $80-100.

BOVINA CENTER

The Swallow's Nest Bed & Breakfast

Bramley Mountain Road, Box 112, 13740
(607) 832-4547

This 1850s Catskill farmhouse sits on 60 acres of tranquility, but for a babbling brook at the front door. A variety of birds can be seen while partaking of a hearty breakfast. College towns of Delhi and Oneonta are within a 30-minute drive, as are fishing, horseback riding, museums, antiques, and auctions. The rooms are spacious, bright, and tastefully decorated. Inquire about accommodations for pets.

Hosts: Walter and Gunhilde Kuhnle
Rooms: 5 (2 PB; 3 SB) $65-70
Full Breakfast
Credit Cards: A, B
Notes: 2, 5, 7, 8, 11, 12, 13

The Swallow's Nest

BURDETT

The Red House Country Inn

4586 Picnic Area Road, 14818
(607) 546-8566; e-mail: redhsinn@aol.com

Restored 1840s farmstead in the national forest, hiking, and cross-country ski trails, in-
ground pool, near wineries. Large country
breakfast. Open year-round. Five acres of
lawns and gardens. Near Corning, Ithaca,
Watkins Glen.

Hosts: Joan Martin and Sandy Schmanke
Rooms: 5 (5 SB) $59-89
Full Breakfast
Credit Cards: A, B, C, D
Notes: 2, 4, 5, 7, 9, 10, 11, 12, 13, 14

The Red House Country Inn

BURNT HILLS

American Country Collection

1353 Union Street, Schenectady, 12308
(518) 370-4948; (800) 810-4948
FAX (518) 393-1634 (call first)
e-mail: Carolbnbres@msn.com
www.bandbreservations.com

114. The oldest part of this home was built in
1796. The main house, a brick center-hall
Colonial, was completed about 150 years ago.
The home is surrounded by trees and old-fashioned flower gardens that abut a 12-acre apple
orchard. Two guest rooms with private baths.
One guest room opens onto a third room to
form a suite. Smoking limited to sitting room
and outdoors. Children school-age and over
welcome. No pets in residence but may accept
guest pet (charge $10). $65-85.

CAMBRIDGE

Battenkill Bed & Breakfast

937 State Route 313, 12816
(518) 677-8868

Guests are invited to experience the river life at
Battenkill Bed and Breakfast. The land borders
the famous trout stream, the Battenkill, which
rises in the Green Mountains of Vermont and
flows into New York State's Hudson River.
The Battenkill is for both the novice or experienced canoeist or fisherman. If one canoes, on
the navigable portion of the river, one will paddle under four covered bridges. The rental shop
has canoes, kayaks, and fishing equipment.

Hosts: Veronica and Walter Piekarz
Rooms: 1 (SB) $65-75
Full Breakfast
Credit Cards: A, B
Notes: 3, 7, 9, 12

CANANDAIGUA

Acorn Inn

4508 Route 64 South, Bristol Center, 14424-9309
(716) 229-2834; FAX (716) 229-5046
www.acorninnbb.com

This 1795 stagecoach inn exudes warmth and
charm. Guest rooms (all with large, private
baths) are soundproofed and furnished with
antiques, canopied beds, comfortable seating,
TVs, VCRs, excellent reading lamps. Two have
fireplaces, one with whirlpool and private terrace

Acorn Inn

and one with large window seat. A Jacuzzi is on a terrace in the beautiful gardens. Full country breakfasts. Complimentary snacks and beverages. Central air. Weeknights and extended stay discounts. AAA-rated four diamonds.

Hosts: Joan and Louis Clark
Rooms: 4 (PB) $105-175
Full Breakfast
Credit Cards: A, B, C, D
Notes: 2, 5, 7, 9, 10, 11, 12, 13, 14

CANTON

Ostrander's Bed & Breakfast

1675 State Highway 68, 13617
(315) 386-2126; (877) 707-2126
FAX (315) 386-3843; www.ostranders.com

Country-style living in 1996 Cape Cod home. Spacious rooms with private baths, telephones, cable TV, room-controlled heating, ceiling fans, air conditioning, and locked entrances. Two rooms in main house and private accommodations in guest house overlooking an acre pond. Spectacular views of maple tree groves and farm fields. Relax on the front porch or back deck. Working sheep and border collie dog farm. Short drive to canoeing, hiking, golf, antique shops, cross-country ski trails, bicycling, and four colleges in Canton and Potsdam. Fax and photocopy service on-site.

Hosts: Rita and Al Ostrander
Rooms: 3 (PB) $55-75
Full Breakfast
Credit Cards: A, B, C
Notes: 2, 5, 7, 9, 11, 12, 14

White Pillars Bed & Breakfast

395 Old State Road, P.O. Box 185, 13617
(315) 386-2353 (phone/FAX); (800) 261-6292

Experience classic antiquity and modern luxury in this beautifully renovated 1850s homestead. Guest room luxuries include whirlpool tub, marble floor, air conditioning, cable TV, and expansive windows overlooking 100 acres of meadows. This quiet rural setting is only six

White Pillars

miles from Canton, home of two colleges. Summer guests are invited to use the facilities of their hosts' seven-acre estate on Trout Lake, 20 minutes away, for private tennis court, hot tub, swimming, canoeing, and fishing.

Hosts: Donna and John Clark
Rooms: 4 (2 PB; 2 SB) $50-75
Full Breakfast
Credit Cards: A, B, C
Notes: 2, 5, 7, 8, 9, 10, 11, 12, 13, 14, 15

CAZENOVIA

Brae Loch Inn

5 Albany Street, US Route 20, 13035
(315) 655-3431

The 15 quiet rooms in this inn are on the second floor of the Brae Loch in the quaint village of Cazenovia by the lake. They feature the old-time charm of antiques, the classic luxury of Stickley furniture, and the modern comfort of some king-size beds in selected rooms. All rooms have private baths, and these rooms are so handsome and so reasonably priced that guests will want to visit over and over again. Inquire about the getaway packages, fireplaces, and Jacuzzi rooms now available.

Hosts: Jim and Val Barr
Rooms: 15 (13 PB; 2 SB) $55-125
Continental Breakfast
Credit Cards: A, B, C
Notes: 4, 5, 8, 9, 10, 11, 12, 13, 14

NOTES: Credit cards accepted: A MasterCard; B Visa; C American Express; D Discover; E Diner's Club; F Other; 2 Personal checks accepted; 3 Lunch available; 4 Dinner available; 5 Open all year; 6 Pets welcome;

The Brewster Inn

6 Ledyard Avenue, P.O. Box 507, 13035
(315) 655-9232

Built in 1890 on the shore of Cazenovia Lake, the Brewster Inn is an elegant country inn known for fine dining, gracious hospitality, and comfortable lodging. Three attractive dining rooms provide a relaxed atmosphere for superb American cuisine and an award-winning wine list. New in June 1998, a superb glass-enclosed terrace bar overlooking the lake offers delicious lighter fare. Seventeen hotel rooms offer variety in decor. Each room has a private bath, TV, air conditioning, and telephone. Four rooms have Jacuzzis. Cazenovia offers quaint shops, swimming, hiking, golfing, cross-country and downhill skiing, and the impressive Chittenango Falls.

Host: Richard Hubbard
Rooms: 17 (PB) $70-160
Penthouse: 3 rooms $225
Continental Breakfast
Credit Cards: A, B, E
Notes: 2, 4, 5, 7, 8, 9, 10, 11, 12, 13, 15

CHAPPAQUA

Crabtree's Kittle House Restaurant & Inn

11 Kittle Road, 10514
(914) 666-8044; FAX (914) 666-2684

Set in the rolling hills of picturesque Chappaqua in beautiful Westchester County, Crabtree's Kittle House, built in 1790, combines country charm and historic character with

Crabtree's Kittle House

world-class American cuisine. Twelve guest rooms with private bath and cable TV are available for overnight accommodations. *New York Times* rated excellent cuisine and Grand Award wine cellar. Ideal setting for weddings and private parties of 20-200 guests. Just off Route 117, Saw Mill River Parkway, exit 33.

Hosts: Dick and John Crabtree
Rooms: 12 (PB) $107.50
Continental Breakfast
Credit Cards: A, B, C, D, E
Notes: 2, 3, 4, 5, 8, 9, 12, 14, 15

CHESTERTOWN

Friends Lake Inn

963 Friends Lake Road, 12817
(518) 494-4751

In the Adirondacks overlooking Friends Lake, this fully restored 19th-century inn is 20 minutes north of Lake George, with Gore Mountain ski center only 15 minutes away. Breakfast and gourmet dinner are served daily accompanied by an award-winning wine list. Canoeing, swimming, hiking, and cross-country skiing and snowshoeing facilities are on the grounds. Children 12 and older welcome.

Hosts: Sharon and Greg Taylor
Rooms: 17 (PB) $155-335
Full Breakfast
Credit Cards: A, B, E, F
Notes: 2, 3, 4, 5, 7, 9, 10, 11, 12, 13, 14

Landon Hill Bed & Breakfast

10 Landon Hill Road, 12817
(518) 494-2599 (phone/FAX); (888) 244-2599
e-mail: landon@bedbreakfast.net
www.bedbreakfast.net

Located at gateway to the southern Adirondack Lakes area. Unique Adirondack Victorian home overlooking scenic Chestertown. Spiral staircase, five distinctive guest rooms, with private baths. Scandinavian woodstove in common area. Perennial rock garden. Full breakfast featuring eggs Benedict, Adirondack quiche,

7 No smoking; 8 Children welcome; 9 Social drinking allowed; 10 Tennis nearby; 11 Swimming nearby; 12 Golf nearby; 13 Skiing nearby; 14 May be booked through a travel agent; 15 Handicapped accessible.

blueberry pancakes. Nearby fine dining, historic Lake George, Gore Mountain (20 minutes), Saratoga Springs, Adirondack Museum (40 minutes), Lake Placid (60 minutes). One mile off I-87, exit 25.

Hosts: Judy and Carl Johnson
Rooms: 5 (4 PB; 1 SB) $70-120
Full Breakfast
Credit Cards: A, B
Notes: 2, 5, 7, 8, 9, 10, 11, 12, 13, 14, 15

CINCINNATUS _____

Elaine's Bed & Breakfast Selections

4987 Kingston Road, Elbridge, 13060
(315) 689-2082 (call between 10:30 A.M.–7:00 P.M.)

This Italianate Victorian was lovingly built for a bride. It is listed in the state and the National Register of Historical Places. Relax in a wicker rocker on the "painted lady" veranda, sip tea in the formal parlor, or enjoy TV in the comfortable common room. Wake up to the aroma of coffee, teas, and muffins just outside the door as a prelude to breakfast awaiting guests in the dining room. Convenient to area colleges: Ithaca, Cornell, Colgate, SUNY Cortland. Sits nestled in the Otselic Valley between the Finger Lakes and Leatherstocking regions. Golfing, skiing, fishing, antiquing, and other recreational activities are all just around the bend. Two lovely, spacious guest rooms with private baths. No smoking. $65-75.

CLARENCE _____

Asa Ransom House

10529 Main Street, 14031
(716) 759-2315; FAX (716) 759-2791
e-mail: asaransom@aol.com
www.asaransom.com

The Asa Ransom House, an intimate village inn in historic Clarence, is just northeast of Buffalo and only 28 miles from Niagara Falls. The inn features nine beautifully appointed guest rooms, each with private bath, and most with fireplace, balcony, or porch. Asa Ransom House has been awarded grand prize as the Waverly *Country Inn* Room of the Year. The grounds feature flower and herb gardens, pond, and the ruins of the first grist mill in the county. Clarence Hollow is known throughout the East for its treasured antique shops and antique expo.

Host: Robert Lenz
Rooms: 9 (PB) $95-145
Full Breakfast
Credit Cards: A, B, D
Notes: 4, 7, 8, 10, 11, 12, 14, 15

CLEVELAND _____

Elaine's Bed & Breakfast Selections

4987 Kingston Road, Elbridge, 13060
(315) 689-2082 (call between 10:30 A.M.–7:00 P.M.)

This 1820 Colonial is on the north shore of Oneida Lake. An open porch welcomes guests with antique wicker and a hammock. Playroom with billiard table, jukebox, many musical instruments. Family room with TV, stereo, and stained-glass leaded window. All rooms have working fireplaces and private baths. The dining room has a working player piano. There are also an organ and a nickelodeon. A furnished beach house is also available for $170. Perfect for small conferences. No pets. No smoking. No children under 16. Swimming pool. $50-75.

CLINTON _____

Bed & Breakfast Leatherstocking Association, Inc.

5 Rundell House, Dolgeville, 13329
(315) 429-3416 (phone/FAX—call first)
(800) 941-BEDS (2337)
www.bedbreakfastnys.com

061. Lots of history in this unmarred and beautifully maintained English Colonial on the vil-

---

NOTES: Credit cards accepted: A MasterCard; B Visa; C American Express; D Discover; E Diner's Club; F Other; 2 Personal checks accepted; 3 Lunch available; 4 Dinner available; 5 Open all year; 6 Pets welcome;

lage commons of a picturesque college town far from the bustle of the busy world. Crystal and brass chandeliers, five commodious rooms with private baths, full breakfasts, wheelchair accessibility. Just a short ride from Utica, all credit cards. Exchange library; gift shop, fireplace, resident cat. $75-95.

Elaine's Bed & Breakfast Selections

4987 Kingston Road, Elbridge, 13060
(315) 689-2082 (call between 10:30 A.M.–7:00 P.M.)

This home, just around the corner from college hill, is well furnished with antiques and good traditional furniture. There are two sitting rooms for guests' use. In the main house is a first-floor suite featuring a private sitting area and private bath with whirlpool. Upstairs two nice guest rooms share a bath. There is a small sitting area outside these rooms. A separate, fully self-contained cottage is also elegantly furnished with a beautiful living room, eat-in kitchen, spacious bedroom, and one and one-half baths. Full from scratch breakfast. Swimming pool. Children eight and older welcome. Possibly pets depending upon the pet. Open year-round. $75-120.

CLINTON CORNERS

American Country Collection

1353 Union Street, Schenectady, 12308
(518) 370-4948; (800) 810-4948
FAX (518) 393-1634 (call first)
e-mail: Carolbnbres@msn.com
www.bandbreservations.com

195. This lakefront home, surrounded by flower gardens, has a common room with cathedral ceiling, Colonial fireplace, and deck overlooking gardens and lake. The two-room suite, which can accommodate three, has TV, skylight, full private bath, and lake-view balcony. The other room has a fireplace, lake view

balcony, and private bath. Furnishings are a mixture of Colonial and handcrafted Van Hoen furniture. Nearby lake for swimming, boating, fishing, and ice skating; also cross-country skiing. Fifteen miles from Rhinebeck, Millbrook, Culinary Institute, Vanderbilt mansion, Roosevelt home and library, Hyde Park, and other attractions. Thirty dollars extra for third person in suite. $110.

COOPERSTOWN

American Country Collection

1353 Union Street, Schenectady, 12308
(518) 370-4948; (800) 810-4948
FAX (518) 393-1634 (call first)
e-mail: Carolbnbres@msn.com
www.bandbreservations.com

128. Enjoy this rural farmhouse on 7.5 acres. Surrounded by a pond, sugar bush, hills, and meadows, this inn offers travelers a parlor room for relaxing or reading, an air-conditioned breakfast room, and an adjoining room with TV. A small self-contained apartment with two bedrooms, living room, and private bath can accommodate up to five people. Two additional rooms that share a bath are available. Smoking outdoors only. Full country breakfast. Children are welcome. $60-125.

Angelholm

14 Elm Street, Box 705, 13326
(607) 547-2483; FAX (607) 547-2309

On a quiet residential street within easy walking distance of the Baseball Hall of Fame, museums, shops, restaurants, and other attractions, Angelholm is a gracious 1805 Federal-period home with comfortably elegant furnishings. Five rooms, all with private baths and air conditioning. Breakfast is served in the formal dining room. Afternoon tea and lemonade are served on the veranda or in the living

---

7 No smoking; 8 Children welcome; 9 Social drinking allowed; 10 Tennis nearby; 11 Swimming nearby; 12 Golf nearby; 13 Skiing nearby; 14 May be booked through a travel agent; 15 Handicapped accessible.

Angelholm

room. Off-street parking available. Cross-country skiing nearby.

Hosts: Jan and Fred Reynolds
Rooms: 5 (PB) $70-110
Full Breakfast
Credit Cards: A, B
Notes: 2, 5, 7, 9, 11, 12, 13, 14

The Cooper Inn

Main & Chestnut Street, 13326
(607) 547-2567; (800) 348-6222
FAX (607) 547-1271
e-mail: reservations@cooperinn.com
www.cooperinn.com

The Cooper Inn offers a selection of 20 reno-vated rooms, each with a private bath, tele-phone, modem jack, cable TV, central heat and air conditioning. The Cooper Inn is a short dis-tance from the many attractions of Cooper-stown including: the National Baseball Hall of Fame, the Farmer's Museum, and Fenimore Art Museum with its American Indian Wing, the shopping district of Cooperstown, Lake Otsego, and the world-renowned Glimmerglass Opera's Summer Festival.

Rooms: 20 (15 PB; 5 SB) $135-155
Continental Breakfast
Credit Cards: A, B, C
Notes: 2, 5, 7, 8, 9, 10, 11, 12, 14

Elaine's Bed & Breakfast Selections

4987 Kingston Road, Elbridge, 13060
(315) 689-2082 (call between 10:30 A.M.–7:00 P.M.)

1. Authentic old farm Colonial, restored out-side and renovated inside. Guest apartment on the second floor has two bedrooms. Large liv-ing room, complete kitchen, and dining ell. Pri-vate deck off living room through glass doors. Ideal for a family or two couples traveling together. Handy to Cooperstown to visit the Baseball Hall of Fame, Fenimore House, the Farmers' Museum, art galleries, boutiques, Otsego Lake, Glimmerglass Opera, and Glim-merglass State Park. Breakfast available on the nightly rate if desired. $125-250.

The Inn at Cooperstown

16 Chestnut Street, 13326
(607) 547-5756; e-mail: theinn@telenet.net
www.cooperstown.net/theinn

The Inn at Cooperstown, built in 1874, contin-ues to provide genuine hospitality within walk-ing distance of major Cooperstown attractions. The 18 guest rooms, all with private baths, are simply decorated with the guests' well-being in mind. Enjoy the comfortable beds and the large, thirsty towels. Relax in a rocking chair on the sweeping veranda shaded by 100-year-old maples or in front of the cozy fireplace in the sitting room. Off-street parking is available behind this award-winning inn. Smoke-free

The Inn at Cooperstown

NOTES: Credit cards accepted: A MasterCard; B Visa; C American Express; D Discover; E Diner's Club; F Other; 2 Personal checks accepted; 3 Lunch available; 4 Dinner available; 5 Open all year; 6 Pets welcome;

rooms available. Smoking permitted in designated areas only. Cross-country skiing, museums, opera, and dining nearby.

Host: Michael Jerome
Rooms: 18 (PB) $98-140
Continental Breakfast
Credit Cards: A, B, C, D, E
Notes: 2, 5, 8, 9, 10, 11, 12, 14, 15

CORINTH

American Country Collection

1353 Union Street, Schenectady, 12308
(518) 370-4948; (800) 810-4948
FAX (518) 393-1634 (call first)
e-mail: Carolbnbres@msn.com
www.bandbreservations.com

151. Travelers are invited to share a most unusual country inn at the gateway to the Adirondacks, only minutes from the villages of Saratoga Springs, Lake George, and Lake Luzerne. Five rooms, all with private baths. Saratoga, the racetracks, Skidmore College, and SPAC all within an easy drive. Breakfast features a fresh fruit platter, juice selection, muffins with jam, Belgian waffles with cinnamon apples or strawberry blend, coffee, and tea. $70-135.

CORNING

1865 White Birch Bed & Breakfast

69 East First Street, 14830
(607) 962-6355

Imagine a friendly, warm atmosphere in an 1865 Victorian setting. Cozy rooms await guests; both private and shared baths. Awake to the tantalizing aromas of a full home-baked breakfast. Walk to museums, historic Market Street, and the Corning Glass Center. Experience it all here.

Hosts: Kathy and Joe Donahue
Rooms: 4 (2 PB; 2 SB) $50-85
Full Breakfast

Credit Cards: A, B, C
Notes: 2, 5, 7, 8, 10, 11, 12, 13, 14

CORNWALL-ON-THE-HUDSON

American Country Collection

1353 Union Street, Schenectady, 12308
(518) 370-4948; (800) 810-4948
FAX (518) 393-1634 (call first)
e-mail: Carolbnbres@msn.com
www.bandbreservations.com

184. Historic country estate built in traditional manor style with elegant Greek Revival front, set on seven acres of woodlands and gardens. Visit the neighboring farm's craft and gift shop, relax by the goldfish pond, or explore the rolling hills and mountains. Stay in one of nine sumptuously appointed, color-coordinated rooms or suites, all containing sitting/reading areas, private baths, and air conditioning. Breakfast is served in the breakfast room or the back veranda. It is only one mile to the Storm King Art Center and Black Rock Forest hiking trails, five miles to West Point and Brotherhood Winery, and 11 miles to Bear Mountain for swimming and hiking. $150-250.

Cromwell Manor Inn

174 Angola Road, 12518
(914) 534-7136

Cromwell Manor Inn is a historic country estate on seven acres of woodlands and gardens. Guests can visit nearby West Point, explore the many sights of the majestic Hudson Highlands or relax for a quiet weekend getaway. Fourteen rooms and suites all with private baths and all beautifully decorated with period antiques and fine furnishings. Many rooms have working wood-burning fireplaces, Jacuzzi, or steam room. Air conditioning.

Hosts: Dale and Barbara O'Hara
Rooms: 13 (PB) $135-275
Full Breakfast
Credit Cards: None
Notes: 2, 5, 7, 9, 10, 11, 12, 13, 14, 15

7 No smoking; 8 Children welcome; 9 Social drinking allowed; 10 Tennis nearby; 11 Swimming nearby; 12 Golf nearby; 13 Skiing nearby; 14 May be booked through a travel agent; 15 Handicapped accessible.

CORTLAND

The Candlelight Inn

49 West Main Street, P.O. Box 1109, Dryden, 13053
(607) 844-4321; (800) 579-4629
e-mail: inn@candlelightinnny.com
www.candlelightinnny.com

Guests are personally welcomed by owners
Doris and Sam. In the National Register of
Historic Places, this antique-furnished circa
1828 Federal-style homestead is subtly elegant
yet unpretentious. Enjoy deluxe rooms and
suites, air conditioning, fireplace, porches,
library, TV, VCR, herb and flower gardens,
afternoon tea, and full breakfast. In-ground
swimming pool. Ten minutes to Cortland,
Ithaca, Cornell, and Greek Peak ski area.
Twenty minutes to wineries and Finger Lakes.
Smoking in designated areas only.

Hosts: Doris and Sam Nitsios
Rooms: 4 (PB) $55-120
Suites: 2 (PB)
Full Breakfast
Credit Cards: A, B, C, D, E
Notes: 2, 5, 8, 9, 10, 11, 12, 13, 14

The Candlelight Inn

CROTON-ON-HUDSON

Alexander Hamilton House

49 Van Wyck Street, 10520
(914) 271-6737
www.alexanderhamiltonhouse.com

Alexander Hamilton House

The Alexander Hamilton House, circa 1889, is
a sprawling Victorian home on a cliff overlooking the Hudson. Grounds include an in-ground
pool. Guest accommodations include a suite
with a fireplaced sitting room, a suite with a
fireplace and small sitting room, two large
rooms, and a bridal chamber with Jacuzzi,
entertainment center, pink marble fireplace, and
lots of skylights. There is also a master suite
with a view of the river. Nearby attractions
include West Point, the Sleepy Hollow restora-
tions, Lyndhurst, Boscobel, the Rockefeller
mansion, hiking, biking, sailing, and New York
City just an hour away. Off-street parking.

Host: Barbara Notarius
Rooms: 7 (PB) $95-250
Full Breakfast
Credit Cards: A, B, C, D, E
Notes: 2, 5, 7, 8, 9, 11, 12, 14

American Country Collection

1353 Union Street, Schenectady, 12308
(518) 370-4948; (800) 810-4948
FAX (518) 393-1634 (call first)
e-mail: Carolbnbres@msn.com
www.bandbreservations.com

157. Perfect for vacations, business travel, and
romantic getaways, this stately Victorian home,
circa 1889, is nestled on a cliff above the Hudson River, only a short walk from the picturesque village of Croton-on-Hudson.
Luxurious without being ornate, this bed and
breakfast offers three suites, each with a private
bath and fireplace, three rooms on the second

NOTES: Credit cards accepted: A MasterCard; B Visa; C American Express; D Discover; E Diner's Club;
F Other; 2 Personal checks accepted; 3 Lunch available; 4 Dinner available; 5 Open all year; 6 Pets welcome;

floor with private baths, and two third-floor suites, each with a fireplace and full Jacuzzi. In-ground swimming pool available for guest use. Full breakfast. Smoking outside only. Train station is close. Children welcome. $95-250.

CROWN POINT

American Country Collection

1353 Union Street, Schenectady, 12308
(518) 370-4948; (800) 810-4948
FAX (518) 393-1634 (call first)
e-mail: Carolbnbres@msn.com
www.bandbreservations.com

095. It took three years for a team of Italian craftsmen to complete this 18-room "painted lady" Victorian mansion, circa 1887, on five and one-half acres in the center of this small town. Carved woodwork, doors, and stair railing from oak, cherry, mahogany, and walnut grace the home. All six guest rooms have private baths. In winter, breakfast is served in front of the fireplace in the dining room. Fort Ticonderoga and Fort Crown Point are nearby. Children are welcome. $80-130.

Crown Point Bed & Breakfast

Box 490, Main Street, Route 9N, 12928
(518) 597-3651; FAX (518) 597-4451
e-mail: mail@crownpointbandb.com
www.ctelco.net/~crwnptbb

Crown Point

The Wyman House (named after its banker-owner) is an elegant "painted lady" Victorian manor house on five and one-half acres. Its gracious interior is filled with period antiques. Each bedchamber is distinctly decorated and has a private bath. The house glows with woodwork panels and stained glass. Blooming gardens and a fountain grace the property. Continental plus breakfast is served in an oak-paneled dining room or on one of the three porches. Picnic lunch is available at an extra cost. Inquire about accommodations for children. Three-room suite available. Bath robes, slippers, hair dryers, shower massage, turndown service with gourmet chocolates complete the amenities package for all rooms.

Hosts: Hugh and Sandy Johnson
Rooms: 6 (PB) $60-80
Suite: $110-130
Continental Breakfast
Credit Cards: A, B, C, D
Notes: 2, 5, 7, 9, 11, 12, 14

DE BRUCE

De Bruce Country Inn on the Willowemoc

De Bruce Road, 12758
(914) 439-3900

In a spectacular 1,000-acre natural setting within the Catskill Forest Preserve, overlooking the Willowemoc trout stream, the inn offers turn-of-the-century charm and hospitality. Terrace dining, wooded trails, wildlife, pool, sauna, outdoor activities in all seasons, fresh air, and mountain water. Fireside lounge, fine wine cellar, and the best food. Two hours from New York City. Inquire about pets. Dinner and breakfast are included.

Hosts: Ron and Marilyn
Rooms: 15 (PB) from $95
Full Breakfast
Credit Cards: None
Notes: 4, 5, 9, 10, 11, 12, 13

7 No smoking; 8 Children welcome; 9 Social drinking allowed; 10 Tennis nearby; 11 Swimming nearby; 12 Golf nearby; 13 Skiing nearby; 14 May be booked through a travel agent; 15 Handicapped accessible.

DEWITT

Elaine's Bed & Breakfast Selections

4987 Kingston Road, Elbridge, 13060
(315) 689-2082 (call between 10:30 A.M.–7:00 P.M.)

A. Near Shoppington, this fine older Colonial is warmly furnished with some antiques. A large front guest room has an antique double bed, and a den with a sofa bed is available for families. $60.

DOLGEVILLE

Bed & Breakfast Leatherstocking Association, Inc.

5 Rundell House, Dolgeville, 13329
(315) 429-3416 (phone/FAX—call first)
(800) 941-BEDS (2337)
www.bedbreakfastnys.com

031. Just 10 minutes from exit 29-A, NYS Thruway (I-90), is this quiet country village and this lovely bed and breakfast, with central air conditioning, three guest rooms, one with a private bath, all decorated and furnished with personal comfort in mind. Bath amenities, and bathrobes are provided for guests. Enjoy a full breakfast by candlelight in the dining room. Convenient to Cooperstown, Utica, Saratoga, and Albany. Visa and MasterCard accepted. Smoking restricted. $45-65

DURHAMVILLE

American Country Collection

1353 Union Street, Schenectady, 12308
(518) 370-4948; (800) 810-4948
FAX (518) 393-1634 (call first)
e-mail: Carolbnbres@msn.com
www.bandbreservations.com

166. Easy access from the New York Thruway and near Colgate and Hamilton Colleges. Completely restored 1800s farmhouse and barn on three tree-shaded acres. Decorated in a country motif and furnished with solid cherry furnishings. Four rooms with queen-size, double, or single beds and two shared baths. Full breakfast; children welcome. Resident barn cat. Smoking in common rooms. $50.

Elaine's Bed & Breakfast Selections

4987 Kingston Road, Elbridge, 13060
(315) 689-2082 (call between 10:30 A.M.–7:00 P.M.)

This stately old farm Colonial sits on its own quiet three acres in the country yet has easy access to all activities in the Oneida Valley: Sylvan Beach, Verona Beach, fishing, boating, Vernon Downs, antique shops, historic Fort Stanwix in Rome, Turning Stone Casino, and several nearby colleges. First-floor suite has private bath, living room with fireplace, TV, and ceiling fan. Second floor has four rooms with two new shared baths. Two second-floor rooms are air conditioned. TV/VCR in living room. MasterCard and Visa. Children under five free. $60-85.

EAST CHATHAM

American Country Collection

1353 Union Street, Schenectady, 12308
(518) 370-4948; (800) 810-4948
FAX (518) 393-1634 (call first)
e-mail: Carolbnbres@msn.com
www.bandbreservations.com

206. This authentic 1790s center-hall Colonial farmhouse is nestled on eight acres and overlooks a wetlands reserve. Inside are Shaker furnishings with touches of Asian art interspersed with country quilts and antiques, wide-board floors, beamed wooden ceilings, and a keeping room with a wood-burning stove. Guests may use an outdoor grill and picnic table or request a catered picnic. Three guest rooms with private baths. Near three Shaker museums, within 20 minutes of Massachusetts Berkshire attrac-

NOTES: Credit cards accepted: A MasterCard; B Visa; C American Express; D Discover; E Diner's Club; F Other; 2 Personal checks accepted; 3 Lunch available; 4 Dinner available; 5 Open all year; 6 Pets welcome;

tions. Cross-country skiing. Smoking permitted in designated areas only. Children and small pets welcome. Full breakfast. $80-95.

EAST HAMPTON

The Maidstone Arms

207 Main Street, 11937
(516) 324-5006; FAX (516) 324-5037
e-mail: maidstay@aol.com
www.maidstonearms.com

This beautifully restored 1740 inn nestled in the charming village of East Hampton offers visitors historic charm with modern comfort. The 19-room inn features guest rooms, suites, and private cottages (with fireplaces) which are all attractively decorated with antique furniture, authentic art and fresh flowers. All rooms include private bath, direct-dial telephone, cable TV, and air conditioning. The first-class restaurant, quoted "the best cuisine in the Hamptons" by Gourmet magazine, serves breakfast, lunch, and dinner. Pristine ocean beaches, boutique shopping, and trendy art galleries all are nearby.

Host: Coke Anne M. Wilcox
Rooms: 19 (PB) $132-395
Continental Breakfast
Credit Cards: A, B, C, E
Notes: 2, 3, 4, 5, 7, 8, 9, 10, 11, 12

Mill House Inn

33 North Main Street, 11937
(516) 324-9766; FAX (516) 324-9793
www.millhouseinn.com
www.tastingthehamptons.com

This 1790 Dutch Colonial house in East Hampton village was fully renovated and refurbished in 1995. Each room has a private bath and is decorated around a Hamptons' theme, such as Sail Away or Hampton Holiday—a popular wedding night and honeymoon room. Guests love the whirlpool tubs and gas fireplaces. Full breakfast features delicious homemade baked goods and seasonal entrées

Mill House Inn

and fruits. Rooms feature telephone with voice mail, air conditioning, and TV. Near gorgeous beaches, shopping, and fine restaurants. Seasonal rates available. Four-night minimum stay on holiday weekends; three-night minimum stay required for summer weekends. Gift certificates available. New this year *Tasting the Hamptons* cookbook and area guide.

Hosts: Katherine and Daniel Hartnett
Rooms: 8 (PB) $150-350
Full Breakfast
Credit Cards: A, B, E
Notes: 2, 5, 7, 8, 9, 10, 11, 12, 15

ELBRIDGE

Elaine's Bed & Breakfast Selections

4987 Kingston Road, 13060
(315) 689-2082 (call between 10:30 A.M.–7:00 P.M.)

Remodeled ranch-style home in the country on five acres, 20 minutes west of Syracuse, seven minutes from downtown Skaneateles, and 12 minutes from Auburn. Two guest rooms sharing one and one-half baths. Smoke free. Resident cat. Continental plus breakfast, more if required. Open year-round. Hostess runs Elaine's Bed and Breakfast Selections. Very close to Skaneateles for Music Festival, Antique Boat Shop, dinner and sightseeing

---

7 No smoking; 8 Children welcome; 9 Social drinking allowed; 10 Tennis nearby; 11 Swimming nearby; 12 Golf nearby; 13 Skiing nearby; 14 May be booked through a travel agent; 15 Handicapped accessible.

cruises, antique shops, restaurants, polo, fishing, swimming, boat launch, boutiques, art galleries, food specialities, arts and crafts in the park, concerts, antique sale in Allyn Arena, historic homes, all lovely. Also just seven miles to Weedsport I-90 interchange and D.I.R.T. racing track and auto museum. $60-65.

ELLICOTTVILLE

Ilex Inn

6416 East Washington Street, P.O. Box 1585, 14731
(716) 699-2002; (800) 496-6307
FAX (716) 699-5539; www.ilexinn.com

A turn-of-the-century Victorian farmhouse fully refurbished in 1990 with private modern baths. Guests are sure to enjoy the immaculate antique adorned interior, the meticulously maintained grounds, and the hot tub spa or heated in-ground swimming pool. Guest rooms feature terry-cloth robes, slippers, fireplaces, and air conditioning. The elegant yet comfortable living room features a fireplace, cable TV, VCR, and video library. The upstairs foyer and gallery offer early morning coffee, parlor games, and a lovely view. Golf or ski packages, bicycles, feather beds, and flannel sheets are available upon request. AAA-approved.

Hosts: Bill Brown and Leslie Cannon
Rooms: 5 (PB) $55-195
Full Breakfast
Credit Cards: A, B, C, F
Notes: 5, 7, 9, 10, 11, 12, 13, 15

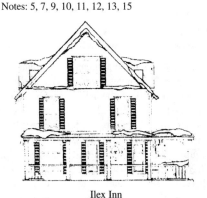

Ilex Inn

ESSEX

American Country Collection

1353 Union Street, Schenectady, 12308
(518) 370-4948; (800) 810-4948
FAX (518) 393-1634 (call first)
e-mail: Carolbnbres@msn.com
www.bandbreservations.com

189. Overlooking Lake Champlain, this charming, fully restored farmhouse dates back to the mid-1800s. The original buildings are in the National Register of Historic Places. Minutes from the ferry to Vermont. A full country or Continental breakfast (guest's choice) is served. Four guest rooms. $80-100.

FAIR HAVEN

Elaine's Bed & Breakfast Selections

4987 Kingston Road, Elbridge, 13060
(315) 689-2082 (call between 10:30 A.M.–7:00 P.M.)

Restored Victorian farmhouse on 20 acres in the country. Four guest rooms are air conditioned; private or shared bath. The main bath has a whirlpool tub as well as shower. Also available is a private cabin with fireplace, great room, and kitchen and sleeps four—a two-night minimum stay in July and August. Snowmobile or cross-country ski from the door. No pets. Children over 12 welcome. No smoking. Full breakfast. Moderate rates.

FAYETTEVILLE

Bed & Breakfast Leatherstocking Association, Inc.

5 Rundell House, Dolgeville, 13329
(315) 429-3416 (phone/FAX—call first)
(800) 941-BEDS (2337)
www.bedbreakfastnys.com

003. Only a few minutes from Syracuse University, this authentic antebellum home, filled

---

NOTES: Credit cards accepted: A MasterCard; B Visa; C American Express; D Discover; E Diner's Club; F Other; 2 Personal checks accepted; 3 Lunch available; 4 Dinner available; 5 Open all year; 6 Pets welcome;

with period antiques and collectibles, sits in the historic section of this pretty suburban town. Also close to Syracuse Airport, Lemoyne College, and Green Lake State Park. Thirty minutes away from Clinton's Hamilton College and Hamilton's Colgate. Walking distance to Fayetteville Mall. Four baths provide optional private bath possibilities to five air-conditioned bedrooms, one with whirlpool. Full breakfast served weekends, Continental breakfast served weekdays. Credit cards okay. Smoking permitted in designated areas only. $45-95.

Elaine's Bed & Breakfast Selections

4987 Kingston Road, Elbridge, 13060
(315) 689-2082 (call between 10:30 A.M.–7:00 P.M.)

A. Italianate brick built in 1830 and 1854. First-floor room has private bath and sitting room. Second floor has four guest rooms and two baths upstairs. Each bedroom has air conditioning. The bridal room has a private bath with two-person whirlpool. In the historic preservation area. Walk to restaurants and stores. $55-95.

B. Colonial home in fine suburb offers one guest room and private access to bath. Single bed available in upstairs den for child if necessary. Smoke-free home. One small resident dog. Ten dollars for additional person with sleeping bag. $65.

FILLMORE

Just a "Plane" Bed 'n Breakfast

11152 Route 19 A, 14735
(716) 567-8338

Enjoy a relaxing, peaceful stay at Just a "Plane" Bed 'n Breakfast. Located seven miles south of Letchworth State Park on the banks of the Genesee Canal. A Dutch Colonial home constructed in 1926 by Craig's grandparents. Well-maintained and very comfortable; deco-

rated with country flair. Airplane rides available for additional fee.

Hosts: Audrey and Craig Smith
Rooms: 4 (PB) $60
Full Breakfast
Credit Cards: A, B, C
Notes: 2, 7, 8, 9, 10, 11, 12, 13, 14

FLEISCHMANNS

American Country Collection

1353 Union Street, Schenectady, 12308
(518) 370-4948; (800) 810-4948
FAX (518) 393-1634 (call first)
e-mail: Carolbnbres@msn.com
www.bandbreservations.com

161. This 1867 classic Victorian summer retreat is at the entrance to the high peaks of the Catskill Mountains. Trout streams and well-marked hiking trails are all nearby. Skiing only five minutes away. Ten rooms, six with private baths, four with shared bath, and one efficiency apartment with private bath. Smoking permitted in apartment only. Handicapped accessible. Children and guest dogs welcome. $70-100.

Elaine's Bed & Breakfast Selections

4987 Kingston Road, Elbridge, 13060
(315) 689-2082 (call between 10:30 A.M.–7:00 P.M.)

This classic Victorian was built in 1887 by a wealthy Griffin Corners resident. There are seven distinctive guest rooms, most with private baths, as well as a lower floor '50s style apartment suite. Full gourmet breakfast. $60-105.

River Run Bed & Breakfast Inn

Main Street, 12430
(914) 254-4884

Exquisite 1887 Queen Anne cottage surrounded by the Catskill Forest Preserve, with its magnificent hiking trails, splendid foliage, and superb skiing. Rejuvenate on a delightful

7 No smoking; 8 Children welcome; 9 Social drinking allowed; 10 Tennis nearby; 11 Swimming nearby; 12 Golf nearby; 13 Skiing nearby; 14 May be booked through a travel agent; 15 Handicapped accessible.

wraparound front porch, acre of streamside property, or book-filled parlor, complete with piano and fireplace. Step into the oak-floored dining room, bathed in colors of the inn's signature stained-glass windows, and enjoy delectable breakfasts and refreshments. New York City bus stops at the front door. Continental plus breakfast.

Host: Larry Miller
Rooms: 10 (6 PB; 4 SB) $60-110
Continental Breakfast
Credit Cards: A, B, C
Notes: 2, 5, 6, 7, 8, 9, 10, 11, 12, 13, 14

FLOYD (ROME)

Bed & Breakfast Leatherstocking Association, Inc.

5 Rundell House, Dolgeville, 13329
(315) 429-3416 (phone/FAX—call first)
(800) 941-BEDS (2337)
www.bedbreakfastnys.com

065. A restored farmhouse on 122 acres of farmland which includes barns and outbuildings for horse stables and some chickens. Main house on groomed landscaped plot has three immaculate guest rooms with shared and optional private baths. Clean, sunny, and airy. No credit cards, close casino, all Utica/Rome activities, area colleges, shopping, and fine dining.

FREDONIA

Brookside Manor Bed & Breakfast

3728 Route 83, 14063-9740
(716) 672-7721; (800) 929-7599

Spacious brick Victorian manor, circa 1875, on five and one-half partially wooded acres, minutes from historic Fredonia, SUNY at Fredonia, Lily Dale, and Lake Erie. Three beautifully appointed guest rooms with private bathrooms, queen-size beds, large windows, antique inside window shutters, ceiling fans, room air condi-

tioners, and hardwood floors plus unique family heirlooms. Gourmet breakfasts are served in the elegant dining room. Outside, a covered patio, woods, a meadow, and a spring-fed brook offer a relaxing atmosphere.

Hosts: Andrea Andrews and Dale Mirth
Rooms: 3 (PB) $75
Full Breakfast
Credit Cards: A, B
Notes: 2, 5, 6, 7, 8, 9, 10, 11, 12, 13

The White Inn

52 East Main Street, 14063
(716) 672-2103; (888) FREDONIA
e-mail: inn@whiteinn.com; www.whiteinn.com

This 23-room inn lies at the center of a vibrant cultural and historical community. Nearby Chautauqua Institution presents lectures and concert performances each summer, and Fredonia State College offers a year-round schedule of cultural and sporting events. Antiques and reproductions adorn the guest rooms, 11 of which are spacious suites. Guests and the public may enjoy gourmet meals at the inn, a charter member of the Duncan Hines "Family of Fine Restaurants." The inn offers fine dining and banquets, as well as cocktails and casual fare in the lounge or on the 100-foot-long veranda. Wineries, state parks, and a variety of shops are all nearby.

Hosts: Robert Contiguglia and Kathleen Dennison
Rooms: 23 (PB) $79-179

The White Inn

NOTES: Credit cards accepted: A MasterCard; B Visa; C American Express; D Discover; E Diner's Club; F Other; 2 Personal checks accepted; 3 Lunch available; 4 Dinner available; 5 Open all year; 6 Pets welcome;

Full Breakfast
Credit Cards: A, B, C, D, E
Notes: 2, 3, 4, 5, 8, 9, 12, 13, 14, 15

GARRISON

The Bird & Bottle Inn

Route 9, Old Albany Post Road, 10524
(914) 424-3000; FAX (914) 424-3283
e-mail: birdbottle@aol.com

Originally known as Warren's Tavern in 1761,
this building was a stagecoach stop along the
Albany Post Road. It is a perfect spot to stay
overnight in one of the three rooms in the main
building, each with a private bath, working fireplace, air conditioning, and canopied bed. A
cottage, steps away from the main building,
offers the same appointments. Near West Point,
Boscobel Restoration, antiquing, and hiking.
Price includes a $75 food credit toward a four-
course gourmet dinner for two and full breakfast Wednesday through Sunday. On Mondays
and Tuesdays, a Continental breakfast is served.
Member Independent Innkeepers Association.

Host: Ira Boyar
Rooms: 4 (PB) $210-240
Full Breakfast
Credit Cards: A, B, C, E
Notes: 2, 3, 4, 5, 9, 10, 11, 12, 13, 14

GENESEO

Conesus Lake Bed & Breakfast

5332 East Lake Road, Conesus, 14435
(716) 346-6526; (800) 724-4841

On beautiful Conesus Lake near Route 390.
Unique European styling with private balconies and flower boxes. Relaxing resort
atmosphere includes large private dock, picnic
pavilion, free use of canoe, paddleboat, or row-
boat, and overnight boat docking with mooring
whips. Each attractive bedroom has queen-size
bed and cable TV. Private bathroom and double
whirlpool tub are available. Near excellent
restaurants. Reservations suggested.

Conesus Lake

Hosts: Dale and Virginia Esse
Rooms: 3 (1 PB; 2 SB) $70-90
Full Breakfast
Credit Cards: A, B, D
Notes: 2, 7, 9, 11, 12, 14

GENEVA

Elaine's Bed & Breakfast Selections

4987 Kingston Road, Elbridge, 13060
(315) 689-2082 (call between 10:30 A.M.–7:00 P.M.)

A. This Federalist house offers first-floor two-
room suite with private bath. Inside room has
single bed for third person in party. Upstairs
two guest rooms and one bath, living room
with TV/VCR. Full breakfast. Fifteen dollars
for third person. $65-75.

B. This mansion was built in 1865. Six bedrooms and two suites. Private and shared baths.
Breakfast is guests' choice when planned
ahead. Children over 12 welcome. No smoking. Guests may have light kitchen use. $50-85.

Geneva On The Lake

1001 Lochland Road, Route 14 South, 14456
(800) 3-GENEVA
www.GenevaOnTheLake.com

Amidst an ambiance of Italian Renaissance
architecture, classical sculptures, and Stickley

7 No smoking; 8 Children welcome; 9 Social drinking allowed; 10 Tennis nearby; 11 Swimming nearby;
12 Golf nearby; 13 Skiing nearby; 14 May be booked through a travel agent; 15 Handicapped accessible.

furnishings, guests from around the world enjoy romantic getaways, family reunions, glorious weddings, and small executive retreats. Named one of "the ten most romantic inns in the United States" Geneva On The Lake offers luxurious suites, gourmet candlelight dining and friendly hospitality. Recipient of the coveted AAA four-diamond award for 17 years.

Host: William J. Schickel
Rooms: 30 (PB) $104-730
Continental Breakfast
Credit Cards: A, B, C, D
Notes: 2, 4, 5, 7, 8, 9, 10, 11, 12, 13, 14

Virginia Deanes Bed & Breakfast

168 Hamilton Street, 14456
(315) 789-6152

This antique-filled Colonial home in the 200-year-old city of Geneva. Next to Hobart and William Smith Colleges. Minnie's Room is a combination bedroom and sitting room. The Victorian Room and Dolly's Bedroom share bath. The Brass Room has an antique brass bed and shared bath. The Little Penthouse has a living room and private bath. All rooms are air conditioned and have TVs.

Hosts: Virginia Deane Cunningham
Rooms: 5 (2 PB; 3 SB) $60-110
Continental Breakfast
Credit Cards: None
Notes: 2, 5, 8, 9, 12, 13

GORHAM

Elaine's Bed & Breakfast Selections

4987 Kingston Road, Elbridge, 13060
(315) 689-2082 (call between 10:30 A.M.–7:00 P.M.)

This 14-room country Colonial-style farmhouse was built before the turn of the century. First-floor guest room has private bath. Two more guest rooms upstairs. Full breakfast on weekends and Continental breakfast weekdays.

Two children over 10 welcome. No pets, but there is a boarding kennel nearby. $70-90.

The Gorham House

4752 East Swamp Road, P.O. Box 43, 14461-0043
(716) 526-4402 (phone/FAX)
e-mail: GORHAM.HOUSE@juno.com
www.angelfire.com/biz/GorhamHouse
www.freeyellow.com/members2/gorham-house

Elegant and historic 1887 Victorian country Colonial farmhouse puts guests in the heart of the Finger Lakes. Nearby restaurants, museums, wineries, beaches, and antique shops. Picnic, walk, or cross-country ski the quiet, serene country acres. Large, spacious, beautifully appointed guest rooms furnished with antiques, country charm, and casual elegance. Private and shared baths. Air conditioning. Luscious gourmet breakfast. Children over 10 welcome.

Hosts: Nancy and Al Rebmann
Rooms: 4 (1 PB; 3 SB) $79-99
Full Breakfast
Credit Cards: None
Notes: 2, 5, 7, 9, 10, 11, 12, 13

The Gorham House

GOWANDA

The Teepee

14396 Four Mile Level Road, 14070-9796
(716) 532-2168

This bed and breakfast is operated by Seneca Indians on the Cattaraugus Indian Reservation near Gowanda. Tours of the reservation and the Amish community nearby are available.

NOTES: Credit cards accepted: A MasterCard; B Visa; C American Express; D Discover; E Diner's Club; F Other; 2 Personal checks accepted; 3 Lunch available; 4 Dinner available; 5 Open all year; 6 Pets welcome;

The Teepee

Hosts: Maxwell and Phyllis Lay
Rooms: 3 (SB) $50
Full Breakfast
Credit Cards: None
Notes: 2, 5, 7, 8, 9, 10, 11, 12

GRAND VIEW-ON-HUDSON

American Country Collection

1353 Union Street, Schenectady, 12308
(518) 370-4948; (800) 810-4948
FAX (518) 393-1634 (call first)
e-mail: Carolbnbres@msn.com
www.bandbreservations.com

218. This is a historic Colonial, circa 1835, that is on and overlooks the Hudson River. In back is a large garden with swimming pool and pool house as well as a breakfast patio and sunken barbecue. Accommodations include two rooms and one studio, which has a private entrance and kitchenette. Bathrobes, hair dryer, and laundry facilities are available. Breakfast is an informal affair in that guests may have it prepared or simply help themselves if they decide to arise later than expected. Smoking is permitted in the kitchen or outside. Children are welcome. There are two cats and one dog in residence. $80-90.

GREENPORT

The Bartlett House Inn, Bed & Breakfast

503 Front Street, 11944
(516) 477-0371
www.greenport.com/bartlett

Built in 1908, the Bartlett House Inn offers elegant comfort for those who prefer the relaxed pace of the north fork of Long Island and visiting local award-winning wineries, antique shops, fine restaurants, and maritime events. The inn was built with Corinthian columns, ornate plaster relief moldings, stained-glass windows, inlaid floors, two fireplaces, and a large front porch. Guests can choose from 10 spacious bedrooms filled with period antiques as well as fresh flowers, air conditioning, and in-room telephones.

Hosts: Diane and Bill May
Rooms: 10 (PB) $80-120
Full Breakfast
Credit Cards: A, B, D
Notes: 5, 7, 9, 10, 11, 12

The Bartlett House Inn

GROTON

Elaine's Bed & Breakfast Selections

4987 Kingston Road, Elbridge, 13060
(315) 689-2082 (call between 10:30 A.M.–7:00 P.M.)

This charming 1867 Victorian in the country has three guest rooms plus a single-size pull-out bed in the TV den upstairs. Full country breakfast on weekends and Continental on weekdays. Children over five years old are welcome. $65.

7 No smoking; 8 Children welcome; 9 Social drinking allowed; 10 Tennis nearby; 11 Swimming nearby; 12 Golf nearby; 13 Skiing nearby; 14 May be booked through a travel agent; 15 Handicapped accessible.

GUILFORD

Bed & Breakfast Leatherstocking Association, Inc.

5 Rundell House, Dolgeville, 13329
(315) 429-3416 (phone/FAX—call first)
(800) 941-BEDS (2337)
www.bedbreakfastnys.com

039. Four bedrooms, all elegantly furnished and decorated, are the essential grace of this 150-year-old country bed and breakfast. Also available is a new solarium with sunny ambiance and three-seat whirlpool tub. Guest rooms have queen-size beds, many antiques, fine fabrics and original art works, shared baths; full breakfasts served in the dining room each morning. Minutes away from colleges and universities: Colgate, Hartwick, SUNY Oneonta, and other attractions like Cooperstown's National Baseball Hall of Fame, Glimmerglass Opera, and, in Oneonta, the Soccer Hall of Fame. No smoking. Children welcome. $50-75.

HADLEY

American Country Collection

1353 Union Street, Schenectady, 12308
(518) 370-4948; (800) 810-4948
FAX (518) 393-1634 (call first)
e-mail: Carolbnbres@msn.com
www.bandbreservations.com

135. Built in the late 1800s, this restored Victorian country inn with full service restaurant is in the southern Adirondacks within easy driving distance to Saratoga, Glens Falls, and Lake George. Six distinctive guest rooms, all with private baths, are individually decorated and offer their own special amenities; two have Jacuzzis and one has a fireplace. Carriage house has two rooms, each with gas fireplace, one with a balcony Jacuzzi. Private dinners and breakfasts can be arranged in the three larger rooms. A gourmet breakfast served each morning. Packages available. $145-175.

Saratoga Rose Inn & Restaurant

4274 Rockwell Street, 12835
(518) 696-2861; (800) 942-5025
e-mail: sararose@capital.net
www.saratogarose.com

Romantic Victorian inn in southern Adirondacks near Saratoga and Lake George. The beautiful Victoria Room has a private indoor hot tub. The Adirondack Room has floor-to-ceiling riverstone fireplace, TV, and log cabin walls. The Carriage House, private and secluded, has it all with fireplace, TV, and outdoor spa. The Garden Room is bright and cheery with a private deck just outside the French doors from the room with own private Jacuzzi. Breakfasts are fabulous with a selection by Chef Anthony. Dinners are outstanding and the menu offers many selections. Discount packages are available.

Hosts: Chef Anthony and Nancy Merlino
Rooms: 6 (PB) $85-175
Full Breakfast
Credit Cards: A, B, D
Notes: 2, 4, 5, 7, 9, 10, 11, 12, 13

Saratoga Rose Inn

HAGUE

American Country Collection

1353 Union Street, Schenectady, 12308
(518) 370-4948; (800) 810-4948
FAX (518) 393-1634 (call first)
e-mail: Carolbnbres@msn.com
www.bandbreservations.com

198. Perched on a ledge above Lake George, this luxurious fieldstone home, circa 1900, boasts a panoramic view of the lake and the surrounding Adirondack Mountains. Four guest rooms with private baths. There are hiking trails, a swimming beach, boat launch, and horseback riding within 5 miles of the house. Lake George village is 22 miles away. Full breakfast. $90-150.

HAMLIN

Sandy Creek Manor House

1960 Redman Road, 14464-9635
(716) 964-7528; (800) 594-0400
e-mail: agreatbnb@aol.com
www.sandycreekbnb.com

Quiet country retreat on six wooded acres. Luxurious hot tub spa. Gift shop and outrageous gourmet breakfasts! Pets welcome. Romance packages, dinner, sleigh rides, and massages. TV, VCR, air conditioning, robes, and slippers. Fly-fishing in the back yard. SUNY Brockport is 7 miles, Rochester is 25 miles. Niagara Falls is 65 miles. Discover why guests say it "…feels like coming home."

Rooms: 4 (1 PB; 3 SB) $70-90
Gourmet Breakfast
Credit Cards: A, B, C, D
Notes: 2, 5, 6, 7, 8, 9, 10, 11, 12, 13, 14

HAMMONDSPORT

The Amity Rosé Bed & Breakfast

8264 Main Street, 14840
(607) 569-3408; (877) 230-5761
FAX (607) 569-3483; e-mail: bbrose@ptd.net
www.amityroseinn.com

Come spend a night in a turn-of-the-century country home. There are four lovely rooms with queen-size beds. All private baths, two with whirlpool soaking tubs. The large parlor invites guests to enjoy the fireplace, soft music, or some conversation. Stroll to the historic village square restaurants, shops, antiquing, or

just relaxing. The bed and breakfast is at the southern end of the Finger Lakes next to Keuka Lake. Winery tours, swimming, beach, boating, Corning, Watkins Glen, Curtis Aviation Museum nearby. Full country breakfast.

Hosts: Frank and Ellen Laufersweiler
Rooms: 4 (PB) $85-125
Full Breakfast
Credit Cards: F
Notes: 2, 7, 9, 10, 11, 12

Blushing Rosé Bed & Breakfast

11 William Street, 14840
(607) 569-3402; (800) 982-8818
FAX (607) 569-2504; e-mail: bbrose@ptd.net
www.blushingroseinn.com/

In the "Finger Lakes of NYS at the southern tip of Keuka lake you'll find a rose "painted lady."' All four of the elegantly appointed rooms have a separate ambiance and color scheme, yet each is supremely inviting and comfortable with pampering personal touches and private baths. Stroll to the historic village square…shops, restaurants, or antiques. Visit wineries, Curtiss Aviation Museum, Corning Glass, or Watkins Glen. Relax in the morning over a full, copious breakfast.

Hosts: Ellen and Frank Laufersweiler
Rooms: 4 (PB) $85-105
Full Breakfast
Credit Cards: F
Notes: 2, 7, 9, 10, 11, 12, 13

HANCOCK

The Cranberry Inn Bed & Breakfast

38 West Main Street, P.O. Box 574, 13783
(607) 637-2788

Built in 1894, this stately turn-of-the-century Victorian is enveloped by the glorious Upper

---

7 No smoking; 8 Children welcome; 9 Social drinking allowed; 10 Tennis nearby; 11 Swimming nearby; 12 Golf nearby; 13 Skiing nearby; 14 May be booked through a travel agent; 15 Handicapped accessible.

The Cranberry Inn

Catskill Mountains, the famous Delaware River, and a great front porch. Inside, enjoy a romantic fireplace, antique and Art Deco design, fine woodwork, and old-style architecture. The inn offers warmth, charm, and hospitality. Come fish and canoe the rivers, bicycle and hike the miles of country roads, or shop for antiques. Seasonal packages are also available.

Hosts: Lorene and George Bang
Rooms: 4 (2 PB; 2 SB) $65-90
Full Breakfast
Credit Cards: A, B
Notes: 2, 3, 4, 5, 7, 8, 11, 12, 13

HARTFORD

American Country Collection

1353 Union Street, Schenectady, 12308
(518) 370-4948; (800) 810-4948
FAX (518) 393-1634 (call first)
e-mail: Carolbnbres@msn.com
www.bandbreservations.com

160. Within a short drive of both Saratoga Springs and Lake George, this historic Colonial tavern offers a relaxed country atmosphere in a quiet, rural setting. A history buff's delight, this restored home was built in 1802 and remodeled in 1878. Three second-floor rooms are available for guests and offer both private and shared baths. A first-floor bedroom has handicapped access, tub rails, and elevated toilet. Full breakfast. $45-65.

HERKIMER

Bed & Breakfast Leatherstocking Association, Inc.

5 Rundell House, Dolgeville, 13329
(315) 429-3416 (phone/FAX—call first)
(800) 941-BEDS (2337)
www.bedbreakfastnys.com

007. Beautiful and spacious Italian brick Colonial, formal gardens, ideal for business, or corporate traveler, providing the ultimate in elegance and clean comfort amid heirloom furnishings. Full breakfasts in formal dining room, off-street parking, private suite with queen-size bed and Jacuzzi, one queen-size and one double bed room; two twin beds (optional king-size) and one day bed (optional king-size)—all with private baths. Major credit cards accepted. No smoking. Only short minutes from I-90, exit 30. $55-125.

HIGH FALLS

Elaine's Bed & Breakfast Selections

4987 Kingston Road, Elbridge, 13060
(315) 689-2082 (call between 10:30 A.M.–7:00 P.M.)

A rustic, rural carriage house with four cozy guest rooms with canopied beds. Some have private balconies. A stream for swimming and fishing is just behind the property. A full six-course gourmet breakfast is served. Only a couple hours from the city make this a very lovely place to spend the weekend.

Locktender Cottage

Route 213, 12440
(914) 687-7700; e-mail: johnnovi@ulster.net

Set along a portion of the old Delaware and Hudson Canal, this Victorian-style cottage offers a choice of bedrooms, each with a private bath, air conditioning, and individually controlled heat in winter. One bedroom has a fireplace; a cozy chef's quarters is complete with kitchenette and Jacuzzi. Explore the Catskills and mid-Hudson Valley; enjoy the scenic back roads, mountains, pick-your-own fruit and vegetable farms, winery tours, hiking trails, and ski areas. Or dine at the world-renowned, four-star Depuy Canal House Restaurant, serving regional and international treats. Since they are not open for breakfast, a $10 voucher per room per night toward dinner at the Depuy Canal House is included in rates.

Rooms: 3 (PB) $65-110
Credit Cards: A, B, C
Notes: 2, 4, 5, 8, 9, 10, 11, 12, 13

HILLSDALE

American Country Collection

1353 Union Street, Schenectady, 12308
(518) 370-4948; (800) 810-4948
FAX (518) 393-1634 (call first)
e-mail: Carolbnbres@msn.com
www.bandbreservations.com

106. Built as a farmhouse around 1830, this inn has four guest rooms, two with private baths. Children over 11 welcome. Two cats in residence. Two-night minimum stay on in-season weekends; three-night minimum stay on holiday weekends. $125.

HOBART

Breezy Acres Farm Bed & Breakfast

Rural Delivery 1, Box 191, 13788
(607) 538-9338

For a respite from a busy, stressful life, visit Breezy Acres. Offering cozy accommodations with private baths in a beautifully renovated 1830s farmhouse. Hosts are known for their friendliness and bountiful homemade breakfasts. Roam the 300-acre crop farm, swing on the wicker swing on the old-fashioned pillared porches, and feel the tension subside. Just

enough to do locally with some museums, antiquing, and four seasons of sports activities. Or choose to do nothing at all, and relax!

Hosts: Joyce and David Barber
Rooms: 3 (PB) $60-75
Full Breakfast
Credit Cards: A, B, C
Notes: 2, 5, 7, 9, 10, 11, 12, 13

HOLLAND PATENT

Bed & Breakfast Leatherstocking Association, Inc.

5 Rundell House, Dolgeville, 13329
(315) 429-3416 (phone/FAX—call first)
(800) 941-BEDS (2337)
www.bedbreakfastnys.com

042. Set upon 35 acres of historic countryside, this 150-year-old restored farmhouse overlooks rolling meadows. It is remote from the bustle of city life, but only minutes away from area colleges: Colgate, Utica College, Hamilton College, as well as Utica shopping malls, theaters, art centers, and fine dining. Three beautifully decorated rooms offered, a two twin-bed room, and two rooms with a full-size bed in each, shared baths. Full breakfast. Visa and MasterCard accepted. No smoking. $50-60.

HOMER

Elaine's Bed & Breakfast Selections

4987 Kingston Road, Elbridge, 13060
(315) 689-2082 (call between 10:30 A.M.–7:00 P.M.)

Built in 1834, this village home was the first brick house in the quaint, picturesque village of Homer. Breakfast served in dining room. Four guest rooms. Children welcome. Homer is just north of Cortland and about halfway between Ithaca and Syracuse. No smoking. $70.

7 No smoking; 8 Children welcome; 9 Social drinking allowed; 10 Tennis nearby; 11 Swimming nearby; 12 Golf nearby; 13 Skiing nearby; 14 May be booked through a travel agent; 15 Handicapped accessible.

HOOSICK

Hoosick Bed & Breakfast

P.O. Box 145, 12089
(518) 686-5875; (888) 686-5875

Hoosick Bed and Breakfast is a family-oriented bed and breakfast on scenic Route 7, 8
miles from historic Bennington, Vermont, 15
miles from Williamstown, Massachusetts, 40
miles from Saratoga Springs, and minutes
away from antique center. This recently
restored 1840s Greek Revival farmhouse has
spacious rooms inside, beautiful views outside.
Enjoy a home-cooked breakfast, evening tea,
use of a full kitchen, and barnyard animals for
children.

Host: Maria Recco
Rooms: 3 (3 SB) $55
Full Breakfast
Credit Cards: None
Notes: 2, 5, 6, 7, 8, 9, 10, 11, 12, 13, 14

HOPEWELL JUNCTION

Nutmeg Bed & Breakfast Agency

P.O. Box 1117, West Hartford, CT 06127-1117
(860) 236-6698; (800) 727-7592
FAX (860) 232-7680
e-mail: nutmegbnb@home.com
www.bnb-link.com

342. Fourteen-room Georgian Colonial built in
1841; six fireplaces, double living rooms, formal dining room for gourmet breakfast, sunroom with wicker furniture overlooking
two-acre lawn, perennial flower gardens, and
pool. All five guest rooms have private baths;
two rooms have fireplaces and another two
rooms have Jacuzzis. Nearby to many historic
Hudson River sites, antiquing, and a superb
four-star restaurant. House is air conditioned
and has a ballroom for weddings up to 100
guests. Full breakfast. No children. No smoking. No resident pets.

ITHACA

Angel Arms Bed & Breakfast & Wellness Center Day Spa

481 Lafayette Road, Groton, 13073
(607) 838-0497; e-mail: angel@lightlink.com
www.lightlink.com/angel

A sanctuary for the soul and body! From rustic
beams to cathedral ceilings, this newly renovated barn says serene. Watch hummingbirds
or warm by the fire. Country acres include
Moon, Perennial, Potager, and Woodland gardens. Close to falls, wineries, food, shopping,
and more! Massage, Reiki, alternative work
and classes available. Alternative lifestyles
welcome. Psychic readings. Sweat lodge. Ski
packages. Fireplaces. Jacuzzi. Full edible
flower/herb breakfast. Dog/cats on premises.
Inquire about accommodations for pets.
Inquire about accommodations for children.
Smoking permitted outside only. Inquire about
handicapped accessibility.

Host: Suzanne E. Camin
Rooms: 5 (3 PB; 2 SB) $60-125
Full Breakfast
Credit Cards: A, B
Notes: 2, 5, 7, 10, 11, 12, 13, 14

The Candlelight Inn

49 West Main Street, P.O. Box 1109, Dryden, 13053
(607) 844-4321; (800) 579-4629
e-mail: inn@candlelightinnny.com
www.candlelightinnny.com

Guests are personally welcomed by owners
Doris and Sam. In the National Register of
Historic Places, this antique-furnished circa
1828 Federal-style homestead is subtly elegant
yet unpretentious. Enjoy deluxe rooms and
suites, air conditioning, fireplace, porches,
library, TV, VCR, herb and flower gardens,
afternoon tea, and full breakfast. In-ground
swimming pool. Ten minutes to Cortland,
Ithaca, Cornell, and Greek Peak ski area.
Twenty minutes to wineries and Finger Lakes.
Smoking in designated areas only.

NOTES: Credit cards accepted: A MasterCard; B Visa; C American Express; D Discover; E Diner's Club;
F Other; 2 Personal checks accepted; 3 Lunch available; 4 Dinner available; 5 Open all year; 6 Pets welcome;

Hosts: Doris and Sam Nitsios
Rooms: 4 (PB) $55-120
Suites: 2 (PB)
Full Breakfast
Credit Cards: A, B, C, D, E
Notes: 2, 5, 8, 9, 10, 11, 12, 13

The Edge of Thyme— A Bed & Breakfast

6 Main Street, Candor, 13743
(607) 659-5155; www.edgeofthyme.baka.com

Featured in *Historic Inns of the Northeast*, this large, gracious Georgian home with leaded-glass-windowed porch, marble fireplaces, period sitting rooms, gardens, and pergola is in a quiet rural village. Epicurean breakfast is served in a genteel manner. Central to Cornell, Ithaca College, Corning, Elmira, Watkins Glen, Binghamton, wineries, and state parks. Gift Shop. High tea by appointment.

Hosts: Prof. Frank and Eva Mae Musgrave
Rooms: 5 (3 PB; 2 SB) $65-135
Suites: 1
Full Breakfast
Credit Cards: A, B, C
Notes: 2, 5, 7, 9, 12, 14

Elaine's Bed & Breakfast Selections

4987 Kingston Road, Elbridge, 13060
(315) 689-2082 (call between 10:30 A.M.–7:00 P.M.)

This renovated barn has five guest rooms with private and shared baths. Full country breakfast. Massage therapy available by appointment. Cat in residence. Seasonal. Moderate to higher rates.

The Federal House

P.O. Box 4914, 14852-4914
(607) 533-7362; (800) 533-7362
e-mail: innkeeper@clarityconnect.com
http: //wordpro.com/fedh/fh.htm

A gracious circa 1815 inn featuring spacious rooms, exquisitely furnished with antiques and hand-carved mantel in the parlor, two suites with TV and fireplace. The inn is in the heart of the Finger Lakes, minutes from Cornell and Ithaca Colleges, downtown, wineries, state parks, and less than two miles from Cayuga Lake. The landscaped grounds, with gardens and gazebo, border the Salmon Creek and Falls, a wonderful, relaxing fishing and biking area. Full breakfast served. Air-conditioned rooms. Midweek packages. Children over four years welcome.

Host: Diane Carroll
Rooms: 4 (PB) $55-175
Full Breakfast
Credit Cards: A, B, C, D
Notes: 2, 5, 7, 9, 10, 11, 12, 14

La Tourelle Country Inn

1150 Danby Road, 14850
(607) 273-2734; (800) 765-1492 (reservations)
FAX (607) 273-4821

Rated highly by AAA and Mobil Travel Guides, La Tourelle is the perfect blend of Old World charm and contemporary comfort. Next to John Thomas Steakhouse. The beautifully appointed guest rooms are reminiscent of the delightful country hotels of Europe, each with private bath, air conditioning, TV, and telephone. Choose one of the king- or queen-size bedrooms or indulge in the Fireplace Suite or romantically exciting Tower Room. The Continental breakfast is not included in rates quoted.

La Tourelle Country Inn

7 No smoking; 8 Children welcome; 9 Social drinking allowed; 10 Tennis nearby; 11 Swimming nearby; 12 Golf nearby; 13 Skiing nearby; 14 May be booked through a travel agent; 15 Handicapped accessible.

Host: Leslie Leonard
Rooms: 35 (PB) $89-150
Continental Breakfast
Credit Cards: A, B, C, E
Notes: 4, 5, 8, 9, 10, 11, 12, 13, 14

Log Country Inn

P.O. Box 581, 14851
(607) 589-4771; (800) 274-4771
FAX (607) 589-6151
e-mail:wanda@logtv.com
www.logtv.com/inn

Escape to the rustic charm of a log house at the edge of 7,000 acres of state forest in the Finger Lakes region. Modern accommodations provided in the spirit of international hospitality. Enjoy full European breakfasts with blintzes or Russian pancakes. Fireplace in the living room, Jacuzzi in the suite, sauna and afternoon tea available. Easy access to hiking and cross-country trails. Families with children are welcome and host will also find a place for guest pets. A perfect place for spiritual retreats or family reunions. Cornell University, Ithaca College, Corning Glass Center, wineries, and antique stores nearby. Smoking in designated areas only.

Host: Wanda Grunberg
Rooms: 5 (3 PB; 2 SB) $55-95
Full Breakfast
Credit Cards: A, B, C
Notes: 2, 5, 6, 8, 9, 10, 11, 12, 13, 14

Rose Inn

Route 34 North, Box 6576, 14851-6576
(607) 533-7905; FAX (607) 533-7908
e-mail: roseinn@clarityconnect.com
www.roseinn.com

An elegant 1840s Italianate mansion on 20 landscaped acres. Fabulous circular staircase of Honduran mahogany. Prix fixe dinner served with advance reservations. Close to Cornell

University. Twice selected by Uncle Ben's as one of the Ten Best Inns in America. New York State's only four-star and four-diamond country inn. Children over 10 welcome. Conference facilities.

Hosts: Sherry and Charles Rosemann
Rooms: 20 (PB) $115-200
Suites: $200-320
Full Breakfast
Credit Cards: A, B
Notes: 2, 4, 5, 7, 9, 10, 11, 12, 13, 14

A Slice of Home

178 North Main Street, Spencer, 14883
(607) 589-6073

A 150-year-old farmhouse with four bedrooms, a cozy cottage, and a full, hearty country breakfast designed so guests won't need lunch. A Slice of Home is just 20 minutes from Ithaca and Watkins Glen and in the center of the Finger Lakes. Hiking, winery tours, biking (day or overnight bicycle tours planned), picnic tables, tenting, and outside grill. Cross-country skiing on-site.

Host: Bea Brownell
Rooms: 5 (PB) $35-150
Full Breakfast
Credit Cards: None
Notes: 2, 5, 6, 7, 8, 9, 10, 11, 12, 13, 14

JAMESVILLE (LAFAYETTE)

Elaine's Bed & Breakfast Selections

4987 Kingston Road, Elbridge, 13060
(315) 689-2082 (call between 10:30 A.M.–7:00 P.M.)

High on a hill with a view for miles, this owner-designed contemporary home offers the ultimate in peace and quiet. Master bedroom with a spacious private whirlpool bath. Two other rooms share a bath. New lower-level apartment. Resident cat. Ten dollars for each additional guest. $75-125.

NOTES: Credit cards accepted: A MasterCard; B Visa; C American Express; D Discover; E Diner's Club; F Other; 2 Personal checks accepted; 3 Lunch available; 4 Dinner available; 5 Open all year; 6 Pets welcome;

JAY

The Book & Blanket Bed & Breakfast

P.O. Box 164, Route 9N, 12941-9998
(518) 946-8323
www.adirondackinns.com/bookandblanket

This charming, 150-year-old Greek Revival is nestled in the quaint hamlet of Jay, just seven miles from Whiteface Mountain and less than 20 minutes from Lake Placid. Walking distance to village green, fishing and swimming in the Ausable River. Living room features a large fireplace; in warmer weather relax on the large porch. A booklover's dream; guest rooms honor Jane Austen, F. Scott Fitzgerald, and Jack London. Borrowers and browsers welcome.

Hosts: Kathy, Fred, Samuel, and Daisy, the basset hound
Rooms: 3 (1 PB; 2 SB) $55-75
Full Breakfast
Credit Cards: C
Notes: 2, 5, 7, 8, 9, 10, 11, 13

JEFFERSONVILLE

The Griffin House

Rural Delivery 1, Box 178, Maple Avenue, 12748
(914) 482-3371
e-mail: info@griffin-house.com
www.griffin-house.com

The Griffin House was featured as New York *Newsday's* Inn of the Week and was also a recipient of four ovations from Innovations, a national inn marketing firm. Noted for architectural excellence by visiting French architects (commending Irene and Paul Griffin for looking after "an American treasure"), this ornate home exemplifies local craftsmanship at its very finest. The Griffin House bed and breakfast also accepts reservations for dinner, thereby providing even greater opportunity to experience this exquisite, historical home of distinction.

Hosts: Irene and Paul Griffin
Rooms: 4 (PB) From $95
Full Breakfast
Credit Cards: A, B
Notes: 2, 3, 4, 5, 7, 9, 10, 11, 12, 13, 14

KINGSTON

Elaine's Bed & Breakfast Selections

4987 Kingston Road, Elbridge, 13060
(315) 689-2082 (call between 10:30 A.M.–7:00 P.M.)

Built in 1906, this pillared Colonial Revival is surrounded by two acres of lawn, gardens, and woods. Two large rooms with private, full-size baths are on the second floor; and on the third floor, two rooms share a full bath and sitting room with TV. All rooms have air conditioning. In colder weather, guests, in addition to arrival refreshments, can be warmed by the great woodstove in the large artistic living room. Hearty breakfasts reflect the hosts' interest in food from many countries. Fresh fruit is always served.

Rondout Bed & Breakfast

88 West Chester Street, 12401
(914) 331-8144; FAX (914) 331-9049
e-mail: calcave@ibm.net
www.pojonews.com/rondout

Spacious, gracious, light-filled 1906 12-room Colonial Revival house on two acres in quiet neighborhood near Hudson River and Catskill Mountains. Hearty breakfasts, evening refreshments, hospitable, knowledgeable hosts. Antiques, near antiques, paintings, posters, ceramics, and plenty of books. Air-conditioned, gardens, fireplaces in common rooms. Excellent restaurants, cruises, antiques, museums, galleries, theaters, and five colleges nearby. Kingston, rich in history and architectural variety, is an urban cultural park. Dogs welcome.

7 No smoking; 8 Children welcome; 9 Social drinking allowed; 10 Tennis nearby; 11 Swimming nearby; 12 Golf nearby; 13 Skiing nearby; 14 May be booked through a travel agent; 15 Handicapped accessible.

Hosts: Adele and Ralph Calcavecchio
Rooms: 4 (2 PB; 2 SB) $75-115
Full Breakfast
Credit Cards: A, B, C
Notes: 2, 5, 7, 8, 9, 0, 10, 11, 12, 13, 14

LAKE CHAMPLAIN

Elaine's Bed & Breakfast Selections

4987 Kingston Road, Elbridge, 13060
(315) 689-2082 (call between 10:30 A.M.–7:00 P.M.)

A. A cozy yet elegant large Dutch Colonial bed and breakfast overlooking Lake Champlain in the historic village of Westport. Several lovely suites with working fireplaces and lake views upstairs and some more modest rooms on the first floor. All have private baths. Full home-made breakfasts. Dinner options available by advance arrangement. Special winter weekend packages offered November through April. Summer season is May 1 through October 31. Group rates and dinner packages available year-round.

B. Authentic Victorian overlooking Lake Champlain in the picturesque village of Westport. Four guest rooms are available in the main house. A full distinctive breakfast is served daily at 8:30 A.M. A proper tea is served between 4:00 and 5:00 P.M. by prior arrangement. A separate carriage house suite is completely private. This is a smoke-free bed and breakfast. For smokers, folks with pets or small children this host also owns a motel on the lake. Host will be happy to schedule tee time for guests at the country club, make dinner reservations, or secure tickets for the Depot Theatre.

LAKE GEORGE

Elaine's Bed & Breakfast Selections

4987 Kingston Road, Elbridge, 13060
(315) 689-2082 (call between 10:30 A.M.–7:00 P.M.)

This spectacular gracious 1907 mansion overlooks beautiful Lake George in the town of Hague. Four gorgeous guest suites all have working fireplaces. Three have balconies. A four-season bed and breakfast in the Adirondack Mountains. Handy to Saratoga Springs, Lake George Village, Glens Falls, Lake Placid, Lake Champlain, Schroon Lake, Fort Ticonderoga, and Vermont. Hot country breakfast served. Seasonal rates. $95-165.

LAKE LUZERNE

The Lamplight Inn Bed & Breakfast

231 Lake Avenue, P.O. Box 70, 12846
(518) 696-5294; (800) 262-4668
e mail: lamp@netheaven.com
www.lamplightinn.com

Romantic, 1890 Victorian, halfway between Saratoga Springs and Lake George. A perfect location for those who want a quiet hideaway with plenty of activity nearby. Swim in Lake Luzerne, raft on the Hudson, walk or cross-country ski the inn's 10 acres. Enjoy rocking on the wraparound porch, or sitting in the elegant great room with two fireplaces, chess, Scrabble board game, and TV. Ten upstairs bedrooms, five with gas fireplaces, telephones, central air, all private baths. Full breakfast, gift shop, wine and beer, elegant dining available at the inn.

The Lamplight Inn

The secluded Carriage House has jet tubs, fireplaces, TV, telephones, private porches, and a handicapped-accessible bedroom.

Hosts: Linda and Gene Merlino
Rooms: 17 (PB) $95-225
Full Breakfast
Credit Cards: A, B, C
Notes: 2, 4, 5, 7, 9, 10, 11, 12, 13, 14, 15

LAKE PLACID

Spruce Lodge Bed & Breakfast

31 Sentinel Road, 12946
(800) 258-9350

Spruce Lodge has been in the Wescott family since 1949. The buildings were erected in the early 1900s. Large lawns extend down to a pond where guests can picnic or fish. Inside Lake Placid and close to all area activities. There is a view of the Sentinel Range and Whiteface from the back of the property.

Rooms: 6 (PB) $45-129
Cottage: 1
Continental Breakfast
Credit Cards: A, B, D
Notes: 2, 5, 7, 8, 9, 10, 11, 12, 13, 14

Stagecoach Inn

370 Old Military Road, 12946
(518) 523-9474

An Adirondack experience since 1833. Quiet, convenient location, close to winter and summer recreation, restaurants, sightseeing, and shopping. Rooms lovingly decorated with quilts, Indian art, and antiques. Outstanding great room and a front porch with rockers and a swing. Two-room family suites are available. Fireplaces.

Host: Peter Moreau
Rooms: 9 (5 PB; 4 SB) $60-85
Full Breakfast
Credit Cards: A, B
Notes: 2, 5, 7, 9, 10, 11, 12, 13, 14

LEROY

Heart's Desire Bed & Breakfast

147 East Main Street, 14482
(716) 768-4486

Genuine hospitality will welcome the guests of Heart's Desire Bed and Breakfast. This 1913 Colonial home is in the quaint village of LeRoy in western New York. Spacious rooms with private baths and queen-size beds. The master suite features a wood-burning fireplace and Jacuzzi. Enjoy an evening snack in the cozy sitting room next to the fire or stroll the lovely tree-lined streets of this historical village. A perfect spot to enjoy the many nearby attractions, such as Niagara Falls, Gaslight Village, Letchworth Falls, and Genesee Country museum.

Hosts: Dale and Mariann Conner; Fred and Susan Holmes
Rooms: 3 (2 PB; 1 SB) $70-95
Full Breakfast
Credit Cards: A, B, D
Notes: 2, 5, 7, 8, 12

Oatka Creek Bed & Breakfast

71 East Main Street, 14482
(716) 768-4609; (877) 768-4609 (toll-free U.S. only)

Enjoy warm hospitality and comfortable accommodations at Oatka Creek Bed and Breakfast in the quaint village of LeRoy—the birthplace of Jello. The air-conditioned guest rooms feature antique and reproduction furnishing—some with queen-size beds. Relax by the fire or stroll the beautiful tree-lined Main Street. Just five minutes off exit 47 of I-90—the perfect overnight hub for exploring Rochester, Buffalo/Niagara Falls, Finger Lakes, museums, antiquing, and Letchworth State Park—"The Grand Canyon of the East."

Hosts: Craig and Lynn Bateman
Rooms: 4 (PB) $65-75
Full Breakfast
Credit Cards: A, B
Notes: 2, 5, 7, 8, 9, 10, 12

7 No smoking; 8 Children welcome; 9 Social drinking allowed; 10 Tennis nearby; 11 Swimming nearby; 12 Golf nearby; 13 Skiing nearby; 14 May be booked through a travel agent; 15 Handicapped accessible.

LITTLE FALLS

Bed & Breakfast Leatherstocking Association, Inc.

5 Rundell House, Dolgeville, 13329
(315) 429-3416 (phone/FAX—call first)
(800) 941-BEDS (2337)
www.bedbreakfastnys.com

006. White wooden Ionic columns decorate this 17-room wood-frame Victorian inside and out. Two grand pianos are in the music salon, and original art hangs in the art salon. Rail lift on main staircase. Three guest rooms with private and shared baths. Enjoy a Continental plus breakfast in the formal dining room, or in the solarium off the huge wraparound porch, or on the rear sun deck. Also full family accommodations for six in a private suite in the carriage house. All credit cards accepted. $55-75.

LIVERPOOL

Elaine's Bed & Breakfast Selections

4987 Kingston Road, Elbridge, 13060
(315) 689-2082 (call between 10:30 A.M.–7:00 P.M.)

This 100-year-old three-story Victorian overlooking the Yacht Club on Onondaga Lake is next to a small antique and craft center. Walk everywhere—restaurants, shops, library, prize-winning Johnson Park, grocery, just a half-block to Onondaga Lake Park. Full country breakfast. Since there is but one modern bath for all three guest rooms, only one room will be booked unless more members of the same party want the other two rooms. Only 10 minutes to Syracuse University.

LOCKPORT

Hambleton House

130 Pine Street, 14221
(716) 439-9507; (716) 634-3650

Hambleton House

Historic home built in the 1850s. Three charming guest rooms with private baths and air conditioning—all with a delicate blending of past and present. The private parlor and dining room are perfect for group get-togethers. Easy walking to the city's Main Street and the historic Erie Canal as well as 18 miles to Niagara Falls and other points of interest.

Rooms: 3 (PB) $50-80
Continental Breakfast
Credit Cards: A, B
Notes: 7, 9, 14

LYONS

Elaine's Bed & Breakfast Selections

4987 Kingston Road, Elbridge, 13060
(315) 689-2082 (call between 10:30 A.M.–7:00 P.M.)

1. Convenient to the popular Finger Lakes region, halfway between Rochester and Syracuse and Lake Ontario and Seneca Lake, this charming brick Greek Revival was built in the mid-1840s. It was remodeled in the 1880s with Victorian touches. Three guest rooms share two and a half baths. Convenient to I-90, on Route 14. Owners are antique dealers and all the furniture is authentic and delightful. $65.

2. A perfect Adirondack-style cottage with full modern kitchen, rustic fireplace, sleeper-sofa,

NOTES: Credit cards accepted: A MasterCard; B Visa; C American Express; D Discover; E Diner's Club; F Other; 2 Personal checks accepted; 3 Lunch available; 4 Dinner available; 5 Open all year; 6 Pets welcome;

and bath. Upstairs are two more bedrooms. This adorable cottage could easily accommodate a family of five. No smoking. New sauna and hot tub. Gourmet dinner for two with champagne can be arranged at an additional charge. Fifteen dollars for each additional person. Weekly rates available. $115.

MADISON

Bed & Breakfast Leatherstocking Association, Inc.

5 Rundell House, Dolgeville, 13329
(315) 429-3416 (phone/FAX—call first)
(800) 941-BEDS (2337)
www.bedbreakfastnys.com

044. Elegant brick Federalist mansion built 1797–1802, on several acres of rolling land, half mile south of Route 20, provides a rare architectural gem—the perfect place to relax in a historic countryside. Only five minutes to Colgate, antiques corridor; hour's ride to Syracuse and Cooperstown. Offering a family suite with adjoining bedrooms, private bath, sitting area; common rooms, full breakfasts. Afternoon tea available. Good for weddings and parties. Open mid-May to Mid-October. Smoking permitted in designated areas only. $75-175.

MARATHON

Elaine's Bed & Breakfast Selections

4987 Kingston Road, Elbridge, 13060
(315) 689-2082 (call between 10:30 A.M.–7:00 P.M.)

This accommodation consists of a main house with master guest room having a private bath and a second guest room with a shared bath. The main feature, however, is the small, rustic guest cottage in this quiet, pleasant country setting. No smoking. Continental breakfast served in the main house. $70-95.

MARGARETVILLE

Elaine's Bed & Breakfast Selections

4987 Kingston Road, Elbridge, 13060
(315) 689-2082 (call between 10:30 A.M.–7:00 P.M.)

Imagine an 1886 Queen Anne Victorian high on a mountainside with stunning view of Catskill Mountain State Park. Seven guest rooms, including two suites, with private baths. Smoke-free environment. A full gourmet breakfast is served. Mobil Travel Guide-approved three stars. Rollaways and cribs available at $10 each. Inquire about accommodations for pets. Open year-round. Close to many area attractions and colleges. $55-125.

MARCELLUS (SKANEATELES)

Elaine's Bed & Breakfast Selections

4987 Kingston Road, Elbridge, 13060
(315) 689-2082 (call between 10:30 A.M.–7:00 P.M.)

Antique-filled, large, turn-of-the-century house in rural setting on several acres with an orchard and view for miles offers four large guest rooms. Two have private baths and two share a bath. Full breakfast in large formal dining room. $75-85.

MAYVILLE

The Village Inn

111 South Erie Street, Route 394, 14757
(716) 753-3583

Spend restful nights in a turn-of-the-century Victorian near the shores of lakes Chautauqua and Erie. The home is furnished with antiques and trimmed in woodwork crafted by European artisans. Near the Chautauqua Institution, antique shops, wineries, swimming, golf,

7 No smoking; 8 Children welcome; 9 Social drinking allowed; 10 Tennis nearby; 11 Swimming nearby; 12 Golf nearby; 13 Skiing nearby; 14 May be booked through a travel agent; 15 Handicapped accessible.

biking, arts and crafts, gliding, and water, downhill, and cross-country skiing.

Host: Dean Hanby
Rooms: 3 (SB) $55-60
Full Breakfast
Credit Cards: C
Notes: 2, 5, 6, 7, ,8, 9, 10, 11, 12, 13, 14

MERIDALE

The Old Stage Line Stop

P.O. Box 125, 13806
(607) 746-6856

This early 1900s farmhouse, once part of a very active dairy farm, sits high on a hill overlooking the peaceful countryside. The comfortable rooms are tastefully decorated with country furnishings. Guests enjoy area attractions, relaxing on the porch, taking walks to absorb the beautiful views. A full breakfast and afternoon treats are served with pleasure. Delhi, Oneonta, and Hartwick Colleges are nearby. A short drive to Cooperstown and many other attractions, i.e., antiques, fairs, auctions, and historic sights. Children over six welcome.

Host: Rose Rosino
Rooms: 4 (1 PB; 3 S2B) $60-75
Full Breakfast
Credit Cards: A, B
Notes: 2, 5, 10, 12, 13

MIDDLEPORT

Canal Country Inn

4021 Peet Street, 14105
(716) 735-7572; FAX (716) 735-0003

Arrive by car or boat at this 1831 home facing the famous Erie Canal. A 70-foot dock with a lower section to accommodate canoeists. Bicyclists and hikers can enjoy the towpath. A basket lunch is available. Large, pleasant rooms, one with fireplace. Breakfast served in guest's room or in the dining room. A large, black walnut-treed yard adds to the

serenity of this bed and breakfast. Approximately 25 miles from Niagara Falls and 35 miles from Buffalo.

Hosts: Wendell and Joan Smith
Rooms: 4 (4 S21/2B) $49
Continental Breakfast
Credit Cards: None
Notes: 2, 3, 5, 6, 8, 9, 12, 14

MOHAWK

Bed & Breakfast Leatherstocking Association, Inc.

5 Rundell House, Dolgeville, 13329
(315) 429-3416 (phone/FAX—call first)
(800) 941-BEDS (2337)
www.bedbreakfastnys.com

015. Private second-floor family suite with private bath and two bedrooms; canopied and four-poster beds available. Fully equipped kitchen, color cable TV, air conditioned. Full breakfasts. Enclosed outdoor spa seats four. Minutes from Cooperstown, Glimmerglass Opera, and area colleges, just two minutes from I-90 exit. Resident cat. Smoking permitted in designated areas only. No pets. $55-75.

MONTAUK

Shepherds Neck Inn

90 Second House Road, P.O. Box 639, 11954
(516) 668-2105

Seventy-room country inn three and one-half blocks to ocean. All rooms have color cable TV, private baths, telephone. Pool, tennis, volley ball court, basketball court, putting green, and chip tee on premises. Restaurant open May through September for full service; off-season it serves breakfast only. Family and school reunions, weddings, and seminars welcome. Lovely lawn and garden setting.

Hosts: George and Marie Hammer
Rooms: 70 (PB) $69-160
Full and Continental Breakfast

NOTES: Credit cards accepted: A MasterCard; B Visa; C American Express; D Discover; E Diner's Club; F Other; 2 Personal checks accepted; 3 Lunch available; 4 Dinner available; 5 Open all year; 6 Pets welcome;

Credit Cards: A, B, D
Notes: 2, 3, 4, 5, 7, 8, 9, 10, 11, 12, 14, 15

MONTGOMERY

American Country Collection

1353 Union Street, Schenectady, 12308
(518) 370-4948; (800) 810-4948
FAX (518) 393-1634 (call first)
e-mail: Carolbnbres@msn.com
www.bandbreservations.com

182. This center-hall Colonial inn was built in stages beginning around 1790. Recently completely renovated, it has the original wideboard oak floors, now covered discreetly with oriental rugs. Decor is French country, and furnishings are a mix of contemporary and antique. The five guest rooms are all large, with sitting area, TV, and air conditioning. Full breakfast served. Three miles to horseback riding, four to hiking, tennis, boating, swimming, and golf, and 10 to 15 to wineries and SUNY at New Paltz. Forty minutes to West Point. $95-155.

NAPLES

Vagabond Inn

3300 Sliter Road, 14512
(716) 554-6271

One name is synonymous with a contemporary, mountaintop resort—the Vagabond! This secluded 7,000-square-foot inn sits amidst 65 acres, one minute to the golf course, seven minutes to Naples. Huge suites with Jacuzzi or hot tub, fireplace, deck, or garden patio, TV/VCRs. Breakfast served 8:00-10:00 A.M. Pool, 400 movies, guest kitchen. Discounted packages for golf, cross-country skiing, honeymoons, shopping, business retreats.

Host: Celeste Stanhope Wiley
Rooms: 5 (PB) $105-192
Breakfast
Credit Cards: A, B
Notes: 4, 5, 7, 9, 11, 12, 13, 14

NELLISTON

Bed & Breakfast Leatherstocking Association, Inc.

5 Rundell House, Dolgeville, 13329
(315) 429-3416 (phone/FAX—call first)
(800) 941-BEDS (2337)
www.bedbreakfastnys.com

009. A lovingly restored limestone mansion from the 1850s Federalist period, now listed in the National Register of Historic Places, provides a home away from home. Full breakfasts served, in the summer on a 50-foot sun deck that overlooks the banks of the Mohawk and lowland farmlands. Original tin ceilings and circular staircase, convenient parking and turnaround. Only short drives to Cooperstown and other museums; Glimmerglass Opera, Howe Caves, SUNY Cobleskill, Fulmont, and the Capital District. Three rooms available, shared baths/optional private on some nights. Visa and MasterCard accepted. Smoking permitted in designated areas only. $50-65.

NEW BALTIMORE

American Country Collection

1353 Union Street, Schenectady, 12308
(518) 370-4948; (800) 810-4948
FAX (518) 393-1634 (call first)
e-mail: Carolbnbres@msn.com
www.bandbreservations.com

089. This 1860s Victorian sits on one and one-half acres of wooded land along the scenic Hudson River, 12 miles south of Albany. Arrive by boat and dock at the marina less than one mile away. Steps are provided to reach the antique canopied four-poster in the River Room. The cannonball bed gives the second room a feel of an earlier period. The living room where guests are invited to gather for refreshments upon arrival has a fireplace and grand piano. A small study with TV is also a guest common room. Walk out to a secret garden and enjoy the natural beauty of the river

7 No smoking; 8 Children welcome; 9 Social drinking allowed; 10 Tennis nearby; 11 Swimming nearby; 12 Golf nearby; 13 Skiing nearby; 14 May be booked through a travel agent; 15 Handicapped accessible.

valley. Private baths. Children over five welcome. Smoking permitted in designated areas. No resident pets. Full breakfast. $70-75.

NEWBURGH

American Country Collection

1353 Union Street, Schenectady, 12308
(518) 370-4948; (800) 810-4948
FAX (518) 393-1634 (call first)
e-mail: Carolbnbres@msn.com
www.bandbreservations.com

213. The house, a contemporary two-story peaked Colonial-Cape, sits well off a rambling, almost country, road, yet only minutes from I-84, the New York Thruway, and a variety of fine restaurants and shops. A candlelight full breakfast is served on the deck or in the dining room. The living room, private for guest use, has a large oriental rug, a piano, and a sizeable collection of books and music. Upstairs are two carpeted guest bedrooms, each with its own sitting area. The bath is private to either room or private to a party of four. Smoking permitted outside. Two cats in residence outside. Dinner available with prior arrangement. $75.

NEW LEBANON

American Country Collection

1353 Union Street, Schenectady, 12308
(518) 370-4948; (800) 810-4948
FAX (518) 393-1634 (call first)
e-mail: Carolbnbres@msn.com
www.bandbreservations.com

132. This historic Colonial was built in 1797 for a preacher and his family. Nestled on 18 acres just outside of town, this country inn is convenient to Lenox, the Berkshires, the capital district, and major ski areas. There is a suite on the first floor with a feather mattress, day bed with a trundle, and a private bath; four bedrooms on the second floor, two with private baths, the other two forming a suite with a

common sitting room and bath. Rooms are light and airy with homemade quilts and period Colonial furniture. A full country breakfast is served on weekends and a Continental breakfast is served on weekdays. Smoking outside only. $75-120.

Elaine's Bed & Breakfast Selections

4987 Kingston Road, Elbridge, 13060
(315) 689-2082 (call between 10:30 A.M.–7:00 P.M.)

A. A cozy home filled with antiques, this rambling farmhouse on 50 acres lies in the heart of Shaker country. It has wide-plank floors, five delightful guest rooms, and three baths. The original house dates back to 1836. Children and pets are welcome. A spacious, handicapped-accessible three-room contemporary apartment in an adjacent building is also available. A fully remodeled creamery adds sleeping facilities for 25 and catering for all guests' special get-togethers, whether for family reunions or business meetings. There is a meeting space with adjacent mini-conference rooms, as well as a dining area, lounge, and complete kitchen. Two attractive apartments above the creamery. Visa and MasterCard accepted. Cot and crib available for an additional $15. $85-150.

Palmer House

14213 Route 22, P.O. Box 422, 12125
(518) 794-9385; FAX (518) 794-8128
e-mail: palmerhouse@taconic.net

Enjoy our 14th season in an 1821 farmhouse and renovated creamery on 50 acres in the heart of Shaker country. Stroll through the gardens and woods. Five rooms and three housekeeping suites. A superb setting for small weddings, reunions, and celebrations. No minimum stay. The Berkshires and Capital District offer year-round cultural and recreational attractions. Easy access to Tanglewood, art galleries, theaters, museums. For the nature

---

NOTES: Credit cards accepted: A MasterCard; B Visa; C American Express; D Discover; E Diner's Club; F Other; 2 Personal checks accepted; 3 Lunch available; 4 Dinner available; 5 Open all year; 6 Pets welcome;

lovers, ski areas and state forests offer adventure. Shopping and antiques abound.

Host: Peggy Hawkins
Rooms: 8 (4 PB; 4 SB) $65-150
Full Breakfast
Credit Cards: A, B, C
Notes: 2, 5, 6, 7, 8, 9, 10, 11, 12, 13, 15

NEW PALTZ

American Country Collection

1353 Union Street, Schenectady, 12308
(518) 370-4948; (800) 810-4948
FAX (518) 393-1634 (call first)
e-mail: Carolbnbres@msn.com
www.bandbreservations.com

116. Rejuvenating one's mind and body can be as simple as strolling through the apple, pear, and quince orchards on a warm summer day, or as fascinating as a session on stress management and holistic health offered by the host. Four guest rooms, two private baths, two shared baths. One room has a double Murphy bed, working fireplace, and private bath. All rooms have air conditioning. A healthful gourmet breakfast is served in the light and airy country kitchen. Smoking in guest rooms and outdoors. Children under seven stay for free. No pets. $85-105.

NEWPORT

Bed & Breakfast Leatherstocking Association, Inc.

5 Rundell House, Dolgeville, 13329
(315) 429-3416 (phone/FAX—call first)
(800) 941-BEDS (2337)
www.bedbreakfastnys.com

010. This Georgian four-square limestone built around 1812 sits far back and high up on a groomed lawn in this pretty little village. All modern conveniences, networked security system, common rooms, and fireplaces; all rooms lovingly decorated. Two rooms, one double, one twin/king-size, both with private bath.

Full breakfasts served. Credit cards accepted. $35-65.

063. Deep in the woods this handsomely constructed log house, complete with its own solar power energy generating facility, awaits all travelers looking for fresh country air mixed with elegant pampering. Complex has two buildings. Main house with two bedrooms/shared bath two-story great room; the other with a family suite: kitchen, private baths, three bedrooms: double, queen-size, and two singles. $175.

NEW ROCHELLE

Rose Hill Guest House

44 Rose Hill Avenue, 10804
(914) 632-6464

The hostess at this beautiful, intimate French Normandy home is a real estate agent and bridge Life Master. Weather permitting, enjoy breakfast on the flower patio or in the chandeliered library/dining room. Thirty minutes to Manhattan by train or car. Safe parking behind house. Two-night minimum stay required for holidays. No smoking in guest rooms. Rates do not include tax.

Host: Marilou Mayetta
Rooms: 2 (SB) $65-75
Full and Continental Breakfast
Credit Cards: C
Notes: 2, 5, 8, 9, 10, 11, 12, 14

NEW YORK

Aaah! Manhattan Bed & Breakfast Registry & Furnished Apartments

P.O. Box 2093, 10108
(212) 246-4000; FAX (212) 765-4229
e-mail: info@nybnb.com; www.nybnb.com

1. East Village 1st Avenue between 1st and 2nd Street. Six guest rooms with shared baths. Full

---

7 No smoking; 8 Children welcome; 9 Social drinking allowed; 10 Tennis nearby; 11 Swimming nearby; 12 Golf nearby; 13 Skiing nearby; 14 May be booked through a travel agent; 15 Handicapped accessible.

kitchens available. The hosts are spiritual and health conscious. Vegetarian restaurant on premises; as well as Yoga Center. Clean, safe comfortable. No smoking or drinking please. Rates include all charges and a full English breakfast. $95.

2. July's midtown, eastside prewar old-money doormanned building. Lovely hostess with private guest room with private bath, TV, private line guest telephone. Smoking permitted. $120.

3. Jeri's upper eastside E80s at 1st Avenue with a guest room with private en suite bath, color cable TV. Nicely furnished. Continental breakfast. Also a second room with shared bath. $110.

4. Central Park South. Private room with en suite private bath. Gorgeous building with 24-hour doorman. Color cable TV. Breakfast included. $125.

5. West 50s. Elevator in building. Immaculate apartment with shared bath. Color cable TV. Telephone in room. Breakfast included. $80.

6. West 50s near Broadway, the heart of the theater district. Private guest room with color cable TV. Shared bath. Charming hostess. $100.

7. West 40s in the theater district. Only block from Broadway. Color cable TV. Also available unhosted as a two-bedroom apartment for up to four people. $100-200.

8. Beautiful Murray Hill East 30s, one minute from Empire State Building. The building has a 24-hour doorman. Enormous suite with shared bath with hostess. Excellent light. TV. Telephone. Also available unhosted for up to four people in two bedrooms. All amenities. $120-200.

9. West 40s third-floor walkup in the theater district. Unhosted. Full kitchen and bath. Color cable TV. Telephone. Full bath. $125.

10. West 30s in theater district. One bedroom totally renovated. Sleeps four comfortably. Full kitchen and bath. Color cable TV. Telephone. Brand new everything. Great value. $125.

Bed & Breakfast (& Books)

35 West 92nd Street, 10025
(212) 865-8740 (phone/FAX)

Sample listings: Beautifully renovated townhouse on quiet tree-lined street near Central Park offers one double-bed room with private bath. Convenient to museums, theaters, shopping, and all transportation. Children welcome in loft areas. $100. Working artist's loft in the heart of SoHo has comfortable twin-bed room, sitting area, and bath en suite. Convenient to SoHo galleries, shops, and restaurants. Sofa opens to sleep two. $100.

Host: Judith Goldberg
Rooms: 50 (45 PB; 5 SB) $80-110
Continental Breakfast
Credit Cards: None
Notes: 5, 14

Bed & Breakfast Network of New York

134 West 32nd Street, Suite 602, 10001
(212) 645-8134; (800) 900-8134

A reservation service for New York City, mostly Manhattan. Accommodations are in some of the most exciting parts of town: Greenwich Village, Midtown, Upper East and West Sides, etc. Ranging from modest to luxurious, from townhouses to lofts to million-dollar high-rise condos. Weekly and monthly rates available. Also represents unhosted furnished apartments and studios ranging $125 to $400. Personal checks accepted for deposit. Inquire about accommodations for pets and children.

Rooms: 300 (100 PB; 200 SB) $100-400
Continental Breakfast
Credit Cards: None
Notes: 5, 14

NOTES: Credit cards accepted: A MasterCard; B Visa; C American Express; D Discover; E Diner's Club; F Other; 2 Personal checks accepted; 3 Lunch available; 4 Dinner available; 5 Open all year; 6 Pets welcome;

A Greenwich Village Habitué

New York's Greenwich Village, 10014
(212) 243-6495; FAX (212) 243-6582
e-mail: gvhabitue@aol.com

A Greenwich Village Habitué has fully appointed private apartments in an owner-occupied 1830s Federal brownstone in historic Greenwich Village. Antique-filled apartments come complete with living room, dining alcove, sleeping alcove, kitchen, and full private bath. As quoted by Mimi Reed of *Food and Wine Magazine*, "It was our delight, an immaculate, graciously stocked and elegantly furnished apartment in a brownstone. It seemed a great bargain." Three-night minimum.

Host: Matthew
Apartments: 3 (PB) $135-145
Credit Cards: None
Notes: 5, 7, 9

Urban Ventures, Inc.

38 West 32, #1412, 10001
(212) 594-5650; FAX (212) 947-9320
e-mail: ann@nyurbanventures.com
www.nyurbanventures.com

Established in 1979, Urban Ventures has about 600 accommodations. Each has been inspected by Urban Ventures. A range of fifth-floor walk-ups to a three-bedroom house in center city. This service can provide unhosted apartments and bed and breakfasts in every area of the city. Guests need only express their needs and they will find them met. In peak seasons, book at least three weeks prior to arrival. Brochure is free. The capable staff has been with this service for years. There are approximately 300 accommodations with private and shared baths. Continental breakfast served. Credit cards and personal checks accepted. Open-year round. Children welcome. Social drinking permitted. May be booked through travel agent.

85. In the Midtown West area on West 49th Street right in the heart of the theater district is a luxurious two-bedroom, one-bath apartment

in a doormanned building. Piano, TV, VCR. Owner is an expert on theater. $260.

166. A beautifully kept townhouse with two suites for guests. Sleeper-sofa in area with high ceilings, polished wood floors. Living room, bedroom, bath. Another suite has a view of gardens, living room with sleeper-sofa. Near Hudson River. $125.

168. On West 81st Street and Columbus Avenues in the Upper West Side area is this beautiful apartment. Duplex with multiple terraces, a greenhouse providing blooming flowers year-round, views of the grand old Museum of Natural History, and Central Park. Two guest rooms with private baths. $110.

230. At Second Avenue and 34th Street in the Midtown East area. Large kitchen; surprisingly quiet. Smoking permitted. Shared bath with host. Three flights of steps to this wooden floor and fireplaced back apartment. No TV. $80.

247. Corner room with a view of the city and the East River in Greenwich Village. East Sixth Street and 1st Avenue puts guests right in the heart of the East Village. Lots of ethnic restaurants, especially Indian restaurants. Near Papps Theatre, sidewalk café, the famous Avenue A Sushi Place, thrift and antique shops, NYU, Washington Square Park, and lots more. Two bedrooms share a bath with host. $80.

253. Four different levels in this delightfully designed village apartment in Greenwich Village. The queen-size-bed level is two levels away from the next sleeping level. On West 10th Street and Greenwich. One room with private bath and the other is shared. $100.

521. On the U.S. list of historic places. Two rooms, each with queen-size bed and fireplace; one also has access to an enormous lawn with lovely plants. $130.

7 No smoking; 8 Children welcome; 9 Social drinking allowed; 10 Tennis nearby; 11 Swimming nearby; 12 Golf nearby; 13 Skiing nearby; 14 May be booked through a travel agent; 15 Handicapped accessible.

581. Top of the line bed and breakfast. A large three-bedroom with two-bath apartment on East 87th Street and York Avenue in door-manned building. Views! Available hosted or unhosted. $180-320.

873. Brand-new building with views stretching out for miles. Terraced. Doorman and concierge. This two-bedroom, two-bath apartment is splendid. At West End Avenue and 73rd Street in the Upper West Side. Directly behind Lincoln Center. $240.

936. Each piece of furniture is a beauty, and each piece is individually carved. From the 23rd floor, one is able to see south a long way. Especially race back for the sunsets. From the terrace guests are able to smoke. Available as bed and breakfast or apartment. $100-140.

1366. Only the second owner of this century-old home. The original detailing and wood is firmly in place. Half block from Central Park. Lots of good restaurants, subway, and bus lines. Beautiful room with private bath with two sinks. $125.

1614. A mansion which has had the great good fortune of belonging to caring owners. Bathrooms in most rooms. Luscious carved wood sparkles, original detailing in place, marble entry. A variety of beautiful rooms. $160.

NIAGARA FALLS

The Cameo Inn

4710 Lower River Road, Route 18F, Lewiston, 14092
(716) 745-3034; e-mail: cameoinn@juno.com
www.cameoinn.com

This stately Queen Anne Victorian commands a majestic view of the lower Niagara River and Canadian shoreline. Lovingly furnished with period antiques and family heirlooms, the Cameo will charm guests with its quiet ele-

The Cameo Inn

gance. Here one can enjoy the ambiance of days past in a peaceful setting far from the bustle of everyday life. Three guest rooms with private or shared baths are available, as well as a three-room private suite that overlooks the river.

Hosts: Greg and Carolyn Fisher
Rooms: 4 (2 PB; 2 SB) $65-115
Full Breakfast
Credit Cards: A, B, D
Notes: 5, 9, 10, 11, 12, 13, 14

Cameo Manor North

3881 Lower River Road, Route 18F, Youngstown, 14174
(716) 745-3034; e-mail: cameoinn@juno.com
www.cameoinn.com

Just eight miles north of Niagara Falls along the lower Niagara River, Cameo Manor offers

Cameo Manor North

NOTES: Credit cards accepted: A MasterCard; B Visa; C American Express; D Discover; E Diner's Club; F Other; 2 Personal checks accepted; 3 Lunch available; 4 Dinner available; 5 Open all year; 6 Pets welcome;

a peaceful setting for those seeking a quiet retreat. Three secluded acres add to its romantic charm, as does the elegantly appointed interior. Choose either a suite with private sunroom and cable TV or a room with shared bath, all furnished with guests' comfort in mind. Relax in the great room or library, both featuring massive stone fireplaces. Come and enjoy.

Hosts: Greg and Carolyn Fisher
Rooms: 5 (3 PB; 2 SB) $65-175
Full Breakfast
Credit Cards: A, B, D
Notes: 5, 9, 10, 11, 12, 13, 14

The Country Club Inn

The Country Club Inn

5170 Lewiston Road, Lewiston, 14092
(716) 285-4869; FAX (716) 285-5614
e-mail: ctyclubinn@conn.net

Six miles from Niagara Falls, the Country Club Inn is a smoke-free bed and breakfast. Three large beautifully decorated rooms with private bath, queen-size bed, and cable TV. A great room with a wood-burning fireplace and pool table leads to a covered patio overlooking the challenging Lewiston golf course. A full breakfast is served at guests' convenience. Conveniently near the NYS Thruway and bridges to Canada. Ample off-street parking.

Hosts: Barbara Ann and Norman Oliver
Rooms: 3 (PB) $80-100
Full Breakfast
Credit Cards: None
Notes: 2, 5, 7, 8, 9, 10, 11, 12, 13, 14

NORTH RIVER

Highwinds Inn

Barton Mines Road, P.O. Box 370, 12856
(518) 251-3760; (800) 241-1923

At an elevation of 2,700 feet on 1,600 acres of land. All guest rooms and the dining area have a spectacular view to the west. On the property there are mountain biking, canoeing, hiking to several peaks and ponds, garnet mine tours, gardens, cross-country ski touring, tennis, swimming, and guided summer and winter midweek trips available. Nearby fly-fishing and spring rafting on the Hudson; Lake George; Octoberfest; down-hill skiing at Gore Mountain. Picnic lunches can be arranged for guests.

Host: Holly Currier
Rooms: 4 (PB) $130-190 MAP
Full Breakfast
Credit Cards: A, B, D
Notes: 2, 3, 4, 5, 7, 8, 9, 10, 11, 12, 13, 14

NORTHVILLE

American Country Collection

1353 Union Street, Schenectady, 12308
(518) 370-4948; (800) 810-4948
FAX (518) 393-1634 (call first)
e-mail: Carolbnbres@msn.com
www.bandbreservations.com

175. In the foothills of the Adirondacks, on the shores of the Great Sacandaga Lake, lies this charming lakefront Victorian inn where visitors can relax in the timely elegance of years gone by. There is a large common room with mahogany staircase, cable TV, and fireplace. Breakfast is available each morning in an adjacent dining room with guest refrigerator. Complimentary refreshments are served in the afternoon. Dinner is available in the evening at an additional cost. Boat docking space is free in season. Arrangements can be made for small private parties, weddings, and business meetings. Six rooms, five on the second floor and one on the first floor, all with private bath.

7 No smoking; 8 Children welcome; 9 Social drinking allowed; 10 Tennis nearby; 11 Swimming nearby; 12 Golf nearby; 13 Skiing nearby; 14 May be booked through a travel agent; 15 Handicapped accessible.

Smoking outside only. Well-behaved children are welcome; children under 12 must room with their parents. $75-95.

Elaine's Bed & Breakfast Selections

4987 Kingston Road, Elbridge, 13060
(315) 689-2082 (call between 10:30 A.M.–7:00 P.M.)

On Great Sacandaga Lake in the southern Adirondack Mountains this authentic three-story Victorian, built in 1903, offers six guest rooms, all with private baths. A first-floor room is handicapped accessed. An interior hydraulic lift at parking lot level raises a wheelchair to the first floor. Excellent location for swimming, boating, fishing, hiking, cross-country and Alpine skiing, tennis courts, and golf. Great homemade breakfasts included. Cable TV. Open year-round. Smoke-free. Moderate rates.

OGDENSBURG

Way Back In Bed & Breakfast

247 Proctor Avenue, 13669
(315) 393-3844

A warm welcome awaits guests at the Way Back In Bed and Breakfast, located on more than three acres. Minutes from the Ogdensburg-Prescott International Bridge. A full breakfast is served in the solarium where guests can see ships ply the seaway. We're minutes away from the Frederic Remington Art Museum and a short drive to colleges in Canton and Potsdam. The 1000 Islands and Ottawa, Ontario, are less than an hour's drive.

Hosts: Rena and Milton Goldberg
Rooms: 2 (1 SB) $60
Full Breakfast
Credit Cards: None
Notes: 2, 5, 7, 9, 10, 11, 12, 13

OLCOTT

Bayside Guest House

1572 Lockport Olcott Road (State Road 78), 14126-0034
(716) 778-7767; (800) 438-2192

Overlooking the harbor and marina, near Lake Ontario, this country-style Victorian home offers fishermen and travelers a comfortable, relaxed stay. Antiques and collectibles furnish this guest house. Great fishing, a county park, and many shops within walking distance. Plenty of restaurants. One-half hour from Niagara Falls, one hour from Buffalo. Smoke free. Friendly cats will make guests feel right at home! Off-street parking and dock rental available—bring own boat!

Host: Jane M. Voelpel
Rooms: 5 (SB) $40
Continental Breakfast
Credit Cards: None
Notes: 2, 5, 6, 7, 8, 9, 10, 11, 12

Bayside Guest House

OLD CHATHAM

Old Chatham Sheepherding Company Inn

99 Shaker Museum Road, 12136
(518) 794-9774; FAX (518) 794-9779
e-mail: oldsheepinn@worldnet.att.net

The inn is a restored 1790 Hudson Valley manor house on 600 pristine acres nestled between the Catskills and the Berkshires. Filled with 18th- and 19th-century antiques, the inn has 13 luxuriously appointed bedrooms, each with a private English tiled bath. Dinner is served Wednesday through Sunday from 5:30 P.M. on. Sunday brunch is from 10 A.M. to 1:30 P.M. Closed for the month of January.

Host: George Shattuck
Room: 13 (PB) $225-800
Continental Breakfast
Credit Cards: A, B, C, E
Notes: 2, 4, 7, 8, 9, 10, 11, 12, 13, 14, 15

OLEAN

Old Library Inn Bed & Breakfast

120 South Union Street, 14760
(716) 373-9804; FAX (716) 373-2462

Adjacent to the renowned Old Library Restaurant, the "pink house" offers eight guest rooms complete with private baths, telephones, TVs, in-room movies, computer hookups, and air conditioning. The exterior of the home remains the same as when built in 1895, with its towering brick chimney, beautiful bay windows, and several ornate cupolas that adorn the roof. The elegant stained-glass windows add an air of romance and history to the building's features. Inside, the rich woodwork, par-

Old Library Inn

quet floors, and antique furnishings provide a warm and inviting atmosphere. Families are welcome. Lunch and dinner are available at the restaurant.

Hosts: The Marra Family— Mary Barbara, Joe, and Susan
Rooms: 8 (PB) $65-125
Full Breakfast
Credit Cards: A, B, C, D
Notes: 2, 5, 7, 8, 9, 10, 11, 12, 13, 14

ONEIDA

Bed & Breakfast Leatherstocking Association, Inc.

5 Rundell House, Dolgeville, 13329
(315) 429-3416 (phone/FAX—call first)
(800) 941-BEDS (2337)
www.bedbreakfastnys.com

035. Here's that marvelous place that gets guests away from the mundane! Its 15 rooms, complete with garret and widow's watch, were the standard of the wealthy of its day for more than 150 years ago. Now, four large bedrooms with private baths provide travelers with state of the art accommodations. All rooms, including one suite, have color cable TV with remote and HBO, air conditioning, telephones, custom-tailored fabrics, and ensembles. Small guest kitchen provides stocked snacks and refreshments. Full breakfasts are served. Major credit cards. $83.50-150.

Elaine's Bed & Breakfast Selections

4987 Kingston Road, Elbridge, 13060-9773
(315) 689-2082 (call between 10:30 A.M.–7:00 P.M.)

This 1848 Federal brick mansion is the epitome of a gracious Victorian bed and breakfast. The four guest rooms, including one suite, have new private baths. A full hearty country breakfast is served in the antique-filled formal dining room on fine china. A very private cupola above the mansard roof affords a place to hide away, dream, meditate, or curl up with a

7 No smoking; 8 Children welcome; 9 Social drinking allowed; 10 Tennis nearby; 11 Swimming nearby; 12 Golf nearby; 13 Skiing nearby; 14 May be booked through a travel agent; 15 Handicapped accessible.

book. All rooms have cable TV, a telephone, and a security lock. The mansion is fully air conditioned. $98-175.

OWASCO LAKE

Elaine's Bed & Breakfast Selections

4987 Kingston Road, Elbridge, 13060-9773
(315) 689-2082 (call between 10:30 A.M.–7:00 P.M.)

This completely furnished year-round lakefront cottage is perfect for a romantic getaway. Totally renovated in 1989 into a bright airy contemporary with a sleeping loft. Wake to a view of the lake and go out and greet the new day on the private loft deck. First-floor living room with dining area opens also onto another roomy deck overlooking the lake. Whimsical decor throughout. Fully equipped kitchen. Private dock. Two-night minimum on weekends Memorial Day through September. Weekly rentals available. $125.

PALMYRA

Canaltown Bed & Breakfast

119 Canandaigua Street, 14522
(315) 597-5553

This 1850s historic village home of Greek Revival architecture is near antique stores, Erie Coverlet Museum, country store museum, Erie Canal hiking trail, canoe rental. Rooms are furnished with rope and brass beds and antiques. Living room with fireplace.

Hosts: Robert and Barbara Leisten
Rooms: 2 (2 SB) $65
Full Breakfast
Credit Cards: C, D
Notes: 2, 5, 7, 8, 9, 10, 12, 13, 14

Elaine's Bed & Breakfast Selections

4987 Kingston Road, Elbridge, 13060-9773
(315) 689-2082 (call between 10:30 A.M.–7:00 P.M.)

An 1855 brick Federal Colonial on 17 peaceful acres. Three guest rooms upstairs. No smoking in house. Full hearty country breakfasts. Wine or homemade cordials served afternoon or evenings. Moderate rates.

PENN YAN

Finton's Landing

661 East Lake Road, 14527
(315) 536-3146

Lakeside lawn leads to Finton's Landing's 165-foot private beach and gazebo. Four guest rooms, all with private baths. A scrumptious breakfast on fine china is relished in the sunny dining room or romantic porch overlooking Keuka Lake's bluff and vineyards. The parlor, with fireplace, is filled with warmth and memories of an 1860 Victorian. Escape to a whimsical, secluded getaway convenient to waterfront restaurants, antiques, and vineyard wine tastings.

Hosts: Doug and Arianne Tepper
Rooms: 4 (PB) $99
Full Breakfast
Credit Cards: A, B
Notes: 2, 7, 9, 10, 11, 12

Wagener Estate Bed & Breakfast

351 Elm Street, 14527
(315) 536-4591

This historic (circa 1796) 15-room home is nestled on a knoll, surrounded by four lovely acres of lawn, stone walls, shade and apple trees in Finger Lakes. The wicker-furnished veranda offers a relaxing spot for enjoying breezes or chats. It's a five-minute walk to the village or a short drive to many wineries, beaches, Watkins Glen, and other state parks.

NOTES: Credit cards accepted: A MasterCard; B Visa; C American Express; D Discover; E Diner's Club; F Other; 2 Personal checks accepted; 3 Lunch available; 4 Dinner available; 5 Open all year; 6 Pets welcome;

Wagener Estate

A scrumptious full breakfast starts guests' day. Children welcome by prior arrangements. Skiing is a 40-minute drive away.

Hosts: Joanne and Scott Murray
Rooms: 6 (4 PB; 2 SB) $75-95
Full Breakfast
Credit Cards: A, B, C, D
Notes: 2, 5, 7, 9, 10, 11, 12

PINE HILL

American Country Collection

1353 Union Street, Schenectady, 12308
(518) 370-4948; (800) 810-4948
FAX (518) 393-1634 (call first)
e-mail: Carolbnbres@msn.com
www.bandbreservations.com

205. Guests are invited to relax in front of the four working fireplaces in the common rooms, on the wraparound porch, or to stroll through the garden. Inside is a vintage billiard room and an adjacent "great hall" and library. Accommodations include one suite on the first floor and five rooms on the second floor, all with private baths. Just a few steps from the bed and breakfast the owners have constructed a private cottage with queen-size bed, wood stove, and kitchenette. For skiing enthusiasts, Belleayre is only a half-mile away with jitney pickup and return service available. Hiking, swimming, tubing, fishing, and horseback riding are within a 5- to 10-minute drive. Smoking permitted in common rooms only. Children

welcome. One dog in residence. Full breakfast. $75-119.

PITTSFORD

Oliver Loud's Inn

1474 Marsh Road, 14534
(716) 248-5200; FAX (716) 248-9970
e-mail: rchi@frontiernet.net

Historic 1812 stagecoach inn elegantly restored. Evocative of an English country house. Garden setting on the Erie Canal. Romantic and well appointed. Continental breakfast hamper delivered to guests' room. Welcome trays in room include homemade cookies. Easily accessible to many area attractions. Private bathrooms, telephones, TV. Richardson's Canal House on premises.

Host: Jill Way
Rooms: 8 (PB) $99-145
Continental Breakfast
Credit Cards: A, B, C, E
Notes: 2, 4, 5, 7, 12, 13, 14, 15

PITTSTOWN

Maggie Towne's Bed & Breakfast

Rural Delivery 2, Box 82, Valley Falls, 12185
(518) 663-8369; (518) 686-7331

An old Colonial amid beautiful lawns and trees, 14 miles east of Troy on NY Route 7. Enjoy tea or wine before the fireplace in the family room. Use the music room or read on the screen porch. The hostess will prepare lunch for guests to take on tour or enjoy at the house. It's 20 miles to historic Bennington, Vermont, and 30 to Saratoga Springs.

Host: Maggie Towne
Rooms: 3 (SB) $35-45
Full Breakfast
Credit Cards: None
Notes: 2, 3, 5, 8, 9, 10, 11, 12, 13

7 No smoking; 8 Children welcome; 9 Social drinking allowed; 10 Tennis nearby; 11 Swimming nearby; 12 Golf nearby; 13 Skiing nearby; 14 May be booked through a travel agent; 15 Handicapped accessible.

PORT ONTARIO

Elaine's Bed & Breakfast Selections

4987 Kingston Road, Elbridge, 13060
(315) 689-2082 (call between 10:30 A.M.–7:00 P.M.)

An authentic stone lighthouse built in 1838 to help guide shipping on Lake Ontario is now completely furnished for nightly or weekly rental. First floor has large kitchen complete with kitchenwares for cooking, living room with fireplace, two bedrooms, and a bath. Second floor has two bedrooms and sitting room or third bedroom. There is a glassed-in cupola that may be accessed by a steel ladder. There are also four housekeeping cabins with three bedrooms each on this six-acre property. They have color cable TV and new rustic furniture. There is also a marina. Fishing guides available. Port Ontario is just three miles west of Pulaski and I-81. Group and weekly rates, including boat, motor, and gas, are available. Closed in the winter. $135-185.

QUEENSBURY

Crislip's Bed and Breakfast

693 Ridge Road, 12804
(518) 793-6869

Just minutes from Saratoga Springs and Lake George in the Adirondack area, this landmark Federal home provides spacious accommodations, complete with period antiques, four-poster beds, and down comforters. The delicious country breakfast menu features buttermilk pancakes, scrambled eggs, and sausages. The hosts invite guests to relax on the porches and enjoy the beautiful mountain view of Vermont. Inquire about accommodations for pets.

Hosts: Ned and Joyce Crislip
Rooms: 3 (PB) $55-85
Full Breakfast
Credit Cards: A, B, D
Notes: 2, 5, 7, 8, 9, 11, 12, 13

RED HOOK

American Country Collection

1353 Union Street, Schenectady, 12308
(518) 370-4948; (800) 810-4948
FAX (518) 393-1634 (call first)
e-mail: Carolbnbres@msn.com
www.bandbreservations.com

223. This 120-year-old mansard roof Victorian has ornate woodwork, high ceilings, parquet floors, and marble fireplaces. Once a hotel, rooming house, and the village school, it is an authentic Victorian restoration. Furnishings are period to enhance the age and elegance of the house. Six guest rooms, four with private baths and two that share. Full breakfast of John Wayne eggs, because "real men don't eat quiche." Close to historic Hyde Park, wineries, and many antique shops. Children over six welcome. Resident dog. $85-125.

RHINEBECK

Olde Rhinebeck Inn c. 1745

37 Wurtemburg Road, 12572
(914) 871-1745; www.rhinebeckinn.com

A fascinating structure of remarkable integrity. This intimate inn is three miles south of the quintessential Hudson Valley historic village of Rhinebeck. An authentic property offering its guests the rare opportunity to appreciate the romance of the past, yet enjoy the luxuries of today. Spacious, elegant suites featuring hand-hewn beams and original buttermilk finishes and fine amenities provide plush accommodations for the perfect retreat. Superb breakfasts. Near many local attractions.

Host: Jonna Paolella
Rooms: 3 (PB) $175-295
Full Breakfast
Credit Cards: A, B, C
Notes: 2, 5, 7, 8, 12

NOTES: Credit cards accepted: A MasterCard; B Visa; C American Express; D Discover; E Diner's Club; F Other; 2 Personal checks accepted; 3 Lunch available; 4 Dinner available; 5 Open all year; 6 Pets welcome;

RICHFIELD SPRINGS

Bed & Breakfast Leatherstocking Association, Inc.

5 Rundell House, Dolgeville, 13329
(315) 429-3416 (phone/FAX—call first)
(800) 941-BEDS (2337)
www.bedbreakfastnys.com

014. Invitingly clean, comfortable, homey atmosphere, suitable for large family gatherings, awaits travelers here in this 14-room former railroad hotel and general store built around the turn of the century. Now converted into a fine family dwelling with modern sun deck and turnaround, accommodations include a family site with two rooms and a sitting room and private bath; three other immaculate guest rooms all with private baths. Children welcome. No smoking. No pets. $70-145.

029. Stately charm describes this 19-room Queen Anne Victorian with portico as it stands on a small but commanding knoll overlooking the main street of this quaint old village. Full breakfasts are served as well as prearranged picnic baskets and formal dining. Washer and dryer available to guests. Five guest rooms are offered, most with private baths. Only short minutes from Glimmerglass Opera, Cooperstown, and Glimmerglass State Park. Visa and MasterCard are accepted. $65-80.

ROCHESTER (MUMFORD)

Genesee Country Inn

948 George Street, Mumford, 14511-0340
(716) 538-2500; FAX (716) 538-4565

Historic stone mill on eight serene acres of woods and waterfalls. All timely conveniences. Tea and gourmet breakfast by candlelight. Italian trahoria dining some weekends. Historic and romance special packages. Year-round trout fishing. Near Genesee Country Museum, Rochester, and Letchworth State Park. Three

hours from Toronto. Chosen by *Country Inns* magazine as one of the 12 best inns in the USA. AAA, Mobil, CIBR, IIA.

Proprietor: Glenda Barklow
Innkeeper: Kim Rasmussen
Rooms: 9 (PB) $85-135
Full Breakfast
Credit Cards: A, B, D, E
Notes: 2, 4, 5, 7, 8, 9, 10, 11, 12, 13, 14

ROME

Elaine's Bed & Breakfast Selections

4987 Kingston Road, Elbridge, 13060
(315) 689-2082 (call between 10:30 A.M.–7:00 P.M.)

A. On six acres near New York State Thruway, this 1840 Cape saltbox is warmly furnished with many antiques and crafts made by the hostess. Full country breakfast of guests' choice. Suite features double bed, sitting area, and private bath. Two other rooms with one double bed each share main bath. Cot available. Perfect stop-off from I-90 about halfway between Boston and Toronto. $45-65.

ST. JOHNSVILLE

Bed & Breakfast Leatherstocking Association, Inc.

5 Rundell House, Dolgeville, 13329
(315) 429-3416 (phone/FAX—call first)
(800) 941-BEDS (2337)
www.bedbreakfastnys.com

037. Historic 1835 grist mill, located in a tranquil park-like setting, with cascading waterfalls, herb, flower and water gardens, offers richly decorated rooms with private baths in a century-old miller's home and 1888 cottage, including a fully stocked kitchen, sitting room, and game parlor. A Continental plus breakfast is served. Guests may browse in the museum-like Emporium or sample complimentary gourmet desserts in the Ice Cream Parlor. No

7 No smoking; 8 Children welcome; 9 Social drinking allowed; 10 Tennis nearby; 11 Swimming nearby; 12 Golf nearby; 13 Skiing nearby; 14 May be booked through a travel agent; 15 Handicapped accessible.

smoking, young children, or pets. Historical tours, afternoon teas, gift certificates are available. $65-120.

SARANAC LAKE

Fogarty's Bed & Breakfast

37 Riverside Drive, 12983
(518) 891-3755; (800) 525-3755

Fogarty's is high on a hill overlooking Lake Flower and Mounts Baker, McKenzie, and Pisgah but is still only three minutes from the center of town. The bed and breakfast's porches, wide doors, and call buttons attest to its past as a cure cottage for treating tuberculosis a century ago. The living room and dining room are uniquely decorated with handsome woodwork, and the bathrooms have the original 1910 fixtures. Swimmers and boaters are welcome to use Fogarty's dock, and cross-country skiers will find trails within a mile.

Hosts: Jack and Emily Fogarty
Rooms: 5 (SB) $60
Full Breakfast
Credit Cards: None
Notes: 2, 5, 7, 8, 9, 10, 11, 12, 13

SARATOGA SPRINGS

American Country Collection

1353 Union Street, Schenectady, 12308
(518) 370-4948; (800) 810-4948
FAX (518) 393-1634 (call first)
e-mail: Carolbnbres@msn.com
www.bandbreservations.com

105. The friendly atmosphere of this working organic farm is a delight for children and adults. The Victorian farmhouse and barns have been restored to offer seven air-conditioned guest rooms, all with private baths. One room has two double beds, private bath, TV, wood-burning stove, and private deck. A gourmet breakfast is served in the Florida room amid flowering plants and the hot tub/Jacuzzi. The Saratoga Performing Arts Center and race-

track are two miles away. Smoking permitted. Children welcome. $100-130.

124. Built in 1770, this home is in the midst of an apple orchard on an elevation overlooking the Hudson River. The mantel holds cannonballs that American troops fired at the house when it served as a hospital for British and Hessian troops during the Revolutionary War. In the main house, there are three guest rooms with shared bath. Two cottages available. Smoking in common areas only. Children welcome in the Island Cottage. They are welcome at the main house and Apple Cottage when the pool is not open. Pets in residence. Full and Continental breakfast offered. $65-175.

180. This Colonial-style cobblestone home is just minutes from Victorian Round Lake and Saratoga. There are four guest rooms on the second floor with private or shared baths. Breakfast is served in the spacious dining room, or in the summer months on the deck. Wake-up coffee is available for early risers, and refreshments are served in the afternoons. Smoking on the deck or porch only. Adults only. $90-135.

224. This contemporary homestay bed and breakfast is less than two miles from the heart of downtown and the many Saratoga Springs attractions. Guests enjoy the privacy of a second-floor air-conditioned suite with private bath and sitting area. Additional travelers can be accommodated on a comfortable sofa bed. An additional guest room with private bath is on the second floor. Private TV, wood-burning stove, and refrigerator. $100-150.

231. Partway between Saratoga Springs and Lake George, this side-hall Colonial, circa 1790, sits on a knoll surrounded by maple trees. The home has been completely restored to its original beauty. The rooms are appointed with various themed antiques from periods spanning the 18th to the 20th centuries, which is not to say there is not 1990s comfort sunk

NOTES: Credit cards accepted: A MasterCard; B Visa; C American Express; D Discover; E Diner's Club; F Other; 2 Personal checks accepted; 3 Lunch available; 4 Dinner available; 5 Open all year; 6 Pets welcome;

deep into each cushy mattress. All rooms carry an enchanting view of the vast and rolling farms of this quiet town. $85-115.

237. Look out the back door and see the clubhouse gate. This 100-year old Victorian was once the site of large greenhouses and nursery started by the original owner. Now it cultivates warm hospitality for guests looking for a comfortable and charming place to enjoy the Saratoga area. Two guest rooms with private baths and air conditioning. A small apartment is also available for a more private stay. $95-195.

242. In historic Round Lake, nine miles south of Saratoga Springs, this gingerbread-trimmed Victorian has a large front porch and second-floor balconies. Walk or bike the narrow streets of this quaint village, once a church camp in the 1880s. View the unique architecture or enjoy a pipe organ concert in the village auditorium. Two guest rooms share a hall bath. Play pool in the parlor or swim in the large in-ground pool. Smoking permitted outside only. No children. No resident pets. Full breakfast. $65-85.

250. Quaint Victorian cottage within walking distance to raceway. One guest room with private bath or for guests traveling together expanded suite accommodating up to five. Continental breakfast. Air conditioned. Adults only. No resident pets. Seasonal rates. $75-300.

Batcheller Mansion Inn

20 Circular Street, 12866
(518) 584-7012; (800) 616-7012
FAX (518) 581-7746
e-mail: mail@batchellermansioninn.com
www.batchellermansioninn.com

In 1873 George S. Batcheller designed and built his fanciful and spectacular home at the southern edge of Congress Park. it remains one of the city's architectural gems, with warm and highly detailed interiors of intricate wood paneling, crystal chandeliers, and 12-foot high

ceilings. Now visitors to Saratoga can relive some of the splendor of the past while enjoying modern comforts. All of the guest rooms are air conditioned, have private baths, telephones, TVs, and convenience refrigerators. Full breakfast served weekends; Continental breakfast served weekdays.

Hosts: Sue McCade or Frank Burns
Rooms: 9 (PB) $125-400
Full and Continental Breakfasts
Credit Cards: A, B, C
Notes: 2, 5, 7, 9, 10, 11, 12, 13, 14

Lombardi Farm Bed & Breakfast

41 Locust Grove Road, 12866
(518) 587-2074

A restored Victorian farm, two miles from the center of historic Saratoga Springs. Air conditioning, private baths, and gourmet breakfast served in the Florida room. Hot tub/Jacuzzi. Recreation center with exercise equipment. Bicycles available for guests' use. A peaceful country setting within two miles of the National Museum of Dance, National Museum of Racing, Thoroughbred racetrack, harness track, polo club, Skidmore College, Yaddo artists' retreat and gardens, and famous Saratoga mineral baths. Open year-round. Listed in AAA tour guidebook. Rates are different during the flat track racing season.

Hosts: Vincent and Kathleen Lombardi
Rooms: 4 (PB) $100
Full Breakfast
Credit Cards: None
Notes: 2, 5, 9, 10, 11, 12, 13, 14, 15

The Mansion Inn

801 Route 29, P.O. Box 77, Rock City Falls, 12863
(518) 885-1607

Elegant, charming Victorian/Italianate 23-room mansion built in 1866. Furnished with beautiful antiques, original brass and copper chandeliers, exquisite 13-foot mirrored marble fireplaces, distinctive woodwork and moldings.

7 No smoking; 8 Children welcome; 9 Social drinking allowed; 10 Tennis nearby; 11 Swimming nearby; 12 Golf nearby; 13 Skiing nearby; 14 May be booked through a travel agent; 15 Handicapped accessible.

Guests luxuriate in the two grand parlors and library and enjoy the spacious porches, grounds, and gardens with views of the Kayaderosseras Creek and magnificent tiger-tail spruce. Adjacent to Saratoga Springs. Horse racing, health spas, museums, Performing Arts Center. The Mansion was selected by *Country Inns* magazine as one the the Top 12 Inns in America in 1991. Full gourmet breakfast served.

Hosts: Louise V. Brown
Rooms: 7 (PB) $95-185
Full Breakfast
Credit Cards: A, B
Notes: 2, 5, 7, 9, 10, 11, 12, 13

Six Sisters Bed & Breakfast

149 Union Avenue, 12866
(518) 583-1173; FAX (518) 587-2470
e-mail: stay@sixsistersbandb.com
www.sixsistersbandb.com

This beautifully appointed 1880 Victorian is on a historic, flower-laden boulevard in the heart of Saratoga Springs. Luxurious, immaculate rooms offer private baths and air conditioning, some with a whirlpool tub. Antiques, oriental carpets, hardwood floors, and Italian marble create a resplendent decor. The inn is close to Skidmore College, convention center, racetracks, Saratoga Performing Arts Center, downtown, museums, spas, antiques, and restaurants. SPAC discounts. The owner is a native of

Six Sisters

Saratoga eager to share local information. Recommended by *Gourmet, McCall's,* and the *New York Times.* Children over eight welcome.

Hosts: Kate Benton and Steve Ramirez
Rooms: 4 (PB) $75-275
Full Breakfast
Credit Cards: A, B, C, D
Notes: 2, 5, 7, 9, 10, 11, 12, 13, 14

The Westchester House

The Westchester House

102 Lincoln Avenue, Box 944, 12866
(518) 587-7613; (800) 581-7613

This gracious 1885 award-winning Queen Anne Victorian inn features elaborate chestnut moldings, antique furnishings, and up-to-date comforts. Elegantly appointed bedrooms have tiled baths and air conditioning. Enjoy the extensive library or play the baby grand piano. Museums, racetracks, boutiques, and restaurants are within an easy walk. After a busy day, relax on the wraparound porch, in the old-fashioned gardens, or in the double Victorian parlors. Two-night minimum stay required for weekends and holidays. AAA-rated three diamonds. Children over 12 welcome. Rates are subject to change during racing and special events.

Hosts: Bob and Stephanie Melvin
Rooms: 7 (PB) $85-265
Continental Breakfast
Credit Cards: A, B, C, D
Notes: 2, 7, 9, 10, 11, 12, 13, 14

NOTES: Credit cards accepted: A MasterCard; B Visa; C American Express; D Discover; E Diner's Club; F Other; 2 Personal checks accepted; 3 Lunch available; 4 Dinner available; 5 Open all year; 6 Pets welcome;

SARATOGA SPRINGS/BALLSTON SPA _____

Apple Tree Bed & Breakfast

49 West High Street, 12020
(518) 885-1113; FAX (518) 885-9758
e-mail: mail@appletreebb.com
www.appletreebb.com

Gracious second empire Victorian home in the historic district, two miles from the Saratoga Performing Arts Center. Close to Saratoga Race Course and other Saratoga attractions. Five rooms with air conditioning, private baths, whirlpool, and full breakfasts. Personal checks accepted for deposit only.

Hosts: Jim and Dolores Taisey
Rooms: 5 (PB) $75-175
Full Breakfast
Credit Cards: A, B, D
Notes: 5, 7, 9, 10, 11, 12, 13, 14

SARATOGA SPRINGS (STILLWATER) _____

American Country Collection

1353 Union Street, Schenectady, 12308
(518) 370-4948; (800) 810-4948
FAX (518) 393-1634 (call first)
e-mail: Carolbnbres@msn.com
www.bandbreservations.com

234. This gracious Tudor-style home was built in the 1930s on the banks of the Hudson River, near the site of the turning point of the American Revolution. Hike the Saratoga battlefield, enjoy concerts at the Performing Arts Center, or watch the Thoroughbreds run at the raceway. Full breakfast. Three air-conditioned rooms. $100-125.

252. Once a church rectory, this large Victorian home sits on the banks of the Hudson River. Watch the boats sail by as you picnic on the banks. Two guest rooms, private baths. Single overflow, all on the first floor. Convenient to National Cemetery and Saratoga Springs. Full breakfast. $85.

SCHENECTADY _____

American Country Collection

1353 Union Street, Schenectady, 12308
(518) 370-4948; (800) 810-4948
FAX (518) 393-1634 (call first)
e-mail: Carolbnbres@msn.com
www.bandbreservations.com

043. This bed and breakfast, formerly a tavern, is in the heart of the city's oldest historic district. The entire house can be rented for overnight lodging, weddings, or long-term stays. Two second-floor guest rooms, each with a TV, share one and one-half baths. One has a working fireplace, and two are air conditioned. The luxurious bath has a Jacuzzi and a separate shower. Within walking distance to theaters, shopping, restaurants, bike trail, train station, and Union College. Smoking limited. Children welcome. No pets. $95-115.

172. Set in the heart of historic Schenectady, one-half mile from Union College, this Craftsman-style home has been meticulously restored to its former charm and grace. Maple, cherry, and walnut antique furnishings with hardwood floors throughout. Large common room with wood-burning fireplace and patio overlooking perennial gardens ensure that "at home" feel. There are two guest rooms with air conditioning and private baths. Full breakfast served in formal dining room or on garden patio. $75.

SCHOHARIE _____

American Country Collection

1353 Union Street, Schenectady, 12308
(518) 370-4948; (800) 810-4948
FAX (518) 393-1634 (call first)
e-mail: Carolbnbres@msn.com
www.bandbreservations.com

219. Built in 1800 and later Victorianized around 1860, this bed and breakfast home offers truly quaint country rooms and the most

---

7 No smoking; 8 Children welcome; 9 Social drinking allowed; 10 Tennis nearby; 11 Swimming nearby; 12 Golf nearby; 13 Skiing nearby; 14 May be booked through a travel agent; 15 Handicapped accessible.

genuine of personal attention and hospitality. Decorated with an eclectic mix of Colonial-Primitive to Victorian pieces and leaded, stained-glass windows. The upstairs guest rooms have queen-size beds and share a bath. The common room has a couch, chair, and TV/VCR. Smoking permitted outside. Children five years and older welcome. Two cats in residence. Full breakfast. $60.

SHELDRAKE

Elaine's Bed & Breakfast Selections

4987 Kingston Road, Elbridge, 13060
(315) 689-2082 (call between 10:30 A.M.–7:00 P.M.)

This 145-year-old Queen Anne house on Cayuga Lake is a destination in itself. Completely renovated in 1993, including new private baths. Two rooms have Jacuzzis and fireplaces, and two have private balconies. There are ceiling fans in all rooms and all upstairs rooms are air conditioned. There is private lake frontage for guests who enjoy swimming and boating. Gourmet breakfast served. Adults only. Next door is a three-bedroom, two-bath house with two decks, four-person hot tub, pool table, fully equipped kitchen, washer/dryer, satellite TV, telephone, and large yard. Available only on a weekly basis. Please inquire about rates for the house. $110-175.

SKANEATELES

Elaine's Bed & Breakfast Selections

4987 Kingston Road, Elbridge, 13060
(315) 689-2082 (call between 10:30 A.M.–7:00 P.M.)

A. Cute, clean, comfortable, convenient, cozy, congenial, casual country atmosphere in a newly remodeled modest ranch on five acres.

Adults preferred. Two modest guest rooms share a new bathroom. Syracuse, Auburn, Skaneateles village are all nearby. Just four miles to village line, to music festival, antique boat show, dinner, lunch, and sightseeing cruises, antique shops, restaurants, polo, fishing, swimming, boat launch, boutiques, art galleries, food specialties, arts and crafts in the park, concerts, annual antique sale in Allyn Arena, historic streets and homes, all lovely. No smoking. Resident cat. $60-65.

B. An adorable up-dated old farmhouse on the edge of the village. Two guest rooms share modern guest bath. Resident cat. Open year-round. Continental breakfast. $75.

C. Newly refurbished and freshly decorated ground-floor brick building has three new spacious suites with separate bedrooms, living rooms, with futons, comfortable chairs, cable color TV, VCRs, telephones, air conditioning, kitchenettes with all kitchenwares. Just one mile west of village. Swimming pool. Open year-round. All credit cards accepted. Available by the month, week, or night. Breakfast food will be in the kitchen for short stays. Totally smoke-free building.

SODUS

Maxwell Creek Inn

7563 Lake Road, 14551
(315) 483-2222; (800) 315-2206

Rich in history, this 1846 cobblestone house is on six acres with panoramic views of Maxwell Bay, Maxwell Creek, and Lake Ontario. Local stories rumor that the house was once part of the Underground Railroad. Shops sailed into Maxwell Bay to trade ale for flour at the old flour mill, which is still part of the property. The inn has its own tennis courts, hiking trails, apple orchard, and is well-known for the stream fishing. Amusement parks, swimming, boating, shopping, and restaurants nearby. Two

---

NOTES: Credit cards accepted: A MasterCard; B Visa; C American Express; D Discover; E Diner's Club; F Other; 2 Personal checks accepted; 3 Lunch available; 4 Dinner available; 5 Open all year; 6 Pets welcome;

miles from Sodus Bay on the Seaway Trail. Honeymoon suite and private cobblestone carriage house are included in the six rooms.

Hosts: Patrick and Belinda McElroy
Rooms: 6 (PB) $70-135
Full Breakfast
Credit Cards: A, B, C, D, F
Notes: 2, 5, 7, 9, 10, 11, 12, 13

SODUS BAY

Elaine's Bed & Breakfast Selections

4987 Kingston Road, Elbridge, 13060
(315) 689-2082 (call between 10:30 A.M.–7:00 P.M.)

This turn-of-the-century waterfront home is on the east side of Sodus Bay. Four large guest rooms, each with private bath, TV, and radio occupy the main house. Also a suite overlooking the bay has a full kitchen, living-dining room, private bath, TV, radio, and cassette player. Also available is the Victorian Summer House with two bedrooms, private baths, a balcony, and porch; and the Caretaker's House, with living room, TV, sleeper-sofa, full kitchen, dining area, bath, and two bedrooms. A rollaway bed is also available. Parking area also accommodates boat and trailer. Full gourmet breakfast served. Air conditioned. Smoking allowed outside only. Resident cat. Credit cards accepted. $85-160.

SODUS POINT

Carriage House Inn

8375 Wickham Boulevard, 14555
(315) 483-2100; (800) 292-2990 (reservations only)

Voted one of the Top 50 Inns in America. Lakefront. Private baths and TVs in all rooms. Full country breakfast. Guests can stay in the Victorian home built in 1870 in a quiet residential area or in the stone carriage house on the shore of Lake Ontario overlooking Sodus Point historic lighthouse. Both homes have

private entrances, private living rooms, and beach access. Within walking distance to area restaurants and charter boats. One block north of Route 14 and scenic Seaway Trail. Halfway between Rochester and Syracuse on Lake Ontario.

Rooms: 8 (PB) $65-90
Full Breakfast
Credit Cards: A, B, C, D
Notes: 3, 8, 9, 10, 11, 12, 13

SOUTH OTSELIC

Elaine's Bed & Breakfast Selections

4987 Kingston Road, Elbridge, 13060
(315) 689-2082 (call between 10:30 A.M.–7:00 P.M.)

Fully restored old farmhouse built in the late 1800s offers a private retreat from the sound and rush of everyday life. At this small working farm guests can enjoy the relaxed atmosphere, complete with a wood-burning stove in the front parlor. A generous country breakfast and afternoon snacks served. Three pleasant bedrooms share a shower bath in footed tub. Long-term discounts available, however not in hunting season. Open year-round. Children welcome. Smoking permitted in designated areas only. Extra person in room $10. $45-50.

SPENCER

Elaine's Bed & Breakfast Selections

4987 Kingston Road, Elbridge, 13060
(315) 689-2082 (call between 10:30 A.M.–7:00 P.M.)

This large updated farmhouse is just 20 minutes south of Ithaca and also convenient to Binghamton, Endicott, Elmira, and Watkins Glen. Bike tours can be arranged. There are hiking trails and cross-country skiing. Children over 12 are welcome. There are outside kennels for roving with Rover. No pets inside. A full, hearty country breakfast is served. No

7 No smoking; 8 Children welcome; 9 Social drinking allowed; 10 Tennis nearby; 11 Swimming nearby; 12 Golf nearby; 13 Skiing nearby; 14 May be booked through a travel agent; 15 Handicapped accessible.

smoking. Open year-round. Separate cottage also available. $85-140.

SPENCERTOWN

American Country Collection

1353 Union Street, Schenectady, 12308
(518) 370-4948; (800) 810-4948
FAX (518) 393-1634 (call first)
e-mail: Carolbnbres@msn.com
www.bandbreservations.com

238. This bed and breakfast rests like an architecturally eclectic jewel amid five acres of rolling farm land. The building is a rambling, gabled old mansion styled in both Federal Colonial and Victorian. Five guest rooms with private baths are decorated with period furnishings. Close to Tanglewood and the other great Berkshire attractions. The current owners welcome guests to visit what their extensive renovations have created. Handicapped-accessible first-floor room and equipped bath. $110-155.

STANFORDVILLE

Lakehouse Inn on Golden Pond

Shelley Hill Road, 12581
(914) 266-8093; e-mail: judy@lakehouseinn.com
www.lakehouseinn.com

The most enchanting lakefront sanctuary in the Hudson River Valley, this inn offers swimming,

Lakehouse Inn on Golden Pond

fishing, boating, suites with private Jacuzzi for two, wood-burning fireplaces, private decks, and stunning views of the lake and woods. Gourmet breakfast delivered to guest room in a covered basket. A unique private inn where guests are free to enjoy a special time in splendid circumstances. Just 90 minutes from Manhattan.

Hosts: Judy and Rich Kohler
Rooms: 9 (PB) $125-650
Full Breakfast
Credit Cards: A, B
Notes: 2, 5, 7, 8, 9, 10, 11, 12, 13, 14

STONE RIDGE

Baker's

Baker's Bed & Breakfast

24 Old Kings Highway, 12484
(914) 687-9795; (888) 623-5513
FAX (914) 687-4153
www.pojonews.com/enjoy/locnums/880248992.htm

Year-round the hosts welcome guests into their home, an 18th-century, restored stone farmhouse in an exquisite country setting. Come and enjoy an elegant breakfast, and fireplaces. All rooms have private baths, air conditioning, and TV, telephone, fax, web line available. Baker's has been featured in *New York Times*, *New York* magazine, *Condé Nast's Traveler*, *Woman's Day*, and most bed and breakfast directories.

Hosts: Doug and Linda Baker
Rooms: 6 (PB) $98-128
Full Breakfast
Credit Cards: A, B
Notes: 2, 5, 7, 9, 10, 11, 12, 13

NOTES: Credit cards accepted: A MasterCard; B Visa; C American Express; D Discover; E Diner's Club; F Other; 2 Personal checks accepted; 3 Lunch available; 4 Dinner available; 5 Open all year; 6 Pets welcome;

SYRACUSE

American Country Collection

1353 Union Street, Schenectady, 12308
(518) 370-4948; (800) 810-4948
FAX (518) 393-1634 (call first)
e-mail: Carolbnbres@msn.com
www.bandbreservations.com

222. This large century-old country home is surrounded by woods on a quiet rural road in the Finger Lakes region, with Skaneateles Lake only five miles away. Trails provide hiking in summer and cross-country skiing on groomed trails in winter. Three guest rooms, one private bath. No smoking. Full traditional-style breakfast served in large country kitchen with fireplace. Children over six welcome. $55-65.

Bed & Breakfast Wellington

707 Danforth Street, 13208-1611
(315) 474-3641; (800) 724-5006
FAX (315) 474-2557
e-mail: BBW@ix.netcom.com
www.flbba.com/wellington

The breakfasts at this circa 1914 national historic Arts and Crafts home feature enticing, healthy dishes. Pear Hawaiian French toast is the house specialty, and innkeeper Wendy Wilber serves fresh fruit she picks herself. Guests are pampered with china table settings and lacy tablecloths. The rich wood interior accentuates the fireplaces, canvas floors, and antiques. The area boasts a zoo, Syracuse University, the Carousel Center, nature centers, and wildlife preserves. Turndown service and TV in room. VCR, fax, and copier on premises. Antiques, fishing, shopping, downhill and cross-country skiing, sporting events, and theater are nearby.

Hosts: Ray Borg and Wendy Wilber
Rooms: 5 (4 PB; 1 SB) $75-125
Full and Continental Breakfasts
Credit Cards: A, B, C, D, E, F
Notes: 2, 5, 7, 8, 9, 10, 12, 13, 14

Elaine's Bed & Breakfast Selections

4987 Kingston Road, Elbridge, 13060
(315) 689-2082 (call between 10:30 A.M.–7:00 P.M.)

A. Convenient to Syracuse University and LeMoyne College, this delightful knotty pine basement apartment can sleep two and has a completely furnished eat-in kitchen and attractive shower bath with many built-ins. The living room/bedroom includes color TV, desk, easy chairs, game table, and much more. Patio and yard. Quiet dead-end street with a great view. Use of laundry facilities for long-term guests. Long-term rates available. $85.

B. Ranch-style house handy to NYS Thruway (I-90). The guest room has air conditioning and color cable TV. Bath is across the hall and is shared with a smaller room that is booked for third person in the same party. A full country breakfast is served. Above-ground pool. Open year-round. Moderate rates.

C. A complete ground-floor apartment in a fine contemporary Colonial house with fantastic view. Full kitchen and bath. Convenient to I-81, Syracuse, Skaneateles, and all Finger Lake activities.

Giddings Garden Bed & Breakfast

290 West Seneca Turnpike, 13207
(800) 377-3452; FAX (315) 492-6389
e-mail: giddingsB-B@webtv.net
ww.giddingsgarden.com

Convenient to all Syracuse and central New York events and locations, this large Federal-style home, formerly Giddings Tavern in 1810, has recently been re-opened as an exquisite bed and breakfast. The home's ambiance is inviting and welcoming from the twinkle of many chandeliers and the glow of the rich douglas fir flooring original to the tavern. The owners have fussed over every detail in the upscale

7 No smoking; 8 Children welcome; 9 Social drinking allowed; 10 Tennis nearby; 11 Swimming nearby; 12 Golf nearby; 13 Skiing nearby; 14 May be booked through a travel agent; 15 Handicapped accessible.

guest quarters, with fabulous marble and mirrored en suite baths, four-poster beds, fireplaces, and fluffy down comforters.

Hosts: Pat and Nancie Roberts
Rooms: 3 (PB) $95-150
Full Breakfast
Credit Cards: A, B, C, D
Notes: 5, 7, 8, 9, 10, 12, 13, 14

High Meadows Bed 'n' Breakfast

3740 Eager Road, Jamesville, 13078
(315) 492-3517; (800) 854-0918
e-mail: nancy@himeadows.com
www.himeadows.com

Guests are invited to enjoy country hospitality, peace and serenity high in the hills just 10 miles south of Syracuse. The hosts offer the en suite complete with a canopied bed and bath with a whirlpool tub. The queen-size bedded Rose Room and double bedded Green Room achieve affordable elegance with beautiful linens and share a bath across the hall. The Executive Suite includes a living room, bedroom, bath, and minikitchen with a full refrigerator and private entrance. It sleeps six, and the hosts encourage families to visit. The wraparound deck offers a magnificent 60-mile view. Breakfast is included. Minutes from family activities, close to lakes, nature centers, and vineyards.

Hosts: Al and Nancy Mentz
Rooms: 3 (1 PB; 2 SB) $55-90
Continental Breakfast
Credit Cards: None
Notes: 2, 5, 7, 8, 10, 11, 12, 13, 14

TANNERSVILLE

The Eggery Inn

County Road 16, Box 4, 12485
(518) 589-5363; FAX (518) 589-5774
www.eggeryinn.com

This restored Dutch Colonial farmhouse is on a 12-acre parcel with sweeping views of Hunter Mountain. All 15 guest rooms with private baths have cable TV, in-room telephones,

and air conditioning. Glowing woodwork amidst furnishings of mission oak lends time for relaxing in the inviting parlor/lounge. Wraparound porch with antique wicker. Full breakfast with choice of menu. Formal dining room. In Catskill Forest Preserve. Near many state hiking trails, antiquing, and the artist colony of Woodstock. AAA- and Mobil-approved. Dinner available for groups. Non-smoking rooms available. May be booked through an AAA travel agent. Limited handicap accessibility.

Hosts: Julie and Abe Abramcryk
Rooms: 15 (PB) $85-125
Full Breakfast
Credit Cards: A, B, C
Notes: 5, 8, 9, 10, 11, 12, 13

TOMKINS COVE

American Country Collection

1353 Union Street, Schenectady, 12308
(518) 370-4948; (800) 810-4948
FAX (518) 393-1634 (call first)
e-mail: Carolbnbres@msn.com
www.bandbreservations.com

217. This contemporary home sits upon a hillside about 200 feet above the Hudson River. Accommodations include a living room with cathedral ceiling, solarium, and air conditioning. Two guest rooms have double beds and share a bath. The third room has a queen-size bed and private bath. Smoking permitted outside. Children 10 and older are welcome. Continental breakfast during the week; full breakfast on weekends. $80-95.

TROY

American Country Collection

1353 Union Street, Schenectady, 12308
(518) 370-4948; (800) 810-4948
FAX (518) 393-1634 (call first)
e-mail: Carolbnbres@msn.com
www.bandbreservations.com

NOTES: Credit cards accepted: A MasterCard; B Visa; C American Express; D Discover; E Diner's Club; F Other; 2 Personal checks accepted; 3 Lunch available; 4 Dinner available; 5 Open all year; 6 Pets welcome;

158. This unique Victorian farmhouse, circa 1849, is above Troy and set back 300 feet from the road with a long circular drive. It is near Rensselaer Polytechnic Institute, the Emma Willard School, Russell Sage College, and the Hudson Valley Community College. Four second-floor guest rooms share two full baths and a first-floor half-bath. Full country breakfast is served each morning. Smoking is allowed in designated areas only. $60.

TULLY-VESPER

Elaine's Bed & Breakfast Selections

4987 Kingston Road, Elbridge, 13060
(315) 689-2082 (call between 10:30 A.M.–7:00 P.M.)

This custom-built ranch offers two bedrooms with a shared bath and a master bedroom with private bath. Full country breakfast. Very close to Song Mountain downhill ski area and a short drive to Labrador and Toggenburg ski areas. Just 25 minutes to the lovely Finger Lakes village of Skaneateles and 20 minutes to Syracuse. Open year-round. $55-70.

UTICA

Bed & Breakfast Leatherstocking Association, Inc.

5 Rundell House, Dolgeville, 13329
(315) 429-3416 (phone/FAX—call first)
(800) 941-BEDS (2337)
www.bedbreakfastnys.com

019. Elegant brick Federalist period home built around 1826, in the National Register of Historic Places, offers a dramatic setting for a home away from home. Pre-arranged private dining and picnic lunches available. Five guest rooms with private and shared baths. Full breakfasts served daily. Lots of history on a quiet street in a busy city in the center of New York State. $50-75.

045. This 1815 brick Colonial, on 22 acres on the north edge of Utica, is only short minutes to exit 31, NYS Thruway (I-90) allowing all kinds of easy access to area attractions and colleges. House is snuggled in a woodsy residential area, retaining its aged character with wide-plank floors, old hardwoods, and homey decor. All modern and immaculate conveniences including two bedrooms with private baths, formal dining, and ample off-street parking. Full breakfasts, fresh fruit in rooms. Crib available. $55-65.

064. Spacious and elegant Victorian mansion, built around 1860, in the historic district. Seven large guest rooms with private baths and ceiling fans are offered. Large common rooms for relaxing by the fire, or reading in the library are at guests' disposal. Gourmet breakfasts served daily. Dining room has five round tables. Off-street, well-lighted, and paved parking. Convenient to fine dining, shopping malls, area colleges, cinemas, museums, performing arts centers, and sports arena. Easy access to I-90, north/south arterials, and Routes 5, 8, and 12. $85-150.

The Iris Stonehouse Bed & Breakfast

16 Derbyshire Place, 13501-4706
(315) 732-6720; (800) 446-1456
FAX (315) 732-6854; e-mail: rskilgore@juno.com

In town, close to everything, this stately stone house with leaded-glass windows has a separate guest sitting room and guest rooms with private and shared baths. Full breakfast from the daily menu, central air conditioning, three miles from I-90, exit 31 (New York State Thruway), one block off Genesee Street, three blocks from the north/south arterial and Routes 5, 8, and 12. No smoking.

Hosts: Jim and Nellie Chanatry
Rooms: 4 (2 PB; 2 SB) $50-80
Full Breakfast
Credit Cards: A, B, C, D
Notes: 2, 5, 7, 9, 12, 13, 14

---

7 No smoking; 8 Children welcome; 9 Social drinking allowed; 10 Tennis nearby; 11 Swimming nearby; 12 Golf nearby; 13 Skiing nearby; 14 May be booked through a travel agent; 15 Handicapped accessible.

VERNON

Elaine's Bed & Breakfast Selections

4987 Kingston Road, Elbridge, 13060
(315) 689-2082 (call between 10:30 A.M.–7:00 P.M.)

A marvelous sprawling Victorian-Italianate manor house atop a knoll on seven acres. Filled with antiques, this home has been featured in several local history books and is a must-see for architecture and history buffs. There are five guest rooms available. Children and well-behaved pets are welcome. Full breakfast is served. Smoking is not allowed in the bedrooms. Open year-round. $80-85.

VERONA

Bed & Breakfast Leatherstocking Association, Inc.

5 Rundell House, Dolgeville, 13329
(315) 429-3416 (phone/FAX—call first)
(800) 941-BEDS (2337)
www.bedbreakfastnys.com

036. Pure country! This 14-room restored 1876 farmhouse, only five miles from exit #33 on the NYS Thruway (I-90), is close to Turning Stone Casino, Vernon Downs Raceway, colleges, and the greater Utica -Rome attractions. A private air-conditioned suite consisting of two bedrooms, private bath, and fully equipped kitchenette is available. Continental breakfast. Common room on the first floor has game/dining table, easy chairs, and large cozy fireplace. Plenty of room to relax in a quiet rural area. $55-105.

WALDEN

American Country Collection

1353 Union Street, Schenectady, 12308
(518) 370-4948; (800) 810-4948
FAX (518) 393-1634 (call first)

e-mail: Carolbnbres@msn.com
www.bandbreservations.com

212. Early 19th-century replica saltbox home on 21 acres of fields and woodlands. One suite has a fireplace, a somma bed, and private bath. Air conditioned. Three additional rooms share a bath. A robe is provided for guests, who share a bath. Smoking permitted outside. Children welcome. One dog and two cats in residence. Guest pets are welcome with prior arrangement. Full breakfast. $85-110.

WARRENSBURG

American Country Collection

1353 Union Street, Schenectady, 12308
(518) 370-4948; (800) 810-4948
FAX (518) 393-1634 (call first)
e-mail: Carolbnbres@msn.com
www.bandbreservations.com

067. This 1850 Greek Revival inn has a new guest house featuring 10 rooms and a Jacuzzi in a plant-filled solarium. The inn itself has a public restaurant, a cozy fireplace tavern, and a common room with TV. Ten rooms and one family suite with private baths, air conditioning, and fireplaces. Handicapped access. Smoking permitted with consideration for nonsmokers. No pets. Children over 11 welcome. Minimum stay of two nights on holiday weekends and on July and August weekends. $95-160.

Country Road Lodge

115 Hickory Hill Road, 12885
(518) 623-2207; FAX (518) 623-4363
e-mail: parisibb@mail.netheaven.com
www.countryroadlodge.com

With a view of the Adirondack Mountains and the Hudson River and minutes from Lake George, the lodge has offered its seclusion and casual comfort since 1974. Homemade bread, hiking, skiing, bird watching, wildflowers, books, board games. Fine restaurants and antiquing nearby.

NOTES: Credit cards accepted: A MasterCard; B Visa; C American Express; D Discover; E Diner's Club; F Other; 2 Personal checks accepted; 3 Lunch available; 4 Dinner available; 5 Open all year; 6 Pets welcome;

Hosts: Steve and Sandi Parisi
Rooms: 4 (2 PB; 2 SB) $57-72
Full Breakfast
Credit Cards: None
Notes: 2, 5, 7, 9, 10, 11, 12, 13, 14

The Merrill Magee House

2 Hudson Street, 12885
(518) 623-2449

From the inviting wicker chairs on the porch to the elegant candlelit dining rooms, this inn offers the romance of a visit to a country estate. Guest rooms abound with 19th-century charm and 20th-century comforts. Guests can relax in the inn's secluded gardens, enjoy the outdoor pool, or shop for antiques in the village. In the Adirondack Park, all outdoor activities are minutes away. Smoking in designated areas only. Inquire about accommodations for children.

Hosts: The Carrington Family
Rooms: 10 (PB) $85-125
Full Breakfast
Credit Cards: A, B, C, D, E
Notes: 2, 4, 5, 9, 10, 11, 12, 13, 14, 15

White House Lodge

3760 Main Street, 12885
(518) 623-3640

An 1847 Victorian in the heart of the Adirondacks. The home is furnished with many antiques. Only five minutes to Lake George village, historic Fort William Henry, and Great Escape Fun Park. Walk to restaurants, antique shops, and shopping areas. Enjoy the comfort of the air-conditioned TV lounge or rock on the front porch. Only 20 minutes to Gore Mountain Ski Lodge and the Adirondack Balloon Festival. Smoking allowed in TV lounge only.

Hosts: James and Ruth Gibson
Rooms: 3 (SB) $85
Continental Breakfast
Credit Cards: A, B
Notes: 5, 11, 12, 13

WATKINS GLEN

Clarke House Bed & Breakfast

102 Durland Avenue, 14891
(607) 535-7965; FAX (607) 535-6230

Charming English Tudor home, circa 1920, in lovely village of Watkins Glen. Walk to famous gorge, restaurants, and activities at Seneca Lake. Short drive to Watkins Glen International Raceway, famous wineries, and Corning Glass. Immaculate bedrooms feature antique decor and new twin or queen-size beds. Hearty breakfast graciously served in the formal dining room. Central air conditioning. Private baths. Irish imports and gifts.

Hosts: Jack and Carolyn Clarke
Rooms: 4 (PB) $79-89
Full Breakfast
Credit Cards: A
Notes: 2, 5, 9, 11, 12, 14

Elaine's Bed & Breakfast Selections

4987 Kingston Road, Elbridge, 13060
(315) 689-2082 (call between 10:30 A.M.–7:00 P.M.)

A brick Colonial built in 1926 by a successful industrialist on this five-acre estate. Guest rooms include a two-room suite and three bedrooms with private baths. A third bedroom, which shares a bath with another room, can be booked as a family suite or as a single room midweek. No smoking. No pets. Inquire about accommodations for children. Open year-round. Excellent rates for the quality.

Farm Sanctuary

3100 Aikens Road, 14891
(607) 583-2225

Vegetarian bed and breakfast. Guests will wake up to crowing roosters on a picturesque 175-acre farm. In the beautiful Finger Lakes region of upstate New York, next to a 10,000-acre state forest. A clean and cozy country cabin awaits guests. Farm Sanctuary, established 1986, is a

7 No smoking; 8 Children welcome; 9 Social drinking allowed; 10 Tennis nearby; 11 Swimming nearby; 12 Golf nearby; 13 Skiing nearby; 14 May be booked through a travel agent; 15 Handicapped accessible.

national, nonprofit organization dedicated to ending farm animal abuse through farm animal rescue efforts, public education programs, investigative campaigns, and media exposés.

Hosts: Farm Sanctuary
Rooms: 3; $60-70
Continental Breakfast
Credit Cards: A, B
Notes: 2, 6, 8, 15

Reading House Bed & Breakfast

P.O. Box 321, 14891
(607) 535-9785; e-mail: readingbb@aol.com
www.bbhost.com/readinghouse

A restored 1820 home with spacious grounds, two ponds, and exceptional views of Seneca Lake. If guests like old houses, antiques, comfortable beds, private baths, delicious full breakfasts, good company, good books, a warm relaxing atmosphere—Reading House has it all. It's an ideal center from which to tour Keuka, Seneca, and Cayuga Lakes; Ithaca, Corning, and Hammonds Bay. Now in their 10th year. Children over eight welcome.

Hosts: Rita and Bill Newell
Rooms: 4 (PB) $70-95
Full Breakfasts
Credit Cards: A, B
Notes: 2, 5, 7, 9, 10, 11, 12, 13

WESTHAMPTON BEACH

1880 House Bed & Breakfast

2 Seafield Lane, 11978
(800) 346-3290

This 100-year-old country retreat is only 90 minutes from Manhattan on Westhampton Beach's exclusive Seafield Lane. A swimming pool and tennis court are on the premises, and it's only a short walk to the beach. The Hamptons offer numerous outstanding restaurants and shops. Indoor tennis is available locally, as is a health spa at Montauk Point. Minimum stay is two nights. ABBA excellent rating.

Host: Elsie Pardee Collins
Suites: 2 (PB) $125-200
Full Breakfast
Credit Cards: A, B
Notes: 5, 7, 9, 10, 11, 12, 14

WESTPORT

All Tucked Inn

53 South Main Street, P.O. Box 324, 12993
(518) 962-4400; (888) ALL-TUCK
www.alltuckedinn.com

All Tucked Inn, on Lake Champlain in the historic hamlet of Westport, is a magical, whimsical place where troubles flee and peace presides. Within walking distance to shops, beaches, golf course, and a scenic drive to Adirondack Mountain hiking and skiing, this four-season inn offers lovely bedrooms, five with lake view, three with fireplace. TV/VCR in fireplaced living room. For beauty, history, and serenity, guests owe it to themselves to discover All Tucked Inn.

Hosts: Claudia Ryan and Tom Haley
Rooms: 9 (PB) $55-110
Full Breakfast
Credit Cards: None
Notes: 2, 4, 5, 7, 9, 10, 11, 12, 13, 14

All Tucked Inn

The Inn on the Library Lawn

1 Washington Street, 12993
(518) 962-8666; (888) 577-7748 (toll free)
www.theinnonthelibrarylawn.com

Restored 1875 Victorian inn overlooks Lake Champlain, nestled between the Green Mountains of Vermont and the Adirondack Mountains of New York. Walk to marina, beach, yacht club, 18-hole golf course and country club, summer concerts, and theater. Spacious rooms with private baths, air conditioning, and lake views. Full breakfast served on the outside deck or in the lake-view dining room. Local crafts and art featured. Browse other fine shops and visit historical sites in the area.

Hosts: Don and Susann Thompson
Rooms: 10 (PB) $69-115
Full Breakfast
Credit Cards: A, B, C, D
Notes: 2, 3, 4, 5, 7, 8, 9, 10, 11, 12, 13

The Victorian Lady

The Victorian Lady

57 South Main Street, 12993
(518) 962-2345

Elegant Victorian, circa 1856, in the historic village of Westport, on Lake Champlain in the Adirondacks. Period-furnished guest accommodations and common rooms. Formal gardens and lovely veranda with lake views. Gourmet breakfast and afternoon tea included. Close to many historic sites and outdoor activities. Lake Placid, the high peaks, Fort Ticonderoga, and Burlington, Vermont, all within one-hour drive. Owners/innkeepers assure a warm welcome. Featured in *Victorian Homes* magazine.

Hosts: Doris and Wayne Deswert
Rooms: 5 (4 PB; 1 SB) $75-110

Full Breakfast
Credit Cards: A, B
Notes: 2, 7, 8, 9, 10, 11, 12, 13

WEST TAGHKANIC

American Country Collection

1353 Union Street, Schenectady, 12308
(518) 370-4948; (800) 810-4948
FAX (518) 393-1634 (call first)
e-mail: Carolbnbres@msn.com
www.bandbreservations.com

211. In what used to be a general store, now resides a special farmhouse bed and breakfast and antique shop. Each of the guest rooms has its own private bath and is air conditioned. Two suites can accommodate three or four guests. The living room has a TV/VCR and is graciously furnished with antiques and a Persian rug. Smoking permitted outside. Enjoy hiking, swimming, or cross-country skiing at nearby Taghkanic State Park. Children are welcome. A full American breakfast is served. $65-95.

WILLET

Woven Waters

6224 Route 41, 13863
(607) 656-8672

A beautifully renovated 100-year-old barn on the shores of a lovely private lake. The beautiful interior is accented with unique antiques and gorgeous imported laces. Relax in the large, comfortable living room with beamed cathedral ceiling and massive stone fireplace or on one of the porches overlooking the lake (one porch is open, one is enclosed). Children over 10 are welcome.

Hosts: John and Erika
Rooms: 3 (3 SB) $68-100
Full Breakfasts
Credit Cards: None
Notes: 2, 5, 11, 12, 13, 14

7 No smoking; 8 Children welcome; 9 Social drinking allowed; 10 Tennis nearby; 11 Swimming nearby; 12 Golf nearby; 13 Skiing nearby; 14 May be booked through a travel agent; 15 Handicapped accessible.

WINDHAM

Albergo Allegria

Route 296, 12496
(518) 734-5560; (800) 625-2374
FAX (518) 734-5570; www.AlbergoUSA.com

Meaning the "Inn of Happiness" in Italian, Albergo Allegria seeks to pamper all that walk through her doors. This sprawling Queen Anne mansion, circa 1876, hosts 16 guest rooms and five luxury suites in her carriage house. All rooms have a full private bath, some with Jacuzzi, whirlpool, and gaslight fireplace. Albergo is a registered historic site nestled in the Catskill Forest Preserve and furnished with period wall paper and antiques. Four-star restaurant across the road.

Hosts: Vito and Lenore Radelich; Leslie and Marianna Leman
Rooms: 21 (PB) $65-225
Full Breakfast
Credit Cards: A, B
Notes: 5, 7, 9, 10, 11, 12, 13, 14, 15

Albergo Allegria

WOODSTOCK

American Country Collection

1353 Union Street, Schenectady, 12308
(518) 370-4948; (800) 810-4948
FAX (518) 393-1634 (call first)
e-mail: Carolbnbres@msn.com
www.bandbreservations.com

249. In the shadow of Hunter Mountain, 10 miles to the village of Woodstock, this Victorian has hiking right out the door. Enjoy mountain views, hot tub on the deck, ski Hunter or Windham Mountains, shop and dine in Woodstock, visit Catskill game farm, hike the many trails, or visit the North Lake State Park. Three guest rooms with private baths and two share the fourth. Suite with Jacuzzi tub, wood stove, and sleeping loft. Full breakfast. Children 13 and older welcome. Smoking permitted on enclosed porch. No resident pets. $60-125.

Bed by the Stream

9 George Sickle Road, Saugerties, 12477
(914) 246-2979

Five acres of streamside property. In-ground pool. Breakfast served on sun porch overlooking stream. Seven miles from Woodstock, three miles from exit 20 on the New York Thruway. All rooms have cable TV and air conditioning. Hiking and biking nearby.

Hosts: Odette and Bill Reinhardt
Rooms: 3 (PB) $60-75
Full Breakfast
Credit Cards: None
Notes: 2, 5, 7, 8, 9, 10, 11, 12, 13

NOTES: Credit cards accepted: A MasterCard; B Visa; C American Express; D Discover; E Diner's Club; F Other; 2 Personal checks accepted; 3 Lunch available; 4 Dinner available; 5 Open all year; 6 Pets welcome;

Pennsylvania

Adamstown Inn

Association of Bed & Breakfasts in Philadelphia, Valley Forge, Brandywine

P.O. Box 562, Valley Forge, 19481-0562
(610) 783-7838; (800) 344-0123
FAX (610) 783-7783
e-mail: pa@bnbassociation.com

1600. This 150-year old restored German schoolhouse is nestled on the side of a mountain on two and one-half acres. There are four bedrooms; all have private baths. A Continental plus breakfast is served each morning. $75-105.

ADAMSTOWN

Adamstown Inn

62 West Main Street, P.O. Box 938, 19501
(717) 484-0800; (800) 594-4808

Experience the simple elegance of the Adamstown Inn, a Victorian bed and breakfast. All seven guest rooms are decorated with family heirlooms, handmade quilts, lace curtains, and many distinctive touches that make any stay special. The accommodations range from antique to king-size beds. All rooms have private baths (six rooms feature two-person Jacuzzis and four rooms feature fireplaces). In the heart of the antique district, only minutes from the Reading outlet centers and Lancaster. Experience the magic of yesteryear.

Hosts: Tom and Wanda Berman
Rooms: 7 (PB) $70-150
Continental Breakfast
Credit Cards: A, B
Notes: 2, 5, 9, 10, 11, 12, 14

ALTOONA

Hoenstine's Bed & Breakfast

418 Montgomery Street, Hollidaysburg, 16648
(814) 695-0632; (888) 550-9655
FAX (814) 696-7310

This inn is any antique lover's dream, in an elegant 1839 townhouse in downtown registered

Hoenstine's

7 No smoking; 8 Children welcome; 9 Social drinking allowed; 10 Tennis nearby; 11 Swimming nearby; 12 Golf nearby; 13 Skiing nearby; 14 May be booked through a travel agent; 15 Handicapped accessible.

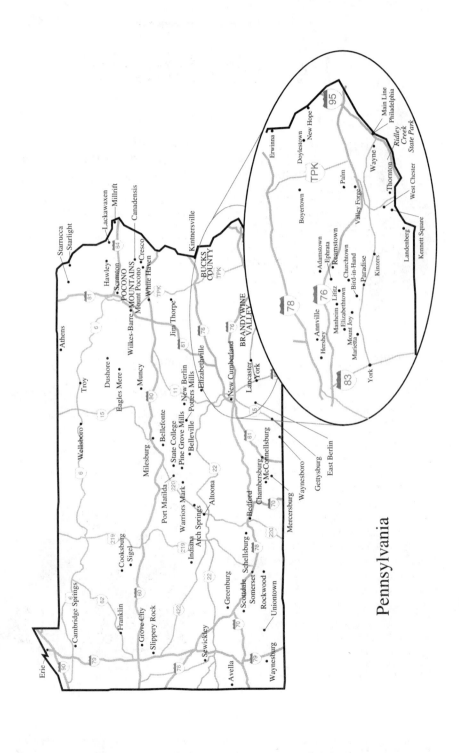

Pennsylvania

historic Hollidaysburg. The hearty breakfast is the whim of the host's fancy and the area's seasonal ingredients. Inquire about accommodations for children and pets. Only three miles to Altoona, and near many antique shops and local parks in a beautiful residential section of Pennsylvania.

Host: Barbara Hoenstine
Rooms: 3 (1 PB; 2 SB) $50-70
Full Breakfast
Credit Cards: A, B
Notes: 2, 7, 9, 10, 12, 13, 14

ANNVILLE

Swatara Creek Inn

Rural Delivery #2, Box 692 (Jamestown Road),
   17003-9211
(717) 865-3259

The mansion was built as the home of wealthy local landowner Jacob Urich about 1860. From 1917 through 1941 it was a Milton S. Hershey boys orphan home. Later after several owners, Dick and Jeannette Hess bought the home in 1986. Historic restaurant within walking distance. AAA-approved diamond rating. Gift certificates available. Fifteen dollars per each additional guest in room. Inquire about accommodations for children. Smoking permitted outside only.

Innkeeper: Mary Evans
Host: Dick Hess
Rooms: 10 (PB) $55-80

Swatara Creek Inn

Full Breakfast
Credit Cards: A, B, C, D, E
Notes: 2, 5, 7, 14, 15

ARCH SPRINGS

Rest & Repast Bed & Breakfast Reservations

Box 126, Pine Grove Mills, 16868
(814) 238-1484; FAX (814) 234-9890
www.iul.com/bnbinpa

The Manor House and the Mill House. Two restored properties directly across a little traveled country road from each other. The Mill House, circa 1799, served as a mill, general store and granary for Sinking Valley. A class-A trout stream runs behind the property. The smaller Mill House has three guest rooms, a parlor with sofa bed, full kitchen, laundry facilities, and two and one-half baths. The grander Manor House has three guest rooms, a child playroom, a formal dining room, and large parlor, each with fireplace, full kitchen, and a finished third-floor suitable for a small conference or business meeting. There are four and one-half baths. Both properties are unhosted, but breakfast is provided. The two facilities booked together can sleep up to seven couples. The Manor House is open year-round. The Mill House is open from April through November. Two-room minimum booking per property. Mill House rates per room $70. Manor House rates per room $110.

ATHENS

Fáilte Inn & Antique Shoppe

Rural Route 2, Box 323, 18810
(570) 358-3899; FAX (570) 358-3387
e-mail: thefailteinn@webtv.net

Nestled in the Susquehanna Valley surrounded by the beautiful Endless Mountains of rural Pennsylvania. Enjoy the unhurried lifestyle of yesterday's Victorian elegance by browsing the

Fáilte Inn

inn's library. Visit the restored speakeasy dating from the days of Prohibition. Breakfast is served in the elegantly appointed dining room or on the wide-screened verandas overlooking beautiful grounds and gardens. Near Pennsylvania's scenic Route 6 and New York's Finger Lakes region. Children over 12 welcome. Smoking and nonsmoking rooms. Visit and browse in the Fáilte Inn antique shop.

Hosts: Jim and Sarah True
Rooms: 5 (PB) $65-70
Full Breakfast
Credit Cards: A, B
Notes: 2, 5, 9, 10, 11, 12, 13

AVELLA

Weatherbury Farm

1061 Sugar Run Road, 15312
(724) 587-3763
www.weatherburyfarm.com

One hundred acres of meadows, gardens, fields, and valleys create a tranquil setting at this award-winning bed and breakfast, the perfect getaway from everyday pressures. Guests' rooms are lovingly furnished with old-fashioned country charm. Guests awaken to a bountiful farm breakfast. Later, guests may get acquainted with the farm's sheep, cattle, and chickens. Opportunities for golfing, fishing, boating, hiking, bicycling, and antiquing abound in the local area. Visit historic Meadowcroft Village. Convenient to Pittsburgh.

Hosts: Dale, Marcy, and Nigel Tudor
Rooms: 5 (PB) $65-75

Suites: 3 (PB) $90-100
Full Breakfast
Credit Cards: A, B, C, D
Notes: 2, 5, 7, 8, 9, 10, 11, 12, 13, 14, 15

BEDFORD

Bedford's Covered Bridge Inn

749 Mill Road, Schellsburg, 15559
(814) 733-4093; www.bedfordcounty.net/cbi.htm

Delightful countryside accommodations in a historic home near a covered bridge afford guests scrumptious full breakfasts and private baths amid a picture-book setting. Hiking, biking, antiquing, fly-fishing, bird watching, and cross-country skiing are all available just outside the door. Old Bedford Village, Blue Knob ski resort, Shawnee State Park, Coral Caverns, and many covered bridges are nearby. Near exit 11, I-76. A cottage also available, which is perfect for families or couples. AAA three-diamonds.

Rooms: 6 (PB) $75-95
Full Breakfast
Credit Cards: A, B, C, D
Notes: 2, 5, 7, 9, 10, 11, 12, 13, 14

Bedford's Covered Bridge Inn

BELLEFONTE

Rest & Repast Bed & Breakfast Reservations

Box 126, Pine Grove Mills, 16868
(814) 238-1484; FAX (814) 234-9890
www.iul.com/bnbinpa

Brockerhoff Mill, formerly an 1800s mill, now brought back to life as a unique bed and break-

NOTES: Credit cards accepted: A MasterCard; B Visa; C American Express; D Discover; E Diner's Club; F Other; 2 Personal checks accepted; 3 Lunch available; 4 Dinner available; 5 Open all year; 6 Pets welcome;

fast with the mill race and stream incorporated inside the lower level. Sit on upper atrium and watch the native trout swim in pond below. Quiet sounds of water rippling offer a soothing backdrop. Two guest rooms, private and shared bath. Near I-80, exit 23. Bellefonte is a beautiful historic town filled with Victorian architecture. $95-110.

BELLEVILLE

Hickory Grove Bed & Breakfast

1861 West Back Mountain Road, 17004
(717) 935-5289; (888) 446-4346

Charming country-style bed and breakfast in the heart of Amish country, only 30 minutes from Penn State University. Other nearby attractions include state parks, the Big Valley Auction and Flea Market, crafts, antiques, gift and quilt shops. Enjoy the flower and vegetable gardens, swing under the grape arbor, picnic on the patio. Homemade muffins and fruit cobbler made from fresh berries raised at Hickory Grove grace the breakfast table. Private entrance, fireplace, and family room.

Hosts: Caleb and Bertha Peachey
Rooms: 5 (1 PB; 4 SB) $45-50
Full Breakfast
Credit Cards: None
Notes: 2, 5, 7, 8

BIRD-IN-HAND

The Village Inn of Bird-in-Hand

2695 Old Philadelphia Pike, P.O. Box 253, 17505
(800) 914-2473; FAX (717) 768-1117
e-mail: lodging@bird-in-hand.com
www.bird-in-hand.com

The Village Inn of Bird-in-Hand was originally built in 1734 and is listed in the National Register of Historic Places. It is in the heart of the Pennsylvania Dutch country. Each morning a Continental breakfast including fresh fruits, pastries, and cereals is served. All guests enjoy

The Village Inn of Bird-in-Hand

free use of the indoor/outdoor swimming pools and tennis courts within walking distance. A complimentary tour of the surrounding Amish farmlands is offered daily, except Sunday.

Host: Rick Meshey
Rooms: 11 (PB) $69-149
Continental Breakfast
Credit Cards: A, B, C, D
Notes: 2, 5, 8, 10, 11, 12

BOALSBURG VILLAGE

Rest & Repast Bed & Breakfast Reservations

Box 126, Pine Grove Mills, 16868
(814) 238-1484; FAX (814) 234-9890
www.iul.com/bnbinpa

The Sign of the Dove. A remodeled carriage house in the middle of the village of colonial Boalsburg where it is claimed the first Memorial Day was celebrated. Charming Williamsburg-like village with shops, restaurants, and museums. Host home has three bedrooms with Amish and country furnishings. Shared bath. $85.

BOILING SPRINGS

The Garmanhaus

217 Front Street, Box 307, 17007
(717) 258-3980

---

7 No smoking; 8 Children welcome; 9 Social drinking allowed; 10 Tennis nearby; 11 Swimming nearby; 12 Golf nearby; 13 Skiing nearby; 14 May be booked through a travel agent; 15 Handicapped accessible.

By the lake in the historic village of Boiling Springs, this gracious Victorian house has four guest rooms of double occupancy. Sitting room, where breakfast is served, overlooks lake. For the fisherman, world famous for its fly-fishing, is Yellow Breeches—a five-minute walk. Antique shops in nearby Carlisle. Excellent gourmet restaurant with an impressive wine list is a two-minute walk. The hosts promise a warm and charming time for all who stay. Children over five welcome.

Hosts: John and Molly Garman
Rooms: 4 (SB) $50
Continental Breakfast
Credit Cards: None
Notes: 2, 5, 7, 9, 10, 11, 12, 13

The Garmanhaus

BOYERTOWN

The Enchanted Cottage

22 Deer Run Road, 19512
(610) 845-8845

Be the only guests in this rustic, romantic, one-and-one-half-story Cotswold-style stone cottage nestled among rolling, wooded acres. Gourmet breakfasts are served in the main house beside the garden or before a blazing fire. Fine restaurant within walking distance. Close to historic sites, country auctions, Amish area, antiques, retail outlets, and flea markets. With fresh flowers and complimentary wine

The Enchanted Cottage

and cheese, this wonderful bed and breakfast offers an informal but gracious lifestyle in a storybook atmosphere.

Hosts: Peg and Richard Groff
Room: 1 (PB) $85-90
Full Breakfast
Credit Cards: None
Notes: 2, 3, 5, 7, 9, 10, 12, 13, 14

BRANDYWINE

Association of Bed & Breakfasts in Philadelphia, Valley Forge, Brandywine

P. O. Box 562, Valley Forge, 19481-0562
(610) 783-7838; (800) 344-0123
FAX (610) 783-7783
e-mail: pa@bnbassociation.com

0800. This circa 1755 country farmhouse has been recognized by the local historic society. New addition was added in 1850. The inn is on wooded acres; surrounded by pastureland, hunt country, and rural dirt roads. Children are welcome. Enjoy TV, VCR, games/cards, the wood-burning stove in the parlor. Fish, hike, or throw horseshoes outdoors. Continental breakfast is served in the morning. $60-90.

NOTES: Credit cards accepted: A MasterCard; B Visa; C American Express; D Discover; E Diner's Club; F Other; 2 Personal checks accepted; 3 Lunch available; 4 Dinner available; 5 Open all year; 6 Pets welcome;

A Bed & Breakfast Connection/ Bed & Breakfast of Philadelphia

P.O. Box 21, Devon, 19333
(610) 687-3565; (800) 448-3619 (outside PA)
FAX (610) 995-9524
e-mail: bnb@bnbphiladelphia.com
www.bnbphiladelphia.com

Hamanassett

G-04. Discover this tucked-away, quietly elegant manor house near the heart of the Brandywine Valley. With 36 acres, historic buildings, gardens, paths, and trails, each season is special at this bed and breakfast. Well-appointed rooms offer canopied king-size beds, queen-size, doubles, twins, or suites. All rooms have TV and private baths. A full country breakfast with homemade breads, muffins, croissants, and other goodies is served each morning. $90-120.

G-05. Step back in time at this 1850 Italian Federal Victorian mansion. High ceilings, oriental rugs, fireplaces, teal paneling, and handcrafted grand staircase decorate the inside of this home. Seven guest rooms decorated in a unique Victorian theme. All share hall bathrooms, except the Darlington Room that, in addition to a private bathroom, offers a working fireplace for evening ambiance. Full breakfast served. $80-110.

BRANDYWINE VALLEY

Hamanassett

P.O. Box 129, Lima, 19037
(610) 459-3000
e-mail: hamanasset@aol.com
www.bbonline.com/pa/hamanassett/

Awarded "Best Bed and Breakfast" by *Main Line Today* magazine. Enjoy an elegantly quiet getaway at this private estate and magnificent 19th-century country mansion with 48 secluded acres of woodlands, gardens, fields, and trails. Near beautiful Brandywine Valley attractions, including Longwood Gardens, Winterthur, Nemours, Hagley, and much more. Excellent local dining. Rooms have king-size, queen-size, double, and twin beds; large, full private baths; TV; and other amenities. Brochure available. Two-night minimum. Children 14 and older welcome.

Host: Evelene Dohan
Rooms: 8 (7 PB; 1 SB)
Full Breakfast
Credit Cards: None
Notes: 2, 7, 9, 12, 14

CAMBRIDGE SPRINGS

Bethany Guest House

325 South Main Street, 16403
(814) 398-2046; (800) 777-2046

Relax in the luxury of an 1876 Italianate home built in a Victorian resort community by one of the area's pioneering families. This home, in the National Register of Historic Places, has been restored to its original elegance and is filled with antiques. It features four guest rooms, a parlor with a pump organ, a drawing room with a period book collection, and a Greek Revival dining room where guests' home-cooked breakfast is served. The Covenant Room, with its double-wide whirlpool tub, is a favorite. Relax while enjoying nearby Lake Erie, wildlife refuges, bicycle trails, amusement parks, antique and specialty stores, or visit Allegheny College or Edinboro University.

Hosts: Dave and Katie White
Rooms: 4 (PB) $35-65
Full Breakfast
Credit Cards: A, B
Notes: 2, 5, 7, 8, 9, 11, 12, 13

7 No smoking; 8 Children welcome; 9 Social drinking allowed; 10 Tennis nearby; 11 Swimming nearby; 12 Golf nearby; 13 Skiing nearby; 14 May be booked through a travel agent; 15 Handicapped accessible.

CANADENSIS _____

Brookview Manor
Bed & Breakfast Inn

Rural Route 1, Box 365, 18325
(570) 595-2451

On four picturesque acres in the Pocono
Mountains, Brookview Manor offers 10 guest
rooms and suites uniquely appointed with
country and Victorian antique furnishings.
Some rooms offer Jacuzzi or fireplace. Enjoy
the wraparound porch, hiking trails, fishing,
and nearby skiing, golf, tennis, boating, and
antiquing. A delicious full breakfast, afternoon
refreshments, and warm hospitality are all
included. Children over 12 are welcome.

Owner: Mary Anne Buckley
Rooms: 10 (PB) $105-150
Full Breakfast
Credit Cards: A, B, C, D
Notes: 5, 9, 10, 11, 12, 13, 14

Dreamy Acres

Box 7, 18325
(570) 595-7115

Dreamy Acres is in the heart of the beautiful
Pocono Mountains vacationland on three acres
of land with a stream flowing into a small
pond. The house is 500 feet back from the
highway, giving a pleasing, quiet atmosphere.
Minimum stay on weekends is two nights; on
holidays, three nights. Continental breakfast
served May through October. Closed Christmas. Children over 12 are welcome.

Hosts: Esther and Bill Pickett
Rooms: 6 (4 PB; 2 SB) $40-60
Continental Breakfast
Credit Cards: None
Notes: 2, 5, 9, 10, 11, 12, 13

The Merry Inn

Route 390, P.O. Box 757, 18325
(570) 595-2011; (800) 858-4182

The Merry Inn is in the heart of the Pocono
Mountains. It is a cozy and affordable home
away from home and is close to all activities.
The hosts encourage their guests to relax in the
Jacuzzi, which is open year-round, or just sit
and enjoy the view on either of the decks.
Good food, great people, and sweet dreams are
what guests will find at the Merry Inn.

Hosts: Meredyth and Chris Huggard
Rooms: 6 (PB) $90-95
Full Breakfast
Credit Cards: A, B
Notes: 2, 5, 8, 9, 10, 11, 12, 13

The Overlook Inn & Lodge

Rural Route 1, Box 680, Dutch Hill Road, 18325
(570) 595-8550

The Overlook has offered a tranquil respite for
guests sine the turn of the century. Take a step
back in time when life was lived more simply.
The inn is a three-storied, turn-of-the-century
structure that incorporates a much older farmhouse. The lodge is nestled on the edge of the
woods, a pathway from the inn. It houses six
bedrooms with private baths, a kitchen, and
living room with fireplace. Locally, there are
fine restaurants, antique and specialty shops,
and the Pocono Playhouse. Skiing, golfing,
fishing, boating, and horseback riding are
available in every direction. Cross-country
trails and walking paths start from the door.
Restaurant on premises.

The Overlook Inn and Lodge

NOTES: Credit cards accepted: A MasterCard; B Visa; C American Express; D Discover; E Diner's Club;
F Other; 2 Personal checks accepted; 3 Lunch available; 4 Dinner available; 5 Open all year; 6 Pets welcome;

Hosts: Frederick Betz and Beverly Post Ketterer
Rooms: 18 (PB) $95-150
Continental Breakfast
Credit Cards: A, B
Notes: 2, 5, 7, 9, 11, 12, 13

Pine Knob Inn

Route 447, 18325
(570) 595-2532; (800) 426-1460
FAX (570) 595-6429
e-mail: innkeepers@pineknobinn.com
www.pinebknobinn.com

A historic Civil War-period inn of distinction. Picturesque setting in the heart of the beautiful Pocono Mountains. Relax in old- time country comfort and indulge in gourmet dining in the Brodhead Room. Fine wine and spirits available in C. J. Mallards Pub. Candlelight dining with five courses served to guests in a relaxed atmosphere. The inn is decorated with an eclectic mix of antiques and handmade arts and crafts. Open year-round.

Hosts: Cheryl and John Garman
Rooms: 25 (19 PB: 6 SB) $85-150
Full Breakfast
Credit Cards: A, B, C, D, E
Notes: 2, 4, 5, 6, 8, 9, 10, 11, 12, 13, 14, 15

CHAMBERSBURG

Amanda's Bed & Breakfast Reservation Service

3538 Lakeway Drive, Ellicott City, MD 21042-1226
(443) 535-0008; (800) 899-7533
FAX (443) 535-0009; e-mail: AmandasRS@aol.com
www.Amandas-BBRS.com

308. A special, spacious residence that was once the summer home of a railroad executive. Original woodwork throughout emphasizes the grandeur of a past era. Eight rooms, each with private bath, some with Jacuzzi and/or a fireplace. Full breakfast is served on weekends. The Victorian era is highlighted every day with a Christmas theme. $89-180.

Distinguished Accommodations in the Potomac Region— (Amanda's Bed & Breakfast Reservation Service)

3538 Lakeway Drive, Ellicott City, MD 21042-1226
(443) 535-0008; (800) 899-7533
FAX (443) 535-0009; e-mail: AmandasRS@aol.com
www.Amandas-BBRS.com

308. Rich in railroad history, this expansive and dramatic setting is a showplace of Victorian splendor. Restored with antiques that honor the exquisite taste and prosperity at the turn of the century. A wraparound porch, hand-carved chestnut staircase, mahogany walls in the living and dining room area, are just a few of the many fine features of this lovely estate. They offer eight rooms of varying sizes, each with a private bath, several with a whirlpool tub and a fireplace. Convenient to Gettysburg, Antietam, and Sharpsburg. A nice drive from the DC or Baltimore area through rich farm country. $89-179.

CHESTNUT HILL

Association of Bed & Breakfasts in Philadelphia, Valley Forge, Brandywine

P.O. Box 562, Valley Forge, 19481-0562
(610) 783-7838; (800) 344-0123
FAX (610) 783-7783
e-mail: pa@bnbassociation.com

1307. Built in 1732 and after a year of careful restoration work, the guest house has five guest rooms. Each room has a private bath, cable TV, radio, telephone, and modem. Kitchen facilities are self-serve 24-hours with refrigerator loaded with beverages. Coffee and tea can be made anytime. Always available are candy, snacks, hot or cold cereal, and by request a hot breakfast can be served. $89-159.

7 No smoking; 8 Children welcome; 9 Social drinking allowed; 10 Tennis nearby; 11 Swimming nearby; 12 Golf nearby; 13 Skiing nearby; 14 May be booked through a travel agent; 15 Handicapped accessible.

COLLEGEVILLE

Association of Bed & Breakfasts in Philadelphia, Valley Forge, Brandywine

P.O. Box 562, Valley Forge, 19481-0562
(610) 783-7838; (800) 344-0123
FAX (610) 783-7783
e-mail: pa@bnbassociation.com

1904. Skilled European and American crafts-men fashioned this 22-room Victorian mansion in 1897. The seven guest rooms all have private baths and air conditioning. Two rooms have whirlpool tubs. Full breakfast. Open year-round for house tours, weddings, and corporate meetings. Twenty dollars for each additional person in room. $90-140.

COOKSBURG

Clarion River Lodge & Riverview Suites

HC 1, Box 22-D, 16217
(800) 648-6743; FAX (814) 744-8553
e-mail: eoday@penn.com

Nestled on 21 wooded acres at the edge of the Cook Forest, the Clarion River Lodge, once a private estate, offers queen- and king-size rooms. A four-star restaurant, lounge, and a cozy library. Guests can enjoy the hot tub and exercise room at the Riverview Suites, which are poised majestically 1,300 feet above the Clarion River and which offer accommoda-tions and a view unsurpassed in western Penn-sylvania. Canoeing and horseback riding are available nearby.

Host: Ellen O'Day
Rooms: 32 (PB) $109-200
Continental Breakfast
Credit Cards: A, B, C, D
Notes: 2, 3, 4, 5, 8, 9, 11, 13, 14, 15

Cook Homestead Bed & Breakfast

P.O. Box 106, 16217
(814) 744-8869; www.cookhomestead.com

Built in 1870, the original Andrew Cook family homestead overlooks the picturesque Clarion River, in the heart of Cook Forest State Park. Nostalgia fills the present-day bed and break-fast, whether it is from the parlor in front of the fireplace, the guest room filled with antiques, or a swing on the front porch, the scenery is spec-tacular in any season. A full country breakfast is served in the formal dining room. The large picture window frames an abundance of forest wildlife that is enjoyed by all. Lunch and dinner are available nearby. Children over 10 wel-come. Cross-country skiing nearby.

Hosts: Denny and Barbara Kocher
Rooms: 9 (4 PB; 5 SB) $75-85
Full Breakfast
Credit Cards: None
Notes: 2, 5, 7, 9, 11, 12, 13

Gateway Lodge

Route 36, Box 125, Cook Forest, 16217
(814) 744-8017 (phone/FAX)
e-mail: info@gatewaylodge.com

Gracious hospitality in an award-winning log cabin inn. Suites with fireside Jacuzzis, king-size beds, air conditioning, indoor pool and

Gateway Lodge

sauna. Cottages, rooms, restaurants, and tavern. Fully equipped 55-seat conference complex. Borders Pennsylvania Cook Forest State Park on Route 36. Open year-round. Color brochures, reservations, or gift certificates. Cross-country skiing nearby.

Hosts: Linda and Joe Burney
Rooms: 35 (30 PB; 5 SB) $85-185
Full Breakfast
Credit Cards: A, B, C, D
Notes: 2, 3, 4, 5, 7, 8, 9, 10, 12, 13, 14, 15

CRESCO

LaAnna Guest House

LaAnna Guest House

Rural Delivery 2, Box 1051, 18326
(570) 676-4225

Built in the 1870s, this Victorian home welcomes guests with large rooms that are furnished in Empire and Victorian antiques. In a quiet mountain village with waterfalls, mountain views, and outdoor activities.

Host: Kay Swingle
Rooms: 4 (SB) $25-40
Continental Breakfast
Credit Cards: None
Notes: 2, 5, 7, 8, 9, 10, 11, 12, 13

DOYLESTOWN

Sign of the Sorrel Horse: A Country Manor Hotel

4424 Old Easton Road, 18901
(215) 230-9999; FAX (215) 230-8053

Built in 1714 as a gristmill in the historic village of Dyerstown near New Hope in the heart of Bucks County, the old mill supplied flour to Washington's troops and provided lodging for Lafayette and his officers during the Revolution. Converted into one of the most gracious inns and awarded "Best Inn Dining of the Year" for 1993-94 by *Country Inns Bed and Breakfast* magazine, DiRoNA Award 1997-98, and Wine Spectator Award of Excellence. Gourmet dining in the Escoffier Room. Weddings are the specialty of this inn. Dining room is handicapped accessible. Closed two weeks in March.

Hosts: Monique Gaumont-Lanvin and Jon Atkin;
    Christian Gaumont-Lanvin
Rooms: 5 (PB) $85-175
Continental Breakfast
Credit Cards: A, B, C, E
Notes: 2, 4, 7, 8, 9, 10, 11, 12, 13

DUSHORE

Cherry Mills Lodge

Rural Route 4, Route 87 South, 18614
(570) 928-8978

This historic inn, circa 1865, is in the scenic Endless Mountains near two beautiful state parks, covered bridges, and many waterfalls. Furnished with antiques, the lodge welcomes guests year-round. Relax with reading, fishing at the creek, and taking country walks in the beautiful valley, once an 1800s logging village. There is mountain biking, hiking, nearby

Cherry Mills Lodge

7 No smoking; 8 Children welcome; 9 Social drinking allowed; 10 Tennis nearby; 11 Swimming nearby; 12 Golf nearby; 13 Skiing nearby; 14 May be booked through a travel agent; 15 Handicapped accessible.

cross-country skiing, tobogganing, hunting, swimming, canoeing, golf, and antiquing. Visit the Victorian town of Eagles Mere.

Hosts: Florence and Julio
Rooms: 8 (1 PB; 7 SB) $55-75
Full Breakfast
Credit Cards: None
Notes: 2, 5, 9, 11, 13

EAGLES MERE

Crestmont Inn

Crestmont Drive, P.O. Box 371, 17731
(570) 525-3519; (800) 522-8767
e-mail: crestmnt@epix.net; www.crestmont-inn.com

Crestmont Inn is a hidden treasure nestled in the Endless Mountains in "the town that time forgot, Eagles Mere, PA." The inn sits on a hilltop, surrounded by state parks, breathtaking vistas, and one of nature's wonders, Eagles Mere Lake. Award-winning cuisine, gracious hospitality, and beautifully decorated rooms await guests. Four seasons of outdoor activities abound at Crestmont, making this inn guests, personal retreat of romance and nature at its very best. AAA three-diamond-rated.

Host: Karen Oliver and Doug Rider
Rooms: 15 (PB) $99-168
Full Breakfast
Credit Cards: A, B
Notes: 2, 4, 5, 8, 9, 10, 11, 12, 13, 14, 15

Shady Lane Bed & Breakfast

314 Allegheny Avenue, P.O. Box 314, 17731
(570) 525-3394; (800) 524-1248
www.pavisnet.com/sullivanbandb

Searching for a place a little out of the ordinary for the next getaway? So pack the bags, and join the hosts at Shady Lane Bed and Breakfast, Eagles Mere's most cozy, comfortable mountaintop bed and breakfast, where guests will feel right at home the moment they walk in. The charming seven-bedroom inn has a mesmerizing view of the Endless Mountains. Shady Lane has developed a loyal clientele

who visit numerous times throughout the year to enjoy the changes that come with each season and the comfortable atmosphere that has made Shady Lane their favorite home away from home. "We invite you to come visit and return often."

Hosts: Pat and Dennis Dougherty
Rooms: 7 (PB) $85
Full Breakfast
Credit Cards: None
Notes: 5, 7, 9, 10, 11, 12, 13, 14

EAST BERLIN

Bechtel Victorian Mansion Inn

400 West King Street, 17316
(717) 259-7760; (800) 331-1108
www.bbonline.com/pa/bechtel/rooms.html
www.gettysburg.com/gcvb/betchel.htm

Visit the charm of yesteryear in this gracious Victorian bed and breakfast in the historic district of East Berlin. All rooms are furnished with antiques and feature original brass chandeliers, wraparound porch with antique wicker. Look for the doll and Boyd's Bears collection throughout the inn. Afternoon tea and refreshments are served. Just a short drive from York and Lancaster, Hershey Park and Gettysburg, antique shopping, golf, fishing, and restaurants.

Hosts: Carol and Richard Carlson
Rooms: 9 (PB) $85-150
Full Breakfast
Credit Cards: A, B, C, D
Notes: 2, 5, 7, 11, 12, 13, 14

Bechtel Victorian Mansion Inn

ELIZABETHTOWN

West Ridge Guest House

1285 West Ridge Road, 17022
(717) 367-7783; (877) 367-7783

Country estate setting midway between Harrisburg and Lancaster. Nine guest rooms, four in main house, five in guest house that offers complete privacy. Some with fireplaces, Jacuzzis, decks; all rooms have telephones, TVs, VCRs (movie library available), private baths. Local attractions—Hershey Park, Lancaster Amish, outlet shopping, Gettysburg. Four-star rated by American Bed and Breakfast Association.

Host: Alice P. Heisey
Rooms: 9 (PB) $60-110
Full Breakfast
Credit Cards: A, B, C, D, E
Notes: 2, 5, 7, 10, 12, 14, 15

ELIZABETHVILLE

Inn at Elizabethville

30 West Main Street, 17023
(717) 362-3476

In the heart of south central Pennsylvania, the inn serves business and leisure travelers. Built in 1883, restored and furnished in Mission oak, antiques, and Stickley furniture, the inn offers seven rooms, each air conditioned with private bath, and indoor/outdoor (porch, patio, yard) dining and relaxing year-round. Convenient to

Inn at Elizabethville

Harrisburg, Routes I-81 and I-83, and superb biking, hiking, fishing, hunting, golf, country fairs and auctions; travelers can use the conference room, fax, telephone, and copy services.

Owner: Jim Facinelli
Innkeepers: Jeff Lentz and Amy Welker
Rooms: 7 (PB) $54-64
Continental Breakfast
Credit Cards: A, B, C, F
Notes: 2, 5, 7, 9, 10, 11, 12, 14, 15

ELVERSON

Association of Bed & Breakfasts in Philadelphia, Valley Forge, Brandywine

P.O. Box 562, Valley Forge, 19481-0562
(610) 783-7838; (800) 344-0123
FAX (610) 783-7783
e-mail: pa@bnbassociation.com

1310. Welcome to this 18th-century farmhouse and barn that was built with mortise and tenon (no nails used here!). The farmhouse has two guest rooms (with two entrances from hall and winding steps from dining room) and a guest cottage which is next to the farmhouse. The entire house and cottage are air conditioned. A bountiful breakfast is served. German is spoken. $85-100.

EPHRATA

Clearview Farm Bed & Breakfast

355 Clearview Road, 17522
(717) 733-6333
www.800padutch.com/clearvw.html

A beautiful limestone farmhouse built in 1814, beautifully restored and lovingly decorated. It is surrounded by a well-kept lawn overlooking a pond with a pair of swans on 200 acres of peaceful farmland. A touch of elegance in a country setting. Featured in

7 No smoking; 8 Children welcome; 9 Social drinking allowed; 10 Tennis nearby; 11 Swimming nearby; 12 Golf nearby; 13 Skiing nearby; 14 May be booked through a travel agent; 15 Handicapped accessible.

Clearview Farm

Country Decorating Ideas and *Country Inns* magazines. AAA four-diamond-rated.

Hosts: Glenn and Mildred Wissler
Rooms: 5 (PB) $95-145
Full Breakfast
Credit Cards: A, B, D
Notes: 2, 5, 7, 9, 10, 11, 12

The Historic Smithton Inn

The Historic Smithton Inn

900 West Main Street, 17522
(717) 733-6094

An American pre-Revolutionary inn open for 235 years, fully restored, with all the amenities, such as whirlpool tubs. In Lancaster County, home of the Pennsylvania Dutch, the Amish, and the Mennonites, who continue to farm with horses. The inn is a classic stone structure, with working fireplaces in every room, also canopied beds, upholstered chairs, quilts, candles, down pillows, night shirts,

flowers, chamber music, and feather beds. Sitting room, library, and Smithton Dahlia Gardens, all open to guests. Inquire about accommodations for pets and children.

Host: Dorothy Graybill
Rooms: 8 (PB) $75-155
Full Breakfast
Credit Cards: A, B, C
Notes: 2, 5, 6, 7, 8, 9, 10, 11, 12

The Inns at Doneckers

318-324 North State Street, 17522
(717) 738-9502; FAX (717) 738-9552
www.doneckers.com

Early American inns in the heart of Pennsylvania Dutch Country, historic Lancaster County. Stay in one of the elegantly-appointed rooms or suites with fireplace and Jacuzzi and enjoy the Doneckers Community: fine dining at the

The Inns at Doneckers

NOTES: Credit cards accepted: A MasterCard; B Visa; C American Express; D Discover; E Diner's Club; F Other; 2 Personal checks accepted; 3 Lunch available; 4 Dinner available; 5 Open all year; 6 Pets welcome;

French/American Restaurant; local artists' studios at the Artworks; distinctive styles for women, men, children, and the home in the upscale fashion store; and nearby antique/collectible markets. Anniversary, birthday, and corporate getaway packages.

Host: H. William Donecker
Rooms: 40 (38 PB; 2 SB) $69-210
Continental Breakfast
Credit Cards: A, B, C, D, E, F
Notes: 2, 5, 7, 8

ERIE

Grape Arbor Inn Bed & Breakfast

51 and 55 East Main Street, North East, 16428
(814) 725-5522; FAX (814) 725-8471
www.grapearborinn.com

Two restored brick mansions, circa 1830, just east of Erie in the historic village of North East. These beautifully decorated homes now serve as a luxurious bed and breakfast in the heart of Pennsylvania wine country with local wineries offering daily tours and tasting. Enjoy a variety of activities including antiquing, biking, skiing, shopping, or visits to nearby Chautauqua Institution, Presque Isle State Park, and Peek 'n' Peak Ski Resort. All suites are spacious and have private bathrooms, air conditioning, telephones, TVs, and antique furnishings. Full breakfast. Children over 10 welcome. Corporate and long-term rates available.

Innkeepers: Robert and Kathleen Mazza; Donald
    and Susan Moore
Manager: Lori Snyder
Rooms: 8 (PB) $100-160
Full Breakfast
Credit Cards: A, B, C, D
Notes: 2, 5, 7, 10, 11, 12, 13, 14

Spencer House Bed & Breakfast

519 West Sixth Street, 16507
(814) 454-5984; (800) 890-7263

FAX (814) 456-5091; e-mail: spencer@erie.net
www.erie.net/~spencer

A unique Victorian mansion in the heart of Erie with 12-foot ceilings and a large front porch. Drive or bike to Presque Isle. Near regional wineries, malls, and fine restaurants. Each of the five rooms has its own individual ambiance and charm; all rooms have private baths, cable TVs, telephones, and air conditioning; some have fireplaces and canopied beds. A full delicious breakfast is served.

Hosts: Pat and Keith Hagenbuch
Rooms: 5 (PB) $85-120
Full Breakfast
Credit Cards: A, B, C, D
Notes: 2, 5, 7, 8, 9, 10, 11, 12, 13, 14

ERWINNA (BUCKS COUNTY)

EverMay-on-the-Delaware

River Road, P.O. Box 60, 18920
(610) 294-9100; FAX (610) 294-8249
e-mail: moffly@evermay.com; www.evermay.com

Lodging is available in manor house, carriage house, cottage, and barn. Liquor license. Parlor with fireplace. A significant, distinguished country retreat on 25 acres of gardens, woodland paths, and pastures between the Delaware River and canal. Dinner served Friday, Saturday, Sunday, and holidays. Minimum stay weekends: two nights. Closed Christmas Eve and Christmas Day.

Hosts: William T. and Danielle Moffly
Rooms: 18 (PB) $110-190
Continental Breakfast

EverMay-on-the-Delaware

Credit Cards: A, B
Notes: 2, 7, 9, 10, 11, 12, 14

FRANKLIN

Quo Vadis

Quo Vadis Bed & Breakfast

1501 Liberty Street, 16323
(814) 432-4208; (800) 360-6598

Quo Vadis is an 1867 Queen Anne with terra cotta tile in a national register historic district. Relive Victorian elegance in a home with heirloom furniture. Breakfast in a splendid mahogany dining room. Enjoy theater, unique museums, oil-heritage-region history. Shop antiques or 130 factory outlets mall. Bicycle trails; fun ride the train. Golf, hike, hunt in the hills. Fish or canoe in the river valleys. Discover northwestern Pennsylvania near crossing of I-79 and I-80.

Hosts: Rachel and Allen
Rooms: 6 (PB) $60-80
Full Breakfast
Credit Cards: A, B, C
Notes: 2, 5, 7, 8, 12, 14

GETTYSBURG

Amanda's Bed & Breakfast Reservation Service

3538 Lakeway Drive, Ellicott City, MD 21042-1226
(443) 535-0008; (800) 899-7533
FAX (443) 535-0009; e-mail: AmandasRS@aol.com
www.Amandas-BBRS.com

125. On Oak Ridge, this restored Colonial offers a splendid view of the town. Enjoy the charm of a bygone era with the comforts of home-cooked breakfasts, cozy quilts, and country antiques. Rooms are decorated with Civil War accents. Nine rooms have private and shared baths. $84-104.

142. Nestled in Gettysburg's downtown historic district, this bed and breakfast offers the comforts of today's living in a style reminiscent of the turn of the century. Guests of the inn can walk to restaurants, attractions, gift and antique shops, and the Gettysburg National Park. Seven rooms and a suite. Two-night minimum on special weekends. Full breakfast. $90-140.

345. A quiet, off-the-beaten-path, woodsy setting. The oldest part of the house served as a field hospital during the Civil War. New additions enhance the former residence. Each room has a private bath. Several new rooms with fireplaces. Small conference facilities available. Full country breakfast. $97-112.

Baladerry Inn at Gettysburg

40 Hospital Road, 17325
(717) 337-1342
e-mail: baladerry@mail.wideopen.net
www.baladerryinn.com

Quiet and private at the edge of the battlefield, this circa 1812 brick Federal home served as a hospital during the Civil War. There are four guest rooms in the main house and a large two-storied great room which serves as both a dining and gathering area. A brick terrace

Baladerry Inn

NOTES: Credit cards accepted: A MasterCard; B Visa; C American Express; D Discover; E Diner's Club; F Other; 2 Personal checks accepted; 3 Lunch available; 4 Dinner available; 5 Open all year; 6 Pets welcome;

provides for outdoor socializing, while a gazebo affords a place of tranquility. The Carriage House has four guest rooms with fireplaces or private patios and a common area featuring a fireplace, sunroom, and brick patio. Private and spacious, this bucolic setting is an ideal choice for small business meetings or reunions. AAA-rated three diamonds, Mobil-rated three stars. Fax available, but call first.

Hosts: Tom and Caryl O'Gara
Rooms: 8 (PB) $94-125
Full Breakfast
Credit Cards: A, B, C, D, E
Notes: 2, 5, 7, 9, 10, 12, 13, 14

Beechmont Inn

Battlefield Bed & Breakfast Inn of Gettysburg, Pennsylvania

2264 Emmitsburg Road, 17325
(717) 334-8804; (888) 766-3897
FAX (717) 334-7330
e-mail: battlefieldinn@hotmail.com
www.gettysburgbattlefield.com

Sleep in an original Civil War home on 46 acres of the Gettysburg Battlefield. Enjoy daily hands-on history programs with muskets, uniforms, artillery, or cavalry demonstrations. Guest carriage rides (April through November, weather permitting) and full breakfast served by costumed staff included in the stay. Eight guest rooms in quiet country setting five minutes from visitors center and historic downtown Gettysburg.

Hosts: Charlie and Florence Tarbox
Rooms: 8 (PB) $129-199
Full Breakfast
Credit Cards: A, B, C, D, E
Notes: 2, 5, 7, 8, 9, 11, 12, 13, 14

Beechmont Inn

315 Broadway, Hanover, 17331
(717) 632-3013; (800) 553-7009
www.virtualcities.com

An elegant 1834 Federal-period inn with seven guest rooms, private baths, fireplaces,

air conditioning, afternoon refreshments, and gourmet breakfast. One large suite has a private whirlpool tub, canopied bed, and fireplace. Gettysburg battlefield, Lake Marburg, golf, and great antiquing nearby. Convenient location for visits to Hershey, York, or Lancaster. Weekend packages and romantic honeymoon or anniversary packages offered. Picnic baskets available. Great area for biking and hiking. AAA- and Mobil-approved. Children over 13 welcome.

Hosts: Susan and William Day
Rooms: 7 (PB) $80-135
Full Breakfast
Credit Cards: A, B, C, D
Notes: 2, 5, 7, 9, 10, 11, 12, 13, 14

The Brafferton Inn

44 York Street, 17325
(717) 337-3423

Enjoy the grace and charm of the oldest house in historic downtown Gettysburg. This 1786 fieldstone home, recently updated, is listed in the National Register of Historic Places. Antiques and stenciling throughout. Featured in the February 1988 issue of *Country Living* magazine. Children over seven welcome.

Hosts: Bill and Maggie Ward
Rooms: 10 (PB) $90-120
Suites: 2 (PB) $115-150
Full Breakfast

7 No smoking; 8 Children welcome; 9 Social drinking allowed; 10 Tennis nearby; 11 Swimming nearby; 12 Golf nearby; 13 Skiing nearby; 14 May be booked through a travel agent; 15 Handicapped accessible.

Brafferton Inn

Credit Cards: A, B, C, D
Notes: 2, 5, 7, 9, 10, 11, 12, 13, 14

Country Escape

275 Old Route 30, P.O. Box 195, McKnightstown,
  17343-0195
(717) 338-0611; (800) 484-3244 CODE 4371
FAX (717) 334-5227; e-mail: merry@innernet.net

Country Escape is a small bed and breakfast
with a laid-back atmosphere in a country setting, just outside of Gettysburg and near the
battlefields. The hosts offer a hot tub under the
stars, a craft shop, cable TV, and video tapes.
Children and families are welcome. A two-
room suite which can accommodate two to
four people is also available.

Hosts: Merry V. Bush and Ross Hetrick
Rooms: 3 (1 PB; 2 SB) $65-80
Suite: $125
Full Breakfast
Credit Cards: A, B, C, D
Notes: 2, 5, 7, 8, 9, 11, 12, 13, 14

Hickory Bridge Farm

96 Hickory Bridge Road, 17353
(717) 642-5261; FAX (717) 642-6491
e-mail: hickory@innbook.com
www.hickorybridgefarm.com

A quiet country setting 12 miles west of Gettysburg. Cottages and rooms in a late 1700s era
farmhouse. Private baths, fireplaces, and
whirlpools. Family-style dinner is served in a
restored 150-year-old barn on Fridays, Saturdays, and Sundays. Many antiques. A truly
unique place. Reservations advised.

Rooms: 9 (PB) $85-150
Full Breakfast
Credit Cards: A, B, D
Notes: 2, 4, 5, 7, 11, 12, 13, 14

Keystone Inn

231 Hanover Street, 17325
(717) 337-3888

Keystone Inn is a large late-Victorian brick
house filled with lots of natural woodwork.
The guest rooms are bright, cheerful, and air
conditioned. The soft pastels and ruffles give
guests a warm welcome. Each room has a
reading nook and writing desk. A suite with
private bath, TV, microwave, and refrigerator
sleeps four. Relax with a book in Aunt
Weasie's Library. Choose a breakfast from the
full menu.

Hosts: Wilmer and Doris Martin
Rooms: 5 (PB) $69-89
Suite: 1(PB) $100
Full Breakfast
Credit Cards: A, B, D
Notes: 2, 5, 7, 8, 10, 11, 12, 13

Keystone Inn

NOTES: Credit cards accepted: A MasterCard; B Visa; C American Express; D Discover; E Diner's Club;
F Other; 2 Personal checks accepted; 3 Lunch available; 4 Dinner available; 5 Open all year; 6 Pets welcome;

The Old Appleford Inn

218 Carlisle Street, 17325
(717) 337-1711; (800) APLEFRD (275-3373)
e-mail: jwiley@cvn.net
www.virtualcities.com/ons/pa/g/pag6602.htm

This elegant 1867 Victorian mansion, Gettysburg's first bed and breakfast inn, offers its guests warm hospitality in an elegant and historic setting. The inn surrounds guests with period antiques, classical music, and collections of antique glass, musical instruments, and needlework samplers. Cozy fireplaces, canopied beds, and sumptuous breakfasts complete a memorable visit to the heart of Gettysburg. Restaurants, shopping, antiquing, and attractions within walking distance. All rooms with private baths and air conditioning. AAA-rated three diamonds.

Hosts: John and Jane Wiley
Rooms: 10 (PB) $80-120
Full Breakfast
Credit Cards: A, B, C, D
Notes: 2, 5, 7, 8, 9, 10, 11, 12, 13, 14

The Tannery Bed & Breakfast

449 Baltimore Street, 17325
(717) 334-2454; e-mail: tannery@cvn.net

The Tannery is a large Gothic Victorian home built in 1868 and is in the heart of Gettysburg. The inn contains seven guest rooms and three suites, all with private baths, and is within easy walking distance to most of Gettysburg's attractions, restaurants, and shops. Original house owner, John Rupp, occupied a steam tannery on the rear of the property at the time of the battle.

Hosts: Jan and George Newton
Rooms: 10 (PB) $79-135
Continental Breakfast
Credit Cards: A, B
Notes: 2, 5, 7, 8, 9, 10, 11, 12, 13

GETTYSBURG BATTLEFIELD

The Doubleday Inn

104 Doubleday Avenue, 17325
(717) 334-9119

Directly on the Gettysburg battlefield, this Colonial inn is beautifully restored with Civil War accents, comfortable antiques, and central air conditioning. Enjoy daily afternoon tea and a delicious candlelit country breakfast in the morning. Roam the lovely grounds and enjoy the splendid views. The inn overlooks historic Gettysburg and the National Military Park. On selected evenings, participate in a discussion with a Civil War historian who brings the battle to life with fascinating stories and accurate accounts. Children over eight are welcome.

Hosts: Charles and Ruth Anne Wilcox
Rooms: 9 (5 PB; 4 SB) $89-109
Full Breakfast
Credit Cards: A, B, D
Notes: 2, 5, 7, 9, 10, 11, 12, 13, 14

The Doubleday Inn

GREENSBURG

Huntland Farm Bed & Breakfast

Rural Delivery 9, Box 21, 15601
(724) 834-8483; FAX (724) 838-8253

The 100-acre Huntland Farm is three miles northeast of Greensburg, a convenient halfway

7 No smoking; 8 Children welcome; 9 Social drinking allowed; 10 Tennis nearby; 11 Swimming nearby; 12 Golf nearby; 13 Skiing nearby; 14 May be booked through a travel agent; 15 Handicapped accessible.

stop between the East Coast and the Midwest. From Pennsylvania Turnpike, exit at New Stanton (east) or Monroeville (west). Circa 1848 house in scenic, historical Laurel Highlands of western Pennsylvania. Four corner bedrooms, two shared baths. Living areas furnished with antiques. Good restaurants and antique shops nearby. Full country breakfast. No smoking indoors. Children over 12 welcome.

Hosts: Robert and Elizabeth Weidlein
Rooms: 4 (4 SB) $85
Full Breakfast
Credit Cards: C
Notes: 2, 5, 7, 9, 12

GROVE CITY

Snow Goose Inn

112 East Main Street, 16127
(724) 458-4644; (800) 317-4644
FAX (724) 458-1686
www.bbonline.com/pa/snowgoose/

Grove City's original bed and breakfast. A former doctor's home, circa 1895. The inn offers four comfortable, air-conditioned guest rooms furnished with antiques and touches of country. Original oak woodwork and fireplace add to the inn's charm. Delicious home-cooked breakfasts are served each morning.

Hosts: Orvil and Dorothy McMillen
Rooms: 4 (PB) $65
Full Breakfast
Credit Cards: A, B, C
Notes: 2, 5, 7, 8, 9, 10, 11, 12, 13, 14

HAWLEY

Academy Street Bed & Breakfast

528 Academy Street, 18428
(570) 226-3430; (609) 395-8590 (winter)
www.academybb.com

Outstanding historic 1863 Italianate Victorian built by a Civil War hero, the first sheriff of Wayne County. Near the largest and most beautiful recreational lake in the state, with all

Academy Street

activities. Convenient to I-84. Lovely furnished inn; full gourmet breakfast and afternoon tea. Air-conditioned rooms. Cable TV. Open May through October. The first and original bed and breakfast in the area.

Host: Judith Lazan
Rooms: 7 (3 PB; 4 SB) $68-90
Full Breakfast
Credit Cards: A, B
Notes: 7, 9, 10, 11, 12, 14

The Settlers Inn at Bingham Park

4 Main Avenue, 18428
(570) 226-2993; (800) 833-8527
FAX (570) 226-1874; e-mail: settler@ptd.net

A fine example of English Arts and Crafts design, this Tudor manor surrounded by herb and flower gardens lends the visitor a sense of peace and serenity. Eighteen guest rooms are decorated with flowered wallpaper, wicker, and comfortable antique furnishings. The inn's tradition of fine dining is highlighted by the artisan bakery and menus influenced by the seasons. Experience the sense of comfort given by the blend of nature, gardens, art, fine food, and personal service.

NOTES: Credit cards accepted: A MasterCard; B Visa; C American Express; D Discover; E Diner's Club; F Other; 2 Personal checks accepted; 3 Lunch available; 4 Dinner available; 5 Open all year; 6 Pets welcome;

Hosts: Grant and Jeanne Genzlinger
Rooms: 18 (PB) $94-155
Full Breakfast
Credit Cards: A, B, C, D
Notes: 3, 4, 5, 7, 8, 9, 10, 11, 12, 13, 14

HERSHEY

Nancy's Guest House

235 Hershey Road, Hummelstown, 17036
(717) 566-9844; e-mail: marnan@paonline.com

Two miles from Hershey Park. Private second-floor entrance to this one-unit furnished apartment. Has two bedrooms, living room, kitchen, and bath with laundry. Color TV, VCR, and air conditioned. Sleeps four. Inquire about personal check acceptance. A 10 percent discount for five nights or more. Three and one-half miles from I-81 on Route 39. Breakfast is not included in rates.

Hosts: Marlin and Nancy Geesaman
Unit: 1 (PB) $65-85
Credit Cards: None
Notes: 7, 8, 10, 11, 12, 13

Pinehurst Inn Bed & Breakfast

50 Northeast Drive, 17033
(717) 533-2603

Spacious brick home surrounded by lawns. Warm, welcoming, many-windowed living room. Large porch with an old-fashioned porch swing. Within walking distance of all Hershey's attractions: Hershey Museum and rose gardens, Hersheypark, Chocolate World, fitness/nature trail, and many golf courses. Less than one hour's drive to Lancaster and Gettysburg. Each room has a queen-size bed with a Hershey Kiss on each pillow. Continental plus breakfast.

Hosts: Roger and Phyllis Ingold
Rooms: 15 (2 PB; 13 SB) $52-85
Continental Breakfast
Credit Cards: A, B
Notes: 2, 5, 7, 8, 9, 10, 11, 12, 14, 15

HOWARD

Rest & Repast Bed & Breakfast Reservations

Box 126, Pine Grove Mills, 16868
(814) 238-1484; (814) 861-6566
FAX (814) 234-9890
www.iul.com/bnbinpa

Friendly tradition in little village of Howard. A modern but antique-filled home. Close to Bald Eagle State Park and marina, near I-80 exits 23 or 24. Two rooms with shared bath. $70.

JIM THORPE

The Harry Packer Mansion

Packer Hill, P.O. Box 458, 18229
(570) 325-8566

This 1874 Second Empire mansion features original appointments and Victorian decor. Completely restored for bed and breakfast, fabulous mystery weekends, and a host of other activities. The adjoining carriage house is decorated in a hunt motif. Guest rooms are elegant but comfortable and feature period antiques. AAA-rated four diamonds. Rates are higher during mystery and ball weekends.

Hosts: Bob and Patricia Handwerk
Rooms: 13 (11 PB; 2 SB) $85-175

The Harry Packer Mansion

---

7 No smoking; 8 Children welcome; 9 Social drinking allowed; 10 Tennis nearby; 11 Swimming nearby; 12 Golf nearby; 13 Skiing nearby; 14 May be booked through a travel agent; 15 Handicapped accessible.

Full Breakfast
Credit Cards: A, B
Notes: 2, 5, 7, 9, 10, 11, 12, 13

The Inn at Jim Thorpe

24 Broadway, 18229
(800) 329-2599; FAX (570) 325-9145
e-mail: innjt@ptd.net; www.innjt.com

The Inn sits in the center of
the historic district of
this quaint little vil-
lage. The rooms com-
bine the splendor of
the Victorian age with
21st-century comforts.
The suites are com-
plete with fireplaces and
whirlpools. Also on-site is
a Victorian dining room and
authentic Irish pub. While in town, take in the
many historic sites including tours of the Asa
Packer Mansion and the Old Jail, or go mountain biking, hiking, or white-water rafting.
Smoking permitted in designated areas only.

Rooms: 37 (PB) $65-250
Continental Breakfast
Credit Cards: A, B, C, D, E
Notes: 2, 3, 4, 5, 8, 11, 12, 13, 14, 15

Victoria Ann's Bed & Breakfast

68 Broadway, 18229
(570) 325-8107 (phone/FAX)
www.thevictoriann.com

The house, built in 1860 by millionaire Nathan
Cortright, is in the heart of the county seat historic district. Guests step back in time with all
the delightful charm of the furnishings,
antiques, lace, and chandeliers that date back to
the days when "Old Mauch Chunk" (Jim
Thorpe's predecessor) was young. Outside,
there are beautiful Victorian porches and garden terraces. Children eight and older welcome. Restaurant on premises—Sequoyah
House, a vegetarian's delight.

Host: Louise Ogilvie
Rooms: 8 (3 PB; 5 SB) $55-85
Suites: $125-170
Full Breakfast
Credit Cards: A, B, C, D
Notes: 3, 4, 5, 7, 9, 10, 11, 12, 13, 14

KENNETT SQUARE

Association of Bed & Breakfasts in Philadelphia, Valley Forge, Brandywine

P.O. Box 562, Valley Forge, 19481-0562
(610) 783-7838; (800) 344-0123
FAX (610) 783-7783
e-mail: pa@bnbassociation.com

0302. This circa 1704 Chester County, solid
fieldstone farmhouse sits on 20 acres of rolling
farmland. Special amenities include pool, hot
tub, and three rooms with a fireplace. Six
guest rooms with private baths. Full breakfast.
Small conference meetings and rental of entire
house welcome. Guest cottage also available.
$125-200.

Bed & Breakfast at Walnut Hill

541 Chandler's Mill Road, Avondale, 19311
(610) 444-3703; e-mail: millsjt@magpage.com

This 1840 antique-filled mill house with warm
country charm is on a crooked country road
facing a horse-filled meadow and stream. Walnut Hill is only minutes from Longwood Gar-

Walnut Hill

dens, Winterthur, and the Brandywine River Museum. The hosts enjoy discussing local lore, mapping out tours and points of interest, and making reservations. A gourmet country breakfast will start guests on their way. Guests may enjoy the hot tub for relaxing moments. Canoeing, horseback riding, and antique shops nearby. Guests say they came as strangers, left as friends.

Hosts: Tom and Sandy Mills
Rooms: 2 (SB) $85-95
Full Breakfast
Credit Cards: None
Notes: 2, 5, 7, 8, 9, 10, 11, 12, 14

Meadow Spring Farm

Meadow Spring Farm

201 East Street Road (Route 926), 19348
(610) 444-3903

The hosts of this 1836 farmhouse on a working farm with animals invite guests to participate in gathering eggs for breakfast. The house is filled with family antiques, Amish quilts, fine linens. The hosts will prepare a gourmet breakfast for guests before they start their day touring the area. Enjoy the pool, hot tub, game room, and solarium. This bed and breakfast has been featured in *Country Inns*, the *New York Times*, and on Washington's Channel 7 TV. In the heart of Brandywine Valley, minutes from Longwood Gardens, Brandywine River Museum, and Winterthur. Afternoon tea is offered. Packed lunch available. Smoking permitted in designated areas only. Carriage rides through the country available.

Host: Anne Hicks
Rooms: 7 (4 PB; 3 SB) $75-85
Full Breakfast
Credit Cards: None
Notes: 2, 8, 9, 10, 11, 12, 14, 15

Scarlett House Bed & Breakfast

503 West State Street, 19348
(610) 444-9592; (800) 820-9592
e-mail: janes10575@aol.com
www.traveloata.com/inns/data/scarlett.html

Elegant and spacious four-square American Victorian in a national historic district. Minutes from Longwood Gardens, Winterthur, Brandywine Museum, and other Brandywine Valley attractions. Gracious antique-filled rooms, sumptuous gourmet breakfasts, complimentary refreshments, special gifts for special occasions. Central to recreational activities, Amish, Philadelphia, Wilmington, and outlets. Enjoy life at a slower pace. Walking tour through historic Kennet, antique shops, restaurants. Wraparound porch for relaxing. Fireplaces, central air. Three-diamond rating from AAA, Mobil Travel Guide.

Hosts: Jane and Sam Snyder
Rooms: 4 (2 PB; 2 SB) $85-135
Full Breakfast
Credit Cards: A, B, C, D
Notes: 2, 5, 7, 9, 10, 11, 12, 14

KINTNERSVILLE

The Bucksville House

Route 412 and Buck Drive
4501 Durham Road, 18930-1610
(610) 847-8948
www.bbgetaways.com/bucksvillehouse

Country charm and a friendly atmosphere await guests at this 1795 Bucks County registered historic landmark. Offering beautifully decorated rooms with many quilts, original art, baskets, queen-size beds, private baths, antiques, and handmade reproductions. Enjoy the seven fireplaces, air conditioning, gazebo, pond, herb garden, and brick courtyard. Near

7 No smoking; 8 Children welcome; 9 Social drinking allowed; 10 Tennis nearby; 11 Swimming nearby; 12 Golf nearby; 13 Skiing nearby; 14 May be booked through a travel agent; 15 Handicapped accessible.

The Bucksville House

New Hope, Peddler's Village, and Nockamixon State Park.

Hosts: Barbara and Joe Szollosi
Rooms: 5 (PB) $100-130
Full Breakfast
Credit Cards: A, B, C, D
Notes: 2, 5, 7, 9, 10, 11, 12, 15

Lightfarm Bed & Breakfast

2042 Berger Road, 18930
(877) 847-3276; FAX (610) 847-8068
e-mail: litefarm@epix.net; www.lightfarm.com

Nestled on a quiet country road between historic Bethlehem and New Hope sits a historic Bucks County plantation, 1738, and stone farmhouse, circa 1811. Sleep comfortably under canopied beds in immaculate period rooms complete with fireplaces, air conditioning, cable, and private baths. Ninety-two breathtaking acres filled with

Lightfarm

sheep, flowers, hills, and creeks. Licensed archeological dig on the original log cabin site (featured in *Early American Life*, October 92). Close to Delaware River country, antiques, biking, historic sites, and Nockamixon State Park. Elite, moderate, and family dining nearby. Children over five welcome.

Hosts: Max and Carol Sempowski
Rooms: 5 (PB) $79-150
Full Breakfast
Credit Cards: A, B, C, D
Notes: 2, 5, 6, 7, 9, 10, 11, 12, 13, 14

KINZERS

Sycamore Haven Farm

35 South Kinzer Road, 17535
(717) 442-4901

This dairy farm is 15 miles east of Lancaster, right in Pennsylvania Dutch country. The rooms are quiet and roomy with a porch in the back of the house with a lovely swing. There is also a balcony with lounge chairs. Forty dairy cows are milked morning and evening. The children will really enjoy the numerous kittens, who like a lot of attention, and the lawn, perfect for play.

Hosts: Charles and Janet Groff
Rooms: 3 (SB) $35
Continental Breakfast
Credit Cards: None
Notes: 2, 5, 6, 7, 8, 10, 11, 12

LACKAWAXEN

Roebling Inn on the Delaware

Scenic Drive, P.O. Box 31, 18435
(570) 685-7900
www.poconos.org/members/roeblinginn

In historic upper Delaware River region, two hours from New York City and two and one-half hours from Philadelphia, the Roebling Inn offers graceful, private living in a classic riverfront gem. In a setting of striking rustic beauty, the area is rich in historical significance, sight-

---

NOTES: Credit cards accepted: A MasterCard; B Visa; C American Express; D Discover; E Diner's Club; F Other; 2 Personal checks accepted; 3 Lunch available; 4 Dinner available; 5 Open all year; 6 Pets welcome;

Roebling Inn on the Delaware

seeing, and activities. Bald eagle viewing in winter, too! All guest rooms are tastefully appointed with private bath, TV, air conditioning, some with fireplaces, and include a sumptuous breakfast. Mobil three-star-rated.

Hosts: Donald and Jo Ann Jahn
Rooms: 5 (PB) $65-120
Full Breakfast
Credit Cards: A, B, C, D
Notes: 2, 5, 9, 10, 11, 12, 13, 14

LAHASKA

The Inn at Lahaska

5775 Route 202, P.O. Box 500, 18931
(215) 794-0440; FAX (215) 794-9063

A country bed and breakfast in the heart of Bucks County. Six comfortable guest rooms include private baths, down comforters, and in-room coffee makers. Buckinham Mountain Restaurant is behind the inn and features its own microbrewery. A short walk to antiques, Peddlars Village, and outlets. Five miles from New Hope.

Host: Heather Craniey
Rooms: 6 (PB) $75-125
Continental Breakfast
Credit Cards: A, B, C
Notes: 2, 3, 4, 5, 7, 9, 10, 11, 12, 14

LANCASTER

Association of Bed & Breakfasts in Philadelphia, Valley Forge, Brandywine

P.O. Box 562, Valley Forge, 19481-0562
(610) 783-7838; (800) 344-0123
FAX (610) 783-7783
e-mail: pa@bnbassociation.com

0304. This restored 1845 country home, which was once a stop on the Underground Railroad, is in the rolling hills of Pennsylvania Dutch country. Five guest rooms, each with a private bath, TV, and air conditioning. Full country breakfast with homemade breads, farm-fresh butter, honey and locally produced fruit jams. Two-night minimum stay on weekends. $95-125.

1001. This 1905 stucco manor house has five guest rooms, with three private and two shared baths, all with color cable TV and air conditioning. Afternoon tea and evening sherry are available. Gourmet breakfasts. $90-115.

1909. A reproduction of an Amish farmhouse, built in 1980, is in the heart of the Pennsylvania Dutch country. Full breakfast. Five guest rooms, each with a private bath and TV, some are handicapped accessible. Central air conditioned. Guests share the home with a resident child and golden retriever. $75.

The Australian Walkabout Inn

837 Village Road, Lampeter, 17537
(717) 464-0707
www.bbonline.com/pa/walkabout/index.html

The Walkabout Inn is an authentic Australian-style bed and breakfast in the heart of Amish country, convenient to all major attractions. The house is a brick 1925 Mennonite farmhouse with wraparound porches. The grounds feature a fountain, wildflower gardens, and goldfish pond. A full candlelight breakfast is served each morning. Guest rooms

7 No smoking; 8 Children welcome; 9 Social drinking allowed; 10 Tennis nearby; 11 Swimming nearby; 12 Golf nearby; 13 Skiing nearby; 14 May be booked through a travel agent; 15 Handicapped accessible.

have private baths, canopied and/or queen-size beds, antiques, cable TVs, fireplaces, whirlpools, and hot tubs. Anniversary/honeymoon suite and fantasy cottage. Smoking outside only. Amish and Victorian dinners arranged. AAA three-diamond-rated.

Hosts: Richard and Margaret Mason
Rooms: 4 (PB) $99-159
Suites: 3 (PB) $139-199
Full Breakfast
Credit Cards: A, B, C
Notes: 2, 4, 5, 7, 9, 10, 11, 12, 14

A Bed & Breakfast Connection/ Bed & Breakfast of Philadelphia

P.O. Box 21, Devon, 19333
(610) 687-3565; (800) 448-3619 (outside PA)
FAX (610) 995-9524
e-mail: bnb@bnbphiladelphia.com
www.bnbphiladelphia.com

H-01. This historic 18th-century house, once a stagecoach stop, is on a working dairy farm surrounded by Amish farms. The three-story home is a showcase for Colonial period furniture and local crafts. There are three large, comfortable guest bedrooms on the second floor, each with private bath. All bedrooms are air conditioned and a color TV is available. Full country breakfast served. Twenty minutes to Amish country, 25 minutes to the Brandywine River area. A Scottish golf course is within a few miles and, if given advance notice, the hostess will arrange for horseback riding or horse-drawn buggy rides. $60-80.

Bed & Breakfast: The Manor Inn

830 Village Road, Route 741
P.O. Box 416, Lampeter, 17537
(717) 464-9564
www.bbdirectory.com/inn/0817.html

In Amish country. This cozy farmhouse is just minutes away from historic sights and attractions. Guests delight in Mary Lou's delicious breakfasts, featuring such treats as eggs Mornay, crêpes or strata, apple cobbler, and homemade jams and breads. Caters to special diets.

A swim in the (20 x 40-foot deluxe in-ground) pool or a nap under one of the many shade trees is the perfect way to cap a day of touring. Amish dinners can be arranged. Groups welcome. Children welcome.

Hosts: Mary Lou Paolini and Jackie Curtis
Rooms: 6 (4 PB; 2 SB) $79-99
Full Breakfast
Credit Cards: None
Notes: 2, 5, 7, 8, 10, 11, 15

Cedar Hill Farm

Cedar Hill Farm

305 Longenecker Road, Mount Joy, 17552-8404
(717) 653-4655
www.800padutch.com/cedarhill.html

The host was born in this 1817 stone farmhouse near Lancaster County Amish farms and Hershey. The working farm offers lovely antique-appointed, air-conditioned rooms, all with private baths. A room for honeymooners has a queen-size canopied bed and opens onto a private balcony overlooking a peaceful stream. One room with king-size bed offers a whirlpool tub. Continental plus breakfast by walk-in fireplace. Farmers' markets, antiquing, and good restaurants nearby. Gift certificates.

Hosts: Russel and Gladys Swarr
Rooms: 5 (PB) $70-80
Continental Breakfast
Credit Cards: A, B, C, D
Notes: 2, 5, 7, 8, 9, 10, 11, 12, 14

NOTES: Credit cards accepted: A MasterCard; B Visa; C American Express; D Discover; E Diner's Club; F Other; 2 Personal checks accepted; 3 Lunch available; 4 Dinner available; 5 Open all year; 6 Pets welcome;

The Columbian

The Columbian— A Bed & Breakfast Inn

360 Chestnut Street, 17512
(717) 684-5869; (800) 422-5869 (reservations)
www.columbianinn.com

This circa 1897 restored turn-of-the-century mansion is a splendid example of Colonial Revival architecture, complete with unique wraparound sun porches, ornate stained-glass window, and magnificent tiered staircase. Uniquely decorated with antiques in Victorian and country style, the spacious air-conditioned rooms offer king- and queen-size beds and private baths. The hearty country breakfast consists of a variety of fresh fruits, hot main dishes, and homemade breads.

Hosts: Becky and Chris Will
Rooms: 8 (PB) $75-125
Full Breakfast
Credit Cards: A, B, D
Notes: 2, 5, 7, 8, 9, 10, 11, 12, 13

Flowers & Thyme Bed & Breakfast

238 Strasburg Pike, 17602-1326
(717) 393-1460; e-mail: padutchbnb@aol.com
www.members.aol.com/padtchbnb

Enjoy a stay at this newly renovated 1941 house that is bordered by farmlands and only minutes from outlets. The gardens bloom with a variety of flowers on beautifully landscaped grounds. Early summer shows a stunning display of Aprium poppies. Relax in clean, comfortable air-conditioned rooms, all with queen-size beds. Furnished in traditional classic decor. Gas fireplace in Garden Room. Baths are private—one with a Jacuzzi. Hearty gourmet breakfasts served in Gathering room. Dinners with Amish family can be arranged. Inquire about accommodations for children.

Hosts: Don and Ruth Harnish
Rooms: 3 (PB) $80-110
Full Breakfast
Credit Cards: A, B, C
Notes: 2, 5, 7, 10, 11, 12, 14

Flowers and Thyme

Gardens of Eden Bed & Breakfast

1894 Eden Road, 17601
(717) 393-5179; FAX (717) 393-7722
www.gardens-of-eden.com

Victorian ironmaster's home built circa 1860 on the banks of the Conestoga River is three miles

Gardens of Eden

7 No smoking; 8 Children welcome; 9 Social drinking allowed; 10 Tennis nearby; 11 Swimming nearby; 12 Golf nearby; 13 Skiing nearby; 14 May be booked through a travel agent; 15 Handicapped accessible.

northeast of Lancaster. Antiques and family collections of quilts and coverlets fill the three guest rooms, all with private baths. The adjoining guest cottage features efficiency kitchen with walk-in fireplace. The three acres of gardens feature herbs, perennials, and wildflowers. Local attractions are personalized by a tour guide service. Two bike trails pass the house. Children are welcome in the guest house.

Hosts: Marilyn and Bill Ebel
Rooms: 3 (PB) $95-110
Cottage: 1-$130
Full Breakfast
Credit Cards: A, B
Notes: 2, 5, 7, 9, 11, 12, 14

Homestead Lodging

Homestead Lodging

184 East Brook Road, Smoketown, 17576
(717) 393-6927

Come to this beautiful Lancaster County setting, where guests hear the clippity-clop of Amish buggies going by and can experience the beautiful farmlands. The clean country rooms provide a homey atmosphere; an Amish farm is adjacent. Within walking distance of restaurants and within minutes of farmers' markets, quilt, antique, and craft shops, outlets, auctions, and museums. All rooms are non-smoking and feature queen-size and double beds, cable TV, refrigerators. Heated and air conditioned. Microwave oven available. Personal checks accepted for advance deposit. Limited handicapped accessibility.

Hosts: Robert and Lori Kepiro
Rooms: 5 (PB) $40-68
Continental Breakfast
Credit Cards: A, B, C, D
Notes: 5, 7, 8, 9, 10, 11, 12, 14

The King's Cottage
A Bed & Breakfast Inn

1049 East King Street, 17602
(800) 747-8717

Traditionally styled elegance, modern comfort, and warm hospitality in Amish country. One of *American Historic Inns'* "Top 10 Inns in U.S." Honeymoon cottage with Jacuzzi and fireplace is a crown jewel. King- and queen-size beds, gourmet breakfasts, and personal service create a friendly atmosphere at this award-winning Spanish-style mansion. Relax by the fire and enjoy afternoon tea in the library while chatting with innkeepers about directions to restaurants and attractions. Special Amish dinners or personal tours arranged. Near farmers' markets, Gettysburg, and Hershey. Listed in the National Register of Historic Places. AAA- and Mobil-listed excellent. One room is handicapped accessible.

Hosts: Karen and Jim Owens
Rooms: 9 (PB) $100-195
Full Breakfast
Credit Cards: A, B, D
Notes: 2, 5, 7, 9, 10, 11, 12, 14

The King's Cottage

Lincoln Haus Inn

Lincoln Haus Inn Bed & Breakfast

1687 Lincoln Highway East, 17602
(717) 392-9412

A suburban home, built in 1915, with distinctive hip roofs in Lancaster County. Front porch for sitting and double lawn swings for relaxing. Inside are natural oak woodwork and gleaming hardwood floors. Antique furniture and rugs are throughout the house. Mary, a member of the Old Order Amish Church, serves a full breakfast family style in her shining, homey dining room. Her specialty is being a great hostess. Amish dinner can be made available with prior notice.

Host: Mary K. Zook
Rooms: 5 (PB) $55-70
Apartment/Suites: 3 (PB) $85
Full Breakfast
Credit Cards: None
Notes: 2, 5, 7, 8, 10, 11, 12, 14, 15

Rose Manor

124 South Linden Street, Manheim, 17545
(717) 664-4932; (800) 666-4932

A 90-year-old manor house, within walking distance of quaint village. Elegant yet comfortable Victorian decor. Antiques, original chestnut woodwork and cabinetry. Relax by the living room fire or in the sunny, plant-filled conservatory. Full breakfast, air conditioned, herb/rose gardens, in-room cable TV, fire-

places, and whirlpool. Services include maps and assistance with sightseeing, dinner arrangements with Amish family. Afternoon tea available. Near Pennsylvania Dutch attractions, Hershey, antiquing, quilting, farmers' markets, outlets, Renaissance Faire, and bike routes. AAA-rated three diamonds.

Hosts: Susan Jenal and Anne Jenal
Rooms: 5 (3 PB: 2 SB) $70-115
Full Breakfast
Credit Cards: A, B
Notes: 2, 5, 7, 8, 9, 12, 14

1725 Historic Witmers Tavern, Inn, & Museum

2014 Old Philadelphia Pike, 17602
(717) 299-5305
www.bbchannel.com/bbc/p204797.asp
www.800padutch.com/1725histwwit.html.

Lancaster's only pre-Revolutionary War inn reflects rural and historic flavor of the area. Fresh flowers, working fireplaces, antique quilts, and antiques in all the romantic rooms. Where wagon trains were assembled for the journeys westward and the Continental Congress was entertained. Hospitable innkeeper offers personal mapping of backroads to historic towns, sites, and other noncommercial points of interest for guests. Innkeeper's sister offers therapeutic massages for inn guests. Special occasion extras available. Pandora's Antique Shop on the premises. In the National Register of Historic Places and a federal

1725 Historic Witmers Tavern

7 No smoking; 8 Children welcome; 9 Social drinking allowed; 10 Tennis nearby; 11 Swimming nearby; 12 Golf nearby; 13 Skiing nearby; 14 May be booked through a travel agent; 15 Handicapped accessible.

landmark. Inquire about accommodations for children. Additional charge for use of fireplaces.

Room: 7 (2 PB; 5 SB) $65-110
Continental Breakfast
Credit Cards: None
Notes: 2, 5, 8, 9, 10, 11, 12, 13, 14

LANCASTER COUNTY

Carriage Corner Bed & Breakfast

3705 East Newport Road, P.O. Box 371, Intercourse, 17534-0371
(717) 768-3059; (800) 209-3059
FAX (717) 768-0691
www.virtualcities.com/ons/pa/r/par9501.htm

With tasteful, handcrafted touches of folk art, this inn offers a relaxing country atmosphere. A five-minute walk takes visitors to Intercourse, which is a bustling village from yesteryear with Amish buggies converging. The inn overlooks the Stoltzfus Farm and accompanying family restaurant. In town, Kitchen Kettle Village lures all visitors to its unique shops. The surrounding area, in the heart of Amish farmlands, has myriad attractions and historic sites. Amish dinners arranged. Children over three welcome. Social drinking allowed but not served. Limited handicapped accessibility.

Hosts: The Schuit Family
Rooms: 5 (PB) $68-85
Full Breakfast
Credit Cards: A, B
Notes: 2, 5, 7, 14

Carriage Corner

LANDENBERG

Amanda's Bed & Breakfast Reservation Service

3538 Lakeway Drive, Ellicott City, MD 21042-1226
(443) 535-0008; (800) 899-7533
FAX (443) 535-0009; e-mail: AmandasRS@aol.com
www.Amandas-BBRS.com

298. Each room's quaint decor is surrounded by a sense of timeless romance. Antiques abound throughout the house with some modern conveniences such as private baths. Colonial in style with fireplaces, full breakfast, bikes for riding, woodlands for hiking, or a swimming pool with Jacuzzi. Two cottages. $125-250.

Cornerstone

Cornerstone Bed & Breakfast

300 Buttonwood Road, 19350
(610) 274-2143; FAX (610) 274-0734
e-mail: corner3000@aol.com

To understand history is to live it. Charming 18th-century country inn with canopied beds, fireplaces in bedrooms, private baths, and antiques galore. Just minutes from Brandywine Valley museums and gardens: Longwood, Winterthur, and Hagley.

Hosts: Linda and Marty
Rooms: 8 (PB) $75-150
Cottages: 8-$125-250
Full Breakfast
Credit Cards: A, B, D
Notes: 2, 5, 7, 8, 9, 10, 11, 12, 14

NOTES: Credit cards accepted: A MasterCard; B Visa; C American Express; D Discover; E Diner's Club; F Other; 2 Personal checks accepted; 3 Lunch available; 4 Dinner available; 5 Open all year; 6 Pets welcome;

MAIN LINE

A Bed & Breakfast Connection/ Bed & Breakfast of Philadelphia

P.O. Box 21, Devon, 19333
(610) 687-3565; (800) 448-3619 (outside PA)
FAX (610) 995-9524
e-mail: bnb@bnbphiladelphia.com
www.bnbphiladelphia.com

From elegant townhouses in history-filled Center City to a manor house in scenic Bucks County; from an elegant home-within-a-barn in the suburbs to charming Victorian inns in York, Bed and Breakfast Connection /Bed and Breakfast of Philadelphia offers a wide variety of styles and locations in its scores of inspected homes, guesthouses, and inns. Choose from accommodations just three blocks from "America's most historic square mile," Independence National Historical Park, within easy distance of Valley Forge Park, or in the heart of the Brandywine Valley area with its magnificent historic estates and museums. Stay on a working farm in the Amish country of Lancaster County. Cover seven counties in the southeastern corner of Pennsylvania offering houses with one guest room and inns with many rooms. Credit cards accepted. Full and Continental breakfasts available. $40-250.

E-9. A 100-year-old carriage house in a lovely residential neighborhood in one of the Main Line's prestigious communities, this bed and breakfast is central for visits to Valley Forge, King of Prussia, Villanova, Haverford, Swarthmore, or Philadelphia. The local train station is just a 15-minute walk away. Also close by are a number of excellent restaurants. $125-200.

E-12. Elegant accommodations in this gracious 40-year-old English Regency-style home. Traditional and antique furniture grace the three second-floor guest rooms. All guest rooms are attractively decorated with floral wallpaper reminiscent of the French countryside. Each

room has a private bath. Feel free to relax with a book in the conservatory or in the first-floor library. There are two resident dogs. No smoking allowed. $80.

MANHEIM

The Loft Inn

1263 South Colebrook Road, 17545
(717) 898-8955

Join the hosts for a relaxing getaway in the country. Strikingly contemporary accommodation nestled in the former loft of a 100-year-old tobacco barn. Large, spacious rooms with all modern conveniences. Master bedroom with queen-size bed and queen-size sleeper-sofa in living room. Wood-burning stove, vaulted ceilings, and fully equipped kitchen. Close to shopping and other attractions but far enough away to enjoy the relaxation of country life.

Hosts: Herb and Miriam Nachbar
Rooms: 1 (PB) $75
Continental Breakfast
Credit Cards: None
Notes: 2, 5, 7, 11

MARIETTA

A Bed & Breakfast Connection/ Bed & Breakfast of Philadelphia

P.O. Box 21, Devon, 19333
(610) 687-3565; (800) 448-3619 (outside PA)
FAX (610) 995-9524
e-mail: bnb@bnbphiladelphia.com
www.bnbphiladelphia.com

H-1. Twelve-foot-high ceilings and stenciled hardwood floors greet guests as they enter the front hallway of this restored Federal brick home, built in 1810. The living room is decorated with an array of antiques. Fresh flowers and original art abound. Upstairs, guests may stay in either of the two charming rooms, each of which has a private bath and one of which

7 No smoking; 8 Children welcome; 9 Social drinking allowed; 10 Tennis nearby; 11 Swimming nearby; 12 Golf nearby; 13 Skiing nearby; 14 May be booked through a travel agent; 15 Handicapped accessible.

has a gas fireplace. The sitting room has a fax and telephone—perfect for the business traveler. A full breakfast is served in the candlelit dining room, and in the living room guests can enjoy a fire, play the piano, read a book, or watch cable TV. $95.

The River Inn

258 West Front Street, 17547-1405
(717) 426-2290; (888) 824-6622

Restored home, circa 1790, in national historic district of Marietta. Along Susquehanna River, near Lancaster, York, and Hershey attractions. Decorated with antiques and reproductions, this home offers three cozy guest rooms. When weather permits, breakfast is served on the screened porch. In the winter, warm the body with the six fireplaces throughout the home. Enjoy the herb and flower gardens. Owner can provide guided boat fishing on river. Air conditioning; cable TV.

Hosts: Joyce and Bob Heiserman
Rooms: 3 (PB) $65-85
Full Breakfast
Credit Cards: A, B, C, D, E
Notes: 2, 5, 7, 9, 12, 14

Vogt Farm Bed & Breakfast

1225 Colebrook Road, 17547
(800) 854-0399; FAX (717) 653-5288
e-mail: vogtfarm@aol.com; www.vogtfarmbnb.com

The hosts welcome guests to a century-old farm and the quietness of the country, where one can see the stars and hear the birds sing. Wake up to the smells of breakfast and a cup of a favorite morning brew. Guests can enjoy the amenities that adults have come to expect at the best bed and breakfasts and also be able to bring the family.

Rooms: 3 (PB) $72-145
Full Breakfast
Credit Cards: A, B, C, D, E
Notes: 2, 5, 7, 8, 9, 10, 11, 12, 14

MCCONNELLSBURG

The McConnellsburg Inn

131 West Market Street, 17233
(717) 485-5495; e-mail: mcinn@cvn.net
www.bbhost.com/mcinn

In the green mountains 90 miles north of Washington, D.C., the McConnellsburg Inn (circa 1903) offers canopied beds, toasty rooms, and private baths in a nationally registered historic district along the Lincoln Highway (Route 30). The gourmet breakfasts feature Burnt Cabins Grist Mill pancakes, locally smoked sausages, and seasonally stirred apple butter. Weekend antique auctions common. Minutes from Whitetail Ski Resort, Cowans Gap State Park (lake swimming and picnicking), Buchanan State Forest (mountain biking, cross-country skiing, and hiking), and fishing. Sixty minutes west of Gettysburg. Air conditioned. Close to Interstates 70 and 81 and Pennsylvania Turnpike (exit 13).

Hosts: Margaret and Timothy Taylor
Rooms: 3 (PB) $75
Full Breakfast
Credit Cards: A, B, C
Notes: 5, 7, 9, 10, 11, 12, 13, 14

MERCERSBURG

Blue Ridge Bed & Breakfast

2458 Castleman Road, Berryville, VA 22611
(540) 955-1246; (800) 296-1246
FAX (540) 955-4240; e-mail: blurdgbb@shentel.net
www.blueridgebb.com

A. This 200-acre farm nestled in the Tuscarora Mountains is near the historic birthplace of James Buchanan. Rope hammock by pond and springhouse. Full tennis court, swimming pool, sun room; fishing in pond stocked with blue gill. Close to C&O Canal. Snowmobiling in winter. Very close to skiing. Crib, high chairs, barbecue, picnic tables, games, and lots of nearby antiquing. Horseback riding and trail rides provided. Fenced-in area for horses. $55-75.

NOTES: Credit cards accepted: A MasterCard; B Visa; C American Express; D Discover; E Diner's Club; F Other; 2 Personal checks accepted; 3 Lunch available; 4 Dinner available; 5 Open all year; 6 Pets welcome;

MILESBURG

Rest & Repast
Bed & Breakfast Reservations

Box 126, Pine Grove Mills, 16868
(814) 238-1484; FAX (814) 234-9890
www.iul.com/bnbinpa

Curtain view, on 20 wooded acres, a modern log home with two guest suites, each sleeping up to four. Private bath in each suite. Home has porch overlooking mountainside where deer and bear come to feed at night. An in-ground pool available for guests. Hiking trails abound. Near several historic sites and state parks with swimming and boating. Off route 150/220, one and one-half miles from I-80, exit 23. Close to historic Bellefonte. $75-125.

MILLRIFT

Bonny Bank Bungalow

145 River Road, P.O. Box 481, 18340
(570) 491-2250

The rush of the rapids lull visitors to sleep in this cottage on the banks of the Upper Delaware National Scenic and Recreational River. Privacy is what you get as the only guests, with own entrance, bath, and river use area. Spectacular views. Canoe, raft rentals nearby. or borrow the hosts' innertubes to float the river. Hike or mountain bike in surrounding state and national parks. View birds, wildlife, scenic, historical, and cultural attractions.

Hosts: Doug and Linda Hay
Room: 1 (PB) $50
Full Breakfast
Credit Cards: None
Notes: 2, 7, 9, 10, 11, 12

MOUNT JOY

Amanda's Bed & Breakfast
Reservation Service

3538 Lakeway Drive, Ellicott City, MD 21042-1226
(443) 535-0008; (800) 899-7533
FAX (443) 535-0009; e-mail: AmandasRS@aol.com
www.Amandas-BBRS.com

264. Lancaster County and Pennsylvania Dutch country area with many activities for children and adults. The area is home to the nation's largest Plain Sect community with its members being of Amish, Brethren, or Mennonite faith. If hustle and bustle are one's style, there are amusement parks, outlet mall shopping, live music theaters, inner tubing, and miniature golf. Eat all one can at one of the tempting Pennsylvania Dutch-style restaurants. Bike along the country roads, glide through the sky in a hot-air balloon, or play golf. Four lovely rooms in the main house plus a luxury cottage with romance in mind. Jacuzzi tub and fireplace. $95-199.

Hillside Farm Bed & Breakfast

607 Eby Chiques Road, 17552-8819
(717) 653-6697; (888) 249-3406
FAX (717) 653-9775; e-mail: hillside3@juno.com
www.hillsidefarmbandb.com

Quiet, secluded 1863 two-acre farm homestead overlooking Chickies Creek with dam and waterfall. Ten miles west of downtown Lancaster, entirely surrounded by farmland. Large barn for exploring with barn cats. Watch a milking at a neighboring farm. Comfortable, country furnishing, dairy antiques, and milk bottles. King-, queen-size, double, and twin beds. Country "all-you-can-eat" breakfast. Six-person Jacuzzi on porch. Close to Amish, Hershey, antique shops, farmers' markets, flea markets, wineries. New cottage with fireplace, whirlpool tub for two and king-size bed available fall of 1999.

Hosts: Gary and Deb Lintner
Rooms: 5 (3 PB: 2 SB) $65-175
Full Breakfast
Credit Cards: A, B, D
Notes: 2, 5, 7, 9, 10, 11, 12, 13, 14

---

7 No smoking; 8 Children welcome; 9 Social drinking allowed; 10 Tennis nearby; 11 Swimming nearby; 12 Golf nearby; 13 Skiing nearby; 14 May be booked through a travel agent; 15 Handicapped accessible.

MOUNT POCONO

Farmhouse Bed & Breakfast

HCR 1, Box 6 B, 18344
(717) 839-0796

An 1850 homestead on six manicured acres. Separate cottage and four suites, all with fireplaces. Farm-style breakfast complete with original country recipes prepared by the host, a professional chef. Enjoy bedtime snacks that are freshly baked each day. Antiques adorn each room, with cleanliness being the order of the day. All accommodations have private baths, queen-size beds, TV, telephones, VCR, and air conditioning. Nonsmokers only.

Hosts: Jack and Donna Asure
Rooms: 5 (PB) $95-115
Full Breakfast
Credit Cards: A, B, C, D
Notes: 5, 7, 9, 10, 11, 12, 13

The Bodine House

Farmhouse

MUNCY

The Bodine House

307 South Main Street, 17756
(570) 546-8949; e-mail: bodine@pcspower.net

Built in 1805 and in the national historic district of Muncy, the Bodine House offers guests the opportunity to enjoy the atmosphere of an earlier age. The comfortable rooms, all with private baths, are individually furnished with antiques, and candlelight is used in the living room by the fireplace, where guests can socialize and enjoy refreshments. Also available is a two-story carriage house which will accommodate up to six persons. Three blocks from town center, movies, restaurants, library, and shops. Children over six are welcome.

Hosts: David and Marie Louise Smith
Rooms: 4 (PB) $60-75
Carriage House: $125
Full Breakfast
Credit Cards: A, B, C, D
Notes: 2, 5, 7, 9, 10, 11, 12, 13, 14

NEW BERLIN

The Inn at Olde New Berlin

321 Market Street, 17855-0390
(570) 966-0321; (800) 797-2350
FAX (570) 966-9557
e-mail: john@newberlin-inn.com
www.newberlin-inn.com

"A luxurious base for indulging in a clutch of quiet pleasures…" (Philadelphia Inquirer). A full-scale country inn in a rural setting offering lodging in three historic buildings—some with canopied beds, whirlpool tubs, and gas fireplaces—fine dining in Gabriel's Restaurant (featured twice on PBS), and Gabriel's Gift

---

NOTES: Credit cards accepted: A MasterCard; B Visa; C American Express; D Discover; E Diner's Club; F Other; 2 Personal checks accepted; 3 Lunch available; 4 Dinner available; 5 Open all year; 6 Pets welcome;

Collection with its Christopher Radko ornament gallery flanked by additional rooms of unique and romantic treasures. Depart feeling nurtured, relaxed, inspired…and ready to return.

Hosts: John and Nancy Showers
Rooms: 7 (PB)
Suites: 2 (PB)
Full Breakfast
Credit Cards: A, B, D
Notes: 2, 3, 4, 5, 7, 8, 9, 10, 11, 12, 13, 14

NEW CUMBERLAND

Farm Fortune

204 Limekiln Road, 17070
(717) 774-2683; FAX (717) 774-5089
e-mail: frmfortune@aol.com

Farm Fortune is a cozy, comfortable bed and breakfast in a 1700s limestone home which sits on a hill overlooking the Yellow Breechus Creek. Close to Harrisburg, York, Carlisle, Hershey, Gettysburg, and Lancaster. Antiques throughout. Small antique shop on property. Business travelers welcome.

Host: Phyllis Combs
Rooms: 4 (PB) $75-95
Full Breakfast
Credit Cards: A, B, C, D, E
Notes: 2, 5, 7, 9, 10, 12, 13, 14

Farm Fortune

NEW HOPE

Centre Bridge Inn

Centre Bridge Inn

2998 North River Road, 18938
(215) 862-9139; (215) 862-2048
FAX (215) 862-3244
www.letsmakeplans.com/centrebridgeinn

"The only thing we overlook is the Delaware River." Relax in the warmth and atmosphere of centuries gone by in quaint lodgings. A romantic country inn overlooking the Delaware River in historic Bucks County, featuring canopied beds and river views. A fine restaurant serving seasonal Continental cuisine in an Old World-style dining room. The river view, the fountain on the terrace, and the candlelit, low-ceilinged dining room with an open hearth fireplace—a relaxing, romantic, historic inn.

Host: Stephen R. DuGan
Rooms: 10 (PB) $80-175
Continental Breakfast
Credit Cards: A, B, C
Notes: 2, 4, 5, 9, 10, 11, 12

The Inn at Phillips Mill

2590 North River Road, 18938
(215) 862-2984

Country French cuisine and lodging in a renovated 18th-century stone barn. Candlelit dining by the fire in winter and on a flower-filled patio

7 No smoking; 8 Children welcome; 9 Social drinking allowed; 10 Tennis nearby; 11 Swimming nearby; 12 Golf nearby; 13 Skiing nearby; 14 May be booked through a travel agent; 15 Handicapped accessible.

in summer. Nearby canal for walking or canoeing. Open seven days a week. One and one-half miles north of New Hope. Smoking permitted in designated areas only.

Hosts: Brooks and Joyce Kaufman
Rooms: 5 (PB) $80-90
Continental Breakfast
Credit Cards: None
Notes: 2, 4, 11

The Mansion Inn

9 South Main Street, 18938
(215) 862-1231; FAX (215) 862-0277
e-mail: mansion@pil.net

This 1865 manor home, historically registered, has been recently restored to its original beauty. This intimate inn encompasses all the amenities for a luxurious and relaxing stay. Spacious suites, all with private baths, some with fireplaces, overlook perennial gardens. In the heart of historic New Hope, the inn is within walking distance of many unique shops and galleries. Enjoy theater at the famous Bucks County Playhouse or a romantic dinner at one of New Hope's exquisite riverfront restaurants. Horse-drawn carriages are available affording panoramic views of the Delaware River. Turn-down service with cookies and early morning coffee tray delivered to guest room.

Rooms: 9 (PB) $160-245
Full Breakfast
Credit Cards: A, B, C
Notes: 2, 5, 7, 11, 12

Pineapple Hill

1324 River Road, 18938
(215) 862-1790; www.pineapplehill.com

Guests will find romantic rooms and gourmet breakfasts at Pineapple Hill. This newly restored manor house rests on almost six acres between New Hope's center and Washington Crossing Park. The eight beautifully decorated rooms and suites each has a fireplace, private balcony, or living room. Most rooms with cable TV and telephones. The hand-tiled

Pineapple Hill

swimming pool is secluded in stone barn walls. Afternoon tea is served on weekends and holidays. Corporate rates and special midweek package are available. AAA three-diamond-rated and Mobil-approved.

Hosts: Charles "Cookie" and Kathryn Triolo
Rooms: 8 (PB) $75-175
Full Breakfast
Credit Cards: A, B, D
Notes: 2, 5, 7, 9, 10, 11, 12, 14

NEW HOPE (BUCKS COUNTY)

Aaron Burr House Inn

80 West Bridge Street, Corner Chestnut Street,
   18938-1401
e-mail: glassmans@evols.com
www.new-hope-inn.com/aaron

This vintage village Victorian "painted lady" sits a block away from the center of New Hope's artist colony and restaurant area. The spirit of Aaron Burr still haunts this historic house, where the infamous vice president fled after his victorious pistol duel with Alexander Hamilton in 1804. Amenities include pool and tennis club privileges plus a barn for guests to store their bicycles. On the busline to New York. Host will gladly pick guests up at the station. Rated excellent by Mobil and AAA. Seminars for aspiring innkeepers offered, too.

Hosts: Jesse and Carl Glassman
Rooms: 8 (PB) $75-195
Full Breakfast
Credit Cards: A, B
Notes: 2, 5, 6, 7, 8, 9, 10, 11, 12, 13, 14, 15

NOTES: Credit cards accepted: A MasterCard; B Visa; C American Express; D Discover; E Diner's Club; F Other; 2 Personal checks accepted; 3 Lunch available; 4 Dinner available; 5 Open all year; 6 Pets welcome;

Tattersall Inn

Tattersall Inn

P.O. Box 569, Point Pleasant, 18950
(215) 297-8233; (800) 297-4988
www.bbhost.com/tattersall_inn
www.travelassist.com/www.visitbucks.com

Overlooking a quaint river village, this 18th century Bucks County manor house features broad porches for relaxation and a walk-in fireplace for cool evenings. Breakfast is served in the dining room or can be taken to guests' room. The guest rooms are antique-furnished, with queen-size beds, private baths, and air conditioning, some with fireplaces. Enjoy the peace and quiet reminiscent of a less hurried time. Close to New Hope. AAA-rated three diamond. Mobil-rated three stars. Smoke free.

Hosts: Donna and Bob Trevorrow
Rooms: 6 (PB) $90-140
Full Breakfast
Credit Cards: A, B, D
Notes: 5, 7, 9, 11, 14

Umpleby House Inn

117 West Bridge Street, 18938
(215) 862-2570 (phone/FAX)
e-mail: stay@new-hope-inn.com
www.new-hope-inn.com/umpleby

About three blocks from Main Street, this quaint plaster-over-fieldstone house was built by a prominent mill owner in 1833 on a foundation dating to the mid-1700s. A delicious home-baked breakfast is served at a common table in the sitting room or the privacy of guests' own room; afternoon tea is offered on Saturday, and refreshments are served upon arrival. For extra privacy, ask for the Carriage House. It has a loft bedroom, second-story deck, kitchenette, sitting area with wood-burning stove, and views of the wildflower garden. Spanish, French, Dutch, and Hebrew spoken. AAA-rated three diamonds and Mobil Guide-rated three stars. Featured on CNN's *Travel-Guide* and Lou Dobbs's *Moneyline*.

Host: JesseRachel Glassman
Rooms: 8 (PB) $80-215
Continental Breakfast
Credit Cards: A, B

Umpleby House Inn

Notes: 2, 5, 6, 7, 8, 9, 10, 11, 12, 13, 14, 15

Wedgwood Inn of New Hope

111 West Bridge Street, 18938-1401
(215) 862-2570 (phone/FAX)
e-mail: stay@new-hope-inn.com
www.new-hope-inn.com

This charming inn was voted Inn of the Year by the readers of inn guidebooks. The Bucks County historic inn is on two acres of landscaped grounds and is only steps from the village center. Antiques, fresh flowers, and Wedgwood china are the rule at the inn, where guests are treated like royalty. Mobil three-star- and AAA three-diamond-rated. Innkeeping seminars are offered. Special packages are available year-round to readers of this guide book.

7 No smoking; 8 Children welcome; 9 Social drinking allowed; 10 Tennis nearby; 11 Swimming nearby; 12 Golf nearby; 13 Skiing nearby; 14 May be booked through a travel agent; 15 Handicapped accessible.

Hosts: Carl A. Glassman and Nadine Silnutzer
Rooms: 12 (PB) $70-199
Continental Breakfast
Credit Cards: A, B, C
Notes: 2, 5, 7, 8, 9, 10, 11, 12, 13, 14

NEW HOPE (WASHINGTON CROSSING) _____

Inn to the Woods

150 Glenwood Drive, Washington Crossing, 18977
(215) 493-1974; (800) 982-7619
www.inn-bucks.com

Hollileif

"Secluded elegance in historic Bucks County." This romantic three-diamond AAA bed and breakfast will enchant guests with seven and one-half acres of forest criss-crosses with deer paths and walking trails. Seven lovely rooms and two master suites. Private baths, TVs, and VCRs. Fireplaces available in several rooms. Outdoor hot tub open all year long. Full gourmet breakfast on weekends. Afternoon teas on Fridays and Saturdays. Enjoy a sip of sherry and a sweet before bedtime. Southern picnic baskets and gift baskets available. Just minutes from New Hope, Princeton, and Yardley. Forty minutes north of Philadelphia. One mile from I-95. Children over 12 welcome.

Hosts: Carol and Chris Bolton
Rooms: 7 (PB) $90-225
Full Breakfast
Credit Cards: A, B
Notes: 2, 5, 7, 11, 12, 13

NEW HOPE (WRIGHTSTOWN) _____

Hollileif Bed & Breakfast Establishment

677 Durham Road (Route 413), Wrightstown, 18940
(215) 598-3100

An 18th-century farmhouse on five and one-half acres of Bucks County countryside with romantic ambiance, gourmet breakfasts, fireplaces, central air conditioning, and private baths. Gracious service is combined with atten-

tion to detail. Each guest room is beautifully appointed with antiques and country furnishings. Enjoy afternoon refreshments by the fireside or on the arbor-covered patio. Relax in a hammock in the meadow overlooking a peaceful stream. View a vibrant sunset and wildlife. Close to New Hope. AAA- and Mobil-rated.

Hosts: Ellen and Richard Butkus
Rooms: 5 (PB) $85-160
Full Breakfast
Credit Cards: A, B, C, D
Notes: 2, 5, 7, 9, 10, 11, 12, 13, 14

OXFORD _____

Association of Bed & Breakfasts in Philadelphia, Valley Forge, Brandywine

P.O. Box 562, Valley Forge, 19481-0562
(610) 783-7838; (800) 344-0123
FAX (610) 783-7783
e-mail: pa@bnbassociation.com

0802. This modern log house, in a quiet wooded area, welcomes families with children. Complimentary beverages and snacks are offered and, each morning, a full hot breakfast is served. One guest room is handicapped accessible. Three guest rooms with private baths. $55.

NOTES: Credit cards accepted: A MasterCard; B Visa; C American Express; D Discover; E Diner's Club; F Other; 2 Personal checks accepted; 3 Lunch available; 4 Dinner available; 5 Open all year; 6 Pets welcome;

PALM (BERKS COUNTY)

Summer Brook Farm

974 Gravel Pike Chapel, 18070
(215) 679-0773

Built in 1796 this historic stone home and former inn is once again welcoming guests. Two
bedrooms with private baths. Cooked gourmet
breakfast served in tavern room. Private sitting
area, completely air conditioned. Afternoon tea
is available on request. Ten miles from Allen-
town, one scenic hour from Amish country,
Lancaster County, and Reading outlets.

Hosts: Joan and Bob Bergey
Rooms: 2 (PB) $70
Full Breakfast
Credit Cards: None
Notes: 2, 5, 7, 9, 10, 11, 12, 13

PARADISE

The Beiler's Bed 'N' Breakfast, Suites, & Efficiencies

3153 Lincoln Highway East, 17562
(717) 687-8612; FAX (717) 687-5145
www.bbde.com/beilersbnb.htm

This bed and breakfast is in the heart of Amish
country. Listen to the mix of the old and the
new with the clip-clop of horse and buggies
passing by alongside normal traffic. Come
enjoy the comfortable rooms and suites, all
with cable TV, VCR, clock radios, private telephone, private entrance, most with private
baths. Suites or full-kitchen units available.

The Beiler's

Continental plus breakfast served in newly
enclosed porch with soothing CD music playing. The hosts will graciously be available to
assist guests in planning their day or to answer
questions about their Amish heritage. Meal
with Amish family and tour of Amish farm can
be arranged. Minutes from many outlets,
antique shops, Strasburg, fishing, golfing, etc.

Hosts: Elam and Barbie Beiler
Rooms: 9 (7 PB; 2 SB) $65-95
Continental Breakfast
Credit Cards: A, B
Notes: 2, 5, 7, 8, 9, 10, 11, 12, 14

PHILADELPHIA

Amanda's Bed & Breakfast Reservation Service

3538 Lakeway Drive, Ellicott City, MD 21042-1226
(443) 535-0008; (800) 899-7533
FAX (443) 535-0009; e-mail: AmandasRS@aol.com
www.Amandas-BBRS.com

600. Center city elegance, off Rittenhouse
Square near Locust. A gracious atmosphere in
a four-story townhouse, antiques, paintings,
objets d'art. Garage for parking nearby. A Continental breakfast is served. Nearby shops, theaters, restaurants, and the civic center. Hostess
knowledgeable about the city. $80-85.

Association of Bed & Breakfasts in Philadelphia, Valley Forge, Brandywine

P.O. Box 562, Valley Forge, 19481-0562
(610) 783-7838; (800) 344-0123
FAX (610) 783-7783
e-mail: pa@bnbassociation.com

0101. This historically certified townhouse was
built in 1790. Each room has color cable TV,
telephone, air conditioning, small refrigerators,
and coffee makers. Breakfast food is provided
in guests' room. The English-style full bathroom separates the two third-floor guest
rooms. A large master suite on the second floor
has a canopied bed, working fireplace, cable

7 No smoking; 8 Children welcome; 9 Social drinking allowed; 10 Tennis nearby; 11 Swimming nearby;
12 Golf nearby; 13 Skiing nearby; 14 May be booked through a travel agent; 15 Handicapped accessible.

TV, telephone, air conditioning. The private bath boasts a separate shower and bathtub. French and Spanish spoken. Rollaway available at an additional charge. $70-115.

0104. This townhouse was built about 1805 as a colonial storefront and rebuilt in 1865 in the Federal style. Each room has bath, individual thermostat control for heat, cable TV, and telephone. Central air conditioning and private garden. Hot breakfast on weekends; Continental plus breakfast served weekdays. Two-night minimum stay. $95.

0400. Two adjacent, circa 1828, townhouses have been joined and renovated as one large townhouse/urban retreat. Two guest rooms, each with fireplace, private bath cable TV/VCR, air conditioning. Full breakfast. $110-145.

0402. This recently renovated three-story brick historical dwelling has balconies and an atrium. Two large guest rooms share a bath. Upon request, a private bath can be arranged. A full, hot, hearty breakfast is served. Within walking distance of several good restaurants. Nearby are the Philadelphia Art Museum, Boathouse Row, Fels Planetarium, the Academy of Science. $65.

0808. This circa 1840 mercantile building is listed in the National Register of Historic Places and is in the historic district section of Old City Philadelphia. The guest apartment has a bedroom, living room, dining area, bath, full kitchen. Other amenities include cable TV, telephone, microwave, whirlpool, central air conditioning, Persian carpets, antiques, washer/dryer, refrigerator, and elevator. Breakfast foods are provided. $125.

A Bed & Breakfast Connection/ Bed & Breakfast of Philadelphia

P.O. Box 21, Devon, 19333
(610) 687-3565; (800) 448-3619 (outside PA)

FAX (610) 995-9524
e-mail: bnb@bnbphiladelphia.com
www.bnbphiladelphia.com

A-01. Built between 1805 and 1810 and redone after the Civil War in Federalist style, this charming Society Hill townhouse saw further renovation when its current owners bought it as a shell some 20 years ago. The second-floor bedrooms offer a color TV, telephone jack, and individual thermostat with a private bath. On the third floor there are two more rooms. Continental breakfast is served in the pleasant kitchen in the winter or on the patio in the warm months. Two-night minimum stay. $95.

B-05. This townhouse is near the Franklin Institute, Museum of Natural History, and the Moore College of Art. The third-floor bedrooms share the bathroom and its old-fashioned claw-foot tub with the hosts. One room offers a double bed and air conditioning for the summer nights. The other has a single bed and is fan cooled. $45-55.

B-09. Victorian Inn. This 16-room mid-Victorian home offers a quiet retreat and the elegance of a Queen Anne Victorian home. Surrounded by the original iron fence and tall hedge, the 1889 home is sheltered by mature species gardens that create a natural seclusion from the urban bustle. The nine magnificently appointed second- and third-floor guest rooms are furnished in period antiques. Most rooms have private baths and some have working fireplaces. Fifteen- to 20-minute drive to center city Philadelphia. $60-100.

B-12. Waverly Walk is an elegant bed and breakfast (circa 1860s) in the Rittenhouse Square area of Philadelphia on a quaint, quiet street. The first-floor apartment has private entrance, stereo system with CDs, living room, complete kitchen, bedroom with cable TV, and private bath. Walk to the restaurants, shops, galleries, and lovely parks. Public transportation to any part of the city is just blocks away.

NOTES: Credit cards accepted: A MasterCard; B Visa; C American Express; D Discover; E Diner's Club; F Other; 2 Personal checks accepted; 3 Lunch available; 4 Dinner available; 5 Open all year; 6 Pets welcome;

Hearty Continental breakfast will be stocked in the kitchen, or, if guests prefer, a gourmet breakfast will be brought to guests' room. Laundry privileges available. Complimentary parking included. $135-150.

D-02. This spacious suburban home in the Chestnut Hill area is set high above the street in a lovely garden. A three-minute walk from commuter rail and bus. Queen-size bed with a private bath, a pair of twins with a shared bath, and a double bed with a shared bath. $60-75.

The Thomas Bond House

The Thomas Bond House Bed & Breakfast

129 South Second Street, 19106
(215) 923-8523; (800) 845-BOND
FAX (215) 923-8504

An elegantly restored, circa 1769, prominent physician's home within Independence National Historical Park, in the old city. Twelve guest rooms, each with private bath, telephone, TV, period furniture, and individually controlled heat and air conditioning. Suites have whirlpool tubs and fireplaces. Rates include breakfast, evening wine and cheese, and beverages. Parking next door. Rated by AAA and Mobil. Featured in *Mid-Atlantic Country* and *Washingtonian* magazines, *Washington Post*, *Boston Sunday Globe*, and others. Muffins and cookies baked daily.

Continental plus breakfast served weekdays; full breakfast served weekends. AAA and government discounts.

Host: Rita McGuire
Rooms: 12 (PB) $95-175
Continental and Full Breakfasts
Credit Cards: A, B, C
Notes: 2, 5, 9, 10, 11, 12, 14

PINE GROVE MILLS (STATE COLLEGE) _____

The Chatelaine Bed & Breakfast

347 West Pine Grove Road, Box 326, 16860
(814) 238-2028; (800) 251-2028
www.virtualcities.com/pa/chatelaine.htm

The Chatelaine Bed and Breakfast at Split-Pine farmhouse is a vintage farmhouse, circa 1830-60, six miles from Pennsylvania State University. Ideal for university parents, business travelers to this dynamic area, antiquers, nature lovers, water sportsmen, festival goers in summer, and Victorian and colonial celebrations in winter. Spacious rooms overlook charming grounds and country vistas. Sumptuous breakfasts. Unique baths. Minutes from the heart of things—miles and miles from guests' concerns. Children over 12 welcome.

Host: Mae McQuade
Rooms: 4 (2 PB; 2 SB) $85-150
Full Breakfast
Credit Cards: A, B, C, D
Notes: 2, 5, 7, 9, 10, 11, 12, 13, 14

Rest & Repast Bed & Breakfast Reservations

Box 126, Pine Grove Mills, 16868
(814) 238-1484; FAX (814) 234-9890
www.iul.com/bnbinpa

Down Home Country Lane. Circa 1825. This restored farmhouse near village of Pine Grove Mills has two bedrooms that share a bath. Received local award for excellent preservation efforts in 1995. Colonial atmosphere. Six miles from Penn State. $95.

POCONO MOUNTAINS

A Bed & Breakfast Connection/ Bed & Breakfast of Philadelphia

P.O. Box 21, Devon, 19333
(610) 687-3565; (800) 448-3619 (outside PA)
FAX (610) 995-9524
e-mail: bnb@bnbphiladelphia.com
www.bnbphiladelphia.com

XC-4. Historic Civil War-period inn, set in the Poconos. Eighteen rooms with private baths decorated with antiques. Two guest houses and a cottage increase capacity up to 50 people. Oversized pool, tennis court, horseshoes, badminton, shuffleboard, and other lawn games. Books and board games. Fishing and golf nearby. Skiers are only five minutes from Alpine Mountain or 20 minutes from Camelback, Shawnee, or Jack Frost ski areas. For cross-country skiing, Promiseland State Park is nearby. Choose bed and breakfast accommodations with a full breakfast or the MAP that includes a five-course gourmet dinner. $90-150.

PORT MATILDA

Rest & Repast Bed & Breakfast Reservations

Box 126, Pine Grove Mills, 16868
(814) 238-1484; FAX (814) 234-9890
www.iul.com/bnbinpa

This 1800s ironmaster's home with stream and hiking available. Three guest rooms, queen-size beds, private baths, one with a fireplace and Jacuzzi. In country setting on 10 acres of landscaped lawns, gazebo, pond, wooded land, walking distance to class-A trout stream. Fifteen-minute drive to PSU. Off I-80, exit 23. $85-120.

POTTERS MILLS

Rest & Repast Bed & Breakfast Reservations

Box 126, Pine Grove Mills, 16868
(814) 238-1484; FAX (814) 234-9890
www.iul.com/bnbinpa

The General Potter Farm. On 14 acres of pastures and streams in country, about 12 miles from State College and Penn State is 1820s farmhouse listed in the national historic register. Carefully restored, many antiques are from England and can be purchased. Offering three bedrooms, queen- and full-size beds. $95-120.

REAMSTOWN

The Jakob Getz House

31-33 East Church Street, P.O. Box 216, 17567
(717) 335-3510

In 1889 Jakob Getz built this classic Victorian home, off Route 272 in Reamstown, Lancaster County, minutes from outlet shopping, historic sites, farmers' markets, and the famous Adamstown Antique Mile. Second-floor rooms offer double or queen-size beds, air conditioning, tasteful stenciling, and 10-feet ceilings. Breakfast is served by candlelight in the dining room, as guests listen for the clippity-clop of buggies going by, driven by Amish and Mennonites who continue to farm the area with horse. Smoking is not permitted in house. Children over 12 welcome.

Hosts: Bob and Loretta Miller
Rooms: 4 (2 PB; 2 SB) $50-65
Full Breakfast
Credit Cash: None
Notes: 2, 5, 7, 10, 11, 12, 14

SCHELLSBURG (BEDFORD AREA)

Amanda's Bed & Breakfast Reservation Service

3538 Lakeway Drive, Ellicott City, MD 21042-1226
(443) 535-0008; (800) 899-7533
FAX (443) 535-0009; e-mail: AmandasRS@aol.com
www.Amandas-BBRS.com

130. A farmhouse with historic credentials, now a lovely bed and breakfast with modern touches. A trout stream and covered bridge, state park, plus other historic, scenic attractions. One hour to Fallingwater, designed by Frank Lloyd Wright. Roast marshmallows by the open fireplace in the smokehouse. A two-bedroom cottage is also available. Full breakfast. $75-190.

SCOTTDALE

Zephyr Glen Bed & Breakfast

205 Dexter Road, 15683-1812
(724) 887-6577

A crackling fireplace, a broad porch with a swing, bright country decor, hundreds of antiques, a restored Federal homestead, lovely grounds for a morning stroll, a hearty home-made breakfast. Zephyr Glen brings guests all this and much more. The hosts want guests to feel relaxed and well cared for. They will share their knowledge of local history, old houses, antiques, cooking, or local attractions includ-

Zephyr Glen

ing skiing, white-water rafting, hiking, biking, Fallingwater, antiquing, and historic sites. Children over 12 welcome.

Hosts: Noreen and Gil McGurl
Rooms: 3 (PB) $75
Full Breakfast
Credit Cards: A, B, D
Notes: 2, 5, 7, 9, 10, 11, 12, 13, 14

SCRANTON

The Weeping Willow Inn

The Weeping Willow Inn

308 North Eaton Road, Tunkhannoch, 18657
(570) 836-7257; e-mail: oaktree1@epix.net

This comfortable Colonial home, circa 1840, has been lovingly restored, and the hosts cordially invite guests to experience its warmth and rich history. Three graciously appointed rooms furnished with a mixture of family treasures and antiques. A hearty country breakfast is served by candlelight. Tunkhannoch abounds in scenic views, beautiful farmland, lovely lakes, and sleepy villages. Come relax, enjoy, and experience yesterday today.

Hosts: Patty and Randy Ehrengeller
Rooms: 4 (2 PB; 2 SB) $60-80
Full Breakfast
Credit Cards: A, B, C, D
Notes: 2, 5, 7, 8, 9, 12

7 No smoking; 8 Children welcome; 9 Social drinking allowed; 10 Tennis nearby; 11 Swimming nearby; 12 Golf nearby; 13 Skiing nearby; 14 May be booked through a travel agent; 15 Handicapped accessible.

SEWICKLEY

The Whistlestop Bed & Breakfast

195 Broad Street, Leetsdale, 15056
(724) 251-0852

The Whistlestop Bed and Breakfast is a quaint brick Victorian built in 1888. It has wide-plank pine floors, original woodwork, and is decorated with country furnishings using a railroad motif. It is on the Ohio River northwest of Pittsburgh, near the classic American village of Sewickley where fine examples of historic architecture are well maintained. Local flavor includes trains whistling nearby and tug boats tootling down the river. Guests will enjoy Old Economy Village two miles north.

Hosts: Stephen and Joyce Smith
Rooms: 4 (2 PB; 2 SB) $60-70
Full Breakfast
Credit Cards: A, B, C, D
Notes: 2, 5, 7, 8, 9, 12

SIGEL

Discoveries Bed & Breakfast

Rural Delivery 1, Box 42, 15860
(814) 752-2632

This Victorian house has four bedrooms and three baths. It has an ambiance of country elegance—bedrooms are beautifully decorated and furnished in antiques. Breakfast is served on the enclosed front porch, with home-cured meats and home-baked breads. Adjacent to the house is a finished crafts and antique shop with fine Victorian furniture and handcrafted items. Six miles from Cook Forest State Park. Route 36 north of I-80, exit 13.

Owner: Pat MacBeth
Rooms: 4 (1 PB; 3 SB) $58-70
Full Breakfast
Credit Cards: None
Notes: 2, 7, 8, 9, 11, 12

SLIPPERY ROCK

Applebutter Inn

666 Centreville Pike, 16057
(724) 794-1844; (888) APLE-INN (275-3466)
www.pathway.net/applebutterinn

Nestled in the rolling green meadows of rural western Pennsylvania, the Applebutter Inn offers a window to the past. Built by Michael Christley in 1844, on land granted to encourage westward settlement, the original six-room farmhouse was restored in 1987. Country charm awaits guests in any of the new rooms added in 1988. From the conference/meeting room with its house plants, to the 11 lovely guest rooms, and spa room, guests will be enchanted by quaint surroundings.

Hosts: The Snyders
Rooms: 11 (PB) $79-125
Full Breakfast
Credit Cards: A, B, C
Notes: 2, 5, 7, 8, 12, 15

Applebutter Inn

SOMERSET

Bayberry Inn Bed & Breakfast

611 North Center Avenue, Route 601, 15501
(814) 445-8471

A romantic, friendly, comfortable inn that pays attention to detail, offering all nonsmoking rooms with private baths. Homemade baked goods served at a table for two. Near exit 10 of the Pennsylvania Turnpike. Close to Seven

NOTES: Credit cards accepted: A MasterCard; B Visa; C American Express; D Discover; E Diner's Club; F Other; 2 Personal checks accepted; 3 Lunch available; 4 Dinner available; 5 Open all year; 6 Pets welcome;

Springs and Hidden Valley resorts, Frank Lloyd Wright's Fallingwater, Ohiopyle whitewater rafting, state parks, antique shops, and outlet malls. Not comfortable for children under 12.

Hosts: Marilyn and Robert Lohr
Rooms: 11 (PB) $50-60
Continental Breakfast
Credit Cards: A, B, C, D
Notes: 2, 5, 7, 9, 10, 11, 12, 13, 14

Quill Haven Country Inn

1519 North Center Avenue, 15501
(814) 443-4514; FAX (814) 445-1376
e-mail: quill@quillhaven.com
www.quillhaven.com

This 1918 gentleman's farmhouse is furnished with antiques and reproductions. Four uniquely decorated guest rooms, each with private bath, air conditioning, cable TV and VCR; common room with fireplace; sunroom where breakfast is served; and private deck with hot tub. AAA-rated three diamonds. Pennsylvania Travel Council-rated. Near Hidden Valley and Seven Springs ski resorts, Frank Lloyd Wright's Fallingwater, Youghiogheny Reservoir, Ohiopyle for hiking, biking, and white-water sports, outlet mall, state parks, golf courses, and antique shops. Only 1.2 miles from the Pennsylvania Turnpike, exit 10.

Hosts: Carol and Rowland Miller
Rooms: 4 (PB) $75-95
Full Breakfast
Credit Cards: A, B, D
Notes: 2, 5, 7, 8, 9, 10, 11, 12, 13

Somerset Country Inn

329 North Center Avenue, 15501
(814) 443-1005

Somerset Country Inn is a spacious five-bedroom Victorian home built in the 1860s. Each room has a private bath. The house is fully furnished with antiques. It is near Seven Springs ski resort, Hidden Valley ski resort, picnic parks, white-water rafting, horseback riding,

an outlet mall, and numerous fine restaurants. The guests will be pleased with the gracious hospitality and full breakfast.

Hosts: H. Joyce Barrett and Dan Jones
Rooms: 5 (PB) $50-70
Full Breakfast
Credit Cards: A, B
Notes: 2, 5, 7, 8, 9, 10, 11, 12, 13, 14

STARLIGHT

The Inn at Starlight Lake

P.O. Box 27, 18461
(570) 798-2519; (800) 248-2519
FAX (570) 798-2672

A classic country inn since 1909 on a clear lake in the rolling hills of northeastern Pennsylvania, with activities for all seasons, from swimming to cross-country skiing. Near the Delaware River for canoeing and fly-fishing. Excellent cuisine and spirits. Public lakeside dining, open daily. Convivial atmosphere. Modified American Plan. Smoking permitted in designated areas only.

Hosts: Jack and Judy McMahon; Patty and Chris Leswing
Rooms: 26 (20 PB; 6 SB) $116-154 MAP
Credit Cards: A, B
Notes: 2, 3, 4, 5, 8, 9, 10, 11, 12, 13, 14

SPRING MILLS

Rest & Repast
Bed & Breakfast Reservations

Box 126, Pine Grove Mills, 16868
(814) 238-1484; FAX (814) 234-9890
www.iul.com/bnbinpa

Eden Croft, 1820s restored stone farmhouse on acres of rolling pasture and meadows. Across the little-traveled country road is a marked hiking trail courtesy of Pennsylvania's 1995 Tree Farmer of the Year. Famous Spruce Creek is two miles away where Jimmy Carter once fly-fished. Home was featured in *Washington Post*

7 No smoking; 8 Children welcome; 9 Social drinking allowed; 10 Tennis nearby; 11 Swimming nearby; 12 Golf nearby; 13 Skiing nearby; 14 May be booked through a travel agent; 15 Handicapped accessible.

travel section. Two to three guest rooms with private and shared baths, queen-size and twin beds. About 30 minutes from Penn State, Juniata College and 10 minutes from Greer Girls School. $75-90.

Grove's Cottage. Less than a mile from Penns Creek in a rural area is a two bedroom cottage, with full kitchen, living room, bath on 14 plus acres. Guests traveling with dogs may make arrangements with host-owned kennel nearby. Quiet, rural property. Breakfast delivered by hosts who live next door. Two-night or two-room minimum booking. $95.

STARRUCCA

Nethercott Inn

Starrucca Creek Road, 18462-0026
(570) 727-2211; FAX (717) 727-3811
e-mail: netheinn@nep.net

This charming country inn is nestled comfortably in the tiny village of Starrucca in the Endless Mountains of Pennsylvania. The inn, decorated in a pleasing combination of antique and country, offers a peaceful setting for rest and relaxation. This is a four-seasons inn, with fishing, hunting, skiing, and golf close to the inn. A new winter loft sleeps eight, with kitchen, three bedrooms, and two baths. Weekend packages available.

Nethercott Inn

Hosts: Charlotte and John Keyser
Rooms: 7 (PB) $75-110
Full Breakfast
Credit Cards: A, B, C, D
Notes: 2, 5, 7, 8, 12, 13, 14

STATE COLLEGE

Rest & Repast
Bed & Breakfast Reservations

Box 126, Pine Grove Mills, 16868
(814) 238-1484; FAX (814) 234-9890
www.iul.com/bnbinpa

Several one- and two-bedroom private apartments that are walking distance to campus, available for either weekend bookings or longer term stays for visiting professors or grad students. All are unhosted, but host lives on premises in separate accommodations. Breakfast is provided for weekend stays. Longer term rates available upon request. $75-125.

Slab Cabin Farm. Large horse farm with circa-1850 farmhouse, two bedroom guest suite with bath, small sitting room with a minirefrigerator, microwave. Pocket doors separate suite from the rest of this large home. Children welcome. Rural location but only four miles from Penn State. Family rates available during off-peak times. $150-160.

STORMSTOWN

Rest & Repast
Bed & Breakfast Reservations

Box 126, Pine Grove Mills, 16868
(814) 238-1484; FAX (814) 234-9890
www.iul.com/bnbinpa

Happy Valley Wooden Treasures Bed and Breakfast. This 1807 home, nine miles from Penn State, has three guest rooms. First-class amenities, shared bath on second floor, gift shop on first floor. Dining room accented by large fireplaces and picture windows looking

NOTES: Credit cards accepted: A MasterCard; B Visa; C American Express; D Discover; E Diner's Club; F Other; 2 Personal checks accepted; 3 Lunch available; 4 Dinner available; 5 Open all year; 6 Pets welcome;

out upon pastoral scene where cows graze. Host offers by reservation only, catered, candlelight gourmet dinners prepared by well-known local chef. $85-110.

THORNTON

Pace One Restaurant & Country Inn

Glen Mills and Thornton Roads, 19373
(610) 459-3702; FAX (610) 558-0825

Each room has a modern private bath and is decorated with a special country flair. Stay includes a Continental breakfast with fresh fruit, orange juice, homemade breakfast breads, coffee, and tea. Whether sightseeing in the Brandywine Valley, attending a business function, or just enjoying a romantic weekend in the country, this inn is the perfect spot to unwind. Lunch is available daily, except Saturdays.

Host: Ted Pace
Rooms: 6 (PB) $75-95
Continental Breakfast
Credit Cards: A, B, C
Notes: 2, 4, 5, 7, 8, 9, 10, 12, 14

TROY

Golden Oak Inn Bed & Breakfast

196 Canton Street, 16947
(570) 297-4315; (800) 326-9834
www.bbonline.com/pa/goldenoak

Experience Victorian elegance accented with Civil War memorabilia, artwork, and a library filled with history books, all nestled in the heart of the Endless Mountains. Antiquing, wineries, and sports for all seasons are within commuting distance. Other attractions include Pennsylvania Grand Canyon, Mount Pisgah State Park, Bradford Basket Company, Finger Lakes, and much more. Gourmet breakfasts prepared by Richard, a Culinary Institute of

Golden Oak Inn

America graduate, served amidst a romantic atmosphere of candlelight and music.

Hosts: Richard and Sharon Frank
Rooms: 4 (SB) $60-75
Suite: $95
Full Breakfast
Credit Cards: A, B, C, D
Notes: 2, 5, 7, 9, 10, 11, 12, 13

UNIONTOWN

Inne at Watson's Choice

234 Balsinger Road, 15401
(724) 437-4999; (888) 820-5380
www.watsonschoice.com

Inn at Waston's Choice is a carefully restored, circa 1820s, western Pennsylvania farmhouse in the Laurel Highlands near Frank Lloyd Wright's Fallingwater and Kentuck Knob. Here family, friends, business acquaintances, and travelers can lodge in the warmth and hospitality of a bed and breakfast. For a night or for a week, a special anniversary, or a weekend getaway, a stay can become a quiet retreat from the bustle of everyday life. Luncheons available. AAA-rated three diamonds. Mobil Travel Guide-rated three stars. Member of PIAA. Inquire about accommodations for children.

Hosts: Bill and Nancy Ross
Rooms: 7 (PB) $89-125
Full Breakfast
Credit Cards: A, B, C, D
Notes: 2, 3, 5, 7, 9, 10, 11, 12, 13, 14, 15

7 No smoking; 8 Children welcome; 9 Social drinking allowed; 10 Tennis nearby; 11 Swimming nearby; 12 Golf nearby; 13 Skiing nearby; 14 May be booked through a travel agent; 15 Handicapped accessible.

VALLEY FORGE

Association of Bed & Breakfasts in Philadelphia, Valley Forge, Brandywine

P.O. Box 562, Valley Forge, 19481-0562
(610) 783-7838; (800) 344-0123
FAX (610) 783-7783
e-mail: pa@bnbassociation.com

0301. A 1928 English Tudor stucco and brick with a massive slate roof, red oak flooring, and stairway. Always a stop on local house tours. Enjoy the comfort and coziness of the large fireplaces or screened-in porch. Gourmet breakfasts served in formal dining room. Complimentary bedtime snack, air conditioning. Six guest rooms, four baths. $50-75.

A Bed & Breakfast Connection/ Bed & Breakfast of Philadelphia

P.O. Box 21, Devon, 19333
(610) 687-3565; (800) 448-3619 (outside PA)
FAX (610) 995-9524
e-mail: bnb@bnbphiladelphia.com
www.bnbphiladelphia.com

F-11. Just minutes from Valley Forge Park, this comfortable old stone home reflects the care and innovation of its carpenter-host. Once a duplex, it now boasts double the space, extra-wide hallways, and creative additions to its guest rooms. Six very inviting second-floor rooms available. A large guest room is beautifully appointed with heirloom antiques, including an impressive oversized four-poster bed, and a private bath. The other five guest rooms, with either air conditioning or ceiling fans, share two hall baths. A portable TV can be provided. $60-75.

WARRIORS MARK

Laurel Ridge Bed & Breakfast

159 Laurel Court, 16877-9733
(814) 632-6813

"Not close to anywhere...On the way to everywhere." The restored Victorian home of antiques and claw-foot tubs...this is not! This home is new, with gleaming baths, firm mattresses, and wooden floors. If guests are looking for a very quiet stay, off the beaten path...call Laurel Ridge. Find a quiet spot on the deck surrounding the house, or glide on the glider beside the water garden with its falls, stream, and pond.

Hosts: Kay and Wally Lester
Rooms: 4 (PB) $50-90
Full Breakfast
Credit Cards: A, B, D
Notes: 2, 5, 7, 9

Rest & Repast Bed & Breakfast Reservations

Box 126, Pine Grove Mills, 16868
(814) 238-1484; FAX (814) 234-9890
www.iul.com/bnbinpa

Private guest cottage with two bedrooms, living room and kitchen. Handicapped-accessible bathroom. Small covered porch. Hostess brings over breakfast basket in morning from main house. Rural country backroads near Spruce Creek and environs in Huntingdon County. Near hiking, fishing, and state parks. Wonderful roads to bicycle. $85.

WAYNE

Association of Bed & Breakfasts in Philadelphia, Valley Forge, Brandywine

P.O. Box 562, Valley Forge, 19481-0562
(610) 783-7838; (800) 344-0123
FAX (610) 783-7783
e-mail: pa@bnbassociation.com

0201. This home is set in a peaceful, heavily wooded neighborhood. Guests are encouraged to use the sitting room with color cable TV, the laundry facilities, and the in-ground Olympic-size swimming pool. Gourmet breakfasts are served. Cat in residence. Four guest rooms

NOTES: Credit cards accepted: A MasterCard; B Visa; C American Express; D Discover; E Diner's Club; F Other; 2 Personal checks accepted; 3 Lunch available; 4 Dinner available; 5 Open all year; 6 Pets welcome;

with private and shared baths and all have air conditioning. $50-65.

WAYNESBURG

Castle Victoria Bed & Breakfast

618 East Greene Street, 15370
(724) 627-5545
www.vicoa.com/castlevic

Come, stroll back to the turn of the century. Enjoy the ambiance of this warmly decorated Victorian mansion. Wander the grounds or relax in one of the comfortably furnished parlors. Enjoy the third-floor billiard parlor, play cards, checkers, or chess, watch TV, play croquet or other yard games, or visit the quaint shops of Waynesburg. End a stay here with a graciously served family breakfast. "Our home is your home for the duration of your stay."

Hosts: Michael and Doreen Klipsie
Rooms: 4 (4 SB) $95
Full Breakfast
Credit Cards: None
Notes: 2, 5, 7, 8, 9, 12, 14

WAYNESBORO

The Shepherd & Ewe Bed & Breakfast

11205 Country Club Road, 17268
(717) 762-8525; (888) WE R 4 EWE (937-4393)
FAX (717) 762-5880

Set high atop lush acres of rolling farmland, it's a year-round getaway where guests will find plenty of peace and rest, warm welcomes, and natural beauty, but they won't find slot machines, pool tables, TVs, traffic, or crowds at this gracious country retreat.

Guests are treated to satisfying full country breakfasts with homemade breads, muffins, fruits, beverages, and other down-home delights included. From the Shepherd and Ewe, it's just a short drive to Gettysburg and other nearby places, which are steeped in early history, architecture, and much more. Fine restaurants, state parks, hiking trails, art and antique galleries are just minutes away. Dinner available by request.

Hosts: Robert and Twila Risser
Rooms: 5 (3 PB; 2 SB) $75-85
Full Breakfast
Credit Cards: A, B, C, D
Notes: 2, 5, 7, 8, 12, 13

WELLSBORO

Kaltenbach's Bed & Breakfast

Rural Delivery 6, Box 106A, Stony Fork Road, 16901
(540) 724-4954; (800) 722-4954
www.pafarmstay.com; www.getawaysmag.com

Flagstone ranch house nestled on 72 acres of rolling hills is in north central Pennsylvania. Ten rooms have a private bath and two rooms are honeymoon suites with oversized tubs for two. Year-round recreation includes skiing at Denton Hill or Sawmill ski areas, cross-country skiing and snowmobiling on trails at the farm, hiking, biking, fishing, and hunting. Visit the nearby Grand Canyon of Pennsylvania, Corning Glass Center, Coudersport Ice Mine, Watkins Glen Raceway, or the Pennsylvania Laurel Festival. Wedding and meeting facilities available. Rails to trails. Two-star rating from Mobil.

Host: Lee Kaltenbach
Rooms: 10 (8 PB; 2 SB) $70-125
Full Breakfast
Credit Cards: A, B, D, F
Notes: 2, 3, 4, 5, 7, 8, 9, 10, 11, 12, 13, 14, 15

7 No smoking; 8 Children welcome; 9 Social drinking allowed; 10 Tennis nearby; 11 Swimming nearby; 12 Golf nearby; 13 Skiing nearby; 14 May be booked through a travel agent; 15 Handicapped accessible.

WEST CHESTER

Association of Bed & Breakfasts in Philadelphia, Valley Forge, Brandywine

P.O. Box 562, Valley Forge, 19481-0562
(610) 783-7838; (800) 344-0123
FAX (610) 783-7783
e-mail: pa@bnbassociation.com

1802. An 1890 Victorian in the National Register of Historic Places. Relax in the large common room or the guests' sitting room, which includes TV and writing desk. On eight wooded acres, the house is surrounded by many shrubs, trees, and wildflowers native to area. Twelve minutes to Longwood Gardens, and four miles to Downingtown and Exton. Children welcome. Three guest rooms with private baths. $75-85.

1901. A Chester County fine gentleman's manor house. Renovated Pennsylvania fieldstone farmhouse, with open beam ceilings, random width floors, dates back to the early 1730s. Former winter kitchen with stone crane fireplace, beehive oven provides the welcoming area. Hospitality center with hot and cold beverages, fruits and treats. Three guest rooms with cable color TV, air conditioning, and private bath. Gourmet breakfast weekends; Continental breakfast weekdays. Twelve minutes to Brandywine attractions. $75-85.

The Bankhouse Bed & Breakfast

875 Hillsdale Road, 19382
(610) 344-7388

An 18th-century bank house nestled in a quiet country setting with view of pond and horse farm. Rooms are charmingly decorated with country antiques and stenciling. Offers a great deal of privacy, including private entrance, porch, sitting room-library, and air condition-

The Bankhouse

ing. Near Longwood Gardens, Brandywine River Museum, and Winterthur. Easy drive to Valley Forge, Lancaster, and Philadelphia. Canoeing, horseback riding, biking, and walking/jogging trails offered in the area. Also, luscious country breakfast and afternoon snacks.

Hosts: Diana and Michael Bove
Rooms: 2 (1 PB; 1 SB) $70-90
Full Breakfast
Credit Cards: None
Notes: 2, 5, 7, 9, 12, 13

The Crooked Windsor

409 South Church Street, 19382
(215) 692-4896

Charming Victorian home in West Chester completely furnished with fine antiques. Full breakfast served, tea time or refreshments for those who so desire. Also pool and garden in season. Points of interest within easy driving distance: Brandywine River Museum, Longwood Gardens, Winterthur Museum, Chester County Historical Society, Brandywine Battlefield, Valley Forge National Park.

Host: Winifred Rupp
Rooms: 4 (2 PB; 4 SB) $75-95
Full Breakfast
Credit Cards: None
Notes: 2, 5, 7, 9, 10, 11, 12, 14

NOTES: Credit cards accepted: A MasterCard; B Visa; C American Express; D Discover; E Diner's Club; F Other; 2 Personal checks accepted; 3 Lunch available; 4 Dinner available; 5 Open all year; 6 Pets welcome;

WHITE HAVEN

Redwood Bed & Breakfast

362 State Street, Rural Route 1, Box 9B, 18661
(570) 443-7186

Three guest rooms available. One room with
antique furniture, one with twin beds, and one
room with waterfall furniture and porch.
Nearby are fishing, discount stores, hiking, biking, horseback riding, white-water rafting,
museums, Eckley Village, state park with beach
and lake. Light breakfast. Redwood Bed and
Breakfast is on the east side of White Haven.

Host: Emma Moore
Rooms 3 (1 PB; 2 SB) $30-45
Continental Breakfast
Credit Card: C
Notes: 2, 5, 7, 8, 11, 12, 13

WILKES BARRE

Ponda-Rowland Bed & Breakfast Inn & Farm Vacations

Rural Route 1, Box 349, Dallas, 18612
(570) 639-3245; (800) 854-3286
FAX (570) 639-5531

A 130-acre, circa 1850 farm, in Endless Mountains of northeast Pennsylvania. Private baths,
air conditioned, fireplaces, king-size beds.
Children welcome. Country antiques. Perfect
romantic getaway, or fun-filled family retreat.
Mountain views. Wildlife sanctuary. Trails to
observe deer, etc. Ponds, meadows, play areas.

Ponda-Rowland

Horses, donkeys, friendly farm dogs, sheep,
goats, chickens, pig, etc. Refreshments. Large
stone fireplace. AAA- and Mobil-rated.

Hosts: Jeanette and Clifford Rowland
Rooms: 5 (PB) $75-115
Full Breakfast
Credit Cards: A, B, C, D
Notes: 2, 5, 7, 8, 9, 11, 12, 13, 14

YORK

A Bed & Breakfast Connection/ Bed & Breakfast of Philadelphia

P.O. Box 21, Devon, 19333
(610) 687-3565; (800) 448-3619 (outside PA)
FAX (610) 995-9524
e-mail: bnb@bnbphiladelphia.com
www.bnbphiladelphia.com

H-10. Secluded on more than 54 scenic acres,
the surrounding woodlands, pastures, streams,
and ponds truly make this 1876 home a bed
and breakfast for all seasons. Forty minutes
from Baltimore, 2 hours from Philadelphia, 30
minutes from Lancaster, 1 hour and 45 minutes
from Washington, D.C., 20 minutes from York,
or 1 hour from Harrisburg, this location is convenient from many points. With tennis and
swimming on the property, public golf courses
nearby, biking (the Northern Central Railroad
Rail Trail is just minutes away), boating, or
skiing, there is something for everyone. Wineries, antique shops, factory outlets, and farmers'
markets are nearby also. A country breakfast
served. $75-135.

H-14. Equidistant from Lancaster, Gettysburg,
Hershey, and Baltimore, this lovely late-1800s
Victorian home is inviting for the traveler just
passing through or as headquarters for sightseeing in the area. Two state parks are nearby.
Relax in the living room with hosts or enjoy
the TV room, which has a microwave for the
use of guests. Four guest rooms share two
baths. Resident cat. $55-75.

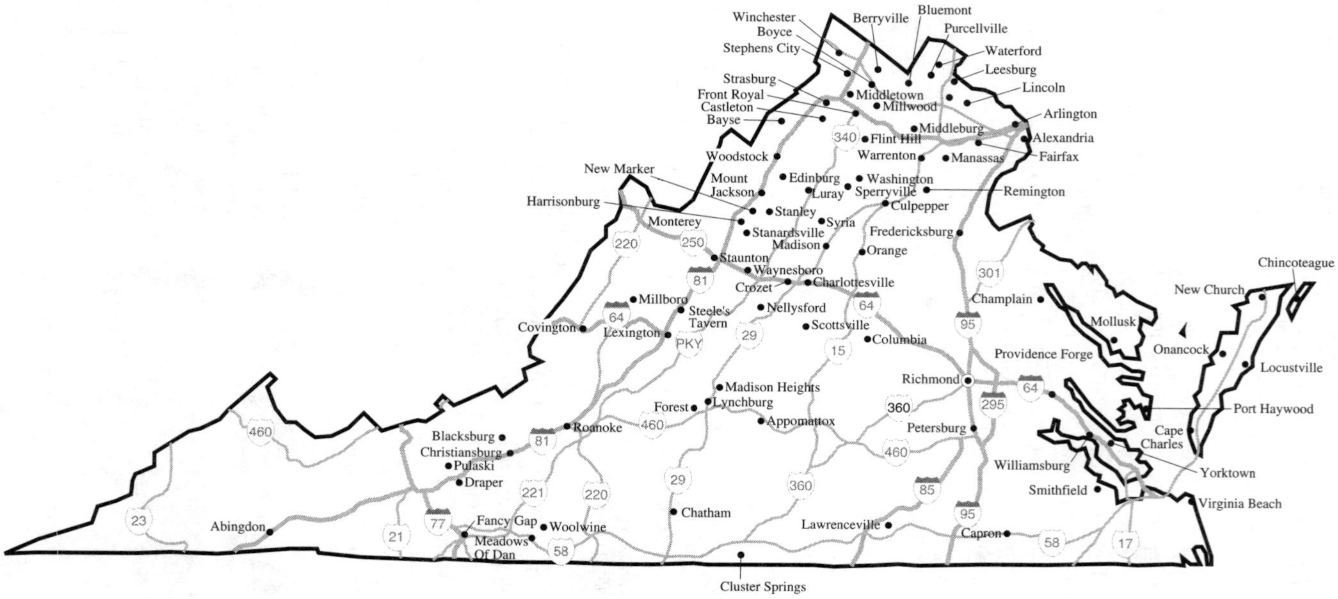

Virginia

Chincoteague
Locustville
Port Haywood
New Church
Onancock
Virginia Beach
Yorktown
Cape Charles
Mollusk
17
Providence Forge
Williamsburg
Smithfield
58
Champlain
64
301
295
Capeon
95
85
Arlington
Alexandria
Fairfax
Manassas
Remington
Washington
Culpepper
Orange
Fredericksburg
Columbia
Richmond
Petersburg
360
460
Leesburg
Lincoln
Waterford
Purcellville
Bluemont
Middleburg
Middletown
Millwood
Flint Hill
Warrenton
Sperryville
Berryville
Boyce
Winchester
Stephens City
Strasburg
Front Royal
Castleton
Bayse
Woodstock
Luray
Edinburg
Stanley
Stanardsville
Madison
Syria
Charlottesville
Scottsville
15
Madison Heights
Appomattox
360
Lawrenceville
Cluster Springs
Mount
Jackson
Monterey
Waynesboro
Crozet
Nellysford
29
64
Forest
Lynchburg
460
Chatham
29
New Market
Harrisonburg
250
81
Millboro
Steeles Tavern
PKY
220
Lexington
64
Covington
Roanoke
81
220
460
221
Woolwine
58
Fancy Gap
Meadows Of Dan
Blacksburg
Christiansburg
Pulaski
Draper
77
21
Abingdon
460
23

Virginia

Inn on Town Creek

ABINGDON

Inn on Town Creek

P.O. Box 1745, 445 East Valley Street, 24212-1745
(540) 628-4560; FAX (540) 628-9611
www.naxs.com/abingdon/innontowncreek/
index.htm

A historic creek is the theme of this bed and
breakfast on four acres of beautifully landscaped property. Multilevel brick patios and
rock gardens provide tranquil privacy; air-conditioned, antique-filled rooms and the cordial-
ity of the innkeepers offer a peaceful getaway
to the discerning guest. Near fine dining, entertainment. Ample parking. Smoking outside.
Children 10 and older welcome.

Hosts: Dr. Roger and Linda Neal
Rooms: 5 (4 PB; 1 SB) $100-250
Full Breakfast
Credit Cards: A, B
Notes: 2, 5, 7, 9, 10, 11, 12, 14

River Garden Bed & Breakfast

19080 North Fork River Road, 24210-4560
(540) 676-0335; (800) 952-4296

River Garden is nestled in the foothills of the
Clinch Mountains, on the bank of the north
fork of the Holston River outside historic
Abingdon. Furnished with traditional, antique,
and period furniture, each room has its own
riverside deck overlooking the gentle rapids.
Private exterior entrance, queen- or king-size
bed, full bath, and central heat and air. Guests
are also granted kitchen privileges. Common
areas include living room, den, dining room,
and recreation room.

Hosts: Carol and Bill Crump
Rooms: 4 (PB) $60-70
Full Breakfast
Credit Cards: None
Notes: 2, 5, 7, 9, 11, 12, 14

Summerfield Inn

101 West Valley Street, 24210
(540) 628-5905; (800) 668-5905;
FAX (540) 628-7515
www.Summerfieldinn.com

Elegant 1920s era home, centrally in Abingdon's historic district, within walking distance
of Barter Theatre, Virginia Creeper Trail,
restaurants, and fine shops. Enjoy American
and European antiques in a quiet and casual
atmosphere. Relax in comfortable parlors,
library, and large wraparound porch with
swing and rockers. Bedrooms are decorated
with floral touches, artwork, oriental carpets,

NOTES: Credit cards accepted: A MasterCard; B Visa; C American Express; D Discover; E Diner's Club;
F Other; 2 Personal checks accepted; 3 Lunch available; 4 Dinner available; 5 Open all year; 6 Pets welcome;
7 No smoking; 8 Children welcome; 9 Social drinking allowed; 10 Tennis nearby; 11 Swimming nearby;
12 Golf nearby; 13 Skiing nearby; 14 May be booked through a travel agent; 15 Handicapped accessible.

Summerfield Inn

brass- or four-poster beds, antiques, and whirlpool baths. Full breakfast.

Hosts: Janice and Jim Cowan
Rooms: 7 (PB) $90-130
Full Breakfast
Credit Cards: A, B, C, D
Notes: 2, 5, 7, 9, 10, 12, 14, 15

ALEXANDRIA

Alexandria and Arlington Bed & Breakfast Network

P.O. Box 25319, 22202-9319
(703) 549-3415; (888) 549-3419
FAX (703) 549-3411; e-mail: aabbn@juno.com

Offering more than 50 private homes, bed and breakfasts, and inns, this network offers something for everyone coming to Washington, D.C., Virginia, and Maryland. Stay in a 1750s Old Town Alexandria townhouse or a glamorous high-rise apartment. Hosts range from retired politicians and admirals to New Age entrepreneurs. All hosts are dedicated to guests' comfort, safety, and enjoyment of a visit in or near Washington, D.C.

Contact: Leslie Garrison
Rooms: 100+ (PB and SB) $60-325
Full and/or Continental Breakfast
Credit Cards: A, B, C
Notes: 2, 5, 6, 8, 9, 10, 11, 12, 14

Amanda's Bed & Breakfast Reservation Service

3538 Lakeway Drive, Ellicott City, MD 21042-1226
(443) 535-0008; (800) 899-7533
FAX (443) 535-0009; e-mail: AmandasRS@aol.com
www.Amandas-BBRS.com

150. In historic Alexandria, a town with an interesting past and current features such as the renovated Torpedo Factory with artist shops and restaurants. The historic buildings and other shops are within easy access. Guests can walk to the Metro with access to Washington, D.C. If driving, there are several areas in the region to tour: Mount Vernon, Arlington Cemetery, and the horse country around Leesburg. Two rooms for bed and breakfast. Two-night minimum. $85-95.

The Morrison House

116 South Alfred Street, 22314
(703) 838-8000; (800)367-0800
FAX (703) 548-2489
e-mail: mhresrv@morrisonhouse.com
www.morrisonhouse.com

This small boutique Mobil four-star, AAA four-diamond inn, built in the style of an 18th-century manor house, offers 45 elegantly appointed guest rooms, 24-hour butler, concierge and room service, and complimentary Continental breakfast served in the parlor each morning. Home of award-winning Elysium Restaurant. It is hard to imagine that one is only minutes from downtown Washington, D.C., strolling along cobblestone streets to one-of-a-kind shops, local "pubs," and historical landmarks just outside the grand entrance.

Rooms: 45 (PB) $150-295
Continental Breakfast
Credit Cards: A, B, C, E
Notes: 2, 3, 4, 5, 7, 8, 9, 10, 11, 12, 14, 15

APPOMATTOX

The Babcock House Bed & Breakfast Inn

Route 6, Box 1421, 106 Oakleigh Avenue, 24522
(804) 352-7532; (800) 689-6208
FAX (804) 352-5754
e-mail: richguild@earthlink.net
www.babcockhouse.com

A restored turn-of-the-century inn in downtown Appomattox, less than three miles from the famous surrender site which ended the Civil War. The inn has five rooms and one suite. All rooms have private baths, ceiling fans, cable TV, and air conditioning.

Hosts: Debbie Powell, Luella Coleman
Rooms: 6 (PB) $85-110
Full Breakfast
Credit Cards: A, B, C, D
Notes: 2, 3, 4, 5, 7, 8, 9, 10, 12, 14, 15

ARLINGTON

The Bed & Breakfast League, Ltd./ Sweet Dreams and Toast, Inc.

P.O. Box 9490, Washington, D.C. 20016-9490
(202) 363-7767; FAX (202) 363-8396
e-mail: bedandbreakfast-washingtondc@erols.com

298. A short ride to the Pentagon and Crystal City, this bed and breakfast is in a quiet, secluded area, but has easy access to Washington. Two pretty, antique-filled guest rooms have a double bed or two twin beds, each with a private bath. The hosts offer the use of a computer and fax in their office and, better still, their lovely garden with a pond. She is a costume historian, he a retired military officer; both are widely traveled, very interesting people. Parking is on-street and easy.

Rates: $70-80
Credit Cards: A, B, C, E
Notes: 2, 5, 7, 9

BASYE

Sky Chalet Mountain Lodges

P.O. Box 300, 22810
(540) 856-2147; (877) 867-8439
FAX (540) 856-2436
e-mail: skychalet@skychalet.com
www.skychalet.com

Romantic, rustic, mountaintop hideaway in the Shenandoah Valley. The property features spectacular, panoramic mountain and valley views. The Ridge Lodge has individual bedrooms with private baths. The Treetop Lodge has bedrooms, private baths, living rooms, working fireplaces, decks, and some kitchens. All are welcome: individuals, couples, honeymooners, families, children, groups, retreats, pets. Continental breakfast delivered to guests. Unique Old World Lodge with unbelievable views for receptions and special events. Hiking, restaurants, resort, attractions, activities, airport nearby. "The Mountain Lovers' Paradise" since 1937.

Hosts: Mona and Ken Seay
Rooms: 10 (PB) $34-79
Continental Breakfast
Credit Cards: A, B, D, E
Notes: 2, 5, 6, 8, 9, 10,11, 12, 13, 14

Sky Chalet Mountain Lodges

BERRYVILLE

Berryville Bed & Breakfast

100 Taylor Street, 22611
(540) 955-2200; (800) 826-7520
e-mail: bvillebb@shentel.net

Enjoy the in-town comfort and elegance of the Berryville Bed and Breakfast while exploring

---

7 No smoking; 8 Children welcome; 9 Social drinking allowed; 10 Tennis nearby; 11 Swimming nearby; 12 Golf nearby; 13 Skiing nearby; 14 May be booked through a travel agent; 15 Handicapped accessible.

Berryville

the small town of Berryville and Clarke County, in the heart of the Shenandoah Valley. Known for its apple orchards and horse farms, it is a perfect area for unwinding after a hectic week or for celebrating a special occasion. The house, built in 1915, is in the English country style and offers an acre of grounds for guests' enjoyment. The master suite features a fireplace. An abundant breakfast is served to each guest, and Berryville and the surrounding area offer restaurants for other meals to suit every taste and price range. "Come join us and name your pleasure."

Hosts: Don and Jan Riviere
Rooms: 4 (2 PB; 2 SB) $85-145
Full Breakfast
Credit Cards: A, B, C, D
Notes: 2, 5, 7, 9, 12

Blue Ridge Bed & Breakfast

2458 Castleman Road, 22611
(540) 955-1246; (800) 296-1246
FAX (540) 955-4240; e-mail: blurdgbb@shentel.net
www.blueridgebb.com

A Colonial Williamsburg reproduction furnished with lovely antiques; near the Shenandoah River on 11 acres complete with Christmas trees. Perfect getaway; ideal for weekend bikers and hikers. Only 90 minutes from Washington, D.C. $65-100.

BLACKSBURG

L'Arche Bed and Breakfast

301 Wall Street, 24060
(703) 951-1808

An oasis of tranquility just one block from the Virginia Tech campus, L'Arche Bed and Breakfast is an elegant turn-of-the-century Federal Revival home among terraced gardens in downtown Blacksburg. Spacious rooms have traditional antiques, family heirlooms, handmade quilts, and private baths. Delicious full breakfasts feature homemade breads, cakes, jams, and jellies.

Host: Vera G. Good
Rooms: 5 (PB) $85
Full Breakfast
Credit Cards: A, B
Notes: 2, 5, 10, 12, 13, 15

L'Arche

BLUEMONT

Blue Ridge Bed & Breakfast

2458 Castleman Road, Berryville, 22611
(540) 955-1246; (800) 296-1246
FAX (540) 955-4240; e-mail: blurdgbb@shentel.net
www.blueridgebb.com

Perfect for hiking the Appalachian Trail or biking. This retreat on the Shenandoah River 50 miles west of Washington D.C., is a restful stopover for a bed and meals. From $30.

NOTES: Credit cards accepted: A MasterCard; B Visa; C American Express; D Discover; E Diner's Club; F Other; 2 Personal checks accepted; 3 Lunch available; 4 Dinner available; 5 Open all year; 6 Pets welcome;

BOYCE

Amanda's Bed and Breakfast Reservation Service

3538 Lakeway Drive, Ellicott City, MD 21042-1226
(443) 535-0008; (800) 899-7533
FAX (443) 535-0009; e-mail: AmandasRS@aol.com
www.Amandas-BBRS.com

333. Near Winchester and Front Royal at the northern end of Skyline Drive and the Shenandoah Valley. A rural getaway on the river, built in 1780 and 1820. Fireplaces and private baths, lots of books, full breakfast, and scenery. $80-125.

Blue Ridge Bed & Breakfast

2458 Castleman Road, Berryville, 22611
(540) 955-1246; (800) 296-1246
FAX (540) 955-4240; e-mail: blurdgbb@shentel.net
www.blueridgebb.com

A. In the heart of fox hunt country. Lovely modern stone and clapboard house has a true western ranch house feel. Complete fox hunting arrangements available seven days a week for experienced riders, including complete care for horse and tack. Groom quarters available. Indoor ring. In the middle of 60 acres with beautiful views of mountains, a swimming pool, stable house, and kennel. $75-115.

B. Historic estate built in 1748 is graced by a lovely English hostess. In the National Register of Historic Places and featured in major books and the *Washington Post*. Over 1,000 spring bulbs, wicker-filled porch, acreage to hike, in-ground pool, and two lakes on property. George Washington really did sleep here, as well as Col. John S. Mosby. $100.

C. Beautiful view of the Blue Ridge to enjoy. Guests might even get a ride in a horse and buggy in this farm country. Less than two hours from the nation's capital. $55.

CAPE CHARLES

Amanda's Bed & Breakfast Reservation Service

3538 Lakeway Drive, Ellicott City, MD 21042-1226
(443) 535-0008; (800) 899-7533
FAX (443) 535-0009; e-mail: AmandasRS@aol.com
www.Amandas-BBRS.com

122. Lovely, quiet, rural setting along the Chesapeake Bay featuring unspoiled land, abundant wildlife, game birds, miles of private beach, and nature's most fabulous sunsets. This two-story brick home has a great view of the bay and is decorated with antiques, reproductions, and collectibles. Four rooms with private baths. Full breakfast. $85.

138. Restored 1910 Colonial Revival. Just steps from a public beach on the bay. Relax on one of the porches, sample the cool breezes off the bay, or bike through the historic town. Guests set their own pace to explore. Four guest rooms share two baths. Full breakfast. $75-85.

183. Cape Charles is the only public beach in area. This majestic home with a wraparound porch is just a few blocks from the beach. Walk and watch the beautiful sunsets over the bay. The Eastern Shore has a unique natural splendor for guests' enjoyment. In the house, the Corinthian columns form the grand staircase leading to some of the bedrooms. A gourmet breakfast is served in the spacious sun-filled dining room. $80-110.

Sea Gate Bed & Breakfast

9 Tazewell Avenue, 23310
(757) 331-2206 (phone/FAX)
e-mail: seagate@pilot.infl.net
www.bbhost.com/seagate

In the sleepy town of Cape Charles, closest to the beach on Chesapeake Bay on Virginia's undiscovered Eastern Shore. The day begins with a country breakfast followed by leisure,

---

7 No smoking; 8 Children welcome; 9 Social drinking allowed; 10 Tennis nearby; 11 Swimming nearby; 12 Golf nearby; 13 Skiing nearby; 14 May be booked through a travel agent; 15 Handicapped accessible.

Sea Gate

hiking, bird watching, bathing, or exploring the historic area. Tea prepares guests for the glorious sunsets over the bay. Sea Gate is the perfect place to rest, relax, and recharge—away from the crush of modern America. Winter special available. Two guest rooms have toilet and sink in room and share a bath across the hall. Smoking restricted. Children seven and older welcome.

Host: Chris Bannon
Rooms: 4 (2 PB; 2 SB) $80-90
Full Breakfast
Credit Cards: None
Notes: 2, 5, 10, 11, 12, 14

Wilson-Lee House Bed & Breakfast

403 Tazewell Avenue, 23310
(757) 331-1WLH (331-1954)
e-mail: WLHBnb@aol.com
www.wilsonleehouse.com

Wilson-Lee House

At the geographic center of historic Cape Charles, Wilson-Lee House is an example of the finest architecture of its time. Built in 1906, this Colonial Revival home is the work of Norfolk architect James W. Lee. A modified four-square house with four rooms per floor, it has been restored to its original elegance and has been configured to accommodate the needs of a late-20th-century bed and breakfast. Six and one-half baths were added for guests' comfort, and the butler's pantry was redesigned with the guests' in mind. The grand foyer with its Ionic colonnade is bright and especially welcoming. The Eastern Shore pace is deliciously slow, and sunsets on the Chesapeake Bay are breathtaking. Come rock on the porch, ride a bicycle built for two, and let the hosts arrange a romantic sunset sail, followed by a relaxing cookout on the deck.

Hosts: David Phillips and Leon Parham
Rooms: 6 (PB) $85-120
Full or Continental Breakfast
Credit Cards: A, B, C
Notes: 2, 5, 7, 9, 10, 11, 12, 14

CAPRON

Sandy Hill Farm Bed & Breakfast

11307 Rivers Mill Road, 23829
(804) 658-4381

Enjoy gracious southern hospitality and experience the pleasures of an unspoiled rural setting at this ranch-style farmhouse. Eleven miles from I-95 at exit 20, this working peanut and cotton farm also offers animals to visit and places to stroll in addition to a lighted tennis court on the grounds. Day trips to Williamsburg, Richmond, and Norfolk are within two hours. Fresh fruits and homemade breads are served at breakfast. Open March 25 through December 10. Reservations necessary.

Host: Anne Kitchen
Rooms: 2 (PB) $50
Full Breakfast
Credit Cards: None
Notes: 3, 4, 6, 8, 9, 10

NOTES: Credit cards accepted: A MasterCard; B Visa; C American Express; D Discover; E Diner's Club; F Other; 2 Personal checks accepted; 3 Lunch available; 4 Dinner available; 5 Open all year; 6 Pets welcome;

CASTLETON

Blue Ridge Bed & Breakfast

2458 Castleman Road, Berryville, 22611
(540) 955-1246; (800) 296-1246
FAX (540) 955-4240; e-mail: blurdgbb@shentel.net
www.blueridgebb.com

A. Fabulous pre-Civil War house built in 1850, in a lovely country setting in the middle of five and one-half acres with small pond. Close to Thornton River, Inn at Little Washington, and Skyline Drive. Lovely mountain views. Two bedrooms and a suite with Jacuzzi are available. $95-125.

CHAMPLAIN

Linden House Bed & Breakfast & Plantation

11770 Tidewater Trail, P.O. Box 23, 22438
(804) 443-1170; (800) 622-1202

Stay in one of the top-rated inns in Virginia. Rated A-plus by the ABBA and three diamonds by AAA. The 250-year-old mansion with carriage house is decorated in 18th-century reproductions and antiques. The beautifully landscaped yard and garden with gazebo and arbor provide room to relax and enjoy the quiet and serene setting. Only 45 minutes south of Fredericksburg and 75 minutes north of Williamsburg. The recently completed Linden House Ball Room with large porches and fountain on the patio overlooking the pond.

Hosts: Ken and Sandra Pounsberry
Rooms: 6 (PB) $85-135
Full Breakfast
Credit Cards: A, B, C, D, F
Notes: 2, 4, 5, 7, 8, 9, 11, 12, 14, 15

CHARLOTTESVILLE

Clifton–The Country Inn

1296 Clifton Inn Drive, 22947
(804) 971-1800; (888)971-1800

FAX (804) 971-7098; e-mail: reserve@cstone.net
www.cliftoninn.com

A restored 18th-century manor house hotel, built by Thomas Jefferson's son-in-law with 14 antique-appointed rooms and suites, all with wood-burning fireplaces. Outdoor pool, heated spa, and clay tennis court, available on 40 wooded and manicured acres, five miles east of downtown Charlottesville. Clifton offers elegant prix-fixe, impeccable service and an award-winning wine list. Midweek rates and bicentennial packages available year round.

Host: Keith Halford
Rooms: 14 (PB) $165-415
Full and Continental Breakfast
Credit Cards: A, B, C, E, F
Notes: 2, 4, 5, 7, 9, 10, 11, 12, 13, 14, 15

Guesthouses Bed & Breakfast

P.O. Box 5737, 22905
(804) 979-7264 (12:00-5:00 P.M. weekdays)
FAX (804) 293-7791
e-mail: guesthouses_bnb_reservations@
    compuserve.com
www.va-guesthouses.com

Afton House. A mountain retreat with panoramic views east to valleys and hills, this spacious home is on the old road up the mountain pass. There are four bedrooms, mostly furnished with antiques. One has a private adjoining bath, and three share two hall baths. Full breakfast is served. Antique shop on the premises and others in the village. $75-80.

Alderman House. This large, formal Georgian home is authentic in style and elegant in decor. It was built by the widow of the first president of the University of Virginia in the early 1900s and is about one mile from the university. Breakfast is served with true southern hospitality. Two guest rooms, each with adjoining private bath. Air conditioning. No smoking in the house. $100.

Auburn Hill. An antebellum cottage on a scenic farm that was part of the original

7 No smoking; 8 Children welcome; 9 Social drinking allowed; 10 Tennis nearby; 11 Swimming nearby; 12 Golf nearby; 13 Skiing nearby; 14 May be booked through a travel agent; 15 Handicapped accessible.

Jefferson plantation. The main house was built by Jefferson for one of his overseers. It is convenient to Monticello and Ash Lawn, just six miles east of the city. The cottage has a sitting room with fireplace, sleeper sofa, bedroom with four-poster bed, and connecting bath and shower. Guests may use the pool in summer. Scenic trails, walks, and views. Air conditioning. No smoking. Supplies provided for guests to prepare breakfast. Weekly rates available. $125-150.

Buck's Elbow Mountain Cottage. Mountaintop retreat with 360-degree views. Buck's Elbow Mountain is the highest point in Albemarle County and looks down on the Skyline Drive and Appalachian Trail, which run adjacent to the farm. Wake up and see the Valley of Virginia without getting out of bed. The cottage is contemporary with lots of glass, a cathedral ceiling in the living room, full kitchen, two bedrooms, and one and one-half baths, one with a Jacuzzi with views. Two-night minimum stay. Air conditioned. $200.

Cross Creek. A spectacular wood, stone, and glass "cottage" on a hilltop nine miles west of Charlottesville, Cross Creek is a perennial favorite. The living room, dining room, half-bath, and kitchen are built around a massive central stone fireplace. A deck provides a wonderful wooded view. Two bedrooms are on the lower level with a full bath across the hall. Air conditioning. Supplies provided for guests to prepare breakfast. $150-200.

Foxbrook. This lovely home just blocks north of the bypass is convenient to either downtown or the university area. Guest quarters consist of a sitting room overlooking a lovely garden, a bedroom, and a large bath with separate shower and sunken tub. Full breakfast. Air conditioned. No smoking. $100.

Indian Springs. This new cottage with a rustic feel is in a lovely wooded setting on a private lake. The lake is stocked and has a small dock for fishing, basking in the sun, or swimming at guests' own risk. There is a large main room, a sitting area with a sofa bed, dining area, kitchen, and bath. This cottage has complete privacy. TV and air conditioning. Supplies are provided for guests to prepare breakfast. $125-200.

Ingwood. In a lovely villa on six wooded acres in one of Charlottesville's most prestigious neighborhoods, Ingwood is an elegant, separate-level suite with its own drive and private entrance. The bedroom is appointed with antiques and has adjoining bath. The sitting room includes a fireplace, pullman kitchen, and sofa for an extra person. A second bedroom with twin beds and private bath is also available. Sliding glass doors open to a secluded terrace with a view of the woods. Air conditioning. Breakfast supplies are left in the suite for guests to prepare. $150-200.

Ivy Rose Cottage. An original cypress cottage, handmade by the host, is surrounded by gardens and offers mountain views. The ground floor has a double drawing room, separated by a screen, with a sitting area and a hand-wrought-iron bed. There is a rainforest sunroom with adjoining kitchen and bath with shower. Upstairs is creatively furnished with stained glass and lace curtains. It has heart-pine floors, an antique bed, and a half-bath. The host is a potter and the cottage showcases her work and that of her father, photographer Stan Jorstad. Full breakfast. Gas log stove. Air conditioned. Smoking outside only. $150-200.

Meadow Run. Enjoy relaxed rural living in this new Contemporary/Classical home six miles west of Charlottesville. Guest rooms share a bath. Guests are welcome to browse in the boat lover's library, play the grand piano, or lounge in the living room. Many windows offer bucolic vistas of the southwest range. Fireplaces in the kitchen and living room add to the homey, friendly feel. Air conditioning. $80-100

Millstream. A lovely, large house about 20 minutes north of Charlottesville up a long driveway lined with old box bushes. The house, with a brick English basement, was built before the Civil War and enlarged in 1866. There are two guest rooms, each with private bath. Guests may enjoy the fireplace in the library or the mountain views from the living room. Full breakfast. No smoking. Air conditioning. $100.

Nicola Log Cabin. This is a romantic 200-year-old log cabin on a 150-acre farm in historic Ivy eight miles west of Charlottesville, with spectacular views of the Blue Ridge Mountains. The one-room cabin has a bedroom, sleeper-sofa, a new bath with shower, microwave oven, refrigerator, and wood-burning stove. Children's playset and tennis court available. Supplies provided for guests to prepare breakfast. $100-150.

Northfields. This gracious home is on the northern edge of Charlottesville. The guest room has a TV, private bath, and air conditioning. There is another bedroom available with a double four-poster bed and private hall bath. A full gourmet breakfast is served. No smoking. $68-72.

Northwood. This 1920s city house is convenient to the historic downtown area of Charlottesville, only a few blocks from Thomas Jefferson's courthouse and the attractive pedestrian mall with many shops and restaurants. The guest quarters have a private adjoining bath. Many of the furnishings are antique, and next to the bedroom there is a small, comfortable sitting room with TV. Window air conditioning. $68-72.

Pocahontas. A large white clapboard house built in the 1920s as a summer retreat in the countryside near Ivy, west of Charlottesville. The large porch and beautiful gardens provide a wonderful place to stop and enjoy life passing by. A large guest room, furnished in Victorian pieces, greets guests with a bright and sunny warmth and offers a private adjoining bath with shower. Other rooms are available for larger groups or families on special weekends. No air conditioning but the house stays cool through the use of attic fans and large, high-ceilinged rooms. $80-100.

Polaris Farm. In the middle of rolling farmland dotted with horses and cattle, this architect-designed brick home offers guests an atmosphere of casual elegance. The accommodations consist of a ground-floor room with an adjoining bath, and two upstairs rooms that share a bath. There are gardens and terraces where one can view the Blue Ridge Mountains; a spring-fed pond for swimming, boating, and fishing; miles of trails for walking or horseback riding (mounts available at nearby stables). Air conditioning. $50-100.

Recoletta. An older Mediterranean-style house built with flair and imagination. The red tile roof, walled gardens with fountain, and artistic design create the impression of a secluded Italian villa within walking distance of the University of Virginia, shopping, and restaurants. Many of the beautiful antique furnishings are from Central America and Europe. The charming guest room has a beautiful brass bed and a private hall bath with shower. Air conditioning. $80-100.

The Rectory. This charming home in a small village five miles west of Charlottesville was a church rectory. It is furnished with lovely antiques and has an English garden in the back. The guest room overlooking the formal rose garden has its own entrance and adjoining full bath. Air conditioning. No smoking allowed. $80-100.

7 No smoking; 8 Children welcome; 9 Social drinking allowed; 10 Tennis nearby; 11 Swimming nearby; 12 Golf nearby; 13 Skiing nearby; 14 May be booked through a travel agent; 15 Handicapped accessible.

Rolling Acres Farm. A lovely brick Colonial home in a wooded setting on a small farm, this guest house has two bedrooms with a hall bath upstairs. The house is furnished with many Victorian pieces. No smoking. Air conditioning. $68-72.

The Rutledge Place. These hosts are only the third family to own this elegant Virginia farmhouse built around 1840 with magnificent mountain views. The original brick structure has been left intact, adding only a bathroom wing. The guest accommodations are light and airy in the English basement and offer a large bedroom, a sitting room, and a full bath. The home is furnished with antiques from the hosts' family homes in the Valley of Virginia. The suite opens to a brick terrace and gardens facing the mountains. Full breakfast. Air conditioned. No smoking allowed. $125.

Upstairs Slave Quarters. A fascinating place to stay if guests want interesting decor with the privacy of their own entrance. There is a harmonious mixture of antiques and art objects. The guest suite consists of a sitting room with a fireplace and two bedrooms with bath (tub only). A sleeper-sofa in the sitting room for extra guests. Adjacent to the University of Virginia and fraternity row, it is especially convenient for university guests. Air conditioning. $120-150.

High Meadows— Virginia's Vineyard Inn

Highmeadows Lane, Scottsville, 24590
(804) 286-2218; (800) 232-1832
e-mail: peterhmi@aol.com
www.highmeadows.com

Enchanting 19th-century European-style auberge with tastefully appointed spacious guest rooms, private baths, and period antiques. Two-room suites available. Several common rooms, fireplaces, and tranquility. Pastoral setting on 50 acres. Privacy, relaxing walks, and

High Meadows

gourmet picnics. Virginia wine tasting and romantic candlelit dining nightly. Virginia Architectural Landmark. National Register of Historic Places. Two-night minimum stay on weekends and holidays. Closed December 24-25. One room is handicapped accessible.

Hosts: Peter Sushka and Mary Jae Abbitt
Rooms: 14 (PB) $90.52-192.42
Full Breakfast
Credit Cards: A, B, C, D, F
Notes: 2, 4, 6, 7, 8, 9, 10, 11, 12, 13, 14

The Inn at the Crossroads

5010 Plank Road, P.O. Box 6519, 22906
(804) 979-6452

Listed in the National Register of Historic Places, the inn has been welcoming travelers since 1820. Today it continues this tradition, offering hospitality and comfort reminiscent of a bygone era. On four acres in the foothills of the Blue Ridge Mountains and convenient to

The Inn at the Crossroads

NOTES: Credit cards accepted: A MasterCard; B Visa; C American Express; D Discover; E Diner's Club; F Other; 2 Personal checks accepted; 3 Lunch available; 4 Dinner available; 5 Open all year; 6 Pets welcome;

Charlottesville, Monticello, and the Skyline Drive. Enjoy magnificent panoramic mountain views and a delicious country breakfast served in the keeping room.

Hosts: John and Maureen Deis
Rooms: 5 (PB) $85-115
Cottage: $125
Full Breakfast
Credit Cards: A, B
Notes: 2, 5, 7, 9, 10, 11, 12, 13, 14

The Inn at Monticello

The Inn at Monticello

Route 20 South, 1188 Scottsville Road, 22902
(804) 979-3593; FAX (804) 296-1344
e-mail: innatmonticello@mindspring.com
www.innatmonticello.com

Just two miles from Jefferson's Monticello, Michie Tavern, and Ash Lawn-Highland, the Inn at Monticello is the perfect place to rest and relax after visiting the historic sites in the area. The 1850 country manor house has five bedrooms, all with private baths, each decorated with antiques and fine reproductions. Each room has a special feature, such as a fireplace, porch, or romantic canopied beds. The comfortable elegance of the inn is enhanced by the gourmet breakfast served each morning, and the Virginia wine tasting offered each afternoon. Limited handicapped accessibility.

Hosts: Norm and Becky Lindway
Rooms: 5 (PB) $125-145
Full Breakfast
Credit Cards: A, B, C
Notes: 2, 5, 7, 9, 10, 12, 13, 14

The Mark Addy

56 Rodes Farm Drive, Nellysford, 22958
(804) 361-1101; (800) 278-2154
FAX (804) 361-2425
www.symweb.com/rockfish/mark.html

Dr. Everett's "most commanding estate in Nelson County" has been beautifully restored and lovingly appointed. The charming rooms and luxurious suites enjoy magnificent views of the beautiful Blue Ridge. The Mark Addy is between Charlottesville and Wintergreen Resort, to encourage either relaxation or adventure. Be surrounded by 12.5 acres of serenity and the romance of a bygone era. The elegant and imaginative "cuisine de grand-mère" will delight all tastes.

Host: John Storck Maddox
Rooms: 9 (PB) $90-135
Full Breakfast
Credit Cards: A, B
Notes: 2, 3, 4, 5, 7, 9, 10, 11, 12, 13, 14, 15

The Mark Addy

Palmer Country Manor

Route 2, Box 1390, Palmyra, 22963
(804) 589-1300; (800) 253-4306
FAX (804) 589-1716

A gracious 1830 estate on 180 secluded acres, Palmer Country Manor is only minutes from historic Charlottesville; Monticello, Thomas Jefferson's beloved home; Ash Lawn, home of James Monroe; Michie Tavern, one of Virginia's oldest homesteads; and some of Virginia's finest wineries. Come and enjoy one of

10 private cottages. Each features a living area with fireplace, color TV, private bath, and a deck. On the grounds, enjoy the swimming pool, five miles of trails, and the fishing pond; use one of the bikes; or take a hot-air balloon ride. Golf is available nearby.

Hosts: Gregory and Kathleen Palmer
Rooms: 12 (10 PB: 2 SB) $77.50-185
Full Breakfast
Credit Cards: A, B, C, D, E
Notes: 2, 3, 4, 5, 8, 9, 11, 12, 14

CHATHAM

Eldon—The Inn at Chatham

1037 Chalk Level Road, State Road 685, 24531
(804) 432-0935

Classically restored 1835 historic plantation manor home. One-half mile from Chatham, "Virginia's prettiest town." Four guest rooms, private baths, and full gourmet country breakfast. Formal garden, wooded country setting with original dependencies (smokehouse, ice house, and servants' cottage). In-ground swimming pool, pergola. Intimate gourmet restaurant with a Culinary Institute of America graduate as chef and CHIC graduate as pastry chef. Former home of Virginia's governor and U.S. secretary of the navy, Claude A. Swanson. Member BBAV. Smoking permitted in designated areas only.

Hosts: Joy and Bob Lemm
Rooms: 4 (3 PB; 1 SB) $65-130
Full Breakfast
Credit Cards: A, B
Notes: 2, 4, 5, 7, 9, 10, 11, 12, 14

Eldon

CHINCOTEAGUE

Amanda's Bed & Breakfast Reservation Service

3538 Lakeway Drive, Ellicott City, MD 21042-1226
(443) 535-0008; (800) 899-7533
FAX (443) 535-0009; e-mail: AmandasRS@aol.com
www.Amandas-BBRS.com

362. Island visitors can enjoy this seaside restored Victorian while sitting on the porch with a cool breeze. The ponies on the island are a must-see along with the many birds and animals at the national wildlife refuge. Rooms are air conditioned should the weather not cooperate. Each room is decorated with antiques, most with private baths. A full breakfast is served as well as afternoon tea. Seasonal rates. $95-135.

369. In town but just a short drive or bike ride to the beach and wildlife area. Walk to shops and restaurants. Charming and romantic ambiance. A brick courtyard, fountains, and a rose garden enhance this large shore home. Rooms are furnished with antiques and art from the 18th and 19th centuries. Once two houses now joined to create one rambling bed and breakfast. $90-150.

Cedar Gables Seaside Inn

6095 Hopkins Lane, P.O. Box 1006, 23336
(757) 336-1096; (888) 491-2944
FAX (757) 336-1291
e-mail: cdrgbl@shore.intercom.net
www.intercom.net/user/cdrgbl

Cedar Gables Seaside Inn is a romantic waterfront bed and breakfast overlooking picturesque Assateague Island. The inn has upscale amenities such as a heated swimming pool, hot tub, dock, secluded shade garden, etc. The rooms all have Jacuzzis, fireplaces, telephones, central heat and air conditioning, TVs, VCRs, exterior and interior entrances, and decks overlooking the water. A must for the discriminating traveler.

NOTES: Credit cards accepted: A MasterCard; B Visa; C American Express; D Discover; E Diner's Club; F Other; 2 Personal checks accepted; 3 Lunch available; 4 Dinner available; 5 Open all year; 6 Pets welcome;

Cedar Gables Seaside Inn

Hosts: Fred and Claudia Greenway
Rooms: 4 (PB) $130-175
Full Breakfast
Credit Cards: A, B, C, D
Notes: 2, 7, 9, 10, 11, 12, 14

The Channel Bass Inn

6228 Church Street, 23336
(757) 336-6148; (800) 249-0818
FAX (757) 336-0600
www.channelbass-inn.com

This imposing house was built in 1892 and became the Channel Bass Inn during the 1920s. Today this elegant Chincoteague landmark has six guest rooms, beautifully furnished, spacious, and quiet. Some rooms have view of Chincoteague Bay; all have comfortable sitting areas for reading and relaxing. Afternoon tea, with "world-famous" scones, and a full breakfast included. Close to wildlife refuge and unspoiled beaches of Assateague Island. Bicycles and beach equipment available for guests' use. Mobil two-star rating. Tea room open to public. Nonsmoking. Children eight and older welcome.

Hosts: David and Barbara Wiedenheft
Rooms: 6 (PB) $89-175
Full Breakfast
Credit Cards: A, B, C, D
Notes: 2, 7, 9, 10, 11, 12, 14

The Garden and the Sea Inn

Virginia Eastern Shore, Route 710
P. O. Box 275, New Church, 23415
(757) 824-0672

Casual elegance and warm hospitality in a charming Victorian inn near Chincoteague and beautiful Assateague wildlife refuges and the beach. Large, luxurious rooms, romantically designed with custom beds, designer fabrics, stained glass, oriental rugs, bay windows, private baths, and skylights. Suites with whirlpools, walk-in showers, and TVs. Hearty Continental breakfast. Romantic, candlelit gourmet dinners created by chef and innkeeper Tom Baker. Patio, gardens, porches. Boating, tennis, and golf nearby. Handicapped suite available. Mobil three-star-rated. Smoking permitted in designated areas only. Children over 12 welcome.

Hosts: Tom and Sara Baker
Rooms: 6 (PB) $75-175
Continental Breakfast
Credit Cards: A, B, C, D
Notes: 2, 4, 6, 9, 10, 11, 12, 14, 15

The Garden and the Sea Inn

Inn at Poplar Corner

4248 Main Street, 23336
(757) 336-6115; (800) 336-6787
FAX (757) 336-5776

The Inn at Poplar Corner is a romantically decorated Victorian home, with marbletop tables

Inn at Poplar Corner

and dressers, high-back walnut beds, and lace curtains. All guest rooms feature whirlpool tubs and are air conditioned for guests' comfort. After enjoying the free use of bicycles to tour Chincoteague National Wildlife Refuge and beach, guests can enjoy afternoon tea on the wraparound veranda featuring wicker rockers, tables, and chairs. Full breakfast.

Room: 4 (PB) $99-149
Full Breakfast
Credit Cards: A, B
Notes: 2, 7, 9, 10, 11, 12, 14

Miss Molly's Inn

4141 Main Street, 23336
(757) 336-6686; (800) 221-5620
FAX (757) 336-0600
e-mail: msmolly@shore.intercom.net
www.missmollys-inn.com

Built in 1886, Miss Molly's Inn is a charming Victorian on the bay, two miles from Chincoteague National Wildlife Refuge and five miles from Assateague National Seashore. All rooms are air conditioned and furnished with

Miss Molly's Inn

period antiques. Room rate includes a traditional English afternoon tea (with Barbara's superlative scones) and a full breakfast. Marguerite Henry stayed in this grand old home while writing *Misty of Chincoteague*. Complimentary bicycles and beach equipment. Mobil two-star rating. Nonsmoking. Children eight and older welcome.

Hosts: David and Barbara Wiedenheft
Rooms: 7 (5 PB: 2 SB) $69-155
Full Breakfast
Credit Cards: A, B, C, D
Notes: 2, 7, 9, 10, 11, 12, 14

The Watson House

The Watson House

4240 North Main Street, 23336
(757) 336-1564; (800) 336-6787
FAX (757) 336-5776

The Watson House has been tastefully restored with Victorian charm. Nestled in the heart of Chincoteague, the home is within walking distance of shops and restaurants. Each room has been comfortably decorated, including air conditioning, private baths, and antiques. A full, hearty breakfast and afternoon tea are served in the dining room or on the veranda. Enjoy free use of bicycles to tour the island. Chincoteague National Wildlife Refuge and its beach are two minutes away, offering nature trails, surf, and Chincoteague's famous wild ponies. AAA-rated three diamonds. Smoking permitted in designated areas only. Inquire about accommodations for children.

NOTES: Credit cards accepted: A MasterCard; B Visa; C American Express; D Discover; E Diner's Club; F Other; 2 Personal checks accepted; 3 Lunch available; 4 Dinner available; 5 Open all year; 6 Pets welcome;

Hosts: David and Jo Anne Snead and Tom and
    Jacque Derrickson
Rooms: 6 (PB) $69-115
Full Breakfast
Credit Cards: A, B
Notes: 2, 7, 9, 10, 11, 12, 14

CHRISTIANSBURG

Evergreen

Evergreen—
The Bell-Capozzi House

201 East Main Street, 24073
(504) 382-7372; (888) 382-7372
FAX (540) 382-0034; www.bnt.com/evergreen

Charming Victorian Inn in Christiansburg's historic East Main Street Area. Close drives to I-81,
the Blue Ridge Parkway, Virginia Tech, and
Radford University. Five guest rooms and one
private cottage. Private baths, air conditioning,
Godiva chocolates. library, VIB bears, concert
grand piano, traditional southern breakfast:
homemade biscuits, country ham, cheese grits,
eggs, pancakes, Gevalia coffee and tea. In-
ground pool, gazebo, swings, and rocking chairs.

Hosts: Rocco Capozzi and Barbara Bell-Capozzi
Rooms: 5 (PB) $95-135.
Full Breakfast
Credit Cards: A, B, C, D, F
Notes: 2, 5, 7, 9, 11, 12, 14

The Oaks Victorian Inn

311 East Main Street, 24073
(540) 381-1500; (800) 336-6257
FAX (540) 381-3036; www.bbhost.com/theoaksinn

Award-winning Queen Anne inn, listed in the
National Register of Historic Places. Warm
hospitality, comfortable, relaxed elegance, and
memorable breakfasts are the hallmark of the
Oaks. Antique-filled rooms with fireplaces,
Jacuzzis, and canopied king- or queen-size
beds. Surrounded by lawns, perennial gardens,
and 300-year-old oak trees, the inn faces Main
Street, once part of the Wilderness Trail blazed
by Daniel Boone and Davy Crockett. Near
Roanoke and the Blue Ridge Parkway. Mountain winery tours nearby, hiking, bike trails,
golf, tennis, fishing, antiquing, and historic
sites in the area. AAA four-diamond award for
four consecutive years. Member of Independent Innkeepers Associations.

Hosts: Margaret and Tom Ray
Rooms: 7 (PB) $125-160
Full Breakfast
Credit Cards: A, B, C, D
Notes: 2, 5, 7, 9, 10, 12, 14

CLUSTER SPRINGS

Oak Grove Plantation

1245 Cluster Springs Road, P.O. Box 45, 24535
(804) 575-7137

Operated from May to September by descen-
dants of the family who built the house in 1820.
Full country breakfast in the Victorian dining
room. Hiking, biking, bird watching, and wildflower walks on 400 acres of grounds. Near
Buggs Island for swimming, boating, and fishing; Danville to tour the last capital of the Con-
federacy; and Appomattox. One hour north of

Oak Grove Plantation

---

7 No smoking; 8 Children welcome; 9 Social drinking allowed; 10 Tennis nearby; 11 Swimming nearby;
12 Golf nearby; 13 Skiing nearby; 14 May be booked through a travel agent; 15 Handicapped accessible.

Raleigh-Durham. One handicapped-accessible room.

Host: Pickett Craddock
Rooms: 4 (1 PB; 3 SB) $55-120
Full Breakfast
Credit Cards: None
Notes: 2, 4, 8, 9, 10, 11, 12, 14

COLUMBIA

Upper Byrd Farm Bed & Breakfast

6452 River Road West, 23038
(804) 842-2240

A turn-of-the-century farmhouse nestled in the Virginia countryside on 26 acres overlooking the James River. Enjoy fishing or tubing. Canoe rentals available. Visit Ash Lawn and Monticello plantations. See the state's capitol, or simply relax by the fire surrounded by antiques and original art from around the world. Breakfast is special. Children 12 and older welcome. Open on weekends only in winter. Winter Green skiing area is one hour away.

Hosts: Ivona Kaz-Jespen and Maya Laurinaitis
Rooms: 4 (SB) $70
Full Breakfast
Credit Cards: None
Notes: 2, 7, 9, 11, 12, 13

COVINGTON

Blue Ridge Bed & Breakfast

2458 Castleman Road, Berryville, 22611
(540) 955-1246; (800) 296-1246
FAX (540) 955-4240; e-mail: blurdgbb@shentel.net
www.blueridgebb.com

A. This Gothic mansion, built in 1874 in the Allegheny Mountains, is nestled within 44 acres of fabulous manicured lawns and formal gardens. It has 14 fireplaces. Close to George Washington National Forest and excellent restaurants. Jacuzzi. Full afternoon tea. $75-140.

Milton Hall

Milton Hall Bed & Breakfast Inn

207 Thorny Lane, 24426
(540) 965-0196; e-mail: milton_h@CFW.com

Milton Hall Bed and Breakfast Inn is a Virginia Historic Landmark, listed in the National Register of Historic Places. This country manor house, built by English nobility in 1874, is on 44 acres adjoining the George Washington National Forest and one mile from I-64, exit 10. Spacious rooms are decorated in the style of the period. All guest rooms have fireplaces and private baths. A full breakfast and afternoon tea are included with a stay.

Hosts: Eric and Suzanne Stratmann;
  George and Pearl Keddie
Rooms: 6 (PB) $85-110
Full Breakfast
Credit Cards: A, B
Notes: 2, 3, 5, 6, 8, 9, 10, 11, 12, 13, 14

CROZET

Guesthouses Bed & Breakfast

P.O. Box 5737, 22905
(804) 979-7264 (12:00-5:00 P.M. weekdays)
FAX (804) 293-7791
e-mail: guesthouses_bnb_reservations@
  compuserve.com
www.va-guesthouses.com

Le Refuge. About 13 miles west of Charlottesville on Buck's Elbow Mountain, this con-

NOTES: Credit cards accepted: A MasterCard; B Visa; C American Express; D Discover; E Diner's Club; F Other; 2 Personal checks accepted; 3 Lunch available; 4 Dinner available; 5 Open all year; 6 Pets welcome;

temporary home was designed by the architect host. The house has a wonderful relaxed, casual atmosphere and magnificent views. It is near the Appalachian Trail and there are plenty of trails for hiking. The upstairs guest suite has a sitting alcove, private bath, and its own balcony. The downstairs guest room, has views in two directions, comfortable seating, and a private hall bath. Resident canines will greet guests and escort them into a house full of art work, eclectic furnishings. and charm. $100-150.

CULPEPER

Fountain Hall Bed & Breakfast

609 South East Street, 22701-3222
(540) 825-8200; (800) 29-VISIT
e-mail: fhbnb@aol.com; www.fountainhall.com

A warm welcome awaits guests. This grand bed and breakfast is highlighted with beautiful antiques, spacious rooms, and formal gardens. Relax on own private porch, stroll the grounds, or curl up with a good book. Enjoy a filling breakfast featuring freshly baked croissants, fresh fruits, yogurt and berries, brewed coffee, and more. Attractions: wineries, hiking, biking, canoeing, museum, battlefields, antique/craft shops, Skyline Drive, Montpelier. Golf courses nearby. Mobil three-star- and AAA three-diamond-rated. BBAV approved. Continental plus breakfast.

Hosts: Steve and Kathi Walker
Rooms: 6 (PB) $95-150

Fountain Hall

Continental Breakfast
Credit Cards: A, B, C, D, E, F
Notes: 2, 5, 7, 12, 13, 14, 15

DRAPER

Claytor Lake Homestead Inn

Route 651, Brown Road, Route 1, Box 184 E5, 24324
(540) 980-6777; (800) 676-LAKE

The inn originated as a two-room log cabin over a century ago. The old Doc Brown house was renovated in 1990. The inn has six guest rooms, four overlooking the lake. The inn offers boating, fishing, and summer swimming on its own beach. Rooms are decorated with antiques, reproductions, and period furnishings from the old Hotel Roanoke. A full country breakfast is served in the dining room overlooking the lake. The inn is only a mile from the New River hiking, biking, and horse trail. The Draper golf course is five miles away. There are 550 feet of waterfront with private sand beach, fishing, and boating. Antique shops are nearby in Pulaski.

Rooms: 6 (3 PB: 3 SB) $95
Full Breakfast
Credit Cards: A, B, C, D
Notes: 2, 4, 5, 7, 8, 9, 11, 12, 13, 14, 15

EDINBURG

Edinburg Inn
Bed & Breakfast, Ltd.

218 South Main Street, 22824
(540) 984-8286

This circa 1850 Victorian home is in the heart of the Shenandoah Valley on the edge of town next to Stoney Creek and the historic Edinburg Mill. The inn is reminiscent of Grandma's country home, with a full country breakfast which includes homemade breads and muffins, local country eggs, bacon and sausage. Game room with board games, new and vintage magazines and books, TV, VCR, and video library. Enjoy outdoor games on spacious grounds and

7 No smoking; 8 Children welcome; 9 Social drinking allowed; 10 Tennis nearby; 11 Swimming nearby; 12 Golf nearby; 13 Skiing nearby; 14 May be booked through a travel agent; 15 Handicapped accessible.

Edinburg Inn

wraparound porch with swing, rockers, and wicker. Walk to nearby restaurant and antique and craft shops. Short drive to caverns, battlefields, fishing, hiking, canoeing, horseback riding, and vineyards. Reservations appreciated.

Hosts: Judy and Clyde Beachy
Rooms: 3 (PB) $75
Full Breakfast
Credit Cards: None
Notes: 2, 5, 7, 8, 9, 10, 11, 12, 13

FAIRFAX

The Bailiwick Inn

4023 Chain Bridge Road, 22030
(703) 691-2266; (800) 366-7666
www.bailiwickinn.com

In the heart of the historic city of Fairfax, 15 miles west of the nation's capital. George

The Bailiwick Inn

Mason University is just down the street, and Mount Vernon and Civil War battlefields are nearby. In the National Register of Historic Places. Fourteen rooms with queen-size feather beds and private baths, fireplaces, Jacuzzis, and bridal suite. Afternoon tea. Candlelight dinner served by reservation. Small meetings and weddings.

Hosts: Annette and Bob Bradley
Rooms: 14 (PB) $135-309
Full Breakfast
Credit Cards: A, B, C
Notes: 2, 4, 5, 7, 8, 12, 14

FANCY GAP

The Doe Run at Groundhog Mountain

Mile Post 189 Blue Ridge Parkway, 24328
(540) 398-2212; (800) 325-6189
FAX (540) 398-2833; FAX (540) 398-3050
e-mail: doerun@tcia.net; www.doerunlodge.com

Romantic getaways, family vacations, business retreats, breathtaking views, quiet pastoral setting. Two-bedroom mountainside chalets with equipped kitchens. Full service restaurant and bar (in season.) Live weekend entertainment (in season.) Three miles from historic Mabry Mill. Heated pool, hiking trails, stocked fish pond, three lit tennis courts, and meeting facilities. Jacuzzis and hot tubs. TV/VCR and fireplace. Reduced rates and services January through March.

Rooms: 100 (PB) $109-260
Continental and Full Breakfast
Credit Cards: A, B, C
Notes: 2, 3, 4, 5, 6, 7, 8, 9, 10, 11, 12, 14

FLINT HILL

Blue Ridge Bed & Breakfast

2458 Castleman Road, Berryville, 22611
(540) 955-1246; (800) 296-1246
FAX (540) 955-4240; e-mail: blurdgbb@shentel.net
www.blueridgebb.com

NOTES: Credit cards accepted: A MasterCard; B Visa; C American Express; D Discover; E Diner's Club; F Other; 2 Personal checks accepted; 3 Lunch available; 4 Dinner available; 5 Open all year; 6 Pets welcome;

A. Lovely stone home built in 1812 with working fireplaces in bedrooms; a working cattle farm adjacent to Shenandoah National Park. With Virginia's Blue Ridge Mountains in the background, this inn offers guests a beautiful setting. Scenic pasture lands are surrounded by stone fences. Close to Inn at Little Washington and Old Rag Mountain. Hot tub. $100-140.

FOREST

Blue Ridge Bed & Breakfast

2458 Castleman Road, Berryville, 22611
(540) 955-1246; (800) 296-1246
FAX (540) 955-4240; e-mail: blurdgbb@shentel.net
www.blueridgebb.com

A. This summer kitchen has been converted to a lovely private cottage. The main mansion was built in 1830. It is in the middle of 600 acres. It has a private Jacuzzi and fireplace. Hostess gives private tours. Close to Thomas Jefferson's birthplace, Peaks of Otter, Blue Ridge Parkway, and Smith Mountain Lake. $135-170.

FREDERICKSBURG

Amanda's Bed & Breakfast Reservation Service

3538 Lakeway Drive, Ellicott City, MD 21042-1226
(443) 535-0008; (800) 899-7533
FAX (443) 535-0009; e-mail: AmandasRS@aol.com
www.Amandas-BBRS.com

310. Combine a visit to the Civil War sites between Antietam-Gettysburg and Fredericksburg. A Classical Revival-style home with high ceilings, wide heart-pine floors, acorn and oak leaf moldings, and a two-story front portico. On 10 acres of grounds filled with a fine balance of mature trees and a pond. Two rooms, each with a private bath. Full breakfast served. $105.

Fredericksburg Colonial Inn

1707 Princess Anne Street, 22401
(540) 371-5666

A restored country inn in the historic district, 32 antique-appointed rooms with private baths, telephones, TVs, refrigerators, and Civil War motif. More than 200 antique dealers, 20 major tourist attractions, and battlefields. Less than one hour from Washington, D.C., Richmond, and Charlottesville. A great getaway. Suites and family rooms available. Wonderful restaurants within walking distance. A nonsmoking facility. Olde Town within walking distance.

Hosts: Brenda Price, Sherrie Beach, and Christine
 Goldsmith
Rooms: 32 (PB) $59-89
Continental Breakfast
Credit Cards: A, B, C
Notes: 5, 7, 15

La Vista Plantation

4420 Guinea Station Road, 22408
(540) 898-8444; (800) 529-2823
e-mail: lavistabb@aol.com
www.bbonline.com/va/lavista/

This lovely 1838 Classical Revival home is just outside historic Fredericksburg. On 10 quiet acres, the grounds present a fine balance of mature trees, flow-  ers, shrubs, and farm fields. The pond is stocked with bass. Choose from a spacious two-bedroom apartment that sleeps six with a kitchen and a fireplace, or a formal room with a king-size mahogany rice-carved four-poster bed, fireplace, and Empire furniture. Homemade jams and farm-fresh eggs for breakfast.

Hosts: Michele and Edward Schiesser
Rooms: 1 (PB) $105
Apartment: 1
Full Breakfast
Credit Cards: A, B
Notes: 2, 5, 7, 8, 9, 10, 12, 14

---

7 No smoking; 8 Children welcome; 9 Social drinking allowed; 10 Tennis nearby; 11 Swimming nearby; 12 Golf nearby; 13 Skiing nearby; 14 May be booked through a travel agent; 15 Handicapped accessible.

FRONT ROYAL

Chester House

43 Chester Street, 22630
(540) 635-3937; (800) 621-0441
FAX (540) 636-8695; www.chesterhouse.com

A stately Georgian mansion with extensive formal gardens on two acres in Front Royal's historic district. Quiet, relaxed atmosphere in elegant surroundings, often described as an oasis in the heart of town. Easy walking distance to antique and gift shops and historic attractions; a short drive to Skyline Caverns, Skyline Drive, Shenandoah River, golf, tennis, hiking, skiing, horseback riding, fine wineries, and excellent restaurants.

Hosts: Bill and Ann Wilson
Rooms: 7 (5 PB; 2 SB) $65-190
Continental Breakfast
Credit Cards: A, B, C
Notes: 2, 5, 9, 10, 11, 12, 14

Killahevlin

1401 North Royal Avenue, 22630
(540) 636-7335; (800) 847-6132
FAX (540) 636-8694; e-mail: kllhvln@shentel.net
www.vairish.com

Historic Edwardian mansion with spectacular views. Spacious bedrooms, professionally designed and restored with working fireplaces,

Killahevlin

private baths, and whirlpool tubs. Private Irish pub for guests. Complimentary beer and wine. Close to Skyline Drive, Shenandoah National Park, hiking, golf, tennis, canoeing, horseback riding, antiquing, fine dining, wineries, and live theater. Property was built in 1905 for William E. Carson, father of Skyline Drive. National Register of Historic Places and Virginia landmarks register.

Hosts: Susan O'Kelly-Lang
Rooms: 6 (PB) $125-225
Full Breakfast
Credit Cards: A, B, C, D, E, F
Notes: 2, 5, 7, 9, 10, 11, 12, 14

HARRISONBURG

Blue Ridge Bed & Breakfast

2458 Castleman Road, Berryville, 22611
(540) 955-1246; (800) 296-1246
FAX (540) 955-4240; e-mail: blurdgbb@shentel.net
www.blueridgebb.com

A. Ten miles west of Harrisonburg off Route 33. Beautiful seven and-a-half-acre estate close to George Washington National Forest. Huge boxwoods with lots of tunnels, terrace, patios, and gazebo; built in 1925 out of matched river rock. There are 128 varieties of wildflowers as well as hiking trails and stocked trout streams. Full breakfast. $65 and up.

Kingsway Bed & Breakfast

3955 Singers Glen Road, 22802
(540) 867-9696

In this private home enjoy the warm hospitality, carpentry, and homemaking skills of your hosts who make guests' comfort their priority. This ranch-style home is in a rural area of the beautiful Shenandoah Valley, just four and one-half miles from downtown. On the mountains to the east, drive the scenic Skyline Drive, visit the caverns, historic Monticello, New Market battlefield, Natural Bridge, antique shops, flea markets, and Valley Mall. Inquire about accommodations for pets. In-ground pool.

NOTES: Credit cards accepted: A MasterCard; B Visa; C American Express; D Discover; E Diner's Club; F Other; 2 Personal checks accepted; 3 Lunch available; 4 Dinner available; 5 Open all year; 6 Pets welcome;

Hosts: Chester and Verna Leaman
Rooms: 2 (PB) $60-65
Full Breakfast
Credit Cards: B
Notes: 2, 5, 6, 7, 8, 11, 12, 13, 14

LAWRENCEVILLE

Blue Ridge Bed & Breakfast

2458 Castleman Road, Berryville, 22611
(540) 955-1246; (800) 296-1246
FAX (540) 955-4240; e-mail: blurdgbb@shentel.net
www.blueridgebb.com

A. Built in 1785, this mansion is filled with all-period antiques. Ideal location between I-85 and I-95. On 27 acres, close to Fort Christina, Civil War battlefield, many Civil War re-enactments, horse racing, and charter fishing on Lake Gaston. Also has two cabins on property complete with fireplaces and small kitchens. Full country breakfasts; will also do dinners and weddings. $95-125.

LEESBURG

The Norris House Inn & Stonehouse Tea Room

108 Loudoun Street, SW, 20175-2909
(703) 777-1806; (800) 644-1806
FAX (703) 771-8051; e-mail: inn@norrishouse.com
www.norrishouse.com

The Norris House Inn

Elegant accommodations in the heart of historic Leesburg. The six charming guest rooms are all furnished with antiques, and three of the rooms have working fireplaces. Full country breakfasts served and evening libations served. Convenient in-town location with several restaurants nearby. Only one hour's drive to Washington, D.C. In the heart of the Virginia hunt country, rich in colonial and Civil War history. Lots of antiquing and wineries. The perfect place for special romantic getaways, small meetings, and weddings. The inn is open daily by reservation. Children over 12 are welcome.

Hosts: Pam and Don McMurray
Rooms: 6 (SB) $95-140
Full Breakfast
Credit Cards: A, B, C, D, E, F
Notes: 2, 5, 7, 9, 10, 11, 12, 14

LEXINGTON

Applewood Inn

Buffalo Bend Road, P.O. Box 1348, 24450
(540) 463-1962; (800) 463-1902
e-mail: applewd@cfw.com
www.applewoodbb.com

Spectacular passive solar country retreat on 35 hilltop acres between the Shenandoah Valley's historic Lexington and Natural Bridge with views of the Blue Ridge Mountains. Romantics and nature lovers alike enjoy the huge porches, quilt-covered queen-size beds, private baths, hot tub, hiking trails, picnic llama treks, poolside barbecues, and hearty whole-grain country breakfasts. Nearby are museums, Washington and Lee University, Virginia Military Institute, the Virginia Horse Center, summer theater, and wonderful scenic back roads.

Hosts: Linda and Chris Best
Rooms: 4 (PB) $80-129
Full Breakfast
Credit Cards: A, B, C
Notes: 2, 5, 6, 7, 8, 11, 12, 15

7 No smoking; 8 Children welcome; 9 Social drinking allowed; 10 Tennis nearby; 11 Swimming nearby; 12 Golf nearby; 13 Skiing nearby; 14 May be booked through a travel agent; 15 Handicapped accessible.

A Bed & Breakfast at Llewellyn Lodge

603 South Main Street, 24450
(540) 463-3235; (800) 882-1145
e-mail: LLL@rockbridge.net; www.LLodge.com

The great in-town location of this charming Colonial, combined with the warm and friendly atmosphere, makes it the perfect home base for exploring this historic town. Ellen and John are "personalized guidebooks" in helping guests get the most out of their visit. Refreshments are served upon arrival and guests receive lots of advice on hiking, cycling, fly-fishing, golf, and other outdoor activities. A full breakfast is served including Belgian waffles, Ellen's special omelets, meats, and homemade muffins. The decor combines traditional with antique furnishings. Walking distance to Lee Chapel, Stonewall Jackson House, Washington and Lee University, and Virginia Military Institute.

Hosts: Ellen and John Roberts
Rooms: 6 (PB) $65-98
Full Breakfast
Credit Cards: A, B, C, D
Notes: 2, 5, 7, 9, 10, 11, 12, 14

Historic Country Inns

11 North Main Street, 24450
(877) 463-2044; FAX (540) 463-7262

Three historic homes restored and furnished with antiques, paintings, and amenities. In center of historic district are Alexander-Withrow, circa 1789, and McCampbell Inn, circa 1809. Museums, shops, Virginia Military Institute, and Washington and Lee University within walking distance. Maple Hall, circa 1850, six miles north of Lexington at the intersection of I-81 and Route 11, offers tennis, swimming, fishing, trails, and working fireplaces. Nightly dining for inn guests and public. Smoking permitted in designated areas only. Limited handicapped accessible.

Hosts: Don Fredenburg (innkeeper);
     The Meredith Family (owners)
Rooms: 44 (PB)
Continental Breakfast
Credit Cards: A, B
Notes: 2, 4, 5, 8, 9, 10, 11, 14

The Hummingbird Inn

The Hummingbird Inn

30 Wood Lane, P.O.Box 147, Goshen, 24439
(540) 997-9065; (800) 397-3214
e-mail: hmgbird@cfw.com
www.hummingbirdinn.com

On a tranquil acre of landscaped grounds, the Hummingbird Inn, a unique carpenter Gothic villa, offers accommodations in an early Victorian setting. Comfortable rooms are furnished with antiques and combine an old-fashioned ambiance with modern convenience. Some have whirlpool tubs and fireplaces. Architectural features include wraparound verandas on the first and second floors, original pine floors of varying widths, a charming rustic den dating from the early 1800s, and a solarium. A wide trout stream defines one of the property lines, and the old red barn was once the town livery. Full breakfasts include unique area recipes.

Hosts: Diana and Jerry Robinson
Rooms: 5 (PB) $85-135
Full Breakfast
Credit Cards: A, B, C, D
Notes: 2, 4, 5, 6, 7, 9, 13, 14

Steeles Tavern Manor

Steeles Tavern Manor Country Inn

P.O. Box 39, Highway 11, 24476
(540) 377-6444; (800) 743-8666
FAX (540) 377-5937; www.steelestavern.com

WDBJ7-TV "A place that specializes in putting the romance back into a relationship." Find romance at the Manor. Guests are spoiled with flowers, afternoon teas, candlelight dinners, as well as sumptuous breakfasts in bed or in the dining room. Languish in a guest room with double Jacuzzis, fireplaces, TV/VCRs. Hike the 55 acres with fishing pond, falls, and panorama of the Blue Ridge Parkway, winery, and much more.

Host: Eileen Hoernlein
Rooms: 5 (PB) $120-185
Full Breakfast
Credit Cards: A, B, D
Notes: 2, 4, 5, 7, 9, 12, 13, 14

Stoneridge Bed & Breakfast

Stoneridge Lane, P.O. Box 38, 24450
(540) 463-4090; (800) 491-2930
FAX (540) 463-6078
www.webfeat-inc.com/stoneridge

Get reacquainted at this romantic 1829 antebellum home on 36 secluded acres. Five guest rooms with private baths, ceiling fans, and queen-size beds, some featuring private balconies, double Jacuzzis, and fireplaces. Relax on the large front porch and enjoy the sunset over Short Hills Mountains. Virginia wines are available and a gourmet country breakfast is served in the candlelit dining room or on the back patio. Central air conditioning. Just five minutes south of historic Lexington.

Hosts: Norm and Barbara Rollenhagen
Rooms: 5 (PB) $95-160
Full Breakfast
Credit Cards: A, B, C, D
Notes: 2, 5, 7, 8, 9, 14

LINCOLN

Springdale Country Inn

Lincoln, 20160 (mailing)
18348 Lincoln Road, Purcellville, 20132 (location)
(540) 338-1832; (800) 388-1832
FAX (540) 338-1839

Restored historic landmark 45 miles west of Washington, D.C., on six acres of secluded terrain with babbling brooks, foot bridges, and terraced gardens. Meal service for groups, e.g. weddings; breakfast included in room price. Fully air conditioned. New heating system and seven fireplaces.

Hosts: Nancy and Roger Fones
Rooms: 9 (6 PB; 3 SB) $95-200
Full Breakfast
Credit Cards: A, B, D
Notes: 2, 5, 7, 8, 9, 10, 11, 12, 14, 15

LOCUSTVILLE

Amanda's Bed & Breakfast Reservation Service

3538 Lakeway Drive, Ellicott City, MD 21042-1226
(443) 535-0008; (800) 899-7533
FAX (443) 535-0009; e-mail: AmandasRS@aol.com
www.Amandas-BBRS.com

143. This 18th-century Colonial is near Wachapreague and just one mile from the ocean. Quiet and comfortable. Water sports nearby. One room with private bath. Continental breakfast. $95.

7 No smoking; 8 Children welcome; 9 Social drinking allowed; 10 Tennis nearby; 11 Swimming nearby; 12 Golf nearby; 13 Skiing nearby; 14 May be booked through a travel agent; 15 Handicapped accessible.

LURAY

Blue Ridge Bed & Breakfast

2458 Castleman Road, Berryville, 22611
(540) 955-1246; (800) 296-1246
FAX (540) 955-4240; e-mail: blurdgbb@shentel.net
www.blueridgebb.com

A. Fabulous mansion built in 1739. Eighteen acres with ponds, in-ground pool, great mountain views, antique furnishings. Two separate cottages also available. $90-150.

B. Large Victorian house with each room providing a private bath and fireplace. Jacuzzi. Bikes and canoes provided. Complete with resident ghost. Full country breakfast and afternoon buffet provided for guests. Mystery weekends available. $98-145.

C. Built in 1931, this grand old inn rests on 14 acres of lawn and formal gardens, delighting its guests with a colonial dining room offering traditional menu. A gallery features the art of P. Buckley Moss, who is often a guest at the inn. The Gilded Cage, specializing in antiques and fine art restoration, is on the lower level. Single, double, and family units available. Also suites with private parlors. This inn boasts a banquet room that will accommodate up to 200 people. A solarium and terrace overlook the formal gardens. Eleanor Roosevelt was an honored guest at this inn. Jacuzzi available. $54-124.

Locust Grove Inn

1456 North Egypt Bend Road, 22835
(540) 743-1804; FAX (540) 843-0751
e-mail: locustg@shentel.net
www.bbonline.com/va/locustgrove/

A time away, a place away—here mountains end, a valley starts, a river runs by. Unforgettable scenery and centuries of history make this restored colonial log house on a large farm a piece of paradise for history and nature lovers.

Five spacious bedrooms, all with private bathrooms, central air conditioning, and beautiful views. Three miles west of Luray on the Shenandoah River. One mile of Shenandoah riverfront.

Hosts: Rod and Isabel Graves
Rooms: 5 (PB) $110-125
Full Breakfast
Credit Cards: A, B, D
Notes: 2, 5, 7, 8, 9, 10, 11, 12, 13, 14

The Woodruff House

The Woodruff House Bed & Breakfast

330 Mechanic Street, 22835
(540) 743-1494

This 1882 fairy-tale Victorian is beautifully appointed with period antiques, hallmarked silver, and fine china. Each room includes working fireplace and private bathroom. Some rooms have Jacuzzis for two. Escape from reality, come into this fairytale where the ambiance never ends! Awaken to freshly brewed coffees delivered to guests' doors; a gourmet candlelit breakfast follows. Sumptuous candlelit high tea buffet dinner included. Relax in the fireside candlelit garden spa. AAA three-diamond-rated. Mobil three-star. Chef owned and operated *Intimate Weddings and Honeymoons* Inquire about accommodations for children.

Hosts: Lucas and Deborah Woodruff
Rooms: 6 (PB) $98-195
Full Breakfast
Credit Cards: A, B, D
Notes: 2, 4, 5, 7, 9, 10, 11, 12, 13, 14

NOTES: Credit cards accepted: A MasterCard; B Visa; C American Express; D Discover; E Diner's Club; F Other; 2 Personal checks accepted; 3 Lunch available; 4 Dinner available; 5 Open all year; 6 Pets welcome;

LYNCHBURG

Blue Ridge Bed & Breakfast

2458 Castleman Road, Berryville, 22611
(540) 955-1246; (800) 296-1246
FAX (540) 955-4240; e-mail: blurdgbb@shentel.net
www.blueridgebb.com

A. Built in 1874, this fabulous Victorian home
is in the National Register of Historic Places
and has received the Merit Award from the
Lynchburg Historic Association for outstanding exterior renovation. Near Blue Ridge Parkway and Appomatox. $65-109.

B. This fabulous house is on a very quiet acre
of land. Beautifully landscaped. Both host and
hostess are interior decorators. House filled
with antiques and reproductions. It is close to
many colleges and universities, the entrance to
the Blue Ridge Parkway, Wintergreen skiing,
and Walton's Mountain. $65-85.

Federal Crest Inn Bed & Breakfast

1101 Federal Street, 24504
(804) 845-6155; (800) 818-6155
FAX (804) 845-1445
www.inmind.com/federalcrest

Relax and unwind in this elegant 1909 Georgian Revival brick home in a historical district.

Federal Crest Inn

Enjoy unique woodwork, bedroom fireplaces,
central air, down comforters, whirlpool tub,
canopied queen-size beds, 1950s café, gift
shop, antiques, country breakfasts, friendly
hosts, and much more. Perhaps there might
even be a special invitation to visit the third-
floor theater where the original owner built a
stage for his children to give plays. Convenient
to Jefferson's Poplar Forest and Appomatox.

Hosts: Ann and Phil Ripley
Rooms: 5 (4 PB; 1 SB) $85-125
Full Breakfast
Credit Cards: A, B, C, D
Notes: 2, 5, 7, 9, 12, 13, 14

Lynchburg Mansion Inn

Lynchburg Mansion Inn Bed & Breakfast

405 Madison Street, 24504
(804) 528-5400; (800) 352-1199
FAX (804) 847-2545; e-mail: Mansioninn@aol.com
www.Lynchburgmansioninn.com

Enjoy luxurious accommodations in a 9,000-
square-foot Spanish Georgian mansion on a
street still paved in turn-of-the-century brick in a
national register historic district. Highly rated
inn, known for attention to detail. Remarkable
interior cherry woodwork. King- and queen-size
beds, lavish linens, private bathrooms, fireplaces, TV, telephones, turn-down with chocolates. Full silver service breakfast. Hot tub.
Suites. Well-supervised children welcome. Near

7 No smoking; 8 Children welcome; 9 Social drinking allowed; 10 Tennis nearby; 11 Swimming nearby;
12 Golf nearby; 13 Skiing nearby; 14 May be booked through a travel agent; 15 Handicapped accessible.

Appomattox, Jefferson's Poplar Forest, summer baseball, Blue Ridge, antiquing, colleges.

Hosts: Bob and Mauranna Sherman
Rooms: 5 (PB) $109-144
Full Breakfast
Credit Cards: A, B, C, E
Notes: 2, 5, 7, 8, 9, 10, 11, 12, 14

MADISON

Guesthouses Bed & Breakfast

P.O. Box 5737, Charlottesville, 22905
(804) 979-7264 (12:00-5:00 P.M. weekdays)
FAX (804) 293-7791
e-mail: guesthouses_bnb_reservations@
    compuserve.com
www.va-guesthouses.com

Laurel Run. A recently built cottage in the woods of Madison County, 30 miles north of Charlottesville. This private cabin offers a great room, kitchen, dining area, and two bedrooms on the first floor. The loft has a double bed and cot. The broad, screened porch offers views of a stream, fields, and woods. Hiking, fishing, and riding are available in nearby Shenandoah National Park. Breakfast supplies are included for the first morning of guests' stay. $100-200.

MADISON HEIGHTS

Blue Ridge Bed & Breakfast

2458 Castleman Road, Berryville, 22611
(540) 955-1246; (800) 296-1246
FAX (540) 955-4240; e-mail: blurdgbb@shentel.net
www.blueridgebb.com

A. This 80-year-old grand southern Colonial mansion is in the middle of 14 acres with fabulous views of Blue Ridge Parkway. Fishing on the James River. Near Appomatox. $69-85.

MANASSAS

Blue Ridge Bed & Breakfast

2458 Castleman Road, Berryville, 22611
(540) 955-1246; (800) 296-1246
FAX (540) 955-4240; e-mail: blurdgbb@shentel.net
www.blueridgebb.com

A. In Manassas battlefields, this beautiful restored farmhouse was built upon General McDowell's campsite. Just five miles from I-66 and 35 minutes from Washington, D.C. Antiques, fireplaces, stone walls, barn livestock, and old gas lamps throughout make this a special treat. $88-100.

MEADOWS OF DAN

Meadowood Bed & Breakfast

6235 Buffalo Mountain Road, SW, 24120
(540) 593-2600; FAX (540) 593-2700

Meadowood is just a short 1,000 feet off the Blue Ridge Parkway (near milepost 174) on 20 beautiful acres of fields and woods with views of the surrounding mountains. Peaceful and quiet, yet only two and one-half miles from the Chateau Morrisette Winery and two miles from famous Mabry Mill. Old split rail fences, spring-fed streams, park benches, and walking trails abound. A 60-foot front porch looks out over the fields and mountains. Large gathering room with library and warm woodstove is provided. Reservations are suggested. "Just what a

Meadowood

NOTES: Credit cards accepted: A MasterCard; B Visa; C American Express; D Discover; E Diner's Club; F Other; 2 Personal checks accepted; 3 Lunch available; 4 Dinner available; 5 Open all year; 6 Pets welcome;

bed and breakfast should be"—*Blue Ridge Country*. "Delightful bed and breakfast just off the Blue Ridge Parkway"—*LA Times*. Children over 12 welcome.

Hosts: Frank and Leona Warren
Rooms: 4-5 (4 PB; 1-2 SB) $75-95
Full Breakfast
Credit Cards: None
Notes: 2, 5, 7, 9, 10, 12

Spangler's Bed & Breakfast

1340 Mayberry Church Road, 24120-9523
(703) 952-2454

On Country Road 602 within view of the Blue Ridge Parkway at milepost 180, four miles from Mabry Mill, this 1904 farmhouse has a kitchen with fireplace, piano, and four porches. There is also an 1826 private log cabin perfect for one couple. An additional 1987 log cabin has two bedrooms, complete kitchen, and wraparound porch. Fishing in the lake, swimming, three boats, bikes, and volleyball. No smoking inside. No pets.

Hosts: Martha and Harold Spangler
Rooms: 7 (2 PB; 5 SB) $50-60
Full Breakfast
Credit Cards: None
Notes: 2, 7, 8, 9, 10, 11, 12

MIDDLEBURG

Blue Ridge Bed & Breakfast

2458 Castleman Road, Berryville, 22611
(540) 955-1246; (800) 296-1246
FAX (540) 955-4240; e-mail: blurdgbb@shentel.net
www.blueridgebb.com

A. Two-hundred-year-old cozy commercial inn in the heart of Middleburg with working fireplaces in all bedrooms. Complete facilities for dinner. Accessible to quaint shops and eateries. $95-275.

The Longbarn

37129 Adams Green Lane, P.O. Box 208, 20118-0208
(540) 687-4137; FAX (504) 687-4044
e-mail:thlongbarn@aol.com
http://member.aol.com/thlongbarn/

Century-old renovated barn in historic Middleburg, VA, surrounded by beautiful woods; European-style garden; swimming, horseback and bicycle riding nearby; golf course available. Air conditioning, fireplaces, and large library for guests' pleasure and comfort. Elegant ambiance in Italian country style; spacious bedrooms with private bath. Delicious breakfast with warm breads and other specialties from Europe. For guests' safety, no indoor smoking.

Host: Chiara Langeley
Rooms: 3 (PB) $105-125
Full Breakfast
Credit Cards: A, B, F
Notes: 2, 5, 7, 9, 10, 11, 12, 14

MIDDLETOWN

Blue Ridge Bed & Breakfast

2458 Castleman Road, Berryville, 22611
(540) 955-1246; (800) 296-1246
FAX (540) 955-4240; e-mail: blurdgbb@shentel.net
www.blueridgebb.com

A. Historic Victorian home on Main Street close to famous restaurant and theatre. All period furniture. Minutes from many antique shops, Passion play, and small lake with beach. $65.

Wayside Inn

7783 Main Street, 22645
(877) 869-1797; (540) 869-1797
FAX (540) 869-6038
e-mail: waysiden@shentel.net

The Wayside Inn is an elegantly restored 18th-century inn nestled in the Shenandoah Valley, exit 302 off of I-81. The inn features period furnishings, rare antiques, and an extensive collection of Americana. There are 22 unique

7 No smoking; 8 Children welcome; 9 Social drinking allowed; 10 Tennis nearby; 11 Swimming nearby; 12 Golf nearby; 13 Skiing nearby; 14 May be booked through a travel agent; 15 Handicapped accessible.

Wayside Inn

guest rooms and suites with private baths, and eight charming dining rooms that feature authentic regional American cuisine. Hiking, swimming, fishing, boating, golfing, skiing, and the Wayside Theatre are all nearby. Small pets welcome.

Rooms: 22 (PB) $110-160
Full Breakfast
Credit Cards: A, B, C, D, E
Notes: 3, 4, 5, 6, 7, 8, 9, 10, 11, 12, 13, 14

MILLWOOD

Blue Ridge Bed & Breakfast

2458 Castleman Road, Berryville, 22611
(540) 955-1246; (800) 296-1246
FAX (540) 955-4240; e-mail: blurdgbb@shentel.net
www.blueridgebb.com

A. Guests in the 1780s section of this stone mansion can enjoy huge fireplaces in every room. There is easy access through a separate entrance to the Shenandoah River. Easy drive to and from Washington, D.C., which is just an hour away. $70-108.

MOLLUSK

Guesthouses on the Water at Greenvale

Route 354, Box 70, 22517
(804) 462-5995

Two separate and private guest houses on 13 acres on the Rappahannock River and Greenvale Creek. Pool, dock, private beach, and bicycles. Each house is furnished with antiques and reproductions and has two bedrooms, two baths, living room, kitchen, and deck. Air conditioned. Enjoy sweeping water views, breathtaking sunsets, and relaxing and peaceful tranquility. Weekly rates available.

Hosts: Pam and Walt Smith
Guest Houses: 2 (PB) $85-125
Continental Breakfast
Credit Cards: A, B
Notes: 2, 5, 9, 11, 12

MONTEREY

Highland Inn

Main Street, P.O. Box 40, 24465
(703) 468-2143; (888) INN-INVA (466-4682)

Classic Victorian inn listed in the National Register of Historic Places. Tranquil location in the picturesque village of Monterey, nestled in the foothills of the Allegheny Mountains. There are 17 individually decorated rooms furnished with antiques and collectibles, each with private bath. Full-service dining room and tavern offer dinner Monday through Saturday and Sunday brunch. Antiquing, hiking, fishing, golf, and mineral baths are nearby.

Host: Michael Strand and Cynthia Peel
Rooms: 17 (PB) $55-85
Continental Breakfast
Credit Cards: A, B, C, D
Notes: 2, 4, 5, 8, 9, 11, 12, 13, 14

Highland Inn

NOTES: Credit cards accepted: A MasterCard; B Visa; C American Express; D Discover; E Diner's Club; F Other; 2 Personal checks accepted; 3 Lunch available; 4 Dinner available; 5 Open all year; 6 Pets welcome;

MOUNT JACKSON

Amanda's Bed & Breakfast Reservation Service

3538 Lakeway Drive, Ellicott City, MD 21042-1226
(443) 535-0008; (800) 899-7533
FAX (443) 535-0009; e-mail: AmandasRS@aol.com
www.Amandas-BBRS.com

181. An 1830 Colonial homestead on seven acres overlooking the George Washington Mountains. Some bedrooms have wood-burning fireplaces, and the antique furniture is for sale. Pool on premises. Area activities include craft fairs, hiking, fishing, tennis, and horseback riding. Five rooms with private baths. Two guest cottages. Full breakfast. $65-85.

Blue Ridge Bed & Breakfast

2458 Castleman Road, Berryville, 22611
(540) 955-1246; (800) 296-1246
FAX (540) 955-4240; e-mail: blurdgbb@shentel.net
www.blueridgebb.com

A. This 1830 stately Colonial is near George Washington Parkway, 10 miles from Bryce. Six bedrooms with working fireplaces. There is also a cozy two and one-half room cottage separate from the main house. Pool. Full breakfast. $65-90.

NELLYSFORD

Distinguished Accommodations in the Potomac Region— (Amanda's Bed & Breakfast Reservation Service)

3538 Lakeway Drive, Ellicott City, MD 21042-1226
(443) 535-0008; (800) 899-7533
FAX (443) 535-0009; e-mail: AmandasRS@aol.com
www.Amandas-BBRS.com

397. Richness and romance of a bygone era, beautifully restored and lovingly appointed. Sitting atop a verdant knoll, this historic home is surrounded by the magnificence of the Blue Ridge Mountains. Charming rooms or luxurious suites offer elegant comfort, romantic privacy, and incredible views. Enjoy serenity and inspiring surroundings from any of the five porches, the hammock, or a peaceful spot on the 13 acres. Some rooms feature a double whirlpool bath or double sauna. Historic sites within a short drive or stay around the property for quiet contemplation. A delicious and satisfying gourmet breakfast is included. A prix fixe lunch or dinner is available by reservations. From $135.

Guesthouses Bed & Breakfast

P.O. Box 5737, Charlottesville 22905
(804) 979-7264 (12:00-5:00 P.M. weekdays)
FAX (804) 293-7791
e-mail: guesthouses_bnb_reservations@
  compuserve.com
www.va-guesthouses.com

The Mark Addy. Near Nellysford in the Rockfish Valley near the foot of Wintergreen, this inn has magnificent mountain views. Relax on one of the porches or in the library or parlor, or stroll around the beautiful grounds. This inn offers eight guest rooms or suites furnished with lovely antiques and collectibles, each with a private bath. Two rooms have Jacuzzis. A bountiful breakfast is served. Smoking outdoors on the porches only. Not suitable for children under 12. Air conditioned. $95-135.

Meander Inn. A 75-year-old Victorian farmhouse on 50 acres of pasture and woods skirted by hiking trails and traversed by the Rockfish River. The inn offers five twin or queen-size bedrooms, some with private baths. A delicious full country breakfast is served each morning. Guests may enjoy the hot tub, woodburning stove, player piano, deck, or front porch. Wintergreen Resort and Stoney Creek golf and tennis facilities are available to guests. Smoking is permitted outdoors only. Air conditioning. $80-100.

7 No smoking; 8 Children welcome; 9 Social drinking allowed; 10 Tennis nearby; 11 Swimming nearby; 12 Golf nearby; 13 Skiing nearby; 14 May be booked through a travel agent; 15 Handicapped accessible.

The Meander Inn

3100 Berry Hill Road, 22959
(804) 361-1121; FAX (806) 361-1380
e-mail: meanderinn@aol.com
www.symweb.com/rockfish/meander.html

Nestled in the foothills of Virginia's Blue Ridge Mountains, in the peaceful surroundings of the Rockfish Valley, the Meander Inn and its 40 acres, welcomes guests to relax in the distinctively French ambiance. Guests can refresh and regroup in the comfort of country farm-style living. Activities in the surrounding area include skiing, hiking, golf, tennis, horseback riding, fishing, swimming, antique shopping. Historic sites such as Charlottesville's Monticello and the University of Virginia are all within 30 minutes' travel.

Hosts: Conte Alain and Francesca San Giorgio
Rooms: 5 (PB) $105-125
Full Breakfast
Credit Cards: A, B, C, D, E, F
Notes: 2, 4, 5, 7, 10, 11, 12, 13

Trillium House

P.O. Box 280, 22958
(804) 325-9126; (800) 325-9126
FAX (804) 325-1099

Trillium House was built in 1983 as a small 12-room country hotel. Relax in the great room, garden room, TV room, or the outstanding library. Available to guests at preferred rates: two golf courses, swimming pool, 30 tennis courts, 25 miles of mapped hiking trails. The entry gate to the Wintergreen Mountain Village is one mile from the Blue Ridge Parkway; motorcycle restrictions. Dinner available Friday and Saturday. Inquire about accommodations for pets.

Rooms: 12 (PB) $100-160
Full Breakfast
Credit Cards: A, B
Notes: 2, 5, 7, 8, 9, 10, 11, 12, 13, 14, 15

NEW CHURCH

Blue Ridge Bed & Breakfast

2458 Castleman Road, Berryville, 22611
(540) 955-1246; (800) 296-1246
FAX (540) 955-4240; e-mail: blurdgbb@shentel.net
www.blueridgebb.com

A. Beautiful Colonial house built in 1790 on 20 acres with fabulous view of Massanetta Mountains, and a fishing creek. Franklin D. Roosevelt slept here in 1936. Ski resort is only 15 miles away. $55-65.

B. Beautiful carriage house built in 1873 offers two rooms in the main house. There is a cottage on the premises that offers two rooms decorated with lovely country decor and many oak and wicker antiques. In the heart of a busy Civil War town within easy walking distance of many quaint country shops and restaurants. $60-65.

C. Gracious manor house in a beautiful garden setting with fabulous mountain views. Built in 1926 in the middle of one and a half acres of land. Gourmet breakfast served: chef attended cooking school in Europe. Afternoon tea included. Activities include antiquing, museums, caverns, Civil War sites, vineyards, and fine restaurants. $55-90.

NEW MARKET

Cross Roads Inn Bed & Breakfast

9222 John Sevier Road, 22844
(540) 740-4157; FAX (540) 740-4255
e-mail: freisitz@shentel.net

This Victorian clapboard home is full of southern hospitality and European charm. The innkeepers serve imported Austrian coffee alongside the homemade breakfasts, and apple strudel is served as an afternoon refreshment. The home is decorated with English floral wallpapers, laced with family antiques, and

---

NOTES: Credit cards accepted: A MasterCard; B Visa; C American Express; D Discover; E Diner's Club; F Other; 2 Personal checks accepted; 3 Lunch available; 4 Dinner available; 5 Open all year; 6 Pets welcome;

Cross Roads Inn

boasts a wonderful view of New Market Gap and Massanutten Mountain. The historic downtown area is within walking distance.

Hosts: Mary-Lloyd and Roland Freisitzer
Rooms: 6 (PB) $55-100
Full Breakfast
Credit Cards: A, B
Notes: 2, 5, 7, 8, 9, 10, 11, 12, 13

ONANCOCK

The Spinning Wheel Bed & Breakfast

31 North Street, 23417
(757) 787-7311
e-mail: BandB@downtownonancock.com
www.downtownonancock.com

An 1890s folk Victorian home with antiques and spinning wheels throughout. Waterfront town listed in the National Register of Historic Places. Calm Eastern Shore getaway from D.C., Virginia, Maryland, Delaware, and New Jersey. Full breakfast. All rooms with private baths, queen-size beds, and air conditioning. Walk to restaurants, shops, and deep-water harbor. Golf and tennis available at private club. Near beach, bay, and ocean. Bicycles, antiques, museums, kayaking, festivals, fishing, wildlife refuge, and Tangier Island cruise. Open May through October. AAA-approved.

Hosts: Karen and David Tweedie
Rooms: 5 (PB) $75-95
Full Breakfast
Credit Cards: A, B, D
Notes: 2, 3, 4, 7, 9, 10, 11, 12, 14

ORANGE

Hidden Inn

249 Caroline Street, 22960
(540) 672-3625; (800) 841-1253
FAX (540) 672-5029
e-mail: hiddeninn@ns.gemlink.com
www.innbook.com/hidden.html

A romantic Victorian featuring 10 guest rooms, each with private bath. Jacuzzis, working fireplaces, and private verandas are available. Wicker and rocking chairs on the wraparound verandas; handmade quilts and canopied beds enhance the Victorian flavor. Full country breakfast, afternoon tea, and candlelight picnics. Minutes from Monticello, Montpelier, and Virginia wineries.

Hosts: Ray and Barbara Lonick
Rooms: 10 (PB) $99-169
Full Breakfast
Credit Cards: A, B, C
Notes: 2, 5, 7, 8, 9, 10, 11, 12, 14

7 No smoking; 8 Children welcome; 9 Social drinking allowed; 10 Tennis nearby; 11 Swimming nearby; 12 Golf nearby; 13 Skiing nearby; 14 May be booked through a travel agent; 15 Handicapped accessible.

PETERSBURG

The High Street Inn–
A Bed & Breakfast

405 High Street, 23803
(804) 733-0505; FAX (804) 861-9433
e-mail: highst@mail.ctg.net; www.ctg.net/owlcat/

An elegant turn-of-the-century Queen Anne
mansion (circa 1899) a few blocks' walk to the
Old Towne historic district, restaurants,
antiques, and Civil War museums. Spacious
guest rooms, most with private baths, air conditioning units, and beautiful wood floors. Full
breakfast. Discounted rates on weekdays. Easy
day trips to Richmond, James River plantations, and Civil War sites. The "purr-fect" base
for guests' southern Virginia discovery. Inquire
about accommodations for pets. Children over
eight welcome.

Hosts: Jim Hillier and Jon Hackett
Rooms: 6 (4 PB: 2 SB) $75-105
Full Breakfast
Credit Cards: A, B, D
Notes: 2, 5, 6, 7, 8, 9, 12, 14

PORT HAYWOOD

Tabb's Creek Inn

Route 14, Mathews County, P.O. Box 219, 23138
(804) 725-5136

Private water-view porches make this an especially attractive getaway for those seeking a
dose of seclusion. On the banks of Tabb's
Creek in Chesapeake Bay, this post-Colonial
farm features a detached guest cottage separated by pool and rose garden. Innkeeper is a
well-known producing artist. The rooms are
decorated with stippling, stenciling, antiques,
and beds that soothe. Canoe and paddle boat
provided so guests can scoot by sea. Lunch and
dinner available upon request. Smoking permitted in designated areas only.

Tabb's Creek Inn

Hosts: Catherine and Cabell Venable
Rooms: 4 (PB) $75-125
Full Breakfast
Credit Cards: None
Notes: 2, 5, 6, 8, 11, 12, 14

PROVIDENCE FORGE

Jasmine Plantation
Bed & Breakfast Inn

4500 North Courthouse Road, 23140
(804) 966-9836; (800) NEW-KENT
FAX (804) 966-5679

Restored 1750s farmhouse on 47 acres with
rooms decorated in various period antiques.
Secluded, yet only three minutes from I-64 and
convenient to Williamsburg, James River Plantations, and Richmond. Fine dining, golf,
sporting clays, fishing, and horse racing

Jasmine Plantation

NOTES: Credit cards accepted: A MasterCard; B Visa; C American Express; D Discover; E Diner's Club;
F Other; 2 Personal checks accepted; 3 Lunch available; 4 Dinner available; 5 Open all year; 6 Pets welcome;

nearby. Nature areas and walking trails. Full country breakfast. No smoking inside.

Hosts: Joyce and Howard Vogt
Rooms: 6 (4 PB; 2 SB) $80-120
Full Breakfast
Credit Cards: A, B, C
Notes: 2, 5, 7, 12, 14

PULASKI

Count Pulaski Bed & Breakfast & Gardens

821 North Jefferson Avenue, 24301
(540) 980-1163; (800) 980-1163

Historic home in quiet neighborhood, Southwest Virginia mountain town. Easy to find, near I-81. In the National Register of Historic Places. Furnished with family antiques, owner's paintings, and items collected from living and traveling around the world. All rooms with new queen- or king- size beds, private baths, tubs and showers, ceiling fans, air conditioning, several fireplaces, continuous beverage center. Gardens in season, arched bridge, patio and outdoor furniture, seed or samples of flowers available. Full gourmet breakfast served at guests' convenience by candlelight, with classical music.

Host: Dr. Florence Byrd Stevenson
Rooms: 3 (PB) $95
Full Breakfast
Credit Cards: A, B
Notes: 5, 7, 9, 10, 11, 12

Count Pulaski

PURCELLVILLE

Amanda's Bed & Breakfast Reservation Service

3538 Lakeway Drive, Ellicott City, MD 21042-1226
(443) 535-0008; (800) 899-7533
FAX (443) 535-0009; e-mail: AmandasRS@aol.com
www.Amandas-BBRS.com

114. A spacious new log home in a meadow setting at the foothills of the Blue Ridge Mountains. Enjoy the sun rise with early morning coffee relaxing in a rocking chair on the front veranda. Convenient to Harpers Ferry and Shepherdstown. Two rooms, each with private bath. One with whirlpool. Continental breakfast. $85-90.

239. Be refreshed by a country setting while staying in an 18th-century home. Guest rooms are welcoming and spacious. The four private-bath bedrooms are pleasingly decorated with comfortable beds and easy chairs. One room has a Jacuzzi and one has a fireplace. A full breakfast is served. $100-125.

Blue Ridge Bed & Breakfast

2458 Castleman Road, Berryville, 22611
(540) 955-1246; (800) 296-1246
FAX (540) 955-4240; e-mail: blurdgbb@shentel.net
www.blueridgebb.com

A. Quaint log house just 10 minutes from Harpers Ferry. Hiking, white-water rafting, great restaurants, and a fun flea market. Mixture of antiques and reproductions. TV, room for all guests. Full country breakfast. Beautiful stone fireplace. Hostess is from Australia. $80-90.

REMINGTON (WARRENTON)

Highland Farm & Inn, L.L.C.

10981 Lees Mill Road, 22734
(540) 439-0088
http: //highlandfarminn.hypermart.net

In Lakota, south of Warrenton, this secluded, 36-acre farm is known for raising thoroughbred

7 No smoking; 8 Children welcome; 9 Social drinking allowed; 10 Tennis nearby; 11 Swimming nearby; 12 Golf nearby; 13 Skiing nearby; 14 May be booked through a travel agent; 15 Handicapped accessible.

Highland Farm

horses and cattle. Often fox and deer share their pastures. The accommodations, with private baths and queen-size beds, are tastefully furnished with family antiques. Guests may enjoy the spacious solarium or comfortable living room for conversation, cozy fires, and spectacular sunsets. Swim in the in-ground pool, walk along the Rappahannock River, or relax by the waterfall and ponds. Antiquing, Civil War battlefields, horse events, wineries, and fine dining are a short drive away. Enjoy afternoon refreshments and a delightful breakfast. One room is handicapped accessible. Dinners by reservation only. Smoking permitted outside.

Hosts: Ralph and Linda Robinson
Rooms: 3 (2 PB; 1 S1/2B) $60-110
Full Breakfast
Credit Cards: None
Notes: 2, 4, 5, 7, 9, 11, 12, 15

RICHMOND

The Emmanuel Hutzler House

2036 Monument Avenue, 23220
(804) 355-4885; (804) 353-6900
e-mail: be.our.guest@bensonhouse.com
www.bensonhouse.com

This large Italian Renaissance-style inn has been totally renovated and offers leaded-glass windows, coffered ceilings, and natural mahogany raised paneling throughout the downstairs, and a large living room with marble fireplace for guests' enjoyment. Four guest rooms on the second floor, each have sitting

area and private bath. One suite has a four-poster bed, love seat, and wing chair. The largest suite has a marble fireplace, four-poster mahogany bed, antique sofa, dresser, and a private bath with shower and Jacuzzi. Resident cat. Nonsmoking environment. Children over 12 welcome.

Hosts: Lyn M. Benson and John E. Richardson
Rooms: 4 (PB) $95-155
Continental and Full Breakfasts
Credit Cards: A, B, C, D, E
Notes: 2, 5, 7, 9, 10, 11, 12, 14

The William Catlin House

2304 East Broad Street, 23223
(804) 780-3746

Antiques and working fireplaces await at the William Catlin House, built in 1845, Richmond's first and oldest in the historic district. The luxury of goose down pillows and evening sherry promises a restful night. Each morning a delicious full breakfast and endless pots of steaming hot coffee or tea await guests in the elegant dining room. Numerous nearby historic sites. As seen in *Colonial Homes*, *Southern Living*, and *Mid-Atlantic* magazines.

The William Catlin House

NOTES: Credit cards accepted: A MasterCard; B Visa; C American Express; D Discover; E Diner's Club; F Other; 2 Personal checks accepted; 3 Lunch available; 4 Dinner available; 5 Open all year; 6 Pets welcome;

Hosts: Robert and Josephine Martin
Rooms: 5 (3 PB; 2 SB) $75-125
Full Breakfast
Credit Cards: A, B, D
Notes: 2, 5, 7, 8, 9, 10, 14

ROANOKE

CrossTrails Bed & Breakfast

5880 Blaksburg Road, Catawba, 24070
(540) 384-8078; (800) 841-8078
e-mail: xtrails@roanoke.infi.net

A mountain valley getaway in scenic Catawba Valley where the Appalachian Trail and TransAmerica Bicycle Trail cross between Roanoke and Blacksburg. World- class hiking and biking just outside the door. The 15 acres adjoining on three sides are national park property. Porches and decks designed to take advantage of commanding views. Rooms have queen-size beds and private baths. Remote carriage house, hot tub, library, cross-country skiing, fly-fishing, shuttles, full breakfast, Homeplace Restaurant nearby.

Hosts: Bill and Katherine Cochran
Rooms: 3 (PB) $70-75
Full Breakfast
Credit Cards: None
Notes: 2, 7, 9, 12

Stone Manor Bed & Breakfast

1135 Stone Manor Place, Smith Mountain Lake, 24095
(540) 297-1414

On beautiful Smith Mountain Lake–690 feet of waterfront, lighted boardwalk, dockage for boats, fishing, in-ground swimming pool, all-season sunroom boasting a panoramic view of the lake. Golf close by. Resort-like atmosphere. Guest rooms highlight themes of the lake activities. Magnificent lake views and sunsets. Near Roanoke and Blue Ridge Parkway. Children over 12 welcome.

Rooms: 3 (PB) $85-105
Credit Cards: A, B, D
Notes: 2, 5, 7, 9, 11, 12, 14

SCOTTSVILLE

Guesthouses Bed & Breakfast

P.O. Box 5737, Charlottesville, 22905
(804) 979-7264 (12:00-5:00 P.M. weekdays)
FAX (804) 293-7791
e-mail: guesthouses_bnb_reservations@
    compuserve.com
www.va-guesthouses.com

Belle Grove. In a beautiful setting on a small farm with gardens and rolling pastures, this upstairs guest suite is in a separate building adjacent to the 1750 home that was the original Scottsville courthouse. These accommodations are light and airy with a large bed-sitting room. There is a queen bed, a kitchenette, and dining area furnished with antiques. There are lovely grounds to wander, and a swimming pool available in season. Continental breakfast supplies are left for you. Air conditioning. No smoking indoors. $125-150.

SMITHFIELD

Isle of Wight Inn

1607 South Church Street, 23430
(757) 357-3176; (757) 357-0777

This luxurious Colonial bed and breakfast inn is found in a delightful historic river-port town. Several suites with fireplaces and Jacuzzis. Antique shop featuring tallcase clocks and period furniture. More than 60 old homes in town dating from 1750. Just 30 minutes and a ferry ride from Williamsburg and Jamestown; less than an hour from James River plantations, Norfolk, Hampton, and Virginia Beach. No smoking allowed in common areas and some rooms.

Hosts: The Harts and the Earls
Rooms: 10 (PB) $59-119
Full Breakfast
Credit Cards: A, B, C, D
Notes: 2, 5, 8, 9, 10, 11, 12, 14

---

7 No smoking; 8 Children welcome; 9 Social drinking allowed; 10 Tennis nearby; 11 Swimming nearby; 12 Golf nearby; 13 Skiing nearby; 14 May be booked through a travel agent; 15 Handicapped accessible.

SPERRYVILLE

Sharp Rock Farm
Bed & Breakfast

5 Sharp Rock Road, 22740
(540) 987-8020; www.bnb-n-va.com/sharp.htm

Sharp Rock Farm is on 23 acres in an unspoiled valley at the foot of the Blue Ridge Mountains with the Hughes River meandering through the property. It embodies the peace and pleasures of country life at its best with trout fishing, swimming, and six-acre vineyard. Hike nearby Old Rag Mountain. There are spectacular views at every turn. Hosts offer a two-bedroom cottage and a carriage house with privacy plus gourmet breakfasts. Smoking permitted outside only. Nestled in beautiful Rappahannock County.

Hosts: Marilyn and David Armor
Rooms: 3 (2 PB; 1 SB) $125-200
Full Breakfast
Credit Cards: A, B
Notes: 2, 5, 7, 8, 9, 11, 12, 14, 15

Sharp Rock Farm

STANARDSVILLE

Edgewood Farm
Bed & Breakfast

1186 Middle River Road, 22973
(800) 985-3782; FAX (804) 985-6275
e-mail: edgewoodfarm@firstva.com
www.firstnetva.com/edgewoodfarm

Edgewood Farm

Beautifully restored circa 1790 farmhouse on 130 acres in the Blue Ridge foothills. Off the beaten path yet near Skyline Drive, wineries, fine restaurants. antique and craft shops as well as Montpelier, Monticello, Ash Lawn, and University of Virginia. Accommodations include spacious, period-decorated bedrooms with private and shared baths and wood-burning fireplaces in each room. A sumptuous breakfast is served each morning on fine china; coffee, tea, or juice is brought to guests' door each morning before breakfast with the newspaper. Sparkling apple cider, cheese and crackers, and fruit served upon arrival. Lovely views, excellent bird watching, quiet and relaxing atmosphere. Skiing is one hour away.

Hosts: Eleanor and Norman Schwartz
Rooms: 3 (2 PB; 2 SB) $90-110
Full Breakfast
Credit Cards: A, B, C
Notes: 2, 5, 7, 8, 9, 11, 12, 14

STANLEY

Jordan Hollow Farm Inn

326 Hawksbill Park Road, 22851
(540) 778-2285; (888) 418-7000
FAX (540) 778-1759
e-mail: jhf@jordanhollow.com

Circa 1700s inn nestled at the base of the Blue Ridge Mountains. Beautiful views, 150 acres to roam, horses to ride. Relax on the spacious porches, walk the trails, and enjoy the llamas

---

NOTES: Credit cards accepted: A MasterCard; B Visa; C American Express; D Discover; E Diner's Club; F Other; 2 Personal checks accepted; 3 Lunch available; 4 Dinner available; 5 Open all year; 6 Pets welcome;

Jordan Hollow Farm Inn

and other farm animals. Fabulous meals in the restaurant—a restored Shenandoah Valley farmhouse. New Luray Caverns, Shenandoah River, snow skiing. "We welcome you with true southern hospitality!"

Hosts: Betsy Anderson and Gail Kyle
Rooms: 14 (PB) $125-200
Full Breakfast
Credit Cards: A, B, D, E
Notes: 2, 3, 4, 5, 7, 8, 9, 10, 11, 12, 13, 14

STAUNTON

Blue Ridge Bed & Breakfast

2458 Castleman Road, Berryville, 22611
(540) 955-1246; (800) 296-1246
FAX (540) 955-4240; e-mail: blurdgbb@shentel.net
www.blueridgebb.com

A. Farm has 190 acres, close to Woodrow Wilson's birthplace. Monticello, Skyline Drive, Blue Ridge Parkway, Shenandoah and Allegheny Mountains all surround this gracious farmhouse. Museum of American Frontier Culture, James Madison University, and Mary Baldwin College, with many antique shops nearby. Weekend packages available. $50-55.

Frederick House

28 North New Street, 24401
(540) 885-4220; (800) 334-5575
FAX (540) 885-5180
e-mail: ejharman@frederickhouse.com
www.frederickhouse.com

A small hotel in the European tradition. Large, comfortable rooms or suites. Amenities include private baths, air conditioning, TV, telephones, robes, private entrances, and antique furnishings. Some balconies or fireplaces. Gourmet breakfast. Award-winning restoration and gardens. Across from Mary Baldwin College. Near shops, restaurants, and the Woodrow Wilson Birthplace. In central Shenandoah Valley near Skyline Drive and Blue Ridge Parkway.

Hosts: Joe and Evy Harman
Rooms: 20 (PB) $75-170
Full Breakfast
Credit Cards: A, B, C, D, E
Notes: 2, 3, 4, 5, 7, 8, 9, 10, 11, 12, 13, 14

Frederick House

The Sampson Eagon Inn

238 East Beverley Street, 24401
(540) 886-8200 (phone/FAX); (800) 597-9722

In the Virginia historic landmark district of Gospel Hill, this gracious, circa 1840, town residence has been thoughtfully restored and transformed into a unique inn offering affordable luxury and personal service in an intimate, inviting atmosphere. Each elegant, spacious, air-conditioned room features private bath, sitting area, canopied bed, TV/VCR, telephone, and antique furnishings. Adjacent to the Woodrow Wilson birthplace and Mary Baldwin College, the inn is within two blocks of downtown dining and attractions.

7 No smoking; 8 Children welcome; 9 Social drinking allowed; 10 Tennis nearby; 11 Swimming nearby; 12 Golf nearby; 13 Skiing nearby; 14 May be booked through a travel agent; 15 Handicapped accessible.

The Sampson Eagon Inn

Hosts: Laura and Frank Mattingly
Rooms: 5 (PB) $95-120
Full Breakfast
Credit Cards: A, B, C
Notes: 2, 5, 7, 9, 10, 11, 12, 13

Thornrose House at Gypsy Hill

531 Thornrose Avenue, 24401
(540) 885-7026

A wraparound veranda and Greek colonnades
distinguish this turn-of-the-century Georgian
residence. Family antiques, a grand piano, and
fireplaces create an elegant, restful atmosphere.
Breakfast specialties served in a formal dining
room energize guests for sightseeing in the beautiful Shenandoah Valley. Beside a 300-acre park
with golf, tennis, swimming, and trails. Other
attractions include the Woodrow Wilson birthplace, the Museum of American Frontier Culture, and the nearby Skyline Drive and Blue
Ridge Parkway. Children six and older welcome.

Hosts: Suzanne and Otis Huston
Rooms: 5 (PB) $60-90
Full Breakfast
Credit Cards: A, B, C
Notes: 2, 5, 7, 9, 10, 11, 12, 13, 14

STEELES TAVERN

Osceola Mill Country Inn

Route 56, 24476
(540) 377-6455

This 1800s grist mill was built by Cyrus
McCormick, the inventor of the reaper. The
mill itself hosts four guest rooms, the Victorian
Manor house has seven, and the Old Mill Store
has been converted into a honeymoon cottage
with Jacuzzi and fireplace. Also in the Mill,
there is a restaurant for dining amongst chestnut timbers and candlelight. The inn is halfway
between the towns of Staunton and Lexington
and is at the foot of the Blue Ridge Mountains,
close to the Appalachian Trail.

Hosts: Mercer Balliro and Brian Domino
Rooms: 12 (PB) $89-169
Full Breakfast
Credit Cards: A, B
Notes: 2, 4, 5, 7, 9, 11, 12, 15

Osceola Mill Country Inn

Sugar Tree Inn

Highway 56, 24476
(540) 377-2197 (phone/FAX); (800) 377-2197
www.sugartreeinn.com

Sugar Tree, Virginia's mountain inn, is nestled
into a mountainside less than a mile from the
Blue Ridge Parkway. Guests find romantic
seclusion here in rustically elegant surroundings. Each spacious room or suite offers a private wood-burning fireplace and beautiful,
comfortable furnishings. There are 40-mile
views from the front porch rockers. Hike
Sugar Tree trails, explore historic Virginia,
shop, or simply relax. Open April 1 through
December 1. Great hiking, antiquing, scenery,
and historic attractions nearby. One smoking
room available; smoking is not permitted in
public rooms.

NOTES: Credit cards accepted: A MasterCard; B Visa; C American Express; D Discover; E Diner's Club;
F Other; 2 Personal checks accepted; 3 Lunch available; 4 Dinner available; 5 Open all year; 6 Pets welcome;

Rooms: 11 (PB) $100-145
Full Breakfast
Credit Cards: A, B, C, D
Notes: 2, 4, 9, 14, 15

STEPHENS CITY

The Inn at Vaucluse Spring

231 Vaucluse Spring Lane, 22655
(540) 869-0200; (800) 869-0525
FAX (540) 869-9546
e-mail: mail@vauclusespring.com
www.vauclusespring.com

Set amidst 100 acres in the orchard country of the Northern Shenandoah Valley, this enclave of four guest houses offers rooms with manor house elegance or log and stone warmth. Ideally located between Winchester's historic sites and Front Royal's Skyline Drive and Shenandoah River. Enjoy fireplaces, Jacuzzis, warm hospitality and gourmet food in an award-winning historic restoration. Beautiful decor and gardens. Large limestone spring. Swimming pool. Dinner available Saturday night.

Hosts: Neil and Barry Myers;
  Karen and Mike Caplanis
Rooms: 12 (PB) $140-250
Full Breakfast
Credit Cards: A, B
Notes: 2, 5, 7, 9, 12, 14

STRASBURG

Hotel Strasburg

213 Holliday Street, 22657
(540) 465-9191; (800) 348-8327
FAX (540) 465-4788; e-mail: thehotel@shentel.net

Like stepping back in time to the 1890s, Hotel Strasburg combines Victorian history and charm to make a special place for lodging and dining. Tastefully decorated with many antique period pieces and an impressive collection of art. Guests are invited to wander through the inn's dining rooms and quaintly renovated sleeping rooms (Jacuzzi suites). Nestled at the foot of Massanutten Mountain near the entrance to the breathtaking Skyline Drive. Inquire about accommodations for pets.

Hosts: Gary and Carol Rutherford
Rooms: 29 (PB) $74-165
Continental Breakfast
Credit Cards: A, B, C, D, E
Notes: 3, 4, 5, 8, 9, 10, 11, 12, 14

SYRIA

Graves' Mountain Lodge

Route 670, 22743
(540) 923-4231; FAX (540) 923-4312
www.gravesmountain.com

This peaceful lodge is on a large cattle and fruit farm in the shadow of the Blue Ridge Mountains next to the Shenandoah National Park. Guests enjoy three meals a day on the American plan while getting rest and relaxation during their visit. Rooms, cabins, and cottages to choose from. Trout stream and farm ponds are available for fishing. Hiking trails and horseback riding are also available for guests' enjoyment. Open mid-March through November. Seasonal rates available. Inquire about accommodations for pets. Both smoking and nonsmoking rooms available.

Hosts: Rachel and Jim Graves
Rooms: 44 (38 PB; 6 SB) $60-100
Cottages: 11 (PB) $55-100
Full Breakfast
Credit Cards: A, B, D
Notes: 2, 3, 4, 6, 7, 8, 9, 10, 11, 12, 14, 15

VIRGINIA BEACH

Angie's Guest Cottage

302 24th Street, 23451
(757) 428-4690
www.bbinternet.com/angies

Angie's Guest Cottage is in the heart of the resort area, just one block from the ocean. Early-20th-century beach house that former guests describe as "cute, cozy, quiet, and extra clean with fresh flowers everywhere!" All

7 No smoking; 8 Children welcome; 9 Social drinking allowed; 10 Tennis nearby; 11 Swimming nearby; 12 Golf nearby; 13 Skiing nearby; 14 May be booked through a travel agent; 15 Handicapped accessible.

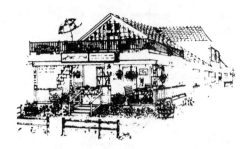

Angie's Guest Cottage

rooms are air conditioned; some have small refrigerators and private entrances. Continental plus breakfast. Sun deck, barbecue pit, and picnic tables. International atmosphere. Closed mid-October through mid-March. Two-night minimum stay. Inquire about accommodations for pets. Also, one- and two-bedroom duplex weekly, and AYH Hostel.

Host: Barbara Yates
Rooms: 6 (1 PB; 5 SB) $60-84
Continental Breakfast
Credit Cards: None
Notes: 7, 8, 9, 10, 11, 12

Barclay Cottage

400 16th Street, 23451
(757) 422-1956; www.barclaycottage.comm
www.inngetaways.com/va/barclay.html

Enjoy casual sophistication in a warm, historic, innlike atmosphere. Two blocks from the beach and in the heart of the Virginia Beach recreational area, the Barclay Cottage has been decorated in turn-of-the-century style with antique

Barclay Cottage

furniture. The hosts welcome guests to the Barclay Cottage where their theme is "We go where our dreams take us." Open April through October. AAA-approved three diamonds.

Hosts: Peter and Claire
Rooms: 5 (3 PB; 2 SB) $78-108
Full Breakfast
Credit Cards: A, B, C
Notes: 7, 9, 10, 11, 12, 14

The Picket Fence

209 43rd Street, 23451
(804) 428-8861

The furnishings in this comfortable Colonial home glow with the patina of loving care. The beach is just one block away, and beach chairs and umbrellas are provided for comfort. Near the new Virginia Marine Science Museum. One room and a suite are available year-round. A guest cottage is open May through October.

Host: Kathleen J. Hall
Room: 1 (PB) $60-90
Suite: 1 (PB)
Cottage: 1 (PB)
Full Breakfast
Credit Cards: None
Notes: 2, 3, 5, 7, 9, 10, 11, 12

WARRENTON

The Black Horse Inn

8393 Meetze Road, 20187
(540) 349-4020; www.blackhorseinn.com

The Black Horse Inn is an elegant Virginia hunt country estate, only 45 minutes from Washington, D.C. Circa 1850, the original portion of this home served as a hospital during the Civil War. Fireplaces, whirlpool baths, four-poster canopied beds complement the serene setting to provide a relaxing respite for guests. The inn provides an elegant setting for family reunions, weddings, and corporate events. Equine guests are welcome. Activities include fox-hunting, horseback riding, wine-tasting, hiking, shopping at antique and spe-

NOTES: Credit cards accepted: A MasterCard; B Visa; C American Express; D Discover; E Diner's Club; F Other; 2 Personal checks accepted; 3 Lunch available; 4 Dinner available; 5 Open all year; 6 Pets welcome;

The Black Horse Inn

cialty shops in Old Town Warrenton, bicycling, and boating.

Host: Lynn A. Pirozzoli
Rooms: 9 (PB) $125-295
Credit Cards: A, B C
Notes: 2, 5, 7, 9, 10, 11, 12, 14

WASHINGTON

Blue Ridge Bed & Breakfast

2458 Castleman Road, Berryville, 22611
(540) 955-1246; (800) 296-1246
FAX (540) 955-4240; e-mail: blurdgbb@shentel.net
www.blueridgebb.com

A. Lovely 1850's house on quiet street with great views of mountains. Easy walk to Inn at Little Washington and local theatre. House has lovely antiques including Rose Kennedy chaise lounge and working fireplace in bedroom. $80-125.

Caledonia Farm—1812

47 Dearing Road, Flint Hill, 22627
(540) 675-3693; (800) BNB-1812

Beautifully restored 1812 stone home and romantic guest house on a farm adjacent to Shenandoah National Park. Listed in the National Register of Historic Places, offers splendor for all seasons in Virginia's Blue Ridge Mountains. Skyline Drive, wineries, caves, historic sites, and superb dining. Fireplaces, air conditioning, hay rides, hot tub, and

bicycles. Only 68 miles to Washington, D.C. Children over 12 welcome.

Host: Phil Irwin
Rooms: 2 (SB) $80
Suites: 2 (PB) $140
Full Breakfast
Credit Cards: A, B, C, D
Notes: 2, 5, 7, 9, 10, 11, 12, 13, 14

Caledonia Farm—1812

The Foster-Harris House

189 Main Street, Box 333, 22747
(800) 666-0153; www.fosterharris.com

A turn-of-the-century home in a historic village nestled in the foothills of the Blue Ridge Mountains, with country antiques, fresh flowers, and outstanding mountain views. Near Shenandoah National Park. Five-star restaurant in town. All rooms feature private baths and central air conditioning.

Hosts: John and Libby Byam
Rooms: 4 (PB) $95-170
Full Breakfast
Credit Cards: A, B, D
Notes: 2, 5, 7, 9, 12, 14

WATERFORD

Milltown Farms Inn

14163 Milltown Road, P.O. Box 34, 20197-0034
(540) 882-4470; (888) 747-3942
e-mail: paul-barbara@erols.com
http://MilltownFarms.com

Paul and Barbara enjoy sharing their world with guests in this 1765 log and stone home set

7 No smoking; 8 Children welcome; 9 Social drinking allowed; 10 Tennis nearby; 11 Swimming nearby; 12 Golf nearby; 13 Skiing nearby; 14 May be booked through a travel agent; 15 Handicapped accessible.

on 300 acres. Period antiques, feather beds, fireplaces, unlimited pastoral views of horses, cattle, sunsets over the Blue Ridge, and a gourmet breakfast. Health is utmost on the innkeepers' minds. Come and join them. One room is handicapped accessible.

Hosts: Paul and Barbara Mayville
Rooms: 3 (PB) $100-135
Full Breakfast
Credit Cards: A, B, C, D
Notes: 2, 5, 7, 9, 10, 11, 12, 14, 15

WAYNESBORO

The Iris Inn

191 Chinquapin Drive, 22980
(540) 943-1991; FAX (540) 942-2093

The Iris Inn, architecturally designed and built in 1991, is on 21 wooded acres on a western slope of the Blue Ridge. It overlooks the historic Shenandoah Valley. Rooms are spacious and comfortable with king- or queen-size beds, all private baths, some whirlpools and fireplaces, porches, rockers, hot tub, full breakfast. Only five minutes to Blue Ridge Parkway and Shenandoah National Park. Near wineries, Monticello, P. Buckley Moss Museum.

Hosts: Wayne and Iris Karl
Rooms: 9 (PB) $80-140
Full Breakfast
Credit Cards: A, B
Notes: 2, 5, 7, 9, 11, 12, 13, 15

WILLIAMSBURG

Aldrich House Bed & Breakfast

505 Capitol Ct., 23185
(757) 229-5422; (877) 745-0887
e-mail: spatton@widomaker
www.aldrichhouse.com

A short stroll from the Aldrich House will transport guests to the 18th-century and the heart of Colonial Williamsburg. This Colonial saltbox home offers spacious accommodations and formal living and dining areas in an unpretentious atmosphere. Innkeepers Tom and Sue Patton will help guests make their visit to the colonial past an enjoyable experience.

Rooms: 2 (PB) $100-115
Full Breakfast
Credit Cards: None
Notes: 2, 5, 7, 8, 10, 11, 12

Amanda's Bed & Breakfast Reservation Service

3538 Lakeway Drive, Ellicott City, MD 21042-1226
(443) 535-0008; (800) 899-7533
FAX (443) 535-0009; e-mail: AmandasRS@aol.com
www.Amandas-BBRS.com

253. This Flemish-bond brick home was one of the first homes built on Richmond Road after the restoration of Colonial Williamsburg began in the late 1920s. The house features 18th-century decor, and the owner's apple collection is evident throughout. Four rooms with private baths. Continental plus breakfast. $95-150.

262. Three blocks from historic area and across from the College of William and Mary's Alumni House and Zable Stadium. Recent renovations have restored the house to its original charm when built in 1926. Antique furnishings throughout. Five guest rooms, each with private bath. $95-115.

361. Williamsburg is well known for its restored historic district and the depth of its history. To take advantage of this, stay a few days in one of Williamsburg's oldest and largest guest houses with 10 guest rooms. Guests are treated to southern hospitality and a full breakfast. Two of the rooms share a bath but this makes a nice family suite. Walk to the historic area and the College of William and Mary. Decorated with 18th-century reproductions and traditional antiques, with canopied or four-poster beds and quilts. $95-160.

Anne Marie's Bed & Breakfast

610 Capitol Landing Road, 23185
(757) 564-0225

Gracious hosts at Anne Marie's have a genuine interest in making a visit to Colonial Williamsburg unforgettable. A three-block stroll and guests are in the quiet restored area where history and shops abound. Evenings at Anne Marie's bring relaxation and comfort. Rooms and suite are tastefully furnished with family heirlooms and antiques. Feather beds are covered with fine linens and await guests' slumber. Guests rave about the exceptional full breakfast and the finest of hospitality.

Hosts: Marie and Ann Supplee
Rooms: 2 (PB) $85-110
Full Breakfast
Credit Cards: A, B
Notes: 2, 5, 7, 8, 9, 10, 11, 12, 14

Candlewick Bed & Breakfast

800 Jamestown Road, 23185
(757) 253-8693; (800) 418-4949

In the heart of Williamsburg, Candlewick invites guests to enjoy the comforts and gracious charm of an earlier era. With 18th-century antiques and reproductions, each of the three guest bedrooms boasts a curtained canopied bed with a plush mattress decked in an antique quilt and absolutely everything necessary for guests' comfort. Following a marvelous night's rest, guests will enjoy a wonderful breakfast in the keeping room. Just a whisper away from the historic area and across the street from College of William and Mary. Children over 12 welcome.

Hosts: Bernie and Mary Peters
Rooms: 3 (PB) $115-125
Full Breakfast
Credit Cards: A, B, C
Notes: 2, 7, 9, 10, 11, 12, 14

The Cedars

616 Jamestown Road, 23185
(757) 229-3591; (800) 296-3591
www.cedarsofwilliamsburg.com

An eight-minute walk to historic Williamsburg and across from the College of William and Mary, this elegant three-story brick Georgian inn offers tradition, gracious hospitality, and comfort. Scrumptious, bountiful breakfasts are served by candlelight on the tavern porch. The porch also serves as a meeting place for cards, chess, or other diversions. Each guest chamber reflects the romance and charm of the colonial era. Cottage with fireplace can accommodate five people. Off-street parking. Williamsburg's oldest, largest bed and breakfast.

Hosts: Carol, Jim, and Brona Malecha
Rooms: 8 (PB) $95-180
Cottage: 1 (PB) $150-275
Full Breakfast
Credit Cards: A, B
Notes: 2, 5, 7, 8, 9, 10, 12, 14

Colonial Gardens Bed & Breakfast

1109 Jamestown Road, 23185
(757) 220-8087; (800) 886-9715
e-mail: colgdns@widomaker.com
www.ontheline.com/cgbb

Colonial Gardens offers the perfect escape in a quiet, woodland setting. The charming interior is beautifully furnished with heirloom antiques and original art. Enjoy breakfast in the sunroom overlooking the beautifully landscaped yard. In the evening relax with other guests in the large living room around the game table and comfortable sitting areas. Ideal for Colonial Williamsburg and all area attractions. Outstanding suites and guest rooms with luxury amenities. TV/VCR, telephones. AAA three-diamond-rated.

Hosts: Scottie and Wilmot Phillips
Rooms: 4 (PB) $115-145
Full Breakfast
Credit Cards: A, B, C, D
Notes: 2, 5, 7, 9, 10, 11, 12, 14

7 No smoking; 8 Children welcome; 9 Social drinking allowed; 10 Tennis nearby; 11 Swimming nearby; 12 Golf nearby; 13 Skiing nearby; 14 May be booked through a travel agent; 15 Handicapped accessible.

Distinguished Accommodations in the Potomac Region— (Amanda's Bed & Breakfast Reservation Service)

1428 Park Avenue, Baltimore, 21217-4203
(410) 728-DAPR (3277); (800) 360 DAPR (3277)
FAX (410) 728-8957; e-mail: amandasrs@aol.com
www.amandas-bbrs.com

561. A three-story brick Georgian home setting the tone of an 18th-century home. Less than a 10-minute walk to historic Williamsburg and across the street from the College of William and Mary. A full breakfast is served. There are eight rooms plus a cottage that are individually and graciously appointed with century reproductions and traditional antiques. Each bedroom has either a canopy or four-poster bed. All rooms have private baths. There is off-street parking. The perfect location for visiting nearby attractions: Jamestown, Yorktown, James River plantations, and Busch Gardens.

For-Cant-Hill Guest Home

4 Canterbury Lane, 23185-3140
(757) 229-6623; FAX (757) 229-1863

This home is in a lovely wooded area, only five to six blocks from the colonial historic area, overlooking a lake, part of the campus of the College of William and Mary, in the heart of town. The rooms are beautifully decorated in antiques and collectibles for guests' complete comfort. The home is central heated and air conditioned with TVs in each room, and a hearty breakfast is served. The hosts make dinner reservations for guests and provide helpful information on the many attractions offered in the area. Telephone and fax are available in the home. Children over eight welcome.

Hosts: Martha and Hugh Easler
Rooms: 2 (PB) $85
Full Breakfast
Credit Cards: None
Notes: 2, 5, 7, 8, 9, 10, 11, 12, 14

Fox & Grape

Fox & Grape Bed & Breakfast

701 Monumental Avenue, 23185
(757) 229-6914; (800) 292-3699
www.foxandgrapebb.com

Genteel accommodations five blocks north of Virginia's restored colonial capital. This lovely two-story Colonial with spacious wraparound porch is a perfect place to enjoy one's morning coffee, plan the day's activities, or relax with a favorite book. Furnishings include antiques, counted cross-stitch, duck decoys, and folk art Noah's arks made by the host.

Hosts: Pat and Bob Orendorff
Rooms: 4 (PB) $100-115
Full Breakfast
Credit Cards: A, B, D
Notes: 5, 7, 9

Hite's Bed & Breakfast

704 Monumental Avenue, 23185
(757) 229-4814

Charming Cape Cod—seven minutes' walk to Colonial Williamsburg. Large rooms cleverly furnished with antiques and collectibles. Each room has a TV, telephone, coffee maker, robes, and beautiful private bathroom with claw-foot tub. In the parlor for guest enjoyment are an antique pump organ and hand-crank Victrola. Guests can relax in the garden and enjoy the swings, birds, flowers, and goldfish pond.

Host: Faye Hite
Rooms: 2 (PB) $90

NOTES: Credit cards accepted: A MasterCard; B Visa; C American Express; D Discover; E Diner's Club; F Other; 2 Personal checks accepted; 3 Lunch available; 4 Dinner available; 5 Open all year; 6 Pets welcome;

Suite: $100
Full Breakfast
Credit Cards: None
Notes: 2, 5, 7, 8, 10, 12, 14

The Homestay

The Homestay Bed & Breakfast

517 Richmond Road, 23185
(757) 229-7468 (information)
(800) 836-7468 (reservations)
e-mail: homestaybb@aol.com
http://williamsburg-virginia.com/homestay

Cozy and convenient. Enjoy the comfort of a lovely Colonial Revival home, furnished with turn-of-the-century family antiques and country charm. It is only four blocks to Colonial Williamsburg and just minutes away from Jamestown, Yorktown, and other local attractions. Adjacent to the College of William and Mary. A full breakfast featuring homemade breads and a delicious hot dish is served in the formal dining room. Children 10 and older welcome.

Hosts: Barbara and Jim Thomassen
Rooms: 3 (PB) $80-110
Full Breakfast
Credit Cards: A, B
Notes: 2, 5, 7, 9, 12, 14

Hughes Guest Home

106 Newport Avenue, 23185-4212
(757) 229-3493
e-mail: LivesIV

Directly opposite the Williamsburg Lodge on Newport Avenue, the Hughes Guest Home has been in operation since 1947. A lovely two-

minute stroll to Colonial Williamsburg's restored district, golfing facilities, and numerous dining facilities including the colonial taverns. The College of William and Mary, Merchant's Square, and several Colonial Williamsburg museums are also within easy walking distance. The house is decorated lavishly with family antiques. Eating facilities are across the street at Williamsburg Lodge and Williamsburg Inn. Lodging only.

Rooms: 3 (1 PB; 2 SB) $60
Credit Cards: None
Notes: 2, 7, 8, 9, 12

Indian Springs Bed & Breakfast

330 Indian Springs Road, 23185
(800) 262-9165; e-mail: indianspgs@tni.net

Indian Springs is in downtown Williamsburg, nestled in a private, wooded glade. Beautiful gardens adorn the view from each guest room. King suites open onto a shady greenery-filled veranda. The Colonial-style cottage features a king-size feather bed loft, fireplace, and wetbar. A small library has holdings for business and leisure activities. A sunny deck is a birdwatcher's haven. In-room amenities include cable, VCR, refrigerator, private bath, and private entrance.

Hosts: Kelly and Paul Supplee
Rooms: 4 (PB) $75-130
Full Breakfast
Credit Cards: A, B
Notes: 2, 5, 7, 8, 9, 10, 11, 12, 14

The Inn at 802

802 Jamestown Road, 23185
(757) 564-0845; (800) 672-4086
FAX (757) 564-7018; e-mail: 105313.42@csi.com
www.bbhost.com/innat802

A four-room bed and breakfast close to Colonial Williamsburg and adjacent to the College of William and Mary. Period decor with down comforters and dust ruffles. Four-poster beds. Large, comfortable, and private rooms, all with private bath/showers. Delicious full

7 No smoking; 8 Children welcome; 9 Social drinking allowed; 10 Tennis nearby; 11 Swimming nearby; 12 Golf nearby; 13 Skiing nearby; 14 May be booked through a travel agent; 15 Handicapped accessible.

breakfast served daily. Two fireplaces, library, sun porch.

Hosts: Don and Jan McGarva
Rooms: 4 (PB) $125-145
Full Breakfast
Credit Cards: A, B, C, D
Notes: 2, 5, 6, 7, 8, 9, 10, 11, 12

Newport House

Newport House

710 South Henry Street, 23185-4113
(757) 229-1775

Newport House was designed in 1756 by Peter Harrison. It is furnished totally in the period, including four-poster canopy beds. Each room has a private bathroom. The full breakfast includes authentic colonial-period recipes. Only five minutes from the historic area (as close as one can walk.) The host is a former museum director and author of many books on colonial history. Enjoy colonial dancing in the ballroom every Tuesday evening.

Hosts: John and Cathy Millar
Rooms: 2 (PB) $130-160
Full Breakfast
Credit Cards: None
Notes: 2, 5, 7, 8, 9, 10, 11, 12, 14

Piney Grove at Southall's Plantation (1790)

P.O. Box 1359, 23187-1359
(804) 829-2480; FAX (804) 829-6888

Piney Grove is just 20 miles west of Williamsburg in the James River plantation country, among working farms, country stores, and historic churches. The elegant accommodations at this National Register of Historic Places property are in two restored antebellum homes (1790 and 1857). Also on the property is Ashland (1835), Dower Quarter (1835), and Duck Church (1917). Guests are welcome to enjoy the parlor-library, gardens, pool, nature trail, farm animals, or a game of croquet or badminton. Upon arrival, guests are served mint juleps and Virginia wine. Restaurants nearby.

Hosts: Brian, Cindy, Joan, and Joseph Gordineer
Rooms: 6 (PB) $130-170
Full Breakfast
Credit Cards: C, D
Notes: 2, 5, 7, 8, 9, 10, 11, 12, 14

Primrose Cottage

706 Richmond Road, 23185
(757) 229-6421; (800) 522-1901
www.primrose-cottage.com

A short walk from Colonial Williamsburg, Primrose Cottage is abloom with pansies, primroses, and thousands of tulips. A French double harpsichord, hand-painted antiques, German dollhouse, and the comforts of home including private baths (two bathrooms have Jacuzzis) and king- or queen-size beds await guests. The aroma of Inge's home-cooked breakfast usually rouses even the sleepiest traveler.

Host: Inge Curtis
Rooms: 4 (PB) $95-125
Full Breakfast
Credit Cards: A, B
Notes: 2, 5, 7, 10, 11, 12, 14

War Hill Inn

4560 Long Hill Road, 23188
(757) 565-0248; (800) 743-0248

Large country estate less than two miles from Williamsburg. Manor House built in 1969 with recycled building materials and patterned after an 18th-century home. Two cottages on grounds, also 18th-century design. Canopy beds, private baths, whirlpool tubs, and fireplaces. Honeymooners as well as families will find their special place at War Hill. AAA three-diamond-rated.

Hosts: Shirley, Bill, Cherie, and Will Lee
Rooms: 7 (PB) $75-100
Suites: 2 (PB) $100-165
Cottage: 2 (PB) $120-180
Full Breakfast
Credit Cards: A, B
Notes: 2, 5, 7, 8, 9, 10, 12, 14

Williamsburg Manor

Williamsburg Manor Bed & Breakfast

600 Richmond Road, 23185
(757) 220-8011; (800) 422-8011

This 1927 Georgian home was built during the reconstruction of historic Colonial Williamsburg. Recently restored to its original elegance and furnished with exquisite pieces, including antiques and collectibles. Five well-appointed guest rooms with private baths, TVs, and central air conditioning. Guests are treated to a lavish fireside breakfast. Home is available for weddings, private parties, dinners, and meetings. Ideal location within walking distance of the historic area. On-site parking. Off-season rates available.

Host: Laura Reeves
Rooms: 5 (PB) $95-150
Full Breakfast
Credit Cards: A, B
Notes: 2, 5, 7, 8, 9, 10, 11, 12, 14

Williamsburg Sampler Bed & Breakfast Inn

922 Jamestown Road, 23185
(757) 253-0398; (800) 722-1169
FAX (757) 253-2669
e-mail: WbgSampler@aol.com
www.WilliamsburgSampler.com

An elegant 18th-century plantation-style six-bedroom Colonial proclaimed by Virginia's governor "Inn of the Year." The *Washington Post* wrote, "decorated with an eclectic assortment of antiques collected by the innkeepers." Lovely rooms and suites with four-poster beds, plus fireplace, wet bar, refrigerator, TV/VCR, and private bath. "Skip lunch"® breakfast. Internationally known as a favorite for honeymoons, anniversaries, or romantic getaways. On-site parking. Walk to historic area. AAA three-diamond and Mobil three-star. Appeared on *CBS This Morning*.

Hosts: Helen and Ike Sisane
Rooms: 2 (PB) $100
Suites: 2 (PB) $150
Full Breakfast
Credit Cards: A, B
Notes: 2, 5, 7, 9, 10, 11, 12, 14

Williamsburg Sampler

7 No smoking; 8 Children welcome; 9 Social drinking allowed; 10 Tennis nearby; 11 Swimming nearby; 12 Golf nearby; 13 Skiing nearby; 14 May be booked through a travel agent; 15 Handicapped accessible.

WINCHESTER

Brownstone Cottage Bed & Breakfast

161 McCarty Lane, 22602
(540) 662-1962
e-mail: brnstone@winchesterva.com
www.nvim.com/brownstonebnb

Guests can enjoy the quiet and peaceful country setting of the Brownstone Cottage, a private home nestled in the Shenandoah Valley outside historic Winchester, Virginia. Hospitality and individual attention highlight a stay with hosts, Chuck and Shiela Brown. Wake to the aroma of freshly brewed coffee and the beginning of a full country breakfast featuring Chuck's homemade pancakes or bread. Smoking outside only. Children over 12 welcome.

Hosts: Charles and Shiela Brown
Rooms: 2 (PB) $95
Full Breakfast
Credit Cards: A, B
Notes: 2, 5, 7, 10, 11, 12

WOODSTOCK

Azalea House

551 South Main Street, 22664
(540) 459-3500
www.shenwebworks.com/azaleahouse

The Azalea House dates back 100 years when it was built in the Victorian tradition and used as a church manse. The guest rooms are pleasing and comfortable, with antique furnishings and mountain views. Situated in the rolling hills of the Shenandoah Valley near fine restaurants, vineyards, shops, caverns, Civil War sites, hiking, and fishing. A great place to relax! Children over six are welcome.

Azalea House

Hosts: Margaret and Price McDonald
Rooms: 4 (PB) $55-75
Full Breakfast
Credit Cards: C
Notes: 2, 7, 8, 9, 10, 11, 12, 13

Blue Ridge Bed & Breakfast

2458 Castleman Road, Berryville, 22611
(540) 955-1246; (800) 296-1246
FAX (540) 955-4240; e-mail: blurdgbb@shentel.net
www.blueridgebb.com

C. Gorgeous mansion built in 1892 filled with antiques and hand-stenciled rooms. Hundreds of azaleas. In-ground swimming pool. $45-75.

WOOLWINE

The Mountain Rose Inn

1787 Charity Highway, 24185
(540) 930-1057; e-mail: mtrosein@swva.net
www.swva.net/mtroseinn

"Historical country elegance in the Blue Ridge Mountains." Once a part of the Mountain Rose Distillery, this Victorian inn, circa 1901, has five spacious rooms with private baths, working

The Mountain Rose Inn

antique-mantled fireplaces, and six porches. Elegant oil-lamp-lit threecourse breakfast. Swimming pool, trout-stocked creek, and 100 acres of hiking and privacy. Convenient to the Blue Ridge Parkway and Chateau Morrisette Winery. AAA three-diamond-rated. Member of BBAV and PAII. Open year-round.

Hosts: Melodie Pogue and Reeves Simms
Rooms: 5 (PB) $79-99
Full Breakfast
Credit Cards: A, B, D
Notes: 2, 5, 7, 8, 9, 10, 11, 12, 14

YORKTOWN

Marl Inn Bed & Breakfast

220 Church Street, P.O. Box 572, 23690
(757) 898-3859; (800) 799-6207
FAX (757) 898-3587
e-mail: EugeneM918@aol.com

Only 20 minutes from Williamsburg. Four rooms with private baths. Two are full suites with a bedroom, living room, kitchen. All rooms are on the second floor and have outside private entrances. Bicycles available for guests to tour battlefields and campgrounds of the Revolutionary armies. The beautiful 13-mile Colonial Parkway linking Yorktown with Williamsburg is a particularly attractive route for bicyclists and touring families. Four restaurants, upscale gift and antique shops are within walking distance, swimming and boating in the York River just two blocks from the house.

Rooms: 4 (PB) $95-120
Continental Breakfast
Credit Cards: A, B, C
Notes: 2, 7, 8, 9, 11, 12, 14

Canada

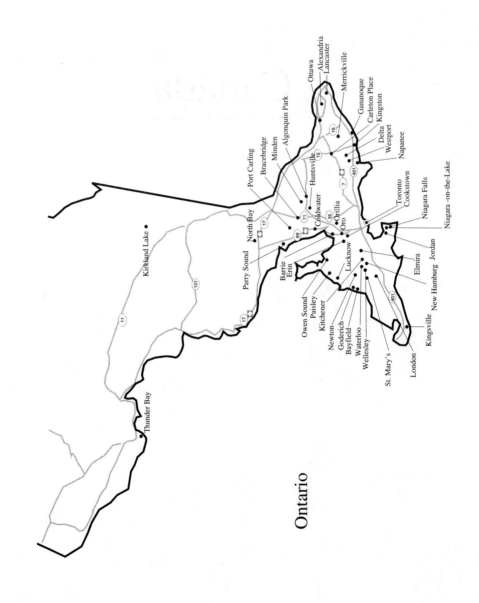

Ontario

Ontario

ALEXANDRIA

Maple Lane Guest Home
Bed & Breakfast

#21320, Glen Robertson Road, K0C 1A0
(613) 525-3205; (905) 666-0517
www.bbcanada.com/1068.html

Century home on 100 acres (built in 1856 by
Scottish settler) with beamed kitchen, pine
floors, antiques, and canopied beds. Truly a
peaceful setting, tucked away down a lane of
maples. Entertainment and Glengarry historical attractions, etc. are nearby. Great location—midway between Ottawa and Montreal
and close to U.S. and Québec borders. Come
sample the bilingual hospitality plus music,
fun, and laughter. It's an ideal adult getaway—
where the past and present blend.

Hosts: Audrey and Ed MacDonald
Rooms: 4 (1 PB; 2-3 SB) $55-65
Full Breakfast
Credit Cards: None
Notes: 3, 4, 7, 12, 14

ALGONQUIN PARK

Arowhon Pines

Algonquin Park, Box 10001, Huntsville, P1H 2G5
(705) 633-5661; (416) 483-4393 (winter)

Rates include three meals per day and use of all
recreational facilities: canoes, sailboats, sail-
boards, hiking trails, tennis courts, sauna, swimming in pristine waters, and games room. Open
June through mid-October. Smoking is not permitted in some cabins. BYOB. Breakfast, lunch,
and dinner are included in room rates.

Hosts: Eugene and Helen Kates
Rooms: 50 (PB) $120-230
Full Breakfast
Credit Cards: A, B
Notes: 2, 3, 4, 8, 10, 11, 12, 14

BARRIE

Cozy Corner

2 Morton Crescent, L4N 7T3
(705) 739-0157

An elegant city home. Old World curtsy and
just nice folks make guests feel spoiled and
pampered. Two spacious suites, Jacuzzi,
queen-size bed, duvet, arm chairs, coffee table,
private TV. Two other bright and comfortable
double bedrooms, writing desk, double dresser,
private TV. The location in the centre of Lakelands, marvel at the pristine beauty of the surroundings, clean air and abundant forests. Chef
Kirby (retired) in residence.

Hosts: Charita and Harry Kirby
Rooms: 2 (S1B) $65
Suite: 2 (PB) $110
Full Breakfast
Credit Cards: B
Notes: 4, 5, 7, 9, 10, 11, 12, 13, 14

Round Table Bed & Breakfast

59 Kinzie Lane, L4M 5Z8
(705) 739-0193; FAX (705) 739-0145

Homey in-town location, one hour north of
Toronto, in historical Huronia cottage country
house surrounded by white picket fence and
English gardens. TV room, TV in each guest
room, fireplace, hot tub, and bicycles. Preserves (jams and pickles) for sale. Twin and

NOTES: Credit cards accepted: A MasterCard; B Visa; C American Express; D Discover; E Diner's Club;
F Other; 2 Personal checks accepted; 3 Lunch available; 4 Dinner available; 5 Open all year; 6 Pets welcome;
7 No smoking; 8 Children welcome; 9 Social drinking allowed; 10 Tennis nearby; 11 Swimming nearby;
12 Golf nearby; 13 Skiing nearby; 14 May be booked through a travel agent; 15 Handicapped accessible.

queen-size beds. Cot available. Cat and dog in residence. Reduced rates for long-term stay (one week or more). Dinner available by reservation only. Children over eight welcome. Smoking permitted outside only.

Host: Diane C. Murray
Rooms: 2 (1 PB; 1 SB) $65
Full Breakfast
Credit Cards: None
Notes: 2, 5, 6, 7, 9, 10, 11, 12, 13

BAYFIELD

The Little Inn of Bayfield

Main Street, P.O. Box 100, N0M 1G0
(519) 565-2611; (800) 565-1832

Originally a stagecoach stop, the inn has been welcoming guests to this picturesque lakeside village since the 1830s. This designated Heritage inn is replete with fireplaces, en suite whirlpools, sauna, games, and books. Fine dining has long been a tradition, with superb meals and imaginative menus. Guests have a perfect base from which to explore the countryside and attend the Stratford and Blyth Festivals. There is much to do any time of the year. pets welcome with prior arrangements. Smoking permitted in designated areas only.

Host: Patrick and Gayle Waters
Rooms: 30 (PB) $110-225
Cards: A, B, C, E
Notes: 2, 3, 4, 5, 8, 10, 11, 12, 13, 14, 15

BRACEBRIDGE

Century House Bed & Breakfast

155 Dill Street, P1L 1E5
(705) 645-9903; e-mail: cnturybb@muskoka.com

"Accommodation for gentlefolk" in this charming, air-conditioned, restored century-old home in the province's premier recreational lake district, a two-hour drive north of Toronto. Sandy's breakfasts are creative and generous. Waffles with local maple syrup are a specialty. Century House is close to shopping, beaches, and many craft stu-

Century House

dios and galleries. Enjoy the sparkling lakes, fall colors, studio tours, and cross-country skiing in the winter. A friendly dog is in residence.

Hosts: Norman Yan and Sandy Yudin
Rooms: 3 (SB) $65-70
Full Breakfast
Credit Cards: B
Notes: 5, 7, 10, 11, 12, 13, 14

CARLETON PLACE

Stewart's Landing Bed & Breakfast

137 Montgomery Park Road, Rural Route 1, K7C 3P1
(613) 257-1285; FAX (613) 257-5828
www.bbcanada.com/1419.html

Right on Mississippi Lake, only three minutes from Carleton Place and 30 minutes from Ottawa. It takes 22 minutes to reach the Corel Centre. Enjoy comfortable smoke-free rooms with lake views. Pedal boating, canoeing, swimming all at the door. Relax on the deck, sip afternoon tea, listen to the loons laugh and watch swallows dip over the lake. Several towns and historical attractions are close by. A full gourmet country breakfast will make taste buds tingle. Warm hospitality makes this spot truly "Close to Heaven."

Hosts: Allen and Peggie Stewart
Rooms: 4 (1 PB; 3 SB) $55-65
Full Breakfast
Credit Cards: None
Notes: 2, 3, 4, 5, 7, 11, 12

NOTES: Credit cards accepted: A MasterCard; B Visa; C American Express; D Discover; E Diner's Club; F Other; 2 Personal checks accepted; 3 Lunch available; 4 Dinner available; 5 Open all year; 6 Pets welcome;

COLDWATER

Inn the Woods

4240 Sixth Line North, Oro-Medonte, L0K 1E0
(705) 835-6193; (800) 289-6295
e-mail: robet.shannon@sympatico.ca

Inn the Woods was designed for comfort, privacy, and relaxation. It combines a peaceful scenic ambiance with the nearby availability of quaint shops, fine restaurants, mountain trails, scenic country roads, fishing streams, and golf courses. A warm welcome awaits guests at this three-level Colonial-style home—on the fringe of Copeland Forest Preserve in a tranquil wooded setting in the heart of the Medonte Hills ski country. Lunch and dinner available upon request.

Hosts: Betty and Bob Shannon
Rooms: 5 (5 SB) $55-75
Full Breakfast
Credit Cards: A, B, C
Notes: 2, 5, 7, 8, 9, 12, 13, 14

COOKSTOWN

Victoria House Bed & Breakfast

36 Victoria Street East, L0L 1L0
(705) 458-0040 (phone/FAX)
e-mail: pine@bconnex.net

In the picturesque village of Cookstown with its many antique and craft shops, this comfortable, well-kept home offers two spacious, very private guest rooms with queen-size beds and en suite baths. Enjoy the garden, decks, and living room with fireplace, TV, VCR, and piano. Easy walk to quaint Cookstown or a short drive to lakes, cottage country, golf, skiing, outlet mall; approximately one hour to downtown Toronto. Highway 400/89/27.

Hosts: Gisele and Alfred Baues
Rooms: 2 (PB) $65
Full Breakfast
Credit Cards: None
Notes: 2, 6, 7, 9, 12, 13

DELTA

Denaut Mansion Country Inn

5 Mathew Street, K0E 1G0
(613) 928-2588 (phone/FAX)
www.denautmansion.com

Restored 1849 stone mansion features art work, pottery, and carpets from around the world. Each room with en suite bath. Imaginatively presented, simply prepared three-course set menu dinners served in the candlelit dining room or enclosed verandah. Licensed. Pool, air conditioning, walking, canoeing, golf, antiquing, hosts' own mapped loop cycle routes. Set on 11 wooded acres in a village setting in the Rideau Lakes, one-half hour from I-81 and the Ivy Lea Bridge. Colour brochure. Continental plus breakfast. Cross-country skiing nearby.

Hosts: Deborah and David Peets
Rooms: 5 (PB) $110-135 Canadian
Continental Breakfast
Credit Cards: A, B
Notes: 4, 5, 7, 8, 11, 12, 13

Denaut Mansion Country Inn

ELMIRA

The Evergreens

Rural Route 1, N3B 2Z1
(519) 669-2471

Welcome to a quiet bed and breakfast nestled among the evergreens. Enjoy long walks through the forest, swimming in the pool, or cross-country skiing in winter. Two comfortable bedrooms with two guest bathrooms, and breakfast with homemade baking and preserves. In Mennonite country, with Elmira, St. Jacobs, and Elora nearby. North of Elmira, east off Regional Road 21 on Woolrich Road

7 No smoking; 8 Children welcome; 9 Social drinking allowed; 10 Tennis nearby; 11 Swimming nearby; 12 Golf nearby; 13 Skiing nearby; 14 May be booked through a travel agent; 15 Handicapped accessible.

3. Smoking is not permitted in home. Open year-round.

Hosts: Rodger and Doris Milliken
Rooms: 2 (SB) $50
Full Breakfast
Credit Cards: None
Notes: 2, 5, 6, 7, 8, 9, 11, 12, 13

GANANOQUE

The Victoria Rose Inn

279 King Street West, K7G 2G7
(613) 382-3368

This stately mansion, with a commanding central tower, was built by the first mayor in 1872. Nine elegant nonsmoking guest rooms with private bath and air conditioning. Two charming guest rooms with shared bath in annex. The honeymoon suite has a marble fireplace and Jacuzzi. Guests are welcome to enjoy the parlor, veranda, patio, and two acres of garden. The ballroom is an ideal location for a family reunion, special party, or business meeting. The Rose Garden Cafe is open April through October for lunch, afternoon tea, and dinner. Close to an excellent selection of restaurants, the summer playhouse, boat tours, and interesting shopping.

Hosts: Liz and Ric Austin
Rooms: 11 (9 PB; 2 SB) $75-155
Full Breakfast
Credit Cards: A, B, C
Notes: 3, 4, 5, 7, 10, 11, 12, 13

GODERICH

Colborne Bed & Breakfast

72 Colborne Street, N7A 2V9
(519) 524-7400; (800) 390-4612
FAX (519) 524-4943
e-mail: kathryn.darby@odyssey.on.ca

This turn-of-the-century home is in Canada's prettiest town, within walking distance of beaches, shopping, restaurants. The bed and breakfast has 10-foot ceilings, foot-high baseboards, stained-glass windows. Enjoy the guest

parlour with fireplace, TV, VCR. The sun porch is enclosed and furnished in wicker. A full distinctive breakfast is offered. All four bedrooms have en suite bathrooms, one twin-, one double-, and two king-size beds, some with gas fireplaces and whirlpool tubs.

Host: Kathryn Darby
Rooms: 4 (PB) $60-95
Full Breakfast
Credit Cards: None
Notes: 3, 5, 7, 9, 10, 11, 12

Kathi's Guest House

Rural Route #4, N7A 3Y1
(519) 524-8587; FAX (519) 524-2969

Welcome to this farm amongst rolling hills. Close to Lake Huron, about 12 kilometers east of Goderich, near Benmiller. Enjoy the privacy of the guest house which has two bedrooms for guests' convenience. A nice place for two couples who share friendship together or young families with children. A crib is available. A full country-style breakfast is served. The host has friendly pets. English and German spoken. Open year-round. Reservations preferred. Deposit required. Special rates for longer stays.

Hosts: Kathi Beyerlein
Rooms: 2 (PB) $60
Full Breakfast
Credit Cards: None
Notes: 5, 8, 11, 12, 13

HUNTSVILLE

Fairy Bay Guest House

228 Cookson Bay Crescent, P1H 1B2
(705) 759-1492; (888) 813-1101
FAX (705) 789-6922
e-mail: hosts@fairybay.ca; www.fairybay.ca
www.muskoka.com/tourism/fairybay

Relax at this charming lakeside country inn. Eight large elegant rooms with en suite baths are equipped for comfortable reading and sleeping. Big windows overlook the lovely treed garden, bird feeders, white-sand beach, and a picturesque, quiet bay. Delicious breakfasts are served by the gracious hosts. Guests may use the two lounges, kitchenette, barbecue, bicycles, dock, and various watercraft. Nearby are five golf courses, Algonquin Park, walking trails, tennis, Pioneer village, fine dining, shopping, driving tours, skiing, and snowmobiling.

Hosts: Rick and Lori Stirling
Rooms: 8 (PB) $105-180
Full Breakfast
Credit Cards: A, B
Notes: 2, 5, 7, 8, 9, 10, 11, 12, 13, 14

JORDAN

The Vintner's Inn

3845 Main Street, L0R 1S0
(905) 562-5336; (800) 701-8074
www.vintnersinn.on.ca.

Elegant country inn in renovated winery building. All rooms have Jacuzzi, fireplace, telephone, and antique appointments. On the same property as an award-winning premium winery and one of Canada's finest regional restaurants, Cave Spring Cellars and On The Twenty, respectively. Village of Jordan has a number of artisan and antique shops. Thirty minutes to Niagara-on-the-Lake, Niagara Falls, and in the heart of Ontario's wine country.

Host: Helen Young
Rooms: 16 (PB) $199-275 Canadian (approx. $145-165 U.S.)
Continental Breakfast
Credit Cards: A, B, C, E
Notes: 3, 4, 5, 7, 8, 9, 10, 12, 14

KINGSTON

Painted Lady Inn

181 William Street, K7L 2E1
(613) 545-0422; www.aracnet/paintedldy

This stately Victorian offers seven elegant rooms, all with private baths, queen-size beds, antiques, and central air. Romance comes alive in luxury rooms with Jacuzzis and fireplaces.

Always lively conversation over scrumptious gourmet breakfasts—waffles, omelets, French toast. Inn is close to restaurants, pubs, Queen's University, Fort Henry, and Thousand Island boats. After a busy day, guests relax on a charming veranda or on sunny balcony. Parking. Four blocks to Lake Ontario.

Host: Carol Franks
Rooms: 7 (PB) $95-155 Canadian
Full Breakfast
Credit Cards: A, B, C
Notes: 2, 5, 7, 9, 10, 11, 12

KINGSVILLE

Kingswood Inn

101 Mill Street West, N9Y 1W4
(519) 733-3248; FAX (519) 733-8734
e-mail: kingswd@mnsi.net
www.lsol.com/kingswood

The ultimate in luxury. This 1859 octagonal manor was built by the founder of Kingsville. Five elegant guest rooms feature fine linens, robes, private baths. Air conditioned. Antiques and canopied beds. Master suite with fireplace and two-person whirlpool. Large drawing room and library with fireplace, TV, VCR, for guest use. Three acres of beautifully landscaped grounds and large in-ground pool. Close to several wineries, Point Pelee National Park, Colasanti's Tropical Gardens, Jack Miner's Bird Sanctuary, and fine dining. Just 45 minutes from Detroit.

Hosts: Barb and Bob Dick; Helen and Jay Koop
Rooms: 5 (PB) $95-280 Canadian
Full and Continental Breakfast
Credit Cards: A, B
Notes: 2, 5, 7, 9, 10, 11, 12, 14

KIRKLAND LAKE

Bed & Breakfast By The River

53 Athenia Boulevard, P. O. Box 96, P0K 1T0
(705) 642-3424 (phone/FAX)

Experience Kirkland Lake's gold mining culture and history, unspoiled rivers and trails, and

7 No smoking; 8 Children welcome; 9 Social drinking allowed; 10 Tennis nearby; 11 Swimming nearby; 12 Golf nearby; 13 Skiing nearby; 14 May be booked through a travel agent; 15 Handicapped accessible.

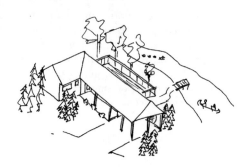

Bed & Breakfast By The River

northern hospitality. Enjoy a panoramic view of the beautiful Blanche River while dining on the gourmet breakfast. Open May through October, reasonable tax-free rates, fireplace, and water-side dock. Culver Park (25 acres), golf, tennis, horse riding, community complex, museum of Northern history, and home of Sir Harry Oakes on the Mile of Gold all close by. A smoke-free and pet-free adult accommodation.

Hosts: Pat and Bill Klass
Rooms: 2 (2 SB) $85-95
Full Breakfast
Credit Cards: B
Notes: 7, 9, 10, 11, 12

KITCHENER

Aram's Roots and Wings Bed & Breakfast

11 Sunbridge Crescent, N2K 1T4
(519) 743-4557; FAX (519) 743-4166

Country living right in the city. Roots and Wings is in the north end of Kitchener on the boundary with Waterloo. Ten minutes from St. Jacobs, universities, and most activities in the Kitchener/Waterloo area. Recreational facilities include a heated pool, Jacuzzi, and walking trails. Ultra whirlpool baths in two bathrooms. Delicious breakfasts start guests on their day's adventures.

Host: Fay Teal-Aram
Rooms: 4 (2 PB: 2 SB) $65-80

Full Breakfast
Credit Cards: A, B
Notes: 5, 6, 8, 9, 10, 11, 12, 15

LANCASTER

MacPine Farms

Box 51, K0C 1N0
(613) 347-2003; FAX (613) 347-2814
e-mail: macpine@glen-net.ca
www.bbcanada.com/688.html

Welcome to MacPine Holstein Farm on the shores of the St. Lawrence River, south of 401, a half-mile east of Lancaster 814 exit, 10 miles from Québec border. Enjoy this modernized century home. Shaded by large old pine trees. Five-minute walk to the cottage on the river, where guests can swim, canoe, paddleboat, relax, and watch the ocean ships go by. Attractions: golf, fishing, boating, nature trails, china outlet, and craft and antique shops. Visit Montréal, Cornwall, or Ottawa. Smoke-free in home; smoking permitted outside only. Children are welcome. Full Breakfast.

Hosts: Guelda and Robert MacRae
Rooms: 3 (SB) $40-50
Full Breakfast
Credit Cards: None
Notes: 2, 5, 7, 8, 9, 11, 12, 13

LONDON

Clermont Place

679 Clermont Avenue, N5X 1N3
(519) 672-0767; FAX (519) 672-2449

A modern home in a parklike setting with its own heated outdoor pool. Central air conditioning, three attractive bedrooms sharing a four-piece bath. A full Canadian breakfast is served in the dining room, by the pool, or in the gardens. Four free tennis courts behind the house; two public golf courses five minutes away. Forty minutes from the Stratford Shakespeare Festival. Close to the University of Western Ontario and University Hospital in northeast London. Cross-country skiing in area.

NOTES: Credit cards accepted: A MasterCard; B Visa; C American Express; D Discover; E Diner's Club; F Other; 2 Personal checks accepted; 3 Lunch available; 4 Dinner available; 5 Open all year; 6 Pets welcome;

Hosts: Doug and Jacki McAndless
Rooms: 3 (SB) $55-65
Full Breakfast
Credit Cards: B, C
Notes: 2, 3, 4, 5, 7, 9, 10, 11, 12, 13

Hilltop

82 Compton Crescent, N6C 4G1
(519) 681-7841

Modern air-conditioned home on quiet crescent in South London. Easy access to Highway 401, downtown London as well as Stratford Huron County Playhouse and Port Stanley. Offers twin and double rooms, each with private bath. Dining room overlooks the city. Outdoor pool available to guests. Nonsmoking adults. No pets.

Host: Beverley Corlett
Rooms: 2 (PB) $60 Canadian
Full Breakfast
Credit Cards: None
Notes: 5, 7, 11

LUCKNOW

Perennial Pleasures Guest Home

558 Rose Street, N0G 2H0
(519) 528-3601

A warm welcome awaits guests at this comfortable, modern bungalow. Attractively decorated, comfortable rooms. Freedom of the

Perennial Pleasures

house and bright, colorful gardens. Perennials for sale. Lucknow is centrally positioned for numerous day trips for antiquing; walking, biking, or swimming at Lake Huron; see Mennonite way of life with farms selling fruit, vegetables, and crafts. Inquire about accommodations for pets.

Host: Mrs. Joan Martin
Rooms: 3 (S2B) $45
Full Breakfast
Credit Cards: None
Notes: 2, 3, 4, 5, 7, 8, 9, 10, 11, 12, 13, 15

MERRICKVILLE

Millisle

Millisle Bed & Breakfast

205 Mill Street, P.O. Box 341, K0G 1N0
(613) 269-3627; FAX (613) 269-4735

Forty-five minutes south of Ottawa, adjacent to the Rideau River and Locks. Three-minute walk to center of village. A restored, turreted Heritage Victorian home (1858). Bedrooms furnished with antiques. Bathrooms private, one with whirlpool for two, two with Victorian claw-foot tubs, and one with shower only. Full breakfast served in Heritage dining room. Dinner package available with nearby restaurant, in a Heritage building. Thirty minutes from U.S. border. Cross-country skiing nearby.

Hosts: Kathy and Derry Thompson
Rooms: 5 (PB) $68 Canadian

7 No smoking; 8 Children welcome; 9 Social drinking allowed; 10 Tennis nearby; 11 Swimming nearby; 12 Golf nearby; 13 Skiing nearby; 14 May be booked through a travel agent; 15 Handicapped accessible.

Full Breakfast
Credit Cards: A, B, C
Notes: 2, 4, 5, 7, 9, 11, 12, 13, 14

MINDEN

The Stone House

Rural Route 2, K0M 2K0
(705) 286-1250

Rustic elegance in secluded, mature woods. Four styles of accommodation, each offering full privacy. The Stone House has two bedrooms, kitchen, and full bath. Large fieldstone fireplace in living room. The Roof Garden is an airy chalet-style studio with two sun decks, full bath, and kitchen. The Gingerbread Cottage has a full bath and a screened porch. The Sugar Cabin has full bath and screened porch. Laundry facilities available, and coffee and tea always on tap. Swimming, boating, and white-water rafting within one mile. Two hours from Toronto. Open May 15 to October 15. Personal checks accepted in advance. Call about pets. Hearty gourmet breakfast served.

Host: Phyllis Howarth
Rooms: 5 (2 PB; 3 SB) $65-75
Continental Breakfast
Credit Cards: None
Notes: 7, 9, 10, 11, 12

NAPANEE

Fairview House
Bed & Breakfast

373 Dundas Street West, P.O. Box 114, K7R 3S5
(613) 354-5142; FAX (613) 354-0609
e-mail: lucas@king.igs.net

Fairview House, built in 1860s by a United Empire Loyalist, is one of Napanee's finest Victorian-style homes. Once a grand estate, it has recently been restored to its original charm and splendor with each guest's comfort in mind. Pine floors, plastered crown mouldings, ceiling fans, and Victorian furnishings await in each guest bedroom. Victorian period furnishings,

modern conveniences, gracious lawns, landscaping, and seasonal facilities, such as an in-ground pool, offer guests complete comforts.

Host: Mr. Shaune E. Lucas
Rooms: 3 (3 SB) $45-65 Canadian
Continental Breakfast
Credit Cards: None
Notes: 5, 7, 8, 10, 11, 12

NEW HAMBURG

The Waterlot Restaurant and
Bed & Breakfast

17 Huron Street, N0B 2G0
(519) 662-2020; FAX (519) 662-2114
e-mail: waterlot@sympatico.ca
www3.sympatico.ca/waterlot

The Waterlot opened in the fall of 1974 and from the outset it has been committed to quality of ambiance and service. Two large and comfortably appointed rooms share a memorable marbled shower, bidet, water closet, wet vanity, and sitting area. Suite has a private bath and a living area. The Waterlot is one of Ontario's finest dining establishments. Twelve miles from world-renowned Stratford Shakespeare Festival May through November.

Host: Gordon and Leslie Elkeer
Rooms: 3 (1 PB; 2 SB) $70-110 Canadian
Continental Breakfast
Credit Cards: A, B, C, E
Notes: 2, 3, 4, 5, 7, 8, 9, 10, 11, 12, 13

The Waterlot

NEWTON

Country Charm

Rural Route #1, Road #129, Emg. #6841, N0K 1R0
(519) 595-8789

Come and enjoy bed and breakfast in the hosts' large Mennonite country home just one kilometer south of Newton. Relax around a campfire (weather permitting) or watch the sunset near the creek. There are a sawmill and a buggy shop at the cross-roads. Skideu Trail, bakery, and cheese factory are favorite spots for guests' enjoyment. Open year-round. "Share a memory with us."

Hosts: Marlene and Ezra Streicher
Rooms: 3 (1 PB; 2 SB) $45
Full Breakfast
Credit Cards: None
Notes: 2, 4, 5, 7, 8, 10, 11, 12, 13

NIAGARA FALLS

Gretna Green

5077 River Road, L2E 3G7
(905) 357-2081; www.bbcanada.com/262.html

This tourist home offers bright, comfortable rooms with en suite bathrooms. All guest rooms are air conditioned and have TV. Families are welcome. This is "a home away from home" where guests are treated to a full, home-

Gretna Green

cooked breakfast that includes muffins, scones, jams, and jellies. Niagara has much to offer: the falls, Skylon Tower, IMAX Theatre, the Floral Clock, the rose gardens, and museums. Bike rentals available. Personal checks accepted for deposit only. Smoking permitted in designated areas only.

Hosts: Stan and Marg Gardiner
Rooms: 4 (PB) $45-75
Full Breakfast
Credit Cards: None
Notes: 8, 10, 12

NIAGARA-ON-THE-LAKE

The Old Bank House

10 Front Street, P.O. Box 1708, L0S 1J0
(905) 468-7136 (phone/FAX)

A gracious 19th-century country inn in the heart of the old town, while overlooking Lake Ontario. Eight tastefully decorated rooms/ suites, air conditioned. Parking. In-season rates include a gourmet breakfast. Attractive off-season rates. A luxury cottage also available upon request. Daily and off-season rates available.

Hosts: Judy and Misha
Rooms: 8 (6 PB; 2 SB) $100-140
Full Breakfast
Credit Cards: A, B, C
Notes: 2, 5, 7, 12, 14

7 No smoking; 8 Children welcome; 9 Social drinking allowed; 10 Tennis nearby; 11 Swimming nearby; 12 Golf nearby; 13 Skiing nearby; 14 May be booked through a travel agent; 15 Handicapped accessible.

NORTH BAY

Hummingbird Hill Bed & Breakfast

254 Edmond Road, Astorville, P0H 1B0
(705) 752-4547; (800) 661-4976
e-mail: mabb@vianet.on.ca
www.bbcanada.com/955.html
www.on-biz.com/hummingbirdhill/

Unique geodesic dome cedar home has outdoor hot tub, sauna, screened cedar gazebo, extensive gardens and pond. Bird watching, privacy. Elegant, spacious accommodations, Victorian Room with en suite, Ivy Room with en suite, and the Loft with shared luxury bath with fireplace. Meals are gourmet, heart smart, low calorie, and vegetarian. Country living at its best. All inclusive spa and gourmet packages.

Hosts: Marianne and Gary Persia
Rooms: 3 (1 PB; 1 SB) $60-75
Full Breakfast
Credit Cards: B
Notes: 2, 3, 4, 5, 7, 8, 9, 10, 11, 12, 13, 14, 15

Hummingbird Hill

ORILLIA

Betty and Tony's Waterside Bed & Breakfast

677 Broadview Avenue, L3V 6P1
(800) 308-2579; FAX (705) 326-2262
e-mail: tony.bridgens@encode.com
www.bbcanada.com/9.html

Betty and Tony's

A modern air-conditioned home in the Lakelands of Ontario, with lawns running down to the 300-mile-long Trent-Severn Waterway. Fishing, swimming, docking for up to 40-foot cruisers, a paddleboat, canoe, and bikes are available. English hosts serve breakfast on Wedgwood bone china. Charming large rooms, guest lounge, books. Nearby are Casino Rama, Stephen Leacock Museum, city parks, and beach. Ice-fishing in the canal.

Hosts: Betty Bridgens, B. Ed. and Tony Bridgens, P. Eng.
Rooms: 3 (1 PB; 2 SB) $60-95 Canadian
Full Breakfast
Credit Cards: A, B, E
Notes: 2, 3, 4, 5, 6, 7, 8, 9, 10, 11, 12, 13

The Verandahs

4 Palm Beach Road, Rural Route 2, Hawkestone, L0L 1T0
(705) 487-1910 (phone/FAX)

Beautiful Victorian-style home with verandas on large landscaped lot 200-feet from Lake Simcoe. Bright, comfortable interior with welcoming ambiance. Guest sitting room with fireplace, TV, books, and games. Ultra-comfortable beds with goose-down duvets. Hearty homemade breakfasts. Summer season May 15 to October 15. Walk to beach and boat launch. Short drive to summer theatre, great restaurants, boat tours. Winter season December 28 to March 31. Close to skiing, snowmobiling and ice fishing for winter enjoyment. Inquire about accommodations for children.

NOTES: Credit cards accepted: A MasterCard; B Visa; C American Express; D Discover; E Diner's Club; F Other; 2 Personal checks accepted; 3 Lunch available; 4 Dinner available; 5 Open all year; 6 Pets welcome;

Hosts: Pearl and Norm Guthrie
Rooms: 3 (PB) $80
Full Breakfast
Credit Cards: A, B
Notes: 2, 7, 9, 11, 12, 13

ORO

Siberi*inn Bed & Breakfast

Rural Route 2, Hawkestone, L0L 1T0
(705) 487-6456; FAX (705) 487-6459
e-mail: siberinn@barint.on.ca
www.barint.on.ca/~siberinn

Relax in the peaceful setting of the panoramic hardwood forest. Take in the fresh air and picturesque natural surroundings. Enjoy affection from the Siberian Huskies who run the place. Year-round outdoor recreation. Hiking trails and skiing from the doorstep. Best snow around! Guest lounge with fireplace. Wraparound veranda. Only 10 minutes west of Orillia, on the scenic 10th Line of Oro.

Hosts: Mike Pidwerbecki and the Siberian Huskies
Rooms: 2 (PB) $65-80 Canadian ($45-55 U.S.)
Full Breakfast
Credit Cards: None
Notes: 5, 7, 12, 13

Siberi*inn

OTTAWA

Albert House Inn

478 Albert Street, K1R 5B5
(613) 236-4479; (800) 267-1982
www.alberthouseinn.on.ca

Albert House Inn

Gracious Victorian inn built in 1875 by a noted Canadian architect. Each room is individually decorated and has private facilities, telephone, TV, and air conditioning. Guest lounge with fireplace. Famous Albert House breakfast. Parking is available, but inn is within walking distance to most attractions.

Hosts: Cathy and John Delroy
Rooms: 17 (PB) $80-125
Full Breakfast
Credit Cards: A, B, C, E
Notes: 5, 9, 13, 14

Auberge McGEE'S Inn (Est. 1984)

185 Daly Avenue, K1N 6E8
(613) 237-6089; (800) 2MCGEES
FAX (613) 237-6201
www.coatesb.demon.co.uk/McGees

Fifteen years of award-winning hospitality. McGEE'S is a smoke-free upscale bed and breakfast inn in downtown Ottawa. Each room features a telephone equipped with computer modem hook up, enabling guests to direct-dial long distance (a savings of 30 percent) and receive messages on personal voice mail. Two Jacuzzi en suite theme rooms. Walking distance of Congress Centre, Parliament, University of

7 No smoking; 8 Children welcome; 9 Social drinking allowed; 10 Tennis nearby; 11 Swimming nearby; 12 Golf nearby; 13 Skiing nearby; 14 May be booked through a travel agent; 15 Handicapped accessible.

Ottawa, Rideau Canal, trendy Byward Market. Ten-minute drive to ski hills. AAA-approved. Meeting rooms for 24 people. Full breakfast.

Hosts: Anne Schutte and Mary Unger
Rooms: 14 (PB) $78-170 Canadian
Full Breakfast
Credit Cards: A, B, C
Notes: 5, 7, 8, 9, 11, 12, 13

Australis Guest House

Australis Guest House

35 Marlborough Avenue, K1N 8E6
(613) 235-8461 (phone/FAX)
e-mail: waters@intranet.ca
www.bbcanada.com/1463.html

This guest house is the oldest established and still operating bed and breakfast in Ottawa. On a quiet, tree-lined street one block from the Rideau River and Strathcona Park, it is a 20-minute walk to the Parliament buildings. The home boasts leaded windows, fireplaces, oak floors, and unique, eight-foot, stained-glass windows. The spacious rooms, including one with private bathroom, feature many collectibles from different parts of the world. The hearty, delicious breakfasts help start the day right. Winner of the Ottawa Gold Award, Star of the City for services to tourism, recommended by *Newsweek* and *Travel Scoop*. Carol Waters is co-author of *The Breakfast Companion*.

Hosts: Brian and Carol Waters
Rooms: 3 (1 PB; 2 SB) $62-78

Full Breakfast
Credit Cards: None
Notes: 5, 7, 10, 11, 12, 13

Bye-the-Way

310 First Avenue, K1S 2G8
(613) 232-6840

Modern, comfortable, and elegant, Bye-the-Way bed and breakfast offers all the conveniences of gracious living in downtown Ottawa. A few minutes' walking distance from the Rideau Canal, city attractions, Carleton University, and world-class museums. The host is happy to guide first-time visitors around Ottawa. Central air conditioning, smoke- and pollen-free.

Hosts: Krystyna, Rafal, and Adam
Rooms: 4 (2 PB; 2 SB) $70-80
Suite: $80
Full Breakfast
Credit Cards: A, B, E, F
Notes: 2, 5, 7, 8, 9, 10, 11, 12, 13, 14

Bye-the-Way

Gasthaus Switzerland Inn

89 Daly Avenue, K1N 6E6
(613) 237-0335; (888) 663-0000
FAX (613) 594-3327; e-mail: switzinn@magi.com
http://infoweb.magi.com/~switzinn/

The Gasthaus Switzerland Inn, in the heart of Canada's capital, offers guests traditional Swiss hospitality. Twenty-two well-appointed air-conditioned rooms, some with fireplace, private bath/Jacuzzi en suite, cable TV, telephone, a smoke-free environment, limited free parking, and a Swiss country breakfast buffet. Recommended by CAA, AAA, Canada Select, and Tourism of Ontario. Honeymoon/romantic getaway suite featuring king-size canopied poster bed, a double Jacuzzi.

Hosts: Josef and Sabina Sauter
Rooms: 22 (PB) $68-188
Full Breakfast
Credit Cards: A, B, C, E
Notes: 5, 7, 10, 11, 12, 13

Lovat

OWEN SOUND

Sunset Farms Bed & Breakfast

Rural Route 6, 398139 28th Avenue East, N4K 5N8
(519) 371-4559; e-mail: moses@bmts.com
www.bmts.com/~moses/

Well-traveled hosts own and operate Owen Sound's longest-established bed and breakfast. Forty picturesque acres just five minutes from the city's center. Ideal for day trips to Manitoulin Island, Georgian Bay touring, and bicycle trips. Bruce Trail access nearby. Gorgeous during autumn. Antique-furnished unique home. Gardens, patios, and pond for outdoor enjoyment. Artistically presented breakfasts featuring garden-fresh produce and flowers. Inquire regarding bringing children and pets.

Hosts: Bill and Cecilie Moses
Rooms: 4 (1 PB; 3 SB) $45-95
Full and Continental Breakfast
Credit Cards: None
Notes: 5, 7, 9, 10, 11, 12, 13, 14

PAISLEY

Lovat Bed & Breakfast

Rural Route 2, N0G 2N0
(519) 353-5534; FAX (519) 353-4195

Come stay at this log home built in the late 1800s. Sleeping accommodations include three bedrooms as well as a fourth bedroom for a family. In winter there are cross-country skiing, snowmobiling, and toboggan hills in the area. Summer is great with an outdoor barbecue. Spend the day on the beach; only 15 to 30 minutes from Lake Huron areas. Guests can travel to Tobermory and enjoy a cruise aboard the MS *Chi-Cheemaun*. Open year-round. Hot tub (new for 1998).

Hosts: Jim and Gail Dalman
Rooms: 4 (SB) $50
Full Breakfast
Credit Cards: None
Notes: 2, 3, 4, 5, 7, 8, 9, 11, 12, 13

PARRY SOUND

Victoria Manor

43 Church Street, P2A 1Y6
(705) 746-5399; e-mail: victoria@zeuter.com

Welcome an era of gracious living in the restored Victorian home. Enjoy our antiques, relax in the cosy library, front parlor or screened veranda. A full breakfast is served in the dining room. We are in the heart of Parry Sound, only a few minutes' walk from the Festival of the Sound, Rainbow Theatre, 30,000 Islands Cruise, shopping, restaurants, and Georgian Bay beaches. Snowmobile and cross-country ski trails and golf are a short drive away. Open year-round. Inquire about accommodations for children.

Hosts: Sharon and John Ranney
Rooms: 5 (1 PB; 4 SB) $60-95
Full Breakfast
Credit Cards: None
Notes: 2, 5, 7, 9, 10, 11, 12, 13

---

7 No smoking; 8 Children welcome; 9 Social drinking allowed; 10 Tennis nearby; 11 Swimming nearby; 12 Golf nearby; 13 Skiing nearby; 14 May be booked through a travel agent; 15 Handicapped accessible.

PORT CARLING

DunRovin

Box 304, P0B 1J0
(705) 765-7317; e-mail: dunrovin@muskoka.com
www.bbcanada.com/615.html

Warmth and charm of a cottage with comforts of home. Lovely wildflower gardens. Large deck overlooking Lake Muskoka. Swim or boat in protected bay. Relax on private boathouse, swing in hammock. Comfortable guest area, hot tub in winter. Queen-size bedroom with romantic half-canopied bed with an en suite. Twin bedroom with great lake view, duvets, and private bath. Heart-healthy breakfasts served upstairs in the great room or on the deck. Two hours north of Toronto.

Hosts: Wilsie and Bob Mann
Rooms: 2 (PB) $80-90 Canadian
Full Breakfast
Credit Cards: None
Notes: 2, 5, 7, 9, 10, 11, 12, 13

DunRovin

ST. MARYS

Eagleview Manor Bed & Breakfast

178 Widder Street East, P.O. box 3183, N4X 1A8
(519) 284-1811

Step back in time at this gracious, smoke-free Queene Anne Victorian home which is perched on a hill overlooking quaint St. Marys, with two rivers, five bridges, waterfalls, and the Canadian Baseball Hall of Fame. There is a

grand sweeping staircase, large rooms, three shared guest bathrooms, Jacuzzi, fireplaces, antique quilts, stained-glass windows, formal oak dining room, guest parlor, menu breakfast, tea table, and in-ground swimming pool. Minutes from Stratford and London.

Hosts: Bob and Pat Young
Rooms: 3 (3 SB) $65-80
Full Breakfast
Credit Cards: A, B
Notes: 2, 5, 7, 8, 9, 10, 11, 12, 13, 14

THUNDER BAY

Pinebrook Bed & Breakfast

Rural Route 16 Mitchell Road, P7B 6B3
(807) 683-6114; FAX (807) 683-8641
e-mail: pinebrok@baynet.net
www.bbcanada.com/1184.html

Warm and friendly cedar chalet. Ten minutes from downtown. Welcoming. Quiet. On 43 rolling acres of meadows and pine forest along more than one-half mile of private river frontage. It is truly a place to rest and relax. Sumptuous meals. Jacuzzi. Three bathrooms. Fireplace room. Sauna by river. Canoeing. Fishing. Meadows and forest trails. Mountain bikes. Library and video library. Children and pets welcome. A home away from home. Smoking permitted outside only.

Hosts: Sara Jeffrey and Armin Weber
Rooms: 4 (1 PB; 3 SB) $45-75 Canadian
Full Breakfast
Credit Cards: A, B, C
Notes: 3, 4, 5, 6, 7, 8, 9, 11, 12, 13

TORONTO

Amblecote

109 Walmer Road, M5R 2X8
(416) 927-1713; FAX (416) 927-0838
e-mail: info@amblecote.com
www.amblecote.com

A restored historical Edwardian home, built in the English cottage style. Wonderful neighbor-

---

NOTES: Credit cards accepted: A MasterCard; B Visa; C American Express; D Discover; E Diner's Club; F Other; 2 Personal checks accepted; 3 Lunch available; 4 Dinner available; 5 Open all year; 6 Pets welcome;

hood. Quiet street yet minutes from the subway, museums, Casa Loma, Yorkville. Plenty of restaurants, café, and shopping within walking distance. The house is furnished with antiques and Persian rugs. The guest rooms are appointed with period furniture and provide comfort and tranquility from another era.

Rooms: 5 (2 PB; 3 SB) $70-95 Canadian
Full or Continental Breakfast
Credit Cards: A, B, C
Notes: 5, 7, 9, 11

Annex House Bed & Breakfast

147 Madison Avenue, M5R 2S6
(416) 920-3922 (telephone/FAX)

Enjoy comfortable bed and breakfast facilities at Annex House, a restored turn-of-the-century Georgian home in the heart of downtown Toronto, with private parking. The tranquility and beauty of the Annex area offers a pleasant 10-minute walk to shops, sights, and restaurants. The best shopping is close by, at Yorkville, Yonge and Bloor Streets, and on Spadina Avenue. Sightseeing opportunities include Casa Loma, the Royal Ontario Museum, McLaughlin Planetarium, historic University of Toronto, and Queen's Park. Subways and buses are three minutes away, making the whole of the city instantly accessible.

Host: Carol (Ricciuto) Davey
Rooms: 3 (PB) $85
Full Breakfast
Credit Cards: None
Notes: 5, 7, 8, 9, 10

Bed & Breakfast Association of Downtown Toronto

P.O. Box 190, Station B, M5T 2W1
(416) 410-3938 (9:00 A.M.-6:00 P.M. Mon-Fri)
    (8:30 A.M.-12:00 P.M. Sat-Sun)
FAX (416) 368-1653
e-mail: bnbtoronto@globalserve.net
www.bnbinfo.com

Representing Toronto's largest selection of fully inspected and privately owned Victorian homes in downtown Toronto. All within 10 minutes of the major tourist attractions. Let the hosts be a guide to the international flavor of Toronto's interesting neighborhoods. Guests can choose a range of accommodations from elegant suites with fireplaces and whirlpool baths to simple, warm guest rooms for the more budget minded. For reservations, free brochure, or any other information one might need, please contact Linda Lippa. There are 50 accommodations with private and shared baths. Full and Continental breakfasts served. All rates include breakfast, taxes, and parking. Visa accepted. $65-120.

Howland at Bloor. An 1800s Georgian two-story flat in the heart of the Annex neighborhood. Walking distance to the Royal Ontario Museum, university, shopping, and great local restaurants. Only a five-minute walk to the Bloor and university subway stations. The home features original moldings, high Georgian ceilings, and much more. The host offers a guest room with TV and private baths. Full breakfast. $75-90.

Howland Street. Renovated Victorian home in the university neighborhood known as the Annex. With its great local restaurants, it is within walking distance to the Royal Ontario Museum, university, public transit to famous Yorkville for shopping, and easy access to the city center. Host offers a second-floor guest room with private bathroom and TV. Full breakfast. $75-90.

Jarvis at Bloor. Beautiful Victorian home in a great downtown neighborhood, only steps from Bloor and Yonge Streets, the shopping center of the city. Only a minute's walk to transit and theaters. Two guest rooms offered. The guest room in the main home has a private bath and the guest room in the coach house has a private bath with a single tub with jets. Breakfast is served in the main house. $75-115.

---

7 No smoking; 8 Children welcome; 9 Social drinking allowed; 10 Tennis nearby; 11 Swimming nearby; 12 Golf nearby; 13 Skiing nearby; 14 May be booked through a travel agent; 15 Handicapped accessible.

King Street West. Beautiful 1800s Victorian home overlooking the lake. On the King street-car line, only 15 minutes from Eaton Centre, and a short walk to the Canadian National Exhibition grounds. Also nearby is a walkway over the expressway to Sunnyside Park on the lake. This home is full of Old World charm, stained-glass windows, hardwood flooring, and floor-to-ceiling bookcases in the library. Hostess offers two suites for guest rooms. Private baths, queen-size beds, and kitchenettes. $55-75.

Oriole Parkway. Wonderful and spacious 1920s home in one of the more elite neighborhoods of the city. Only a 15-minute walk to the Yonge and Davisville subway or 10 minutes down to St. Clair and Avenue Roads. There is also a bus right out front. Beautifully decorated. Relax in a spacious sitting area in front of the fireplace or outside on the deck. Three guest rooms with private and shared baths. All rooms have TVs. $65-85.

Phoebe Street. Lovely new brownstone in the heart of Queen Street West Village, known for its trendier shopping and cafés. Only steps from Spadina and Queen, easy access to public transit, and a 10-minute walk from Eaton Centre and theaters. Two second-floor guest rooms, each with private bath. $55-85.

St. George. Beautiful early 1900s Edwardian home in the heart of the Annex neighborhood, only a 10-minute walk to the university, Royal Ontario Museum, Yorkville, and Casa Loma. Also only a five-minute walk to the Dupont subway stop, making easy access to the rest of the city's attractions. This home features Old World charm, antiques, nooks with leaded bay windows, and fireplaces throughout. Four guest rooms, with two common baths. $65-90.

Seaton Street. Spacious restored Victorian home in downtown, only a 10-minute walk to Eaton Centre and Pantages Theatre, and a minute's walk to public transit. This home fea-

tures antiques, pine and hardwood flooring throughout, and has been totally renovated. The hosts offer a third-floor suite. It has a sitting area with fireplace, private bath with a large single tub with jets, and lots of light from large skylights. $120.

Shaw Street. This quaint home is only a five-minute walk to the Bloor subway line at Ossington station, and only 10 minutes to public transit to the city center, to the Royal Ontario Museum, University of Toronto, and Yorkville Village. This immaculate home, with hardwood flooring and antiques throughout, offers a second-floor guest room with a private bath. Continental breakfast. $50-70.

Soho at Queen. A beautiful brownstone, only steps from Spadina Avenue and Queen Street, a trendy area for shopping and wonderful eateries. Only a 10-minute walk to the Sheraton Centre and Metro Convention Centre, and to the Royal Alexandra and Princess of Wales theaters. A spacious second-floor guest room with an en suite bath is offered. Continental plus breakfast. Parking not included in rates. $60-80.

Bed & Breakfast Homes of Toronto

P.O. Box 46093, College Park, M5B 2L8
(416) 363-6362

Alcina's. (416) 656-6400; www.bbcanada. com/1104.html. This gracious, old Victorian brick house is on a shady tree-lined street in the exclusive Wychwood Park neighborhood. Enjoy casual elegance: indoors, soft furnishings and oak; outdoors an old-fashioned English Garden. Close to Spadina House and ever-popular Casa Loma. Subway, bus, and streetcar are all in walking distance. Casual eateries can be found locally. Continental breakfast. Parking available. Resident cat, Cina. Seasonal rates. Smoking allowed in back yard seating area. $65-80.

NOTES: Credit cards accepted: A MasterCard; B Visa; C American Express; D Discover; E Diner's Club; F Other; 2 Personal checks accepted; 3 Lunch available; 4 Dinner available; 5 Open all year; 6 Pets welcome;

Colwood. (416) 234-9988; FAX (416) 234-1554; e-mail: jgartner@idirect.com; www.bbcanada.com/1100.html. Stunningly renovated traditional home in a prestigious area close to both the airport and downtown; both 10 to 15 minutes away by car. It is near and easily accessible to all major highways. Public transit with direct access to the subway is a short walk. A full range of amenities and restaurants are nearby as are James Gardens and the Humber River park system with its bike and walking trails. The home is bright and sunny with an outdoor swimming pool set amid a beautiful landscaped garden. Breakfasts are served in the dining room or on the deck; tea and coffee are complimentary. Rooms are air conditioned and have ceiling fams. On-site parking is free. Smoke-free. Resident Labrador retriever. $75-105 Canadian.

Feathers May and Max. (416) 534-1923 or (416) 534-2388; www.bbcanada. com/1115.html. A charming, spacious Victorian home in the popular Annex, only a five-minute walk from Bathurst subway and Bloor Street. Guests are two blocks away from one of Toronto's most delightful areas of cosmopolitan restaurants and cafés, film and live theaters, bookstores and antique shops. Nineteenth-century European and oriental furnishings, china, delicate tapestries, and an unusual collection of antique puppets lend a unique atmosphere to this interesting and beautifully restored home. Continental breakfast. Discount offered if no breakfast desired. Central air. Color TV in guest rooms. No smoking in house, please. English, Dutch, French, and German spoken. Free parking. $70-80 Canadian.

Greener-Gunn. (416) 698-9061 (phone/fax); e-mail: greener-gunner@sympatico.ca; www.bbcanada.com/1113.html. In the increasingly popular Beaches area of Toronto, east of downtown, this home offers guests friendly hospitality and a good homemade breakfast in a relaxed, casual atmosphere, served in the dining room or, weather permitting, just outside on the front deck. A two-minute walk will take guests down to Queen Street, where they can find cafés, boutiques, craft shops, small art and antique galleries, and many fine restaurants and night spots. Downtown is accessible by car in 10 to 15 minutes, or by a leisurely 20-minute trolley-car ride. Front driveway parking. Smoking on the deck only. Bathroom shared by guests. Dog in residence. Seasonal discounts. $50-70 Canadian.

Helga's Place. (416) 633-5951; FAX (416) 636-3050; e-mail: helgaplace@hotmail. com. A country home in the city with wood stoves and fireplace, terrazzo floors, and antiques all surrounded by natural wood. Large front porch overlooks the rock garden in a quiet, well-treed neighborhood. A variety of interesting restaurants, shops, and cinemas are within easy walking distance, while a five-minute walk takes guests to the Bloor subway and easy access to downtown. Generous and nutritious breakfsats are served with dietary preferences being catered to. Parking. Smoking permitted on front porch. Airport pick-up and drop-off can be arranged. $60-80 Candian.

Inverness. (416) 769-2028 (phone/FAX). e-mail: ewleslie@interlog.com; http: //bbcanada.com/2918.com. A country home in the city. Antiques, woodstoves, terrazo floors, and lots of natural wood, create a warm and inviting home. Only a five-minute walk to the subway and to High Park, Toronto's largest and greenest park. Walk to a variety of interesting restaurants, shops, and movies. Either downtown or the airport only a 15-minute car ride. Parking available. Generous, nutrituous breakfsats served by candlelight. $50-70 Canadian.

Kingslake Korners. (416) 491-4759; www.bbcanada.com/477.html. Comfort, relaxation, and hospitality await guests in a cheerful, quiet residential area of north Toronto in a family home setting, 20-30 minutes to downtown, depending on traffic flow. Relax in clean, spacious, and tastefully decorated guest rooms— one with private bath and the other with en suite

7 No smoking; 8 Children welcome; 9 Social drinking allowed; 10 Tennis nearby; 11 Swimming nearby; 12 Golf nearby; 13 Skiing nearby; 14 May be booked through a travel agent; 15 Handicapped accessible.

bath, color cable TV and VCR. Children welcome; crib and highchair are available and playground and parks are nearby. Full breakfast is served in the dining room. Special diets can be accommodated. Central air. On-site parking. Smoke-free. Dog and cat in residence; no guest pets, please. $50-60 Canadian.

Martyniuk. (416) 603-2128 (phone/FAX) ; e-mail: martyniukbb@home.com; www.bbcanada.com/1105.html. This home, more than 100 years old, in the Kensington Market area, is quite modest in style and decor, but at prices well below average, it is an excellent choice for the budget traveler, especially for those without cars. The Martyniuk home is exactly one mile from the Eaton Centre, bus terminal, or Elgin and Pantages Theatres. European-style restaurants and Toronto Western Hospital are within walking distance. The full breakfast is served in the kitchen. English, Ukrainian, Polish, and German spoken. Very limited smoking permitted. Ten percent discount from October to March if over seven days. Rooms individually air conditioned. Parking extra $5 per day. $45-55 Canadian.

Morning Glory. (416) 533-6120; www.bbcanada.com/1103.html. This Edwardian home has high ceilings, maple trim, and stained-glass windows. Little Italy and Bloor Street are within walking distance and there is easy access to Chinatown, theaters, concert halls, art galleries, and most other major attractions. Public transportation is very close at hand. A generous, delicious breakfast is served. Convenient highway access; garage available for parking. Smoke-free home. Smoking area on patio. English, French, German, and Dutch spoken. $55-70 Canadian.

Oriole Gardens. (416) 924-4736; www.bbcanada.com/1108.html. Enjoy a warm, friendly atmosphere in this gracious family home on an upscale, tree-lined residential street. A few minutes' walk from St. Clair sub-

way station and Yonge Street buses, and within easy reach of Toronto's major attractions. The location offers an interesting variety of restaurants, pubs, fashion stores, bakeries, bookstores, and cinemas. Historic Casa Loma and Spadina House are approximately 15 to 20 minutes' walking distance. A full and healthy breakfast is served. On-site parking. Cat and dog in residence. $60-85 Canadian.

Sundown. (416) 657-1900; www.bbcanada.com/1102.html. A bright, spacious home on a quiet tree-lined boulevard, a block away from the colorful and lively Corso Italia with its small outdoor bistros and bustling shops. A five-minute streetcar ride takes guests right into the St. Clair W. subway. Minutes to theaters. The generous breakfast consists of hot and cold dishes and is served in the dining room. Cable TV and VCR. Parking. Central air. Smoking on the front veranda. Discounts for long stays. $59-99 Canadian.

Vanderkooy. (416) 925-8765; FAX (416) 925-8557; e-mail: jvanderkooy@ hotmail.com; www.bbcanada.com/ 1107.html. This charming older, traditional home is in an excellent location on a lovely tree-lined street close to Summerhill subway, a choice of good restaurants, and fine boutiques. The house is bright and sunny, with stained-glass windows, and features some original artwork. One of the bedrooms has a private three-piece bathroom and the other has a shared bath. The atmosphere of this home is relaxed and casual. A full breakfast is served on a round oak table overlooking the garden. Parking. Air conditioning. Cat in residence. No smoking. Easy access to all downtown attractions. $70-80 Canadian.

Winchester Square. (416) 928-0827; www.bbcanada.com/1111.html. This recently restored late 1800s three-story brick residence is in Cabbagetown, a quiet downtown Toronto neighborhood of Victorian and Edwardian homes. Round-the-clock public transportation stops a block away, or guests can walk a few

---

NOTES: Credit cards accepted: A MasterCard; B Visa; C American Express; D Discover; E Diner's Club; F Other; 2 Personal checks accepted; 3 Lunch available; 4 Dinner available; 5 Open all year; 6 Pets welcome;

steps to the many charming shops and restaurants or enjoy the gardens and architecture of Heritage homes that make up the heart of Cabbagetown. A healthy Continental breakfast is served. The guest kitchen is conveniently equipped with a dishwasher and laundry facilities for extended stays. Visiting professionals, lecturers, and families take note: Polish is a second language. Air-conditioned suite. Smoking is allowed only on the open-air deck. Free parking. Bathroom shared by only two guest rooms and one en suite. $50-99 Canadian.

Craig House Bed & Breakfast

78 Spruce Hill Road, M4E 3G3
(416) 698-3916; FAX (416) 698-8506
www.bbcanada.com/1222.html

Guests will be welcomed to a large traditional beach home with its beautiful flower gardens from spring to fall. Craig House is in a popular neighbourhood with the air of a small town resort by the lake, a superb location close enough to downtown that guests can be there in 10 minutes by car or by a leisurely street car ride 25 of minutes on the 24-hour public transportation. The guest rooms are on a private second floor. There is a kitchen for the use of guests making light snacks, tea, or coffee. The third floor is a one-bedroom apartment that sleeps four with private bath and TV. Craig House is CAA/AAA-approved.

Host: Dorothy Maguire
Rooms: 4 (2 PB; 2 SB) $65-90
Full Breakfast
Credit Cards: None
Notes: 7, 9, 10, 11, 14

The Homewood Inn

65 Homewood Avenue, M4Y 2K1
(416) 920-7944; FAX (416) 920-4091
e-mail: nickwood@interlog.com
www.interlog.com/~nickwood/homewood.html

Three beautiful Victorian houses converted into a typical English bed and breakfast. Ten minutes walking distance from Eaton Centre

and seven minutes from subway stations. All rooms have color TV and refrigerators. Air conditioning, maid service, free parking, and laundry facilities. Airport bus service. Self-contained and deluxe suites available. Smoking and nonsmoking rooms. Full English breakfast. Guest kitchen available.

Hosts: Nick and Dolores Thompson-Wood
Rooms: 30 (3 PB; 27 SB) $60-90
Full Breakfast
Credit Cards: A, B, C
Notes: 5, 6, 8, 9, 10, 11, 12, 14

Palmerston Inn

322 Palmerston Boulevard, M6G 2N6
(416) 920-7842; FAX (416) 960-9529

Palmerston Inn is an elegant Georgian-style mansion circa 1906. Flanked by large white pillars, it sits majestically on a stately tree-lined boulevard in the heart of one of downtown Toronto's most interesting neighborhoods, close to all amenities. The guest rooms feature traditional furnishings, some period pieces, fresh flowers, bath robes, ceiling fans, clock radios. All double rooms are air conditioned. A full hot breakfast features fresh fruit salad, home baking, and creative egg dishes. Private parking. No smokers.

Hosts: Judy Carr
Rooms: 8 (3 PB; 5 SB) $110-195 Canadian
Full Breakfast
Credit Cards: A, B
Notes: 5, 7, 9, 10, 11, 12, 13, 14

The Red Door Bed & Breakfast

301 Indian Road, M6R 2X7
(416) 604-0544; e-mail: reddor@idirect.com
http: //webhome.idirect.com/~reddoor/

Elegant, spacious accommodation on a quiet, tree-lined residential street. The bedrooms have queen-size beds, air conditioning, TV, clock radio, and comfortable chairs. The bed and breakfast is a five-minute walk from the subway, which will take guests to the centre of downtown in 10 minutes. Guests are served a

7 No smoking; 8 Children welcome; 9 Social drinking allowed; 10 Tennis nearby; 11 Swimming nearby; 12 Golf nearby; 13 Skiing nearby; 14 May be booked through a travel agent; 15 Handicapped accessible.

The Red Door

gourmet breakfast in the spacious dining room and can read and relax in the large, comfortable living room filled with art and antiques.

Hosts: Jean and Paul Pedersen
Rooms: 4 (2 PB; 2 SB) $85-100 Canadian
Full Breakfast
Credit Cards: B
Notes: 2, 5, 7, 10, 11, 12

Vanderkooy Bed & Breakfast

53 Walker Avenue, M4V 1G3
(416) 925-8765; FAX (925) 8557
e-mail: jvanderkooy@hotmail.com

Joan and the resident cat, welcome guests to this charming home where they will enjoy comfortable guest rooms and breakfast served in an open dining room overlooking the garden. A short walk to Summerhill station on the Younge subway line allows easy access to downtown attractions, including the Harbourfront, Skydome, the Eaton Centre, and theaters. Restaurants and shopping districts are all within walking distance. Feel free to watch TV by the fire, enjoy the waterfall and pond in the garden, or relax on the flower-filled deck in the summer. Children over 12 welcome.

Host: Joan Vanderkooy
Rooms: 3 (1 PB; 2 SB) $70-80 Canadian
Full Breakfast
Credit Cards: None
Notes: 5, 7, 9,

WATERLOO

Les Diplomates Bed & Breakfast (Executive Guest House)

100 Blythwood Road, N2L 4A2
(519) 725-3184; (800) 645-9457
e-mail: bmateyk@easynet.ca
www.trqavelinx.com/les_diplomates
www.bbcanada.com/222.html

Classic elegance for executive travellers and romantic getaways. A re-created 19th-century French/English ambiance. Nestled among the serene woods right in the heart of Waterloo. Minutes from universities, Kitchener, St. Jacobs, Farmers Market, and Oktoberfest*ivities*. Very large bedrooms all with en suite/private bathrooms. Full use of spacious parlor and dining room. Caters to special events and elegant smaller weddings. Prices include five-course gourmet breakfast and afternoon Victorian tea. Inquire about accommodations for pets.

Hosts: Hoda and Bob Mateyk
Rooms: 3 (PB) $69-115
Full Breakfast
Credit Cards: A, B
Notes: 2, 5, 7, 8, 9, 10, 11, 12, 13, 14

WELLESLEY

Firella Creek Farm

Rural Route 2, N0B 2T0
(519) 656-2974 (phone/FAX)

Retreat to nature in the heart of Mennonite farming country. Country breakfast with a view of trout pond, stream, and apple orchard. Relax beside the fireplace or explore hiking and cross-country ski trails through ancient forest. Birds, animals, and wildflowers abound. Excellent cycling roads. German and Canadian cuisine served. Air conditioned, smoke-free rooms. On Regional Road 5 between Wellesley and Crosshill, 25 minutes from Stratford, Kitchener, or St. Jacobs Farmers' Market.

Hosts: Adolph and Emily Hafemann
Rooms: 3 (PB) $50-55 Canadian

NOTES: Credit cards accepted: A MasterCard; B Visa; C American Express; D Discover; E Diner's Club; F Other; 2 Personal checks accepted; 3 Lunch available; 4 Dinner available; 5 Open all year; 6 Pets welcome;

Full Breakfast
Credit Cards: None
Notes: 2, 5, 7, 8, 9, 10, 11, 12, 13

Stepping Stone Bed & Breakfast Inn

328 Centreville Road, Rural Route 2, K0G 1X0
(613) 273-3806; FAX (613) 273-3331
e-mail: stepping@rideau.net
www.steppingstoneinn.com

Retreat to this peaceful, safe haven. Get back to nature. Beautiful seven-room 1840 Victorian Heritage inn on 150 acres. Relax by spring-fed pond and walk through magnificent gardens and nature trails; enjoy horses, cows, birds, skiing, golfing, and swimming. Weddings with memories for a lifetime; intimate/family dinners, mouth-watering gourmet breakfasts; corporate retreats, seminars. Come capture winter, summer, spring, or fall in all their glory. Between Ottawa and Kingston. Cozy cabin sleeps two with private shower in main building.

Host: Madeline Saunders
Rooms: 7 (4 PB: 3 SB) $75-150 Canadian
Full Breakfast
Credit Cards: A, B, C
Notes: 3, 4, 5, 7, 8, 9, 10, 11, 12, 13, 14, 15

7 No smoking; 8 Children welcome; 9 Social drinking allowed; 10 Tennis nearby; 11 Swimming nearby; 12 Golf nearby; 13 Skiing nearby; 14 May be booked through a travel agent; 15 Handicapped accessible.

RECOMMENDATION FORM

As *The Annual Directory of American and Canadian Bed & Breakfasts* gains approval from the traveling public, more and more bed and breakfast establishments are asking to be included on our mailing list. If you know of another bed and breakfast which may not be on our list, give them a great outreach and advertising opportunity by providing us with the following information:

1) B&B Name _____

Host's Name _____

Address _____

City _____ State _____ Zip Code _____

Telephone _____ FAX _____

2) B&B Name _____

Host's Name _____

Address _____

City _____ State _____ Zip Code _____

Telephone _____ FAX _____

3) B&B Name _____

Host's Name _____

Address _____

City _____ State _____ Zip Code _____

Telephone _____ FAX _____

Please return this form to: Barbour Publishing, Inc.
P.O. Box 719, Uhrichsville, OH 44683
(740) 922-6045; FAX (740) 922-5948

Planning the perfect vacation?

Find all the best lodging in

The Annual Directory of American and Canadian Bed & Breakfasts

Five volumes in the series:

New England (Volume I)—includes Connecticut, Maine, Massachusetts, New Hampshire, Rhode Island, Vermont, New Brunswick, Nova Scotia, Prince Edward Island, and Quebec. 304 pages, $9.95 ($15.50 in Canada), ISBN 1-57748-771-0

Mid-Atlantic Region (Volume II)—includes Delaware, District of Columbia, Maryland, New Jersey, New York, Pennsylvania, Virginia, Ontario. 272 pages, $9.95 ($15.50 in Canada), ISBN 1-57748-772-9

The South (Volume III)—includes Alabama, Arkansas, Florida, Georgia, Kentucky, Louisiana, Mississippi, North Carolina, South Carolina, Tennessee, Texas, Virginia, West Virginia, Puerto Rico, and the Virgin Islands. 288 pages, $9.95 ($15.50 in Canada), ISBN 1-57748-773-7

The Midwest (Volume IV)—includes Illinois, Indiana, Iowa, Kansas, Michigan, Minnesota, Missouri, Nebraska, North Dakota, Ohio, Oklahoma, South Dakota, Wisconsin, Manitoba, and Ontario. 192 pages, $9.95 ($15.50 in Canada), ISBN 1-57748-774-5

The West (Volume V)—includes Alaska, Arizona, California, Colorado, Hawaii, Idaho, Montana, Nevada, New Mexico, Oregon, Texas, Utah, Washington, Wyoming, Alberta, British Columbia, and Saskatchewan. 448 pages, $12.95 ($19.95 in Canada), ISBN 1-57748-775-3

Available wherever books are sold.
Or order from:
Barbour Publishing, Inc.
P.O. Box 719
Uhrichsville, Ohio 44683
http://www.barbourbooks.com

If you order by mail, add $2.00 to your order for shipping.
Prices subject to change without notice.